NOT BY POLITICS ALONE

Not by Politics Alone

The Enduring Influence
of the Christian Right

Sara Diamond

The Guilford Press
New York   London

Published by The Guilford Press
A Division of Guilford Publications, Inc.
72 Spring Street, New York, NY 10012
http://www.guilford.com

Printed in the United States of America

This book is printed on acid-free paper.

Last digit is print number: 9 8 7 6 5 4 3 2 1

Library of Congress Cataloging-in-Publication Data

Diamond, Sara.
    Not by politics alone : the enduring influence of the
Christian right / Sara Diamond.
        p.   cm.
    Includes bibliographical references and index.
    ISBN 1-57230-385-9 (hardcover)
    1. Evangelicalism—Political aspects—United States—
History—20th century. 2. Conservatism—Religious aspects—
Christianity—History—20th century. 3. Christianity and
politics—United States—History—20th century.   I. Title.
BR1642.U5D52 1998   98-24502
322.4'4'0973—dc21   CIP

*For the sowers of peace
and for the place of peace*

Preface

More than any other public display in recent years, the Promise Keepers' Stand in the Gap rally, held in Washington, DC, in the fall of 1997, symbolized the enduring political and cultural influence of conservative evangelical Christians. Estimates of the men assembled for the six-hour prayer meeting—one of the largest religious gatherings in U.S. history—ranged from seven hundred thousand to over one million men. They packed the bit of land between the Washington Monument and the Capitol. One in five were men of color, and there were supportive women on hand as volunteers. The men huddled in small groups for prayer and Bible studies, and then as one speaker after the next exhorted them for their moral failures, they held their arms up skyward and begged for divine forgiveness. They said they were there to repent for the sins of neglecting their families, and for the collective sins of racism and dissension within the church.

What they truly stand for and why exactly the Promise Keepers (PK) came to Washington, DC, sparked a flurry of controversy in the weeks leading up to the event. Detractors insisted that the rally was part of a covert political agenda, or at least a morale booster for the Christian Right during an off-election year. PK founder Bill McCartney is on the record for his opposition to abortion and gay rights, and yet his politics alone do not explain the popularity of an organization that, over and over, stresses nonpartisan themes of racial reconciliation and men's responsibility to be better fathers and husbands.

PK president Randy Phillips opened the Stand in the Gap rally by denying any political motive. "Are we here to demonstrate political might? No! Is it to take back the nation by imposing our religious values on others? No! We have not come to demonstrate our power to influence men. We have come to display our spiritual poverty, that Almighty God might influence us."

It is precisely this display of religiosity that repels PK's critics. Outside the rally, about one hundred National Organization for Women (NOW) protesters held signs accusing PK of racism, sexism, and homophobia. NOW president Patricia Ireland said that when the Promise Keepers talk about taking responsibility, what they mean is taking charge. "I see the Promise Keepers and I am afraid. I am very afraid, and I am very angry," Ireland said.

Expressions of fear and anger make for headlines and tensions between polarized camps, as do declarations of piety, and charges and countercharges of political opportunism. After the rally, debate continued on whether PK is or is not a political animal, and whether it is or is not inherently "sexist" for masses of men to gather and proclaim themselves responsible for redeeming society. Lost in this debate, though, was much gray area. Can PK be political by virtue of its endorsement of the traditional family and also very personal—even therapeutic—in addressing men's desire for self-improvement? Like many projects sponsored by conservative evangelicals, PK blurs the lines between politics and culture, between old-fashioned dogma and some new ways of looking at things.

A man might attend PK meetings because his marriage has gone sour, but while there he might learn about the legislative lobbying of the Family Research Council. He might get involved in Republican Party politics. He might start attending an interracial church. He might become more emotionally responsive to his wife and kids. The realms of the personal and the political do not correlate neatly or predictably. Yet one of the secrets of a successful social movement is the degree to which it meets the multiple needs of its constituents.

⮠

This book is part of an effort to understand the cultural underpinnings of the Christian Right. Beyond the next election campaign, what accounts for the movement's endurance are its deep roots in the subcultural institutions of evangelical Christianity. Throughout this book, I take at face value the salience such institutions as Christian broadcasting and entertainment media, homeschooling, and missionary projects have for believers. At the same time, I analyze the relevance of these endeavors in mobilizing and maintaining conservative political thought and action.

I began studying the Christian Right during the early 1980s when I learned that leaders of the movement were working collaboratively with the Reagan administration to wage counterinsurgency wars against progressive forces abroad. Later, in my book *Roads to Dominion,* I attributed the success of the post–World War II Right to patterns of interaction between right-wing organizations, political elites, and government agencies. I still think that successful political movements are those that somehow entwine themselves with or become reliable allies for a faction of the ruling political class. The ballot-box marriage between the Republican Party and the Christian Right supports that theory.

But what I have come to understand is that underlying the direct political muscle of an election-friendly movement such as the Christian Right, lies something even more profound: the power to keep a movement base in motion even during times of apparent political setbacks. The Clinton years have provided a sort of test environment for some of my ideas on this point.

The Clinton administration has served as an enormous bull's-eye for the arrows of the Christian Right. It epitomizes everything the Right hates about liberalism, and that has paid off handsomely. From the opening fray over homosexuals in the military, through the continuing legislative wrangling over late-term abortions, Christian Right organizations have lined their coffers and raised the national temperature with the rhetoric of family values. In 1994, backed strongly by Christian Right voters, the Republican Party took control of Congress, and thereby not only crippled whatever progressive policy initiatives the Clinton administration might have launched, but enabled willing Democrats to take extremely regressive positions, particularly on crime and welfare. Here the Right has won by establishing standards to which many liberals have acceded. In many cases now, Democratic and Republican candidates are almost indistinguishable but for their views on abortion, a private problem now elevated as a top issue in national elections.

The Christian Right's ability to adapt to this political reality is largely a function of its having many different organizations. If one political strategy or style fails to work or inspire supporters, another is waiting in the wings.

This holds true, too, for movement projects that are less overtly partisan. I have observed during the Clinton years that failures in the legislative realm can have the effect of channeling Christian Right activists' resources away from short-term political conflicts and toward more long-term educational work. In this book, I give a number of examples of how activists spread their energies widely. In the public schools, for example, we see perennial conflicts about sex education curricula and organized school prayer. Yet a good chunk of the conservative evangelical constituency has opted out of the public schools altogether and is, instead, educating a new generation via homeschooling. On abortion, there are state and national lobbies entrenched to fight for bills such as those outlawing late-term abortions. There are also quieter, less visible activists staffing crisis pregnancy centers and doing postabortion counseling. By both aggressive and subtle means, issues are kept alive.

In this book, I focus on the major cultural projects of conservative evangelicals because, at this juncture in the Christian Right's history, it is worth asking: What accounts for a social movement's longevity? It is now more than two decades since the New Right began organizing with evangelicals to change the shape of American politics. Many organizations and leaders have come and gone. Many also have endured, as has the movement as a whole. In my own view, the Christian Right stays in motion both because it works complimentarily with the Republican Party—through which it achieves partial success—and because the movement's subcultural institutions provide a safe haven to which activists can return to renew their strength.

✑

The sheer size, diversity, and perpetually changing nature of the Christian Right raises questions about how best to study such a social movement. For my purposes, I have found it most reliable to base my writing and analyses on printed primary source materials issued by organizations and their leaders. I also use, selectively, newspaper reports and information gleaned from secondary source books about the Right and politics generally. One obvious advantage of this method is that it enables me to cite tangible sources that readers can locate at libraries, if they are interested. (My own archives are permanently housed in the Bancroft Library at the University of California, Berkeley.)

Some readers may wonder why this book does not rely on interview material. There would have been two possible types of interviews to conduct, and I chose to do neither. In a study of a social movement, one can interview many rank-and-file members to find out what makes them tick. But, as I say in Chapter 1, this is not a book about why people, as individuals, join and participate in social movements. This book is about how and why the Christian Right has endured and remained influential, and that topic is largely a political and organizational question. For this purpose, I might have interviewed organizational leaders, but here the problems of reliability become trickier. Over the years, I have done a great deal of journalistic work, in which it is appropriate and desirable to seek out people at the center of a news story and get their immediate reactions. At conferences and by phone, I have interviewed a large number of Christian Right activists. Sometimes, a reporter gets a quick, ill-considered remark. More often, especially from polished leaders of the Christian Right, one gets a version of what that person has already said in a prepared speech or in an article for his or her own publication. To get information about the public positions of people in movements, I find it much more reliable to use printed sources, which are less idiosyncratic than off-the-cuff interview material. By studying printed source material, one can see how movements evolve strategically and ideologically over time. In movement newsletters, activist leaders do not reveal their deepest, darkest sentiments—but that is not what I am after. What they do convey are consistently held perceptions plus arguments assumed to be persuasive among readers already committed to the cause, and others who might be in the future.

My intention in this book is to portray some of the complexities of the Christian Right, particularly the ways in which the movement integrates cultural practices with hardball politics. It is the Christian Right's dual nature as subculture and political faction that has made it such a potent force, one likely to adapt and endure in the years to come.

Acknowledgments

I wish to offer my grateful thanks to the people who helped make it possible for me to complete this book.

Jean Hardisty and Chip Berlet of Political Research Associates gave me a generous grant that enabled me to purchase some of the research materials I needed for this book. Many thanks to Jean and Chip for their encouragement of my work over the years.

Thanks also to Professor Catherine Lugg of Rutgers University and to an anonymous reviewer for The Guilford Press for constructive criticism of the manuscript.

Thanks to Richard Hatch, without whom it would not have been possible for me to pursue my writing career and many years' worth of research on the Right.

Upon completion of the manuscript, I donated my large archive of primary source materials on the Right to the Bancroft Library of the University of California, Berkeley. Scholars and the general public may now have access to the literature I collected over a fourteen-year period. I would like to thank the staff of the Bancroft Library for creating a permanent home for the Sara Diamond Collection on the U.S. Right.

Following publication of *Roads to Dominion* in 1995, there were a number of reasons why I decided to publish a second book with The Guilford Press. Seymour Weingarten and Bob Matloff have been exceptionally generous and supportive of my work. It has been a pleasure to work with them, as well as Marian Robinson and Debra Finkelstein, both of whom took great care to promote *Roads*.

My major reason for returning to Guilford is my editor Peter Wissoker. Of all the book and periodical editors I've ever worked with, Peter is the best. He's one of the smartest people I know and a writer's dream. He makes sharp critiques of my work, but always with respect for my prerogative. He shepherds a book through all of its phases. He has become a good friend.

Here in the Bay Area, I have been fortunate to find a close and inspiring circle of friends. They shall go nameless here because, while they talk to me about all kinds of subjects, they have not shared my professional interest in the right wing. Instead, their friendship and guidance helped me maintain a state of happiness and balance as I completed this work.

Contents

Chapter 1

〆

Introduction

This is a book about the character and capacity of the Christian Right at the end of the twentieth century. Its successful mobilization has been decades in the making, has been the result of astute planning by movement leaders and the commitment of tens of thousands of adherents, who draw strength largely from sources outside the formal halls of power. The Christian Right remains among the most powerful, active forces in U.S. politics today, partly because the movement delivers votes to the Republican Party. But the Christian Right is much more than an electoral faction.

It is a political movement rooted in a rich evangelical subculture, one that offers participants both the means and the motivation to try to take dominion over secular society. The means include a phenomenal number of religious broadcast stations, publishing houses, churches, and grassroots lobbies. The motivation is to preach the Gospel and to save souls, but also, with equal urgency, to remake contemporary moral culture in the image of Christian Scripture. On the front lines of our persisting battle over what kind of society we are and will become, the Christian Right wages political conflict not just through the ballot box but also through the movement's very own cultural institutions.

One of these is Focus on the Family, the syndicated radio ministry headed by child psychologist Dr. James Dobson. In January 1990 Dobson's Focus on the Family published a special issue of its *Citizen* magazine, proclaiming that the 1990s would become "the Civil War Decade." Dobson made this announcement at a time when the political lens in the United States was shifting toward a near exclusive focus on domestic policy matters. The end of the United States' obsession with communism coincided with the growth and entrenchment of the Christian Right as a permanent fixture within the policymaking arena. Starting in the late 1980s, the movement began to direct its energies toward state and local politics and not just toward the affairs of Congress.

Comparing our times to the turbulent decade leading up to the Civil War over slavery, Dr. Dobson's *Citizen* magazine identified brewing controversies over homosexual rights, abortion, and public education as the terrain on which Christians would be called to "serve as foot soldiers" in what Focus described as a new Civil War of values. *Citizen* heralded a second wave of Christian Right activism, not headed by big names like Pat Robertson and Jerry Falwell, but led by a fresh crop of energetic leaders active mostly at the local level. The big, centralized organizations such as Concerned Women for America and the National Right to Life Committee would still provide training and leadership, but the new wave of activism would encourage the growth of grassroots talent.[1]

The new breed of activists would not carry the stigma of the 1980s preacher scandals, nor would they be dependent on the prerogatives of established national organizations. Instead, they would face new challenges, some of which were outlined by Thomas Atwood who wrote, also in 1990, for the Heritage Foundation's influential *Policy Review* magazine. At the time, Atwood was a Virginia Republican Party activist who had helped organize Pat Robertson's 1988 presidential race and who had since grown sharply critical of the Christian Right's tendency to ignore "basic rules of politics, such as respect for opposing views, an emphasis on coalition-building and compromise, and careful rhetoric." Instead, Atwood wrote, by overestimating their own strength, conservative evangelicals "often came across as authoritarian, intolerant, and boastful, even to natural constituents." Atwood urged fellow evangelical Christians to tone down their inflammatory and apocalyptic rhetoric; to stop calling for "spiritual warfare" against everyone and everything they opposed; and to start building alliances, particularly with black evangelicals and political moderates sympathetic toward one or more pieces of the Christian Right's agenda.[2]

Several years later, though, the Christian Right's warfare rhetoric was no less strident. A writer for the conservative magazine *Christianity Today* singled out James Dobson and Focus on the Family as leading promoters of a warfare mentality among fellow evangelicals. The writer suggested that it was unchristian and counterproductive to the family values agenda[3] to mix political advocacy with metaphors of violence.[4] Dobson responded in a guest editorial for *Christianity Today* with a lengthy defense of his "spiritual warfare" rhetoric. Not only is it traditional for Christians to sing such hymns as "Onward Christian Soldiers," Dobson wrote, but the warfare terminology is an accurate description of the conflict in which Christian Right activists are engaged. "The heated dispute over values in Western nations is simply a continuation of the age-old struggle between the principles of righteousness and the kingdom of darkness," Dobson noted. "Thus when we oppose hardcore and violent pornography, the killing of unborn babies, the provision of immoral advice to teenagers, the threat of euthanasia, and so on, we are engaged in a battle—not primarily with our philosophical opponents—but against Satan, who leads the whole world astray" (Rev. 12:9).[5]

In justifying his own rhetoric, Dobson reveals the essence of the Christian Right's collective mindset. The strength and longevity of the Christian Right, which is the subject of this book, is best understood as a series of efforts by a religiously inspired political force to make the rest of society conform to its ideas of correct belief and behavior. More than a conflict over this or that policy matter, the movement is about protecting guarded notions of what it means to be a good family member and a good citizen in God's Kingdom. For believers, it is about winning an eternal struggle between the forces of good and evil—if not this year, then maybe the next; if not through the ballot box, then by other means.

∽

The 1990s have yielded mixed results in the Christian Right's Civil War for family values. There have been few unmitigated victories, but neither have the movement's many setbacks proven fatal. In 1994, the leading Christian Right organizations helped elect a Republican Congressional majority for the first time in four decades. That victory, however, translated into few immediate legislative gains, and by 1996 the reelection of President Clinton relegated the likes of House Speaker Newt Gingrich to diminishing influence. For the Christian Right, Republican Party politics has proven time and again to be a double-edged sword.

For the movement, it has been imperative to court power within one of the established parties; otherwise nothing of legislative substance can be accomplished. For the Republican Party, the Christian Right represents a uniquely large and reliable voting bloc, one that cannot be ignored lest the Republicans forfeit majority party status. Electoral politics is about numbers. Yet the numbers game, in a system controlled by two ideologically similar parties, tends to push each side to moderate its rhetoric and agenda. The winner is whichever party appears the least objectionable to the fraction of eligible votes willing to participate. Therein lies the conundrum for the Christian Right–Republican Party alliance. On some issues and in some races at the local and state levels, the party cannot win without the movement, which conducts useful voter mobilization campaigns. At the national level, however, the movement has become a public relations liability. Voting majorities in presidential and many Congressional races reject the movement's agenda, especially on abortion.

In 1996, the party tried to paper over its rocky relationship with the movement. During the primaries some movement leaders favored Senator Robert Dole as the best hope for defeating Clinton. But Dole epitomized the professional politician's tendency to hedge on controversial issues such as abortion. As a result, Patrick Buchanan repeated his 1992 performance as a standard-bearer for the grassroots activist Right. Buchanan's strong showings in the primaries helped to galvanize the party's prolifers, who organized to ensure their dominance among delegates to the Republican Party convention in San Diego. There the prolife delegate majority forced Dole to abandon talk of removing the antiabortion plank in the party platform, and thus the Christian Right declared victory on that score. For mass-media consumption, the movement was denied representation in the lineup of televised convention speakers. But Dole's selection of prolife running mate Jack Kemp was, in part, an appeal to evangelical voters.

In the end, Republican jockeying over abortion probably had a negligible effect on the 1996 election. The general electorate was neither enthusiastic about nor particularly dissatisfied with the incumbent Clinton administration. Dole's lackluster campaign gave conservative Christians nothing to cheer about, but most of them voted Republican anyway. One postelection survey showed that, against the backdrop of generally low voter turnout, about 29% of those who did vote in 1996 were self-identified born-again Christians who frequently attend church.[6] Another exit poll indicated that white, self-identified constituents of the Christian Right represented 17% of all voters. Among this 17% bloc, 65% voted for Dole and 26% for Clinton,[7] meaning that Dole would have fared far worse without loyal Christian Right voters. Ralph Reed was widely quoted in the press, to the effect that a Republican Congress would not have been reelected for the first time in sixty-eight years without the Christian Right bloc. "Conservative evangelicals were the firewall that prevented a Bob Dole defeat from mushrooming into a meltdown all the way down the ballot," Reed said, in a heated reminder to Republicans who survived the 1996 Democratic victory.

Other Christian Right leaders were less eager than Reed to put a happy spin on the 1996 election results. Reed's own boss Pat Robertson took to the microphones of his *700 Club* TV show and called 1996 "the second consecutive time where a Republican candidate for president lost the election because he muted the social issues in favor of money issues."[8] In an interview with the *New York Times*, Robertson warned that in the year 2000 the Christian Right would play a more proactive role in selecting a Republican nominee. "We're not going to sit by as good soldiers and take whatever is given us," Robertson said. "We were not consulted on this campaign. We were peripheral."[9]

Just how peripheral the Christian Right is to the political process is a matter of one's perspective. Pat Robertson, James Dobson, and his associate

Gary Bauer of the Family Research Council all lamented their "peripheral" status even while the Republican Party had no choice but to cater to its most conservative, antiabortion wing. Much of this book is about how people within the Christian Right view themselves as outsiders even as they wield political strength disproportionate to their numbers. The perception among evangelicals that they are underdogs, ignored if not abused by the establishment, is part of a mindset that keeps activists from becoming complacent. In order to explain the enduring influence of the Christian Right, this book looks from various angles at the ways in which social movement actors define their own roles on the political stage—and how they then act accordingly.

This book traces the recent political history of the Christian Right. But while looking at this movement's ideology and its most successful organizational vehicles, one inevitably concludes that politics reaches far beyond the polling station. When political activists think of themselves as peripheral—even if they are not—what sustains their long-term commitment is nothing short of faith: in each other, in a worldview or lifestyle set apart from the dominant culture, and in a collective power to reshape society. While this book is a case study of the Christian Right, it is also an exploration of some of the ways in which politics and culture converge.

∽

Over the past two decades, social movements scholarship has proliferated. Today it is one of the most vital fields within the social sciences because the extent and nature of social change is, naturally, determined by the ways in which specific groups of people act in concert. Amid the many insightful theories and empirical case studies of social movements, my own approach is aligned with a theoretical perspective that emphasizes three sets of factors. These are (1) the political opportunities afforded by both long-term trends and short-term features of the prevailing political–economic system; (2) the effectiveness of all the organizations and informal networks through which social movements mobilize and sustain activism; and (3) the ways in which groups interpret the meaning of their grievances and their possibilities for action, all toward the end of continually readjusting their strategies. In the jargon of social movements theorists, the shorthand names for these three sets of factors are *political opportunities, mobilizing structures,* and *framing processes.*[10]

Political opportunities refers to the variable ways in which social hierarchies are constructed between one society and the next, as well as to the inevitability of change over time. Political opportunities can include everything from long- and short-term economic trends to policy controversies to realignments within and between the two parties. *Mobilizing structures* are organizations with physical offices and a stated agenda, for example, the Christian Coalition. Theorists of social movements also include under the rubric of mobilizing structures the many informal networks of friends, coworkers, and parishioners who act collectively. Social movements researchers want to know what kinds of organizational resources a movement has at its disposal. How do organizations inform their constituents and channel their grievances into action? What forms does the action take? How do outside forces influence the development of movement organizations? Is a movement able to plug into one of the leading parties? Does the movement face legal obstacles such as bans on some forms of protest? All of these questions are relevant to the study of the Christian Right which, compared to other modern social movements in the United States, has been highly successful in building numerous types of organizations, from church networks to religious media outlets to think tanks, law firms, lobbies, and voter education drives. In addressing the questions of how and why the Christian Right has become such an influential social movement, this book focuses to a large extent on movement organizations.

While they pressure policymakers, organizations are also key sites for the *framing processes* of interest to social movements scholars. *Framing* is about how members or supporters of a movement conceptualize the grievances they hope to rectify through strategies they consider feasible. Lacking shared grievances or a sense of efficacy, people are unlikely to organize for action even if the political context is advantageous. *Framing* is a *process* because over time movement participants, through trial and error and shifting responses from opponents, change their ideas about what needs to be done and what can be done.

The concept of framing suggests that people organized in social movements have grievances, and therefore they must be *opposed* to the prevailing political system and/or cultural norms of their society. One leading theorist defines social movements in terms of *insurgent realities* as "collective challenges to mainstream conceptions of how society ought to be organized and how people ought to live."[11] This definition is problematic. If applied to the Christian Right, it captures those parts of the movement's ideology at odds with whatever the social scientist chooses to define as "mainstream." But the conception of social movements as insurgencies or challenges to the status quo precludes one from seeing when, how, and to what extent some movements act as bulwarks against social change. In a previous book, *Roads to Dominion*, I relied on the recent history of the U.S. Right to document and analyze the ways in which right-wing social movements function, often simultaneously, as both opponents and supporters of political elites, and more generally of the reigning system.

In *Roads to Dominion* I asserted that movements of the Right are partially *oppositional* and partially what I called *system-supportive*. To be characteristically "right-wing" is to endorse some government functions and policies and to oppose others. Typically, the Right favors a strong government role as *enforcer* of order at home and abroad, by means of religiously inspired codes of conduct, police power, and the military. The Right usually opposes the government in its role as *distributor* of wealth, power, and legal rights more equitably throughout society. There are exceptions to these general patterns. But more often than not, the Christian Right, in particular, favors government policies that would enforce traditional norms of sexual behavior and traditional hierarchical relations between men and women, parents and children. The Christian Right opposes action by government agencies that would extend civil rights protections to homosexuals or that would (seemingly) usurp parental rights. Activists in the antiabortion movement know that women have abortions even where they are illegal; the political struggle is about whether government should or should not *enforce* the religious belief that abortion is murder.

These are just a few examples. The point is that the Christian Right is not, contrary to the epithets used by many of the movement's critics, a "radical" force intent on a thorough overhaul of society. This is a social movement focused fairly narrowly on questions of proper family structure and "moral," that is, sexual behavior. Since the 1980s, when leaders of the Christian Right worked with the Reagan administration to support anticommunist paramilitary groups around the globe, there has been little movement focus on international affairs. (Some Christian Right groups, in the late 1990s, have protested the United States' rapprochement with China for its violations of religious liberty.) With the important exception of Patrick Buchanan, leaders of the Christian Right have had little to say about the increasing globalization of the capitalist economy, nor about the growing disparities between rich and poor. Unlike movements of the Right, a truly radical social movement is one that works to eradicate inequality and injustice. More often than not, the Right treats poverty not as a matter of systemic injustice but as a result of the bad luck and/or bad behavior of individuals and groups who lack proper values.

Were the Christian Right to achieve its wish list of policy goals, things would certainly be different. For starters, abortion would be illegal. Homosexuals would be, if not invisible, then certainly unprotected from all types of discrimination. Children would pray in the schools, which would be run privately or by local school districts, with no government-mandated curricula. The entertainment media would voluntarily eliminate profanity from the airwaves and movie scripts. The range of ideas and images accessible in bookstores, libraries, magazines, and art exhibits would be sharply curtailed.

The agenda of the Christian Right is severe but it is not radical. It is about halting or rolling back social change, not about forging ahead. Moreover, many of the Christian Right's preoccupations are in sync with what outside observers might call the "mainstream." Who in society is fully comfortable with the rapid pace of social and technological changes, with high rates of divorce and illiteracy, with not knowing one's neighbors or knowing what the future will bring?

The "Ozzie and Harriet" type of family was never as prevalent in real life as it was on television in the 1950s.[12] But the family values theme resonates as a nostalgic wish for a return to a time that seemed simpler. Rather than accept a new, wider range of family arrangements and gender roles, the Christian Right has entrenched itself for a fight to preserve an idyllic past. What distinguishes people in the Christian Right from the rest of us is their selection of designated culprits to blame for their insecurity about social and familial change. It must be the fault of the feminists, the sex educators, the gay rights marchers, the liberal politicians. These are ready-made targets, and it is expedient to organize against enemies that seem powerful. Pat Robertson and others like him can tell their audiences that they are "peripheral" even while the Republican wing of the political establishment welcomes the votes and enthusiasm of people who act as if they are under siege.

༄

By framing themselves as underdogs, and by rationalizing their agenda as a defensive response, activists in the Christian Right have built the kind of formidable organizations suited to existing political opportunities. Working effectively within the confines of the two-party electoral system, the movement has made itself central, not peripheral, to the politics and culture of the United States.

In the middle of the 1996 campaign season, the Pew Research Center for the People and the Press released a study that found that conservative, white, evangelical Protestants are "the most powerful religious force in politics today," representing 24% of registered voters, up from 19% in 1987.[13] But, the Pew study also found that only about 7% of the public consider themselves members of the "religious right."[14] This data is roughly consistent with a 1994 *New York Times*–CBS News survey that found about 9% of the public identifying themselves as part of the "religious right."[15] No doubt, among the 7–9% who claim an affiliation with the Christian Right, a much smaller percentage is continuously active between election cycles. But what makes the Christian Right such a potent political force is not just the numbers of supporters or hard-core activists. It is the availability of a consistently large segment of the population ready to vote as a bloc around salient profamily issues. The Pew study found that, regardless of denomination, the more committed evangelicals are to their religion, the more likely they are to be politically conservative.[16] Thus, it is the strength of evangelicalism as a cultural phenomenon that gives the Christian Right an enduring base of political support.

In general, religion offers people emotional sustenance and social ties, thus making them capable of doing activist work. In this book, I use the terms *born-again* and *evangelical* interchangeably, though they have slightly different connotations. The term *born-again* refers to the millions of Americans who say that they have had a conversion experience in which they made a personal commitment to Jesus Christ. To be an *evangelical* implies a more profound, ongoing relationship to the faith. Evangelicals may be either conservative or liberal in their politics or theology. In general, evangelicals are Christians, Catholic as well as Protestant, who have had a born-again experience. They believe the Bible is the accurate, inspired word of God, and they also believe that the only way to salvation is through belief in Christ's divinity and resurrection. Evangelicals believe they are required to share their faith with nonbelievers in an effort to win new converts to Christ.[17] The evangelical tradition of proselytizing makes it especially compatible with political activism. Evangelicals are encouraged to put aside their shyness when approaching newcomers with controversial ideas, and the missionary mindset encourages an attitude of tenacity in waiting for the fruits of one's labor to pay off.

Since the late 1970s, the Gallup Poll organization has publicized surveys showing that between one-fifth and about one-third of adult Americans identify themselves as born-again Christians.[18] Gallup's surveys ask people simply: "Would you describe yourself as a 'born-again' or evangelical Christian?" In a 1993 sample, 42% said yes,[19] but that response reveals nothing about the degree of commitment people have, let alone how religion correlates with politics.

George Barna, an evangelical who directs his own reputable polling firm, conducts surveys that are a bit more revealing. In a compilation of survey data on religion for his 1996 book *The Index of Leading Spiritual Indicators*, Barna found that two out of three, or 66%, of American adults say that they have made a "personal commitment to Jesus Christ that is still important in their life today," up from 60% in the 1980s. Barna found that smaller numbers of respondents go beyond simply viewing themselves as Christians. Forty-one percent say they are "absolutely committed" to Christianity. About one-quarter say they are "always" mindful of being Christ's representatives.[20] Church attendance rates have fluctuated between 42 and 49% over the past decade. On average, Barna found, about one-third of the public attends church every week; about one-third attends one to three times a month; and about one-third attends rarely or never.[21] Evangelicals interpret these numbers pessimistically, as evidence of low church participation.[22] But at a time when society is supposedly becoming more secular, these figures indicate that church attendance is surprisingly widespread and stable.

Numbers, however, do not begin to tell the story of the changing landscape of evangelicalism. Mark Shibley, a sociologist of religion, was intrigued by data showing that between 1971 and 1990 evangelical churches added more than 6 million new members while the so-called mainline moderate and liberal Protestant churches lost about 2.6 million members. In the western region of the United States, evangelical churches have grown at a rate greater than in the traditional southern Bible Belt.[23] Shibley wondered whether the spread of evangelical churches had to do with migrations of people out of the South. But, he found the migration of southerners to be only one factor when he studied the spread of denominational and nondenominational evangelical churches in the Midwest and on the West Coast. The evangelical churches experiencing the greatest growth are those, such as the Vineyard Christian Fellowship and Calvary Chapel, that began in southern California during the 1970s Jesus movement, and that deviate noticeably from traditional southern evangelical churches. Shibley found that Vineyard, Calvary, and other evangelical churches that are growing and thriving are those that best adapt to contemporary non–southern culture. Successful evangelical churches are more likely to have worship services with popular rock music and casual dress codes, and ministries catering to youth, singles, newlyweds, and people with specific hobbies. Shibley concludes that successful evangelical churches "are growing because they have found ways to meet the existential needs of modern individuals better than other churches, not because they are 'strict'; they grow by becoming more like the culture, not less."[24]

Sociologists of religion want to know why some religious institutions thrive while others flounder. The answer has to do with how well churches adapt to their surrounding culture and how well churches meet people's needs: for spiritual expression, but also for friendship and advice.

This book is about the Christian Right and not about evangelicalism in general. But to understand the endurance of the Christian Right, one must consider the essential role of the evangelical subculture. Shibley found no direct correlation between participation in an evangelical church and participation in conservative politics. Nor is it my contention that evangelicalism leads people invariably to get involved with the Christian Right. I do conclude that a social movement is successful, in part, to the extent that it meets people's personal and social needs. The culture of evangelicalism encourages people to take political action, should they choose to. They are more likely to choose to do so if they know people who are active and if they can take action in ways that are religiously comfortable: for example, by handing out voter guides at church or by calling Congress after hearing something on a Christian radio station.

For most people, political action begins and ends with voting, but I define the realm of the *political* very broadly. To the extent that one's religion keeps one content with the status quo, that is a political process, too. For the Christian Right, the range of political preoccupations derives from a biblical view of proper social order. The movement targets abortion, gay rights, and sex education in the public schools because these are the concerns raised by the religious milieu of evangelicalism. The movement establishes an agenda to which politicians and the rest of secular society must then respond. The agenda is set by the evangelical subculture, which thrives through an array of institutions that may not, on the surface, seem political. These include Christian broadcasting, literature and music, Promise Keepers rallies, and the practice of homeschooling. In this book, I use a broad brush in dealing with the evangelical cultural milieu, but not by any means because all evangelicals are part of the Christian Right—they are not. I focus on the evangelical subculture because it is like a big ocean in which the Christian Right's activist fish swim—and spawn.

ᵔᵔ

When one speaks publicly about the Christian Right, there are two kinds of questions that usually come up, and this book purports to answer neither. The first goes something like this: "Aren't people in the Christian Right psychologically disturbed? Don't they have authoritarian personalities, wanting to control everyone, perhaps because of the way they were raised?" To this question, I always answer that I have met people in the Christian Right with all sorts of personalities. As human beings, most seem reasonable, regardless of my own disagreements with their politics. I reject the idea of explaining political ideology and activism through some form of psychoanalysis. I assume that people join social movements because they share with fellow members a collective set of goals, be they political or religious, and because the organized activities within that movement provide people with some sense of satisfaction. Otherwise, they would go do something else. In this book, I do not speculate on the individual psychological reasons why individuals are drawn to the Christian Right.

Nor do I deal with the second frequently asked question about the Christian Right: "Where do they get their money?" This is an important question because it is directly relevant to the success of any social movement. I mention, in passing, the budgets of various organizations. Well-heeled outfits such as the Christian Coalition, Focus on the Family, and Promise Keepers wield influence consistent with their large coffers. But it is not because of *particular* large donors that these organizations are successful. The question "Where do they get their money?" implies that if we somehow learn which corporate foundation or wealthy individual gives

X amount of money to groups Y and Z, that such information will explain the success of groups Y and Z. I do not share this view. I assume that wealthy individuals and corporations—the names and faces are interchangeable—will donate to politically like-minded groups. It is no great surprise that rich people finance institutions that will preserve the status quo. Yet the centrist watchdog groups opposed to the Christian Right play a game of "exposing" the names of the Right's rich donors as if that somehow explains the success of a social movement. It does not. Groups such as People for the American Way, the Planned Parenthood Federation, and similar outfits are also sustained by large donors. This is why the centrist opponents of the Christian Right do not critique the existing political–economic system, but instead try to portray their right-wing enemies as subversive threats to "democracy." In point of fact, the centrists and the conservatives agree in their overall endorsement of the capitalist economy and state. They differ principally on social policy.

Where the Christian Right differs both from centrist lobbies such as People for the American Way and Planned Parenthood, and from elite right-wing institutions such as the Heritage Foundation, is in the role of large numbers of rank-and-file donors. Typically, centrist and liberal critics do not like to highlight the fact that Christian Right organizations enjoy genuinely large constituencies. For its financial well-being, the Christian Right relies on modest donations from hundreds of thousands of people. Typically, the amount of money required to receive a movement publication, and be counted as a member of an organization, is in the neighborhood of $20 to $30 a year. This is true for the Christian Coalition, Concerned Women for America, Focus on the Family, the National Right to Life Committee, and many other groups. Apart from the Christian Coalition's inflated claims that it has nearly two million members, it is true that several hundred thousand people subscribe to the Coalition's bimonthly magazine. Beyond a minimum of $20 a year, no doubt many of these same Coalition members respond to additional direct mail appeals throughout the year. I have been on the membership rosters of many Christian Right organizations, at a cost of several hundred dollars per year—a modest amount from a middle-class person with a commitment to a cause. Who funds the Christian Right? Mostly the money comes from hundreds of thousands of average people who pay dues, buy subscriptions, and respond to fundraising letters.

ᦈ

Before previewing the chapters that follow, I wish to make an additional caveat. When one writes in the present tense, as I do in this book, one risks the possibility of early obsolescence. The names of organizations and social movement leaders change quicker than an author would like. Yet what is most salient about the Christian Right is its longevity and adaptability. While I was writing this book, Ralph Reed announced his plan to resign as executive director of the Christian Coalition and start his own consulting firm. No doubt, other personalities named in this book will also change jobs. This book names numerous activists and organizations because they are the lifeblood of a social movement.

As I wrote in my first book, *Spiritual Warfare*, published in 1989, religious broadcasting has been the single most important ingredient in the rise of the Christian Right. Since the years immediately after World War II, the industry has grown up in tandem with the spread of politically engaged evangelicalism. In Chapter 2, I highlight the evolution of Pat Robertson's Christian Broadcasting Network and Dr. James Dobson's Focus on the Family, the two giants in television and radio, respectively. Robertson and Dobson are preachers, shrewd businessmen, good performers, and political catalysts, all at the same time. I attribute the success of their programs to a careful blend of personal and political content. With religious broadcasting in general, it is the scope and variety of the programming that makes the medium a useful political asset. When people are inspired and entertained, also become receptive to political messages.

In previous writings, I have focused solely on the news and public affairs content of religious broadcasting. In this book, I devote a chapter to what might more properly be thought of as entertainment media. Extending my point that inspiration and enjoyment facilitate political awareness and action, in Chapter 3 I address the political undercurrents found in popular evangelical fiction, magazines, and music. My point is not that one's consumption of cultural products forms one's ideology in any kind of inevitable way. However, I do think that moral precepts and images embedded in cultural artifacts help to reinforce one's political tendencies. If we want to know why people in the Christian Right think as they do, we need to look at the ideas that circulate in the population of the Christian Right.

Chapters 4 and 5 deal explicitly with politics. Readers well versed in the history of the Christian Right may choose to skip the first half of Chapter 4, which is a summary of the movement's development through the end of the 1980s. Also, in Chapters 4 and 5, I discuss different aspects of the Christian Coalition. First, in Chapter 4, I show how the organization has justified some of its tactics by deploying the notion that Christians are "persecuted" by secular society. This theme has been useful, too, in the establishment of a number of Christian Right legal firms, which I deal with also in Chapter 4. In the future, we can expect that the movement will fight its policy battles in the courts as well as through elections.

My intention, in both Chapters 4 and 5, is to show how the

movement continually shifts its strategies in response to new political opportunities and obstacles. Chapter 5 is about electoral politics in the 1990s, including the 1992 and 1996 presidential campaigns of Patrick Buchanan. In neither race was the Christian Right the sole source of support for Buchanan. But in both campaigns, and during the intervening years, movement leaders had to figure out how to make themselves indispensable to the Republican Party without, at the same time, compromising to the point of alienating grassroots constituents. Ralph Reed was central in this interplay, with the effect of solidifying Christian Right influence at the 1996 Republican Party convention and beyond. Before Reed left the helm of the Christian Coalition in 1997, he tried to steer the organization toward a new focus on issues of urban poverty, which was consistent with other efforts by Christian Right leaders to network across racial lines. Given that supporters of the Christian Right are driven mostly by concerns about "immorality" and threats to the traditional family, it remains to be seen how far the movement's newfound interest in poor people might go.

Chapters 6, 7, 8, and 9 are a unit of sorts. They all deal squarely with issues that fall under the *family values* rubric. "Family values" is like a Rorschach inkblot test: one can project onto it just about any notion of what makes a good family. But for the Christian Right, *family values* means some specific things, particularly about relations between parents and children, husbands and wives. In Chapter 6, I discuss the movement's concept of *parental rights*, which is now taking shape in proposed legislation at the state and federal levels. Local battles over public school curricula, which I reserve for Chapter 9, can best be understood as a drive by conservative Christian parents to assert the primacy of their legal rights as parents, in the face of perceived encroachments by the secular state. Purported threats take many forms: from sex education programs to young people's access to "obscene" library books, to the power of social service agencies to intervene on behalf of abused children. The parental rights project is about reestablishing traditional family hierarchy. Similarly, some Christian Right leaders want to add to their social policy agenda an effort to make divorce more cumbersome. Here the movement has a hard row to hoe. Divorce is widespread among the general public, among politicians, and among evangelicals themselves. It is unlikely that the Christian Right will succeed in restoring old stigmas to the practice of divorce. However, internally, within the movement, rhetorical attacks on divorce are part of a discourse about strengthening traditional male and female gender roles. Even while many of the Christian Right's best leaders are women, the evangelical subculture perpetuates the view that wives must be "submissive" to their husbands. This tenet underlies the Christian Right's persistent condemnations of organized feminism. In the long run, though, antifeminism is a losing battle, as I discuss in Chapter 11 in connection with the Promise Keepers men's movement.

Some observers see antiabortion sentiment as a direct outgrowth of the Christian Right's hostility to feminism. I prefer to see opposition to abortion and to feminism as two separate, though not contradictory, pieces of the family values ideological package. I take it at face value that people oppose abortion because they believe it is a form of murder. If one truly considers abortion to be murder, then it is incumbent upon one to take action accordingly. The antiabortion movement functions as a submovement of the larger Christian Right, though there are many Catholic antiabortion activists who do not find common cause with the Right on other matters. In Chapter 7, I detail the politics of the antiabortion movement: the ways in which it has become both influential within and dependent on electoral politics. I devote much of the chapter to an analysis of how the direct-action wing of the antiabortion movement has evolved since the 1980s, from the onset of Operation Rescue to the development of a small faction that espouses the killing of abortion doctors. I also look at how the antiabortion movement casts women as "victims" of abortion in need of "rescue" through various forms of counseling.

Part of what I call the "antigay agenda" is about counseling gays and lesbians out of their so-called lifestyle. There is nothing innocuous about this seemingly low-key form of antigay organizing; it perpetuates stereotypes and stigma and may cause lasting psychological damage to its clients. It is the soft side of an agenda intended to prevent the extension of civil rights laws to homosexuals. Opponents of gay rights want to preserve the right to discriminate against gay people, particularly in the workplace and in the housing market, but really wherever gay people are publicly present. In recent years, the Christian Right has sponsored a series of anti–gay rights ballot measures in several states. The results at the polls were mixed, but that is now a moot point, as the Supreme Court in 1996 ruled such ballot measures unconstitutional. Since then the focus has shifted to the realm of legal recognition of same-sex marriages. Conflict on this front promises to be protracted. In the mean time, though, Christian Right campaigns against gay rights go hand in hand with the circulation of virulent antigay propaganda. Throughout Chapter 8 I pay attention to the ways in which propaganda about gay people as diseased and excessively powerful gives rise to the notion of homosexuality as a threat to social order.

What links the disparate issues in the family values package is the idea that secular government is persecuting Christians by siding with immoral enemies, be they abortion doctors, liberal schoolteachers, or gay employees. Because so much of the family values project is cast in terms of defending innocent children, education is a central site of struggle. In recent years, the Christian Right has focused on electing its own partisans to local school boards. There have been many battles over curricula, especially in the area of sex education, and over the content of textbooks. Conflicts in the public schools would be much fiercer, I am convinced, were it not for the thousands of Christian Right families who opt for homeschooling, which I also cover in Chapter 9. Homeschooling is a respected practice within the evangelical subculture, and it is not without merit as a means of teaching children the three R's. But homeschooling is not as "private" as one might think. Homeschool families are very well organized, and though they may not articulate it this way, they understand the ideological importance of shaping and restricting their children's experiences. They assert *parental rights* to, effectively, keep their children from being exposed to objectionable ideas and people.

Again, the protection of young minds is the justification for the Christian Right's periodic campaigns against public art and television content. At the forefront of these efforts is the American Family Association (AFA). Along with the Christian Coalition and other groups, the AFA led the charge in the early 1990s against federal funding for artists labeled "obscene." With the aid of Republican budget-cutters, the Christian Right has successfully fostered the idea that there should be no government role in supporting the arts. But the Christian Right has had less success challenging the content of network television, which is driven by what advertisers will allow—and they will allow whatever keeps the largest numbers of viewers from changing the channel. But for the AFA, it matters little if ABC, CBS, and NBC ever stop airing nighttime shows with sexually suggestive scripts. The prevalence of such "obscenity" keeps the troops on permanent alert.

Efforts to censor art and media reinforce for true believers the sense that they are in irresolvable conflict with secular enemies. This mindset is useful for political organizers but it is difficult to sustain over the long term. In Chapter 10, I suggest that some of the more idiosyncratic elements of evangelical belief and religious activity help sustain the momentum and commitment of people in the Christian Right. Specifically, I address the role of *eschatology* (the study of end-times prophecy), missionary work, and controversial practices that go on inside charismatic churches. My goal is not to highlight seemingly bizarre beliefs and actions in a gratuitous way, although I do take exception to missionary projects aimed at people who already have their own religions. My real interest in the religious practices of conservative Christians is not about doctrine but about how a movement sustains belief in its own righteousness and chances for success. As with my chapter on entertainment media, my point is that a successful social movement is one that gives people a sense of personal satisfaction as well as political efficacy.

Chapter 11 may be read as my most controversial chapter because it is about changes underway within the evangelical subculture on matters of race and gender. I deviate from predictable leftist views of the Right in that I do not think the latter represents, simply, a backlash to progressive change. On matters of race and gender, there are genuine changes underway within the Christian Right. I urge progressives to pay attention. Many white evangelical churches are beginning to repent for their own role in perpetuating racism. The Promise Keepers (PK) movement has made a top priority of what it calls *racial reconciliation*. To some extent, this idea takes form in a tokenistic way. PK events feature a carefully stage-managed racial mix among podium speakers even while most of the men in attendance are still white. But PK is just the beginning of a shift in how boundaries are drawn. By erasing the color line, the men of PK reinforce other lines of division, namely, the gender line and the line between "saved," born-again Christians and the "unsaved." About PK, I conclude that it is largely an effort by conservative Christian men to cope with the irrevocable gains of feminism. By reasserting their roles as strong husbands and fathers, they strengthen their belief in inherent male supremacy, but in a new and less aggressive form.

PK is a classic example of a popular evangelical cultural project that also bears watching for its political implications; in this case, the ways in which PK men are accommodating to society's slow but gradual shift toward gender equality. Some critics of PK choose to see it as a smokescreen for an unstated electoral agenda. My view is less cynical, and it is consistent with my point throughout this book.

If we want to understand the longevity of the Christian Right, we need to appreciate both the polarizing and vote-driven nature of our existing two-party politics, as well as the appeal conservative evangelicalism holds for millions of people. During times when the most hotly contested legislative issues are on the back burner, what keeps the movement alive is as much cultural and personal as political. When little is going on in the public arena, people in the Christian Right nevertheless share each other's views on the basics of marriage, childrearing, right and wrong. They sing and pray in church together, and gird themselves for battles to come.

Chapter 2

ᕤ

Staying Tuned

Where does one begin the project of trying to determine how and why the Christian Right has become a political powerhouse? One might look to the sorts of people involved in this social movement, their grievances, their motivations. This would be a difficult approach because while the movement is somewhat diverse demographically—meaning that it encompasses people from all regions of the country and from all walks of life—it is also homogeneous in terms of race, religious affiliation, and political viewpoint. The agenda of the movement, in terms of what it hopes to achieve, is broad and continually in flux. One year various groups unite to focus on Issue X. The next year the agenda shifts to Issue Y, and then to Issue Z. It makes little sense to try to psychoanalyze the millions of people who have found an affinity with the Christian Right. Their personalities are as varied and their motivations are as complex as those of any broad segment of the population.

Another way to approach the question of a social movement's success would be to try to measure the movement's influence on a series of salient public issues. But this approach would miss much about why people participate in movements in the first place. Movements are not necessarily out to respond to priorities already deemed worthy by the rest of society. Movements seek to reformulate public priorities, to win support for possibilities the rest of us oppose, or have not yet even considered. As such, a movement has to be judged on its own terms. Success may not entail outright victory but simply the power to shift the terrain on which other societal forces must pursue their goals.

This leads to my preferred way of looking at a social movement, in this case the Christian Right. A social movement is a set of interrelated *projects,* meaning a concerted effort and a plan to achieve a given goal. A set of projects implies the existence of some overarching goals which, in turn, involve incremental steps along the way. For the Christian Right, we could say, the primary project is to remake society in light of one particular reading of Christian doctrine: to make laws and institutions conform to biblical mandates. More specifically, this project involves countless subprojects: outlawing abortion, restoring the male-headed nuclear family, suppressing homosexual rights, removing objectionable materials from schools and art galleries, and so forth. Each of these projects can only be achieved to the extent that the movement creates effective organizations, the more the better.

But, along the way, the organizations of any enduring social movement take on lives of their own. They exist not only to achieve already-agreed-upon goals but also to forge ahead once one set of goals is achieved or abandoned. Organizations, therefore, are projects unto themselves. Yet the longevity of organizations depends on their continuing relevance to other projects, such as changing public opinion or changing the laws of the land. Sometimes a single organization carries water for a movement on a particular issue. More often than not, a successful movement involves multiple organizations working more or less in concert, united by similar beliefs, but employing often very different tactics. Inevitable conflicts between organizations do not spell the demise of a movement. If conflict means that one movement faction will fail, chances are that another faction will land on its feet. Organizations, like other living creatures, survive by evolving and adapting to their (political) climate.

In this book, I use the notion of a movement as a set of projects to analyze the Christian Right. Here we have a movement that encompasses a wide array of religious, political, cultural, and organizational projects. It is the potent mix of all these that has made the movement attractive to millions of participants and that has guaranteed it at least partial success. Yet factors internal to a social movement do not alone yield influence. Equally important is the broader societal context within which movements must contend for power. For the Christian Right, it is the combination of organizational resources, a motivating worldview, and a hospitable political environment that makes the movement a force to be reckoned with. In this chapter I look primarily at the role of religious broadcasting in this equation. Religious broadcasting stands apart from its secular counterparts. Historically, it has been the movement's most important resource. It provides audiences with a sense of shared goals and alerts them to issues they might not otherwise have thought about. In the following pages, I review some of the historical antecedents to the rise of Christian broadcasting.

Spreading the Gospel

∾

The Christian Right emerged out of an evangelical subculture that, until recent decades, was not attentive to partisan politics but instead was concerned primarily with spreading the Gospel.[1] The gradual shift toward political involvement began after World War II, when growth in the reach of broadcast media gave some evangelicals a new impetus to win converts. To ensure at least their fair share of access to the nation's TV and radio airwaves, evangelicals formed two related lobbies, the National Association of Evangelicals and the National Religious Broadcasters association. During the Cold War era, when communist nations were closed to Christian missionaries, and fear gripped the right wing in the United States, evangelicals worried that even the U.S. government might one day restrict their freedom to preach. This fear of religious persecution made it imperative to pay attention to the affairs of government. The cultural project of evangelism facilitated the slow but steady development of a political project.

Evangelicals want to make converts, and during the early post–World War II period they established some new and effective organizations to do just that. Over time they concluded that in order to keep society open to their brand of the Gospel, they would need to challenge trends they perceived as negative; changes in gender and family relations and society's growing secularism were the most pertinent. Gradually the definition of "the Gospel" itself expanded. It was not enough just to preach the story of Christ as savior. By the 1970s, many evangelicals felt a calling to preach on social issues as an integral part of their religious mission. The overarching project of the nascent Christian Right was to insist that questions of faith, morality, and even private conduct belong in the public sphere. Thus, it became part of "the Gospel" to try to outlaw abortion, to reinstate prayer in public schools, and to stop the extension of civil rights to homosexuals.

This political agenda has never been separate from the goal of winning new religious converts. It is no coincidence that two of the movement's most powerful organizations, the Christian Coalition and Focus on the Family, are outgrowths of broadcast ministries. As we will see in this chapter, a combination of factors gives religious broadcasting its potency. At one level, the broadcast ministries are successful business operations run by shrewd and popular individuals. More importantly, the media outlets feed adherents a steady diet of information, entertainment, and spiritual uplift—just the right mix to keep people tuned in, loyal, and ready to act on what they hear.

In Chapter 3, I deal separately with those aspects of the evangelical media culture that qualify more properly as entertainment, including the

Christian book and music industries, and I will show how these, too, carry a political subtext. In this chapter, my focus is on the more overtly political Christian media projects. I highlight Pat Robertson's Christian Broadcasting Network and Dr. James Dobson's Focus on the Family radio ministry because these are exemplary. But I will also deal with other players within the religious broadcasting industry in order to show the strength and diversity of this resource.

The Media and the Messengers

∾

Two aspects of the religious broadcasting industry have made it powerful. One is the sheer scope of the broadcasts in terms of numbers of stations and their reach into most U.S. households. The other is the diversity of formats and personalities found on the airwaves. Radio in particular is a medium that allows for a round-the-clock combination of preaching, interview, and call-in shows.

In 1972, there were 399 full- or part-time Christian radio stations on the air. By 1996, that figure had risen to 1,463,[2] and by 1997 the number of full-time Christian radio stations reached 1,648.[3] In the 1990s, Christian radio has been the third most common radio format in the United States, its popularity surpassed only by country music and adult contemporary music. In 1993, one in ten U.S. radio stations identified its programming as "religious," up 33% from 1980.[4]

On television, by 1997, there were 257 full- and part-time Christian stations.[5] Even more significantly, Christian TV is available as a selection on most cable systems. In 1996, Pat Robertson's Family Channel was carried via ten thousand cable systems into fifty-nine million homes.[6] Of these, more than two million people watched Robertson's weekday *700 Club* program. The Trinity Broadcasting Network, with its two-hour nightly talk show and the rest of the twenty-four hours filled with syndicated interview, Bible study, and music shows, reached into twenty-seven million homes through cable and through several hundred affiliated stations that carry some of its programming.[7]

Most of what airs on Christian TV and radio outlets is not overtly political, and when it is, the message is not a blatant call to vote Republican. The content is mostly biblical teachings, combined with programs offering practical advice on personal and family problems. But, typically, Christian radio stations also include several hours of programming on topics geared toward political activism. Radio station KFAX in the San Francisco area, for example, is part of the large Salem Communications group of stations around the country. On KFAX the schedule includes an early morning block of syndicated preacher shows plus the half-hour daily Focus on the Family program, which is often political in content. The midday schedule includes a rebroadcast of Focus on the Family plus the syndicated half-hour *Beverly LaHaye Live,* produced by Concerned Women for America. This show is almost always political in content; listeners are frequently urged to lobby their legislators on issues ranging from Supreme Court nominees to antiabortion and antigay legislation. In the late afternoon, KFAX, like many Christian stations, hosts its own locally produced drivetime call-in interview show with a mix of topics ranging from church controversies to nitty-gritty politics. The evening schedule is a block of popular syndicated preachers. Each day listeners can hear their pick of favorite Bible teachers plus political programming, and if they so choose, can call the station to interact with guests and fellow listeners.

On TV the content is similarly both inspirational and political. As discussed below, Pat Robertson's *700 Club* distinguishes itself as both a conservative Christian alternative to the network news and a place where viewers can call to pray with telephone counselors. On Trinity Broadcasting Network (TBN), the flagship program is the nightly *Praise the Lord* interview show, on which hosts Paul and Jan Crouch interview a mix of charismatic celebrities and Christian Right organizers. One of the regular shows on TBN is hosted by Jay Sekulow, the lead attorney at Pat Robertson's American Center for Law and Justice. Sekulow's program updates viewers on the latest court cases involving Christians, for example, cases concerning the rights to publicly preach, pray in school, or protest outside abortion clinics.

All in all, it is the mix of programming content that makes religious broadcasting popular. During the 1970s, when the religious broadcasting industry was growing by leaps and bounds, there was widespread concern that Christian TV viewing would cause people to stop attending church. To study the problem, in 1980, a coalition of groups that included evangelicals, mainline Protestant denominations, and Catholics, as well as the National Religious Broadcasters, jointly paid for a study to determine the effects of Christian TV on church attendance. The study, conducted by the Gallup organization and the Annenberg School of Communications, found that religious broadcasting was *not* causing a decline in church attendance. The research indicated that viewers of Christian TV tended to be active churchgoers and generous contributors to their churches. In other words, religious television viewing was an adjunct to, not a substitute for, genuine church involvement. The study also found that the religious TV audience was predominantly female, older, less educated, and more concerned about society's declining morality than viewers of secular network television. The overall audience size was estimated at about thirteen and a half million people who watched at least fifteen minutes of Christian TV on a weekly basis.[8] This was a far cry from some of the inflated claims made by some of the TV preachers themselves. In 1980, Jerry Falwell claimed he had an audience of twenty-five million for his *Old Time Gospel Hour* alone.[9] The audience size debate was never fully resolved because various studies, including one sponsored by Pat Robertson's own Christian Broadcasting Network, used inconsistent methodology. Some studies counted all respondents who said they had watched a single religious program in a given month. Some did not correct for duplication, that is, viewers who watched more than one program regularly. Reported figures ranged wildly into the tens of millions,[10] though the most credible estimate was probably in the range of several million regular viewers, including people who watched multiple programs.

Religious broadcasting and face-to-face interaction within a real church serve different purposes for people. The churches and the broadcast industry have their own separate histories. Much of the growth spurt for evangelicalism, beginning in the 1970s, came about through the youthful Jesus movement. These young converts came to the Lord mostly through friendship networks and not because they were glued to the TV set. The establishment of the religious broadcasting industry largely predated both the Jesus movement and the turn toward conservative political activism among evangelicals.

Religious broadcasting grew out a missionary tradition among evangelicals and fundamentalists. The first wave began in the 1920s when the medium was radio. The first Christian radio broadcast aired in 1921 over KDKA in Pittsburgh. At the time there was little government regulation of radio. Then, in 1927, Congress established the Federal Radio Commission (FRC), later replaced by the Federal Communications Commission (FCC). The FRC issued licenses and allocated channels and frequencies. Consequently, it became more difficult to get on the air, and only a handful of religious radio programs thrived in the 1920s. Then, in the 1930s, a controversy arose over the question of whether stations should sell airtime or give it away free to religious broadcasters. The Federal Council of Churches, which represented the liberal mainline churches, agreed with the federal government that for religious programs airtime should be donated by radio stations as a means to prevent corruption of the religious message. But most evangelical broadcasters were not members of organized denominations, and they feared that the established churches would get the lion's share of donated airtime. The evangelicals wanted the right to buy as much airtime as they could afford. To ensure access and to lobby for a shift toward paid-time programming, they formed the National Religious Broadcasters association in 1944, under the auspices of the National Association of Evangelicals which had formed in 1942. By the end of the 1940s, the

networks began to reverse their ban on selling airtime for religious programs.[11] Thus began a long process by which radio and TV preachers
willing and able to raise money on the air came to dominate the airwaves.
Preacher–performers such as Billy Graham, Rex Humbard, and Oral
Roberts, and, later, Pat Robertson and Jim Bakker, were simply more
entertaining than the ministers associated with the mainline denominations.

TV became a major project for evangelicals, and they were good at it.
Pat Robertson, in particular, took advantage of new technological break-
throughs, including the use of live-by-satellite interviews and, later, cable
TV. As we will see in the next sections of this chapter, Christian broadcasting thrives for several reasons. Smart businessmen—among whom Pat
Robertson and James Dobson are the best known—used tax-exempt
donations to build their respective media outlets into nation-spanning, even
global, soapboxes. But they could not have done it without responsive
audiences, large numbers of people eager for a message that combines
preaching with practical advice and a conservative spin on news events. As
I highlight throughout this book, Christian radio and TV often makes a
crucial difference in mobilizing evangelical activists to vote and lobby in
particular ways. Religious broadcasting is the single-most-important resource for the Christian Right. This is because of the kind of information
delivered over the airwaves. It is also because the most successful of the
Christian broadcast media emphasize connections between the minutiae of
people's personal lives and the larger mission of effecting worldly affairs.

The Christian Broadcasting Network (CBN)

ഇ

Most of the public knew little about Pat Robertson prior to his 1988
presidential campaign, and his entry into that campaign was less than
optimal. Robertson exposed himself to the national media limelight precisely at a time when scandals surrounding TV preachers Oral Roberts, Jim
Bakker, and Jimmy Swaggart created the impression that anyone appearing
on camera with a Bible in hand was cut from the same roguish cloth.
Robertson himself was no stranger to eccentricity. One of his best known
antics occurred in 1985, when he prayed on-air that a hurricane headed
for his Virginia Beach studios would change its course and strike elsewhere.
But Robertson's TV ministry, unlike some others, survived the preacher
scandals and thrived in the 1990s because he runs a solvent and innovative
broadcast operation. He was the pioneer of religious television. He was the
first to deviate from standard pulpit preaching on TV by launching the
original Christian news-and-interview show.

Business-wise, Robertson runs a tight ship. He made his millions neither by crying on cue nor by selling vacation time-shares for theme-park condominiums. Robertson's secret was to get in on the ground floor of the burgeoning cable TV industry and, later, to reap millions in windfall profits from an ethically dubious stock deal involving the network he built from tax-deductible donations. Robertson is every bit as much a businessman as a politician or a preacher. Like any successful businessman, he knows how to spot a good deal, and he also knows how to satisfy his customers.

The Robertson empire began when he bought a run-down television station in Portsmouth, Virginia, in 1959. In his autobiography *Shout It from the Housetops,* Robertson tells the story of how he opened the first bank account for the Christian Broadcasting Network (CBN) with three $1 bills. With help from local Christians, Robertson refurbished the station and, in 1961, he began broadcasting several hours a day. During a 1966 on-air telethon, Robertson came upon the idea for the *700 Club,* which became the title of his long-running weekday TV show. He announced that he needed seven hundred viewers who would donate $10 per month to keep the station solvent. By 1978, CBN had three hundred thousand donors. Of these, about one hundred and forty thousand were *700 Club* members, which meant that the minimum monthly intake was $1.4 million. By 1985, CBN had an annual budget of about $230 million, and from a single station, the *700 Club* spread to two hundred U.S. TV stations, and was also broadcast in some sixty foreign countries.[12]

From the beginning, one secret to Robertson's popularity was his decision not to mimic the standard fare of Sunday-morning TV preachers. Robertson used a set that looked like the one used for the *Johnny Carson Show.* Instead of standing at a pulpit, Robertson sat behind a desk; instead of preaching fire and brimstone, he interviewed popular Christian leaders and hosted Christian musical groups. Robertson is at the helm, but he is not the sole focus of attention, which makes the *700 Club* more interesting than other religious shows. Except during semiannual telethons, Robertson rarely begs for money on air. Instead, he pioneered the use of the phone-in counseling center. While they are watching, viewers are encouraged to call in to request prayer from counselors and to report miracles achieved through prayer. CBN counselors document each call, generating addresses for direct mail fundraising.

In 1978, CBN began a news department headed by Robert Slosser, a former editor for the *New York Times* who had become a born-again Christian.[13] The news feeds and the increasingly serious tone of the program were made possible thanks to the advent of satellite technology that allowed Robertson to expand his guest list. Instead of relying solely on guests willing to come to Virginia, Robertson set up bureaus in Washington, DC, and New York, from which he was able to interview politicians and other notables, thus making the *700 Club* look more and more like the *Good Morning America* genre of breakfast-hour magazine shows.

But not exactly. Even though, by the 1980s, the ninety-minute *700 Club* typically began with news and interview segments, creative forms of preaching remained central to the program. The daily repertoire in the 1980s and 1990s included segments reporting the good fortune of audience members who had tuned in to the *700 Club,* had prayed on the telephone with a CBN counselor, and had subsequently experienced a miracle: for example, the healing of an illness, a long-awaited check in the mail, the resolution of a family dispute, or some such divine intervention. Robertson worked with two cohosts, an African American man named Ben Kinchlow and a series of attractive, intelligent females. Together the three often sat around a small table praying out loud to receive what was called a "word of knowledge," a supernatural message that a viewer in a particular city was about to receive a miracle for a designated problem. Viewers were instructed to "claim" these miracles and call the CBN switchboard to report them.

One who did was a middle-aged housewife in Dallas named Mary Brown. She was sick and home from work one day. Her doctor had diagnosed her with a malignant uterine tumor. As she sat working on needlepoint and flipping through TV channels, she found the *700 Club*. It was the first time she had seen the program. She watched in amazement as one of the men on the screen said, "God has just spoken to me. There is a woman in Dallas, Texas, sitting in front of her TV with needlepoint in her lap. The doctors have just told you of a tumor on your uterus. God loves you. He is healing you right now." Mary Brown described feeling a "gentle warmth pass through her body." When she later went to her doctor, the tumor had miraculously disappeared.[14]

The story was recounted in a charismatic magazine profile of CBN. Countless similar stories have been recounted on the *700 Club* itself, often through dramatic vignettes using actors to re-create the tales. It is traditional within the pentecostal/charismatic subculture for believers to publicly testify as to what the Lord has done in their lives. The more detailed the testimony, the better: the further the depths to which one has sunk— through drug use, marital infidelity, or catastrophic disease—the greater the amazing grace that saves. On other Christian networks, such as Paul and Jan Crouch's Trinity Broadcasting Network, the guests simply sit on the couch with the hosts and tell their long, drawn-out salvation stories.

The *700 Club* raised the tradition to a new standard by turning the stories into scripted morality plays. Salvation stories are often used to personalize topics dealt with in the news segments of the show. For example, news reports on the AIDS epidemic in the 1980s were typically followed by a story of a "former" gay man who, in his youth, had moved to San Francisco to dabble with drugs and perversion. But after watching so many of his friends die of AIDS, he had renounced his homosexual "lifestyle" and converted to Christ. Thus the salvation story reinforces a worldview that frames social problems—and their resolutions—primarily as matters of individual behavior and/or supernatural forces, not problems to be addressed through collective social responsibility.

The prayer messages, the phone-in counselors, and the dramatized salvation stories have made the *700 Club* a highly personal medium. At a time when many people feel disconnected from real communities and real churches, Robertson and his cohosts project the message that they truly care about their audience. The segments devoted to personal salvation and healing make for a receptive audience likely to sit still when the program takes up political topics.

For secular news consumers, there are many less cluttered ways to get one's daily dose of information and analysis. For the general public, there is no shortage of newspapers, TV, and radio talk shows. But for many of the evangelical faithful, it is preferable to bypass the secular spin and get one's news from a reliable fellow believer. Robertson has marketed the *700 Club* to a narrow but underserved niche of the national TV audience. He recognized early on that the success of cable TV is based on cornering the market with specialized audiences.

Robertson understood niche marketing as early as the 1970s when he began moving the content of the *700 Club* in an increasingly political direction. Robertson used the program to host up-and-coming leaders of the New Right and to interpret affairs in the Middle East in light of biblical prophecy.[15] One of Robertson's persistent themes in the 1970s was that the world was moving toward a nuclear war centered in the Middle East. "When the smoke clears," Robertson once wrote, "Soviet Russia will be reduced to a fourth-rate power and Israel will be the wonder of the world. That is what the Bible tells us will happen, and it will happen!"[16] Robertson's religious views at the time coincided with escalating real-world tensions in the Middle East and with a stepped-up arms race between the United States and the Soviet Union. In an interview with the liberal evangelical magazine *Sojourners,* Robertson said he thought a U.S. war with the Soviet Union was inevitable and that the fall of the Shah of Iran in 1979 was a prelude to this war. But he also predicted that the arms race would burden the Soviet economy and that "by 1990 that system is going to fall of its own weight."[17]

In the 1980s, Robertson largely abandoned talk of the end-times and instead used the *700 Club* to air propaganda on behalf of Reagan administration policy in Central America. White House officials appeared frequently on the show, where they gave an otherwise ill-informed audience a distorted picture of the region's politics, all by way of justifying U.S.

support for dictators and assassins. CBN was among a number of private organizations that raised money for the Nicaraguan Contra terrorists at a time when a Congressional ban on funding for the Contras threatened to thwart the Reagan administration's goal of overthrowing the Nicaraguan government. Robertson also backed the Salvadoran and Guatemalan military dictatorships at a time when they were responsible for death-squad killings of thousands of their own citizens. For years, CBN ran newscasts slanted to favor Central America's right-wing military forces. During El Salvador's 1984 elections, for example, Robertson ran favorable coverage of that country's most violent and brutal right-wing factions, and repeatedly urged his viewers to lobby their Congressmembers for continued U.S. military aid to the regime there.[18]

During the Reagan era, Robertson also maintained his keen interest in Middle Eastern affairs. News reports on the *700 Club* were consistently skewed in favor of the Israeli government despite its consistent human rights abuses. Similarly, the *700 Club* in the 1980s reported favorably on right-wing paramilitary forces that wreaked havoc in southern Africa: UNITA in Angola and RENAMO in Mozambique. Robertson's journalistic advocacy on behalf of these mercenary armies—courtesy of tax-deductible donations sent to CBN—came at a time when the U.S. government was committed to supporting a series of so-called freedom fighter wars, which took their tolls mostly in civilian casualties. Robertson consistently sided with egregious killers, all in the name of fighting "communism," and all with the veneer of news reporting from a Christian perspective.

For the hundreds of thousands of regular *700 Club* viewers, the political world according to Robertson makes sense because it is packaged up along with religious ideas they already see as valid. It was only a matter of time before Robertson would use the broadcast ministry for his own political aspirations. It was his TV popularity that made it possible for him to even consider a presidential race. After that, the longevity and visibility of CBN made possible the speedy mobilization of the Christian Coalition.

Between ministry and politics, CBN is also a profitable business. In 1977, when cable TV was still in its infancy, Robertson started an around-the-clock satellite network that was, for a time, the second largest cable TV network in the United States. On this new network, Robertson could have chosen to supplement his own weekday *700 Club* program with other syndicated religious programs. That is what Paul Crouch of the Trinity Broadcasting Network and Jim Bakker of the PTL Network did when they entered the cable market. Robertson went a different route, adopting a strategy designed to expand CBN's audience beyond strictly religious viewers. CBN Cable, later renamed the Family Channel, competed with the new secular cable networks by purchasing the rights to reruns of old situation comedies and movie classics. These shows are inexpensive to acquire and are guaranteed to draw at least a small audience, some of whom might stay tuned for rebroadcasts of the morning *700 Club* show.

By 1987, CBN Cable had an audience of about thirty-four million viewers. Only about 25% of the network's daily schedule was devoted to religious programming. The other 75% of secular programming allowed CBN Cable to attract big-name advertisers.[19] Robertson's business plan allowed CBN to preach the Gospel *and* to grow into a highly valuable asset. Audience donations to the *700 Club* took a temporary dip during 1988 while Robertson campaigned for the presidency. By the early 1990s, pledges returned to mid-1980s levels, when a typical two-week telethon raised between $20 and $30 million. For the fiscal year ending in March 1993, donations to CBN totaled about $97 million.[20]

In the 1990s, the CBN media empire began to reap huge dividends for Robertson and his son, Tim. In 1989, the father–son team formed International Family Entertainment (IFE) as a separate corporation, which then purchased the Family Channel cable network for $250 million in 1990. One reason for the purchase was that the "nonprofit" CBN operation was not legally allowed to receive more than a fixed percentage of its income from a profit-making operation. The new Family Entertainment holding company allowed the nominally separate "nonprofit" CBN to continue to broadcast on the cable network free of charge several hours a day.[21] By separating the assets, the "nonprofit" piece of the empire continued to legally accept tax-deductible donations, while the Robertsons used the explicitly for-profit network to bankroll further ventures.

When the Robertsons formed IFE in 1989, they did so by going into partnership with Tele-Communications Inc. (TCI), the largest cable stem operator in the United States. This partnership signaled to other would-be investors that the Robertson venture was solid. Pat and Tim Robertson paid $183,000 to purchase six million shares of IFE stock, giving them the controlling interest. Then backed by the TCI investment in IFE, they purchased the for-profit Family Channel. The value of IFE's stock rose as advertising revenues climbed from about $40 million in 1990 to $71 million in 1991. Then the Robertsons took IFE stock public, and the market value of their six million shares, originally purchased for $183,000, skyrocketed to a whopping $90 million. The deal was technically legal though ethically questionable. In brief, over the years, Robertson had used tax-free money to create a "religious" ministry, which he then used as collateral to create a commercial cable network, the value of which mushroomed after the Robertsons became the controlling stockholders.[22]

Nor was the stock deal the sole source of continuing revenue for the CBN empire. The tangle of corporations run by Pat Robertson includes the United States Media Corporation, through which Robertson in 1992 made an aborted bid to purchase the United Press International (UPI) wire service;

the Founders Inn and Conference Center, a four-star hotel located at CBN headquarters; International Jet Charters, a small charter airline in Virginia; the Standard News radio wire service; and a proposed Founders Village retirement community.[23]

In 1997, there was talk of a possible merger between Robertson and media giant Rupert Murdoch, this despite the salacious programs (e.g., *Married with Children* and *Melrose Place*) that air on Murdoch's Fox Network. Murdoch reportedly was willing to purchase a 30% share of IFE, the parent company of Robertson's Family Channel, offering as payment preferred stock in Murdoch's gigantic News Corporation. This mutually beneficial deal would enable Murdoch to air Fox's children programming on the Family Channel, while Robertson would make a fortune with the stock deal.[24]

With all of his wheeling and dealing, Robertson has little time to devote to the day-to-day operations of CBN, so, in 1993, he named long-time CBN executive Michael Little as the new president of CBN.[25] Robertson's own attention is divided between appearing on the *700 Club*, overseeing the Family Channel, heading the American Center for Law and Justice legal firm, running the Christian Coalition, and administering Robertson's own Regent University.

The political projects owe their existence to the earlier success of CBN. Without the *700 Club*, Robertson could not have recruited a constituency, nor have raised the necessary funds, to build his empire. One cannot measure the effect of Robertson's conservative political journalism, day in and day out, on a small but loyal audience of several hundred thousand viewers. One can say that Robertson established for the Christian Right the standard message of tying one's personal redemption to a gospel of political participation.

Focus on the Family

⸂

Tune in to just about any Christian radio station and once, twice, even three times a day, one could well hear the soft, avuncular voice of Dr. James Dobson, dispensing homespun wisdom on everything from patching up a husband–wife spat to quelling a toddler's fear of the dark. Like Pat Robertson, James Dobson started small. Over two decades, the Focus on the Family radio broadcast grew into a media empire—and an affiliated lobbying project—that gets the attention of politicians. Dobson is to Christian radio what Robertson is to Christian TV. For both men, politics came as an outgrowth of their earlier work.

Dobson is the son of a Church of the Nazarene minister, and he was a successful child psychologist years before he took to the airwaves. He earned a Ph.D. in child development from the University of Southern California (USC) in 1967. Then he was a professor of pediatrics at the USC School of Medicine while he also worked at the Los Angeles Children's Hospital. At USC, he conducted research on some of the factors involved in childhood mental retardation.[26] In 1970, he published his first book, *Dare to Discipline,* with Tyndale House, an evangelical press. It quickly became a bestseller—it has now sold more than three million copies.

In *Dare to Discipline* Dobson tells parents to spank their kids, not on a whim and not as a sole form of punishment, but as something essential to good parenting. No doubt, some parents might read *Dare to Discipline* as a license for abuse. But Dobson writes that parents should spank infrequently, only on the buttocks, and not just for any old infraction—but only when children refuse to *obey.* On a regular basis, Dobson encourages parents to heap on their kids as much praise and love as possible. Dobson believes that a truly loving parent is one who will instill in children a healthy fear of authority, which he views as the basis for becoming righteous citizens and God-fearing Christians.[27]

Dare to Discipline first hit the market at a time when much of the public was appalled by the perceived excesses of the 1960s. By 1970, the baby-boomer generation, reared with a much less authoritarian parenting style than Dobson's, was rebelling on college campuses and heading for hippie communes. Dobson's book was a forerunner to the widely held view that a retreat from "traditional family values" is at the root of current social problems. His book reduces the complexities of raising children to the single notion that parents must take charge of their offspring inside their own four walls. Noticeably absent from *Dare to Discipline* is any thinking about whether spanking kids into obedience might produce adults overly submissive to secular, governmental authority. Instead, Dobson's popularity stems from the very simplicity of his message.

In 1977, overwhelmed by too many speaking requests, Dobson started a half-hour weekly radio program which he sent to a few dozen stations. By 1978, his public seminars were drawing as many as three thousand people a week and becoming so lucrative that he quit his USC job and started the not-for-profit Focus on the Family.[28] Twenty years later, the radio ministry remains central to Focus. By the mid-1990s, Dobson's half-hour interview and advice program was broadcast on about four thousand stations (counting some that aired the program more than once daily). An additional ninety-second daily Family Commentary aired on dozens of secular radio stations. The flagship *Focus on the Family* magazine is sent to nearly two million listeners, and a long list of more specialized *Focus* magazines caters to particular segments of the audience. The monthly political *Citizen* magazine, with a mid-1990s circulation of about one hundred and thirty thousand, is full of news reports and suggestions for activism. There are magazines for young children, for kids ages eight to twelve, and for teenage boys and for teenage girls, all of which mix Bible teaching with age-appropriate entertaining stories. There are special magazines for parents, teachers, and physicians.[29] Each month Dobson sends a letter to all the people on his mailing list, in which he outlines his thoughts on current political controversies. As of the mid-1990s, Focus had an annual budget of over $100 million. Most of that went to radio production and publishing. But about $4 million of the annual budget went to a "public policy" category that included lobbying and voter education.[30]

Dr. Dobson's success, like Pat Robertson's, derives from a combination of good business sense and a supportive constituency. In 1979, Dobson first got involved in politics. President Jimmy Carter was planning a White House Conference on the Family, and a number of already active New Right leaders were asked to participate. Dobson told his radio audience that he would like to be nominated as a representative; after eighty thousand letters poured in to the White House, he was asked to join the series of meetings.[31] The Conference on the Family ultimately yielded nothing in the way of legislative policy but it was, for many in the Christian Right, a first foray into the idea of using politics to bolster traditional family values.

Dobson himself became more interested in politics as the 1980s progressed. In 1988, Focus on the Family merged with the Family Research Council (FRC) which was then a tiny Washington, DC–based think tank headed by Gary Bauer, a former Reagan administration aide. Bauer had served in the Department of Education, and he knew the ropes of Capitol Hill lobbying. The association with Dobson gave the FRC new visibility. After 1988, Bauer became a regular guest on the Focus radio programs. The two organizations shared mailing lists. In 1992, Focus and the FRC severed legal ties so as not to jeopardize the tax-exempt educational status of Focus. But Bauer's think tank continues to work closely with Focus and with a loose network of several dozen state-based lobbies geared toward their respective state legislatures. These organizations were formed at a time when high-profile national Christian Right organizations, most notably the Moral Majority, had receded from influence. The Christian Right was becoming more decentralized, more focused at the state and local level, though still reliant on information and direction from national leaders like Dobson and Bauer.

In 1989, Dobson gained national name recognition when he interviewed Ted Bundy just hours before the notorious serial killer was executed. From prison, Bundy had written to Dr. Dobson after learning of the radio broadcast and publications. Bundy knew that Dobson had served on Attorney General Edwin Meese's Commission on Pornography, and Bundy had a confession to make, so Dobson struck up a correspondence with him. In the videotaped interview—which Dobson sold for $25 until he took criticism for being too greedy—Bundy blamed his crimes on his addiction to hard-core pornography.[32] This was music to the ears of conservative Christians, eager for evidence of a direct link between pornography and violent behavior.

For Dobson, the Bundy interview was a rare adventure in sensationalism. Mostly the popularity of Focus on the Family rests on Dobson's soft-spoken offerings of practical advice. He is the evangelical answer to Dr. Spock; at a time when real doctors no longer make housecalls, Dobson enters listeners' homes via radio and assures them that they can find solutions to their problems. The radio advice is supplemented with a question-and-answer column Dobson writes and syndicates in Christian newspapers, and with the monthly *Focus on the Family* magazine. The magazine features highly personal, down-to-earth stories by readers who share their solutions to family problems. There are articles on how to prepare young children for an overnight stay at the hospital; how to form a support group for stay-at-home moms; how to warn kids about drugs; and how to cope with messy family members. One frequent theme concerns readers coping with their inability to have children. This is a revealing subject. No doubt, infertility is a disappointment for those who want children. But in the world of Focus on the Family, it is assumed that childlessness is a tragedy, just as it is assumed that the best families are those in which father, mother, and kids play traditional roles. Without heavy-handedness, Focus repeatedly reinforces narrow notions of proper family relations, thus laying a groundwork for a further imperative to defend the traditional family through political action.

The attention Focus gives to people's mundane problems is what makes them committed to the ministry, and thus willing to listen when Dr. Dobson pontificates on political issues. Focus receives several hundred thousand letters from listeners each month. They are answered by staffers trained to look for emergency cases, such as people liable to commit suicide, who are contacted directly and given referrals to professional counselors. But, most of the letters are about common problems such as infidelity, custody disputes, workaholism, and the like. Staffers answer these letters using paragraphs from generic letters Dobson compiles. Staff members also send along recommendations for helpful books and tapes, thus giving afflicted letter writers specific tidbits of usable advice.[33] The Focus on the Family correspondents are similar to the prayer counselors who staff the phones at CBN. Both setups provide a bit of solace for people's emotional needs at a time when the rest of society seems to be falling apart. One can live on the same street for twenty years without knowing one's neighbors, and yet one can find some social connection through a Christian radio or TV ministry.

Focus on the Family is more than just a radio program and a publishing house. It is a mindset that moves seamlessly from the details of daily life to the ominous tasks of changing politics. One day Dobson might answer a question about potty training; the next day he might talk about a new Christian legal firm. In God's Kingdom, everything matters, and that is a vital message to convey to listeners not already skilled at changing the course of history. They are encouraged to believe that professional politicos, such as Gary Bauer, are working on their behalf in Washington, DC, and in their state capitols. But they are also taught that humble actions like writing letters to Congress will preserve the traditional family against a putative attack by secular forces.

In 1989, Dr. Dobson outlined how Focus on the Family could increase its political influence in the 1990s. He noted that in 1988 the ministry had directed a million calls and letters to Congress on two separate issues: the nomination of Robert Bork to the Supreme Court and a federal civil rights bill that expanded protections for minorities and the disabled, including people with AIDS, thus making it more difficult for private businesses to discriminate. The profamily movement lost on both scores, though not for lack of effort. Lobbying by Focus listeners was a quick strike but it was not the kind of sustained action that could set a national agenda even before controversies arise. To do that, Dobson offered a four-part program. Part 1 involved the Focus merger with Gary Bauer's Family Research Council. Bauer would "build relationships with legislators, policymakers, and journalists in the nation's capitol" to "help pro-family activists by providing timely, relevant, well researched information." Part 2 was the formation of think tanks to lobby state legislatures. Part 3 involved the *Citizen* magazine, which began publishing a monthly four-page insert written by the state think tanks so that readers could lobby on issues close to home. And as Part 4, Focus began *Family News in Focus,* a new radio spot with breaking political news for Christian radio listeners. Dobson promised that he personally would not abandon his primary mission of helping families solve problems.[34] But it was clear that Dobson also intended Focus to become a major player in the culture wars of the 1990s.

One way Focus has been involved is through Community Impact Seminars, coordinated by the state think tanks and sympathetic local churches, with speakers and literature sent from Focus headquarters in Colorado Springs. In 1994, I attended a Community Impact Seminar in California, along with two hundred other participants, and found it to be very different from the nuts-and-bolts training seminars offered by the Christian Coalition. It was as if Focus assumed its listeners were still amateurs and even gun-shy about politics. The full-day session was run by two motivational speakers who posed the basic question, "Why should Christians be socially and politically involved?" Fear, anger, and hatred are the wrong reasons, the speakers said. Christians should be motivated by a biblical "love of neighbor" to more effectively evangelize and save souls, and by a biblical obligation to be good citizens. The speeches all reinforced the idea that Christians should insert themselves into political institutions, and not fear opposition from secular society. There were no precise instructions given on voter registration and lobbying, nor on specific candidates or issues. Those details were left to subsequent seminars arranged by the leaders of the state think tanks who were best able to decide which seminar participants would make the best recruits.

In this way, Focus on the Family itself does not appear to be meddling in partisan politics. Focus does the educational work and then mostly leaves people to their own devices. This makes it difficult to judge the precise impact of Focus, though occasionally the ministry takes credit for its work. One Focus project has been the production of 60-second radio spots in conjunction with the state think tanks, aired locally on stations that offer free airtime. In Washington State, for example, Focus produced a spot, "A Woman's Right to Know," on proposed legislation that would have required abortion doctors to tell patients about risks. The leader of the affiliated Washington for Family Values received five hundred calls after the spot aired. A similar spot in Ohio yielded fifteen hundred calls for the Ohio Roundtable, which was sponsoring legislation to restrict sex education curricula.[35] Through such public service announcements Focus provides invaluable help to state and local organizers, including those who lack the skills and recording equipment to do their own media outreach.

In 1992, Focus helped Colorado for Family Values (CFV), the group that sponsored the anti–gay rights Amendment 2 ballot initiative. The signature drive to qualify Amendment 2 was floundering until Dr. Dobson aired a nationwide program on it. Immediately, recalled CFV organizer Kevin Tebedo, "Our phones began ringing off the wall. We had volunteers suddenly begging to carry petitions."[36] After that, Focus helped CFV produce public service announcements that aired on nearly every radio station in Colorado.[37]

Aside from focusing on particular campaigns, Dobson primarily plays an agenda-setting and figurehead role within the Christian Right. Politicians know that Dobson has millions of loyal listeners. It made a difference, then, when Dobson began protesting Republican rumblings about watering down the party's prolife plank before the 1996 election.

Normally Dobson does not speak or write in partisan terms. But in his March 1995 letter to his supporters, he threw down the gauntlet. He wrote that the Republican Party was becoming "increasingly squishy on the issue of abortion." He worried aloud that Senator Bob Dole refused to apply an antiabortion litmus test to possible vice presidential candidates. Dobson said he personally would not continue to vote for lesser-of-two-evils candidates when it came to abortion:

I am committed never again to cast a vote for a politician who would kill one innocent baby. These little ones have no defense except that which we provide for them. Never will I use my influence, however remotely, to support the shedding of their blood. . . .

By voting for a moderate pro-abortionist who might be more desirable in the short run, we squander our influence on decision makers. Rather, when a significant number of votes are cast for a third party/pro-life candidate, even in a losing cause, that fact will not go unnoticed by political leaders. They will be more likely to court our support in the future, especially if they lost the last election. That's the way the game is played.[38]

Thus more than a year before the 1996 general election, Dobson raised the specter that supporters of the Christian Right might refuse to vote Republican unless the party remained unequivocally antiabortion. To underscore the point, in March 1995, Dobson publicized a letter he had written to Republican National Committee chair Haley Barbour, reminding Barbour that prolife Christian voters were pivotal in the 1994 Republican Congressional sweep and warning that the party had better not take them for granted. Dobson's letter sparked similar public statements from Dobson's colleague Gary Bauer, from Concerned Women for America president Beverly LaHaye, and from Phyllis Schlafly of the Eagle Forum. Very early in the election cycle, all of them made it clear that the Christian Right would not accept anything less than a staunchly antiabortion ticket.[39] They worried, too, that the Christian Coalition might sell the movement out to "moderate" Republicans. Gary Bauer, in particular, took issue with the Coalition's *Contract with the American Family,* because its ten-point legislative wish list did not include a denunciation of gay rights and because it took aim against late-term abortions without calling for a ban on all abortions.[40]

To the extent that Dobson and Bauer know "the way the game is played," their game has different rules than that of the Christian Coalition. Focus on the Family and the Family Research Council are not terribly interested in winning immediate and direct influence with the existing cast of elected officeholders. While the Christian Coalition wants to help elect Republicans next month or next year, Dobson and Bauer take a longer view. Relieved of the urgent demands of electoral politics, Dobson and others who are primarily broadcasters and opinion-shapers have the luxury of sticking more closely to their principles.

Something for Everyone

⌘

It is taking the long view that makes religious broadcasting a successful industry and also a project essential to the continuing clout of the

Christian Right. There is a range in the political intensity of the various programs.

Trinity Broadcasting Network (TBN), with its nightly *Praise the Lord* interview-and-music show, is much more entertainment-oriented than Pat Robertson's *700 Club*. TBN began broadcasting in the late 1970s from a station in Orange County, California. Twenty years later, thanks to the demise of Jim Bakker's PTL Network, TBN ranked second only to CBN. Paul and Jan Crouch built TBN by adding to their own show a full schedule of syndicated preachers who paid for their airtime. TBN aired on some cable systems and on dozens of local stations owned by or affiliated with TBN.

The *Praise the Lord* program tends to be gaudier than other Christian TV shows. From the flagship station KTBN in Orange County, California, the glitzy mock-living-room set includes a fake fireplace, stained-glass windows, a grand piano, a chandelier, gold-painted furniture, and a big artificial flower arrangement on the coffee table.[41] To the sound of triumphant music, hosts Paul and Jan Crouch make a theatrical entrance. Paul has a full head of white hair and wears bright-colored, double-breasted suits. Jan wears a big platinum-blonde wig, thick false eyelashes, and an endless supply of southern belle dresses complete with hoop skirts, puffed sleeves, lace, and embroidery. From their overstuffed sofa, Paul and Jan conduct long, chatty interviews with a who's who of charismatic celebrities passing through southern California. Jan often dabs at her weeping eyes and looks up Bible passages while Paul asks the questions. A single interview may go on for two hours. Often the hosts and guests gather around a standing globe, lay their hands on a particular part of the map and pray that God will pierce the darkness and let the Gospel reach the region's unsaved masses.

Prayers around the globe usually coincide with Paul Crouch's latest trips abroad. Crouch travels energetically, and frequently reports on the deals he has made with foreign leaders to broadcast TBN in their countries. The monthly TBN newsletter carries photos of Paul meeting with heads of state from Central America to the former Soviet Union. Crouch even met with Yasser Arafat to discuss broadcasting TBN in the Palestinian territory.[42]

Crouch's trips abroad allow him to come back and pontificate on international affairs. Otherwise the political content on *Praise the Lord* is determined by the guest list. There are occasional interviews with elected officials, "recovered" homosexuals, antiabortion activists, and people concerned about "obscenity" in the entertainment media. But mostly *Praise the Lord* is late-night entertainment for pentecostals. There is raucous music. Jan often reads the prayer requests of viewers afflicted with disease and personal travails. The political content on TBN is left for the experts.

Attorney Jay Sekulow hosts a weekly program on legal issues. Dr. D. James Kennedy of Coral Ridge Ministries in Florida has a program combining Bible preaching with alerts about homosexuals, the American Civil Liberties Union (ACLU), Planned Parenthood, and other dangerous liberal organizations.

This is tame compared to some of what has passed for "religious" programming in recent years. While the secular talk shows became increasingly vulgar in the 1990s, the same was true of some Christian programming. Jerry Falwell tried to make a political comeback by using his *Old Time Gospel Hour* to rail against President Clinton, first over charges of sexual harassment, then by hawking a pair of videotapes alleging that Clinton was involved in unsolved murders and drug dealing back in Arkansas. The broadcasts were so disreputable that a Florida station pulled the plug on Falwell's show.[43]

But that did not stifle Operation Rescue leader Randall Terry, who sold the same tapes and used his weekday radio program to denounce Clinton, leaders of both political parties, and all sorts of other targets on a daily basis. In May 1996, when the Supreme Court ruled against a Colorado anti–gay rights law, Terry took to the airwaves enraged. He condemned to Hell, by name, each of the six justices who had ruled against the Colorado law, and he charged them with fomenting a cultural war in the United States. This was standard fare on *Randall Terry Live,* syndicated on several dozen stations.

Each of the radio stations can pick and choose from the many agitators eager to seat themselves before the microphone. Yet there is a trend in Christian radio similar to the changes underway in the commercial broadcast media. Just as an increasingly smaller number of corporations are assuming ownership of secular outlets, there is also a trend toward more concentrated ownership of Christian radio stations. By 1995, about fifty Christian radio groups, each working in at least three different regions, owned four hundred stations, or about one-fourth of the stations in the country.[44] The largest networks included Bott Broadcasting, Crawford Broadcasting, and Salem Communications.[45] Along with more concentrated ownership, there is also a shift in the stations' key source of revenue, from sale of airtime to numerous syndicated program producers, to an increased dependence on local advertising. There has been a drop in the sheer number of program producers. In 1991, the National Religious Broadcasters listed 742 radio producers; by 1994, there were only 383 listed, a decrease of nearly 50%.[46] The smaller number of programs, each heard on a greater number of stations, does not necessarily mean a loss of diversity because many of the inspirational half-hour broadcasts are barely distinguishable one from the next. What the trends do indicate, however, is that Christian radio is profitable and competitive, and subject to a drift toward homogenous programming across the country. That is good news for popular, politically minded broadcasters, such as James Dobson, Marlin Maddoux, and Beverly LaHaye. When controversies arise—for example, over gays in the military or proposed restrictions on homeschool teachers—they are able to mobilize listeners quickly because they have such large audiences.

There is also a trend toward more call-in programs, reflecting the popularity of the secular talk medium. As I mentioned earlier, Christian radio stations typically include one or more of their own call-in shows, often aired during drivetime and usually with a political bent. One Christian talk show host, Warren Duffy of KKLA in Los Angeles, explained that this type of radio is popular because his listeners see that "their Christian values are being attacked in the political arena on many levels [and] that an active faith requires involvement in the political and social causes that affect our freedom to live godly lives."[47] Along with his counterparts throughout California, in 1994, Duffy's show was instrumental in getting listeners to lobby successfully against a controversial public school achievement test.[48]

As I said with regard to Pat Robertson and James Dobson, it is the seamless content of religious broadcasting that makes it useful for political mobilization. Programs or segments of shows that seem merely to entertain or offer personal advice are, in fact, instrumental in keeping people tuned in and ready to absorb more challenging political material. When people feel connected to a favorite talk show host, when they enjoy hearing their own views repeated by other listeners, they are more likely to want to participate in suggested collective action, for example, calling or writing an elected official.

Part of a Package

Through a revolving door, leaders of the Christian Right often find themselves becoming radio and TV hosts, and vice versa. Organizations rely on the Christian media to reach their constituents, and the media outlets rely on activist spokespersons, lest they have nothing to put on the air.

The backbone of the movement is a multitiered complex of organizations. There are large national outfits geared toward lobbying and distributing information to profamily supporters. Some of the big national lobbies work through state branches and local chapters. Also at the local level, groups form to wage specific campaigns: against abortion clinics or to sponsor anti–gay rights measures, for example. As with any successful social movement, there is a dense overlap with people working for and donating to multiple organizations. Each group has its own prerogatives. But each group is also part of a larger project, whether the goal is to win an election or to make Christians more aware of the political process.

In Chapter 4, as I trace the recent history of the Christian Right, I show how the movement's major political organizations have evolved. The Christian Coalition, the Family Research Council, and other established outfits have an explicitly political agenda. But what makes their message reverberate loudly goes beyond Christian TV and radio. It includes seemingly less political forms of media, including fiction, magazines, and music. Evangelicalism is a cultural phenomenon and, as we will see in the next chapter and elsewhere in this book, its political themes are amplified as much through entertainment as through direct forms of organizing. Songs and suspense can influence minds just as surely as a handbill.

Chapter 3

Hearts and Minds

*I*n *Left Behind,* one of the bestselling Christian novels of the late 1990s, Captain Rayford Steele is an airline pilot who has been enjoying lascivious thoughts about a certain female flight attendant. Rayford's wife, Irene, is a born-again Christian. She keeps trying to drag Rayford to church, and he keeps refusing. Then on board a routine flight one day, about a third of the passengers suddenly vanish into thin air. Panic sets in as the flight crew learns from ground control that the same thing has happened on every plane in the sky and, in fact, all over the world. Rayford lands at the Chicago airport and rushes home, only to find his dear wife's empty nightgown lying between the bed sheets. She and their young son have disappeared in what Rayford comes to believe was the Rapture. All true Christian believers and very young children have been swept up into Heaven, while everyone left behind—including plenty of people who went to church but never really gave their hearts to Jesus—fumbles to figure out what will happen next. As it happens, an enterprising young magazine reporter named Buck Williams was on the flight with Rayford and had promised the same female flight attendant that he would stay in touch with her. Buck is hot on the trail of an international cabal that wants to unify the world's currency and reorganize the United Nations. Some of Buck's friends in the media and foreign intelligence agencies die mysteriously while trying to uncover the conspirators. Rayford and his college-age daughter, Chloe, study the Bible with a member of Irene's church who was left behind. They repent for their past disbelief and hope for a second chance to join Irene and their son/little brother in heaven. Buck meets up with the Steeles while they are on a stopover in New York. Buck falls in love with Chloe, and eventually converts to Christ. Then Buck succeeds in proving—at least to himself, if not to his editor—that the newly elected, blonde, and blue-eyed president of Romania, Nicholas Carpathia, has come to New

York to seize control of the United Nations. Carpathia is the Antichrist who will rule the world while Rayford, Chloe, and Buck will try to convert others during the coming period of social upheaval.

Left Behind was written by long-time Christian Right leader Tim LaHaye and fiction writer Jerry Jenkins. It was LaHaye's first novel, following dozens of other books on family life, politics, and biblical prophecy, some coauthored with wife Beverly LaHaye, president of Concerned Women for America. For years, the LaHayes have led American Christians on trips to the Holy Land to study signs of the coming fulfillment of Bible prophecy. The novel, published in 1995, was an immediate bestseller, no doubt because of LaHaye's reputation in the Christian Right world and because the book enjoyed heavy promotion on the *Beverly LaHaye Live* radio program. *Left Behind* was written for Christians to enjoy themselves and to give to their "unsaved" friends in an effort to convert them. It is a skillfully written story, one that offers more hope than fear. Its message is that unbelievers—unless they repent and convert now—will have to endure a disastrous period called "the Tribulation." But after the Rapture, they will have a second chance to repent and, if they do repent, after they die they will be reunited with their loved ones in heaven.

They will have to be wary, though. The novel's not-so-delicate subtext concerns the international machinations we are instructed to see as signs of the coming Rapture, Tribulation, and a final battle between the forces of good and evil. Hidden conspirators have ensconced themselves within the United Nations, and they are hell-bent on destroying the sovereignty of the United States. Under the rubric of peacemaking, a thriving global economy, and interreligious ecumenicism, an Antichrist is gaining power to control the hearts and minds of all people who are not protected by salvation in Christ. Look out for the seemingly noble deeds of political leaders. They may be enemies of God, no less.

∾

The political impact of religious broadcasting is undeniable. Without the likes of Pat Robertson, Dr. James Dobson, Beverly LaHaye, Randall Terry, and scores of lesser known talk show hosts, Christian Right activists would have difficulty staying abreast of issues and keeping inspired to act collectively. Most of what airs on Christian TV and radio is more religious than political. It is about getting saved from sin and lack of faith. It is about straightening out one's finances and marriages. But once convinced of their own moral righteousness, the audience is ready to hear about saving and straightening out the rest of the country. The religious content of religious broadcasting opens people's ears for direct political appeals from trusted fellow believers.

Most of what is read and heard elsewhere within the evangelical subculture is more properly religious than political, but there is usually a link between religion and politics. Religion is a cultural expression. What distinguishes one brand of Christianity from another is the way in which each crafts messages about human relations: about authority and obedience, good and evil, success and failure, violence, gender roles, racial distinctions—in other words, everything that matters. Christian TV and radio handles these subjects via two formats, through traditional preaching and through news and public affairs formats, including talk shows. That is not enough to satisfy the desire of audiences to be simultaneously informed, inspired, and entertained. A gripping novel packs at least as much political punch as a homily from James Dobson.

In this chapter, I examine the parts of the evangelical media culture not typically thought of as "political" in content or impact. Here I include, but do not purport to treat in exhaustive detail, Christian periodicals, Christian music, and the Christian book business. My point is not that all subcultural productions reflect or endorse a political agenda. As I said in the previous chapter, to the extent that believers find their personal needs met within the evangelical subculture, they are more likely to be eager for action when political opportunities present themselves. They are more likely to think and act in sync with the same leaders and organizations that inspire them on a personal level. To remain committed to a social movement over a long stretch of time, one must find some sense of fulfillment, even fun. For the entrepreneurs working in electronic and print media, the products they produce and broadcast must be profitable. Not everything that is fun has a price tag. But within the evangelical world, what sells is what makes ideological sense to people who see themselves both engaged with and at odds with the rest of mainstream culture. In this chapter, I look at evangelical cultural productions as both an industry and as a factor in the efficacy of the Christian Right.

Sizing Up the Market
❧

A typical Christian bookstore is like a small department store. There are racks of Bibles, greeting cards, and calendars; aisles full of T-shirts, compact discs, and cassettes; and display cases for jewelry and embroidered nickknacks. There is a trend toward converting bookstores into one-stop superstores, though publishing is still the driving force behind the thriving $3 billion a year Christian bookstore business. The Bible—in every shape, size, and binding imaginable—is an eternal bestseller, as are children's books, adult fiction, and manifestoes on why Christians should be involved in politics. The popularity of Christian TV and radio does not hurt book sales but instead seems to create a book market driven by evangelical celebrities: Tim LaHaye, James Dobson, Pat Robertson, and Charles Colson, to name a few. Books promoted through religious broadcasting are guaranteed success at the retail outlets.

In the 1990s, revenues in the Christian publishing industry have grown steadily. *Christianity Today* magazine reported that between 1991 and 1994, religious book publishing increased by 92%, from 36.7 million books to 70.5 million books.[1] The popularity of evangelical books sustains some twenty-five hundred Christian bookstores, and the secular chains, too, now carry the bestselling Christian titles.[2]

Christian publishing owes its success in part to the ease of niche marketing. Publishers know which popular Christian magazines to advertise in, which Christian talk show hosts have the biggest audiences, and which specialized Christian mailing match their target audience. Just as the National Religious Broadcasters association serves evangelical TV and radio entrepreneurs, the Christian Booksellers Association (CBA) facilitates the coordination of the evangelical publishing industry. The CBA was formed in 1950 at a time when only a handful of businesspeople managed Christian bookstores. Among the founders were directors of several evangelical publishing houses, including Moody Press. The idea was for retailers to share information with each other and get to know the publishers.[3] Eventually, CBA began publishing a glossy magazine for everyone in the Christian media business. For many years, it was called *Bookstore Journal* and then, in 1997, the name was changed to *Marketplace*, reflecting the fact that books are but one commodity in Christian retailing. *Marketplace* is the Christian counterpart to *Publishers Weekly*, full of ads, reviews, and tips on the latest trends in marketing. Since the 1950s, the CBA has held an annual convention, which is now one of the two hundred largest trade shows in the United States. The CBA makes an effort to invite stars and executives from the religious broadcasting industry to its conventions.[4] Sending authors out on the TV and radio circuits is key to the publishers' success.

Aside from its annual convention, the CBA is pivotal to the industry in other respects. *Marketplace* is a goldmine of information not otherwise available to the managers of Christian bookstores. Each issue offers the latest research data on sales trends and tips on how to market books to specific age, gender, and ethnic groups. The popularity of the Promise Keepers (PK) men's rallies, for example, has coincided with the release of dozens of new men's books. The CBA follows this trend and encourages retailers to cater to male customers even though, the CBA reports, women account for 80% of the sales in Christian retail stores.[5] In 1997, the CBA reported a 49.5% increase over the previous year's sales of men's books, and attributed the growth directly to the popularity of the PK rallies. The CBA encouraged booksellers to get ready for upcoming PK events, especially the national gathering in Washington, DC, in the fall of 1997. "As record numbers of Christian men gather in the nation's capitol for prayer, expect a storm of media attention," one *Marketplace* article advised. "That and the prayer gathering's historic impact are likely to drive both curious and devoted men into your store."[6]

Aside from tips on how to create a more man-friendly store environment—by downplaying frilly window displays and beefing up men's racks with Bible-study software—CBA recommends that store owners "more aggressively seek out the African-American consumer." One way to attract blacks is to feature books by Tony Evans, T. D. Jakes, and other African American men who speak at PK rallies. The CBA encourages retailers to tap into the $400 billion worth of African American purchasing power by courting black clergy. "If you can get the pastor as a regular customer in your store," the CBA recommends, "he can become an opinion leader. This is more so than with Anglo leaders because the black pastor is one of the few voices of authority in the black community."[7]

Another hot market is homeschooling families. Reportedly, homeschooling families purchase five to six times as many books as other customers. In the 1990s, the CBA reports, the numbers of homeschooling families grew by about 20% a year.[8] Because homeschool parents tend to be solidly middle class or upper middle class and spend about $500 per year per child on school supplies, the CBA recommends that retailers cater to these customers by staying in contact with local homeschool associations.[9] The CBA notes that once homeschool parents are in the store, they are likely to buy more than just books for their children.

Like other publishers, Christian publishers depend on a few bestsellers to sustain the rest of their lists. Word Publishing, for example, specializes in celebrity bestsellers. In late 1995, three of the five bestselling Christian novels were Word books: Frank Peretti's *The Oath*, Pat Robertson's *The End of the Age*, and Charles Colson's *Gideon's Torch*.[10] The CBA calls Christian publishing a "backlist-driven industry" because a handful of popular titles continue to sell well year after year. In 1996, the top one hundred titles together sold nearly ten million copies, with the top eight titles selling more than two hundred thousand copies each.

The books sold can be divided into several categories. Bible study and devotional books accounted for about 20% of sales, up from 16% in 1995, and inspirational titles accounted for 8% of sales. A group of "gift titles" made up 15% of sales. "Christian living" books accounted for 16% of sales, and books on love, marriage, or parenting another 6%. Men's titles accounted for 4% of sales. Fifteen percent of the titles sold were works of fiction. Smaller percentages of books were sold in the categories of prophecy, autobiography, financial management, and health.[11] Within each of these categories, a few titles distinguish themselves. In 1995, the best-selling book was Dr. James Dobson's *Life on the Edge* about issues effecting young adults. Two books by Hal Lindsey about the coming end of the millenium were among the top twenty, and the Promise Keepers movement's manual, *The Seven Promises of a Promise Keeper*, was number fifteen on the list.[12] In 1996, the top three books were all little collections of devotional themes. Number four was John Hagee's *The Beginning of the End*, which looks at current events in Israel as signs of biblical prophecy. The novel *Left Behind* ranked seventieth on the bestseller list.[13]

Christian booksellers see themselves as promoters not just of commodities but also of moral values and enduring truths. The annual CBA conventions are occasions at which industry luminaries pontificate on moral decay within the secular culture. For example, at the CBA's 1995 convention, Charles Colson delivered the keynote address. In the 1970s, Colson went to jail for his role in the Nixon administration's Watergate scandal. Subsequently, Colson became a born-again Christian, the director of a prison counseling ministry, and a bestselling author of inspirational books. Just prior to the release of his first novel, *Gideon's Torch*, Colson spoke to the CBA audience about morality, and said that "a society that has confused liberty and license . . . [is] a grave danger to the liberties that we enjoy here in America."[14] As in the secular media world, the viewpoints of celebrity authors are considered inherently newsworthy. In the 1990s, Colson has spoken at conferences for the Christian Coalition and Concerned Women for America, not because he is still a political operative, but because he has assumed a sort of folk hero status. He was a sinner when he worked in the White House, but now that he has submitted himself to the will of God, he performs deeds of charity and yet he can recall firsthand the corruption of which he speaks.

The Printed Word

∽

The prominence of Charles Colson (and others like him) is partly the function of the kind of cross-promotion involved in selling any kind of books. The broadcasting networks are naturally the biggest soapboxes for the promotion of Christian blockbusters. Lesser known is the evangelical periodical medium. The most popular magazine is the monthly *Charisma*, with a circulation near a quarter million.[15] *Charisma* looks like a cross between *People* magazine and *Reader's Digest*. It is loaded with photographs and short, easy-to-read stories. It features flattering promotional articles on all the latest celebrities in the evangelical subculture: TV preachers, authors, musicians, missionaries, political movers and shakers. *Charisma* is packed with ads and reviews of books and recordings. It is a key link in the chain between consumers and publishers, recording companies, and retail outlets.

Charisma gives readers a sense of what is happening among fellow Christians across the country. At the local level, about fifty independent monthly evangelical newspapers serve a similar role. The newspapers are available by subscription or are given away free at Christian bookstores. Display advertisements from local Christian-owned businesses absorb much of the page space and pay the costs of publication. Ads for bookstores, private schools, car dealerships, and real estate agencies reflect the degree to which evangelicals can, if they choose, live as a closed society and deal only with fellow believers. The *Southern California Times* is big enough to sustain three versions, one each for San Diego, Orange County, and Los Angeles. San Diego has such a large evangelical community that it is also home to another monthly newspaper, *Good News, Etc.* The typical format for these papers is about thirty pages in a tabloid-sized format. There is the *Colorado Christian News*, the *Dallas/Ft. Worth Heritage*, the *Good News* in Tucson, and another *Good News* in Eugene, Oregon. The papers are all similar in content. They lean heavily toward local reporting from pastors, parishioners, and profamily activists. Each paper also has its own calendar of upcoming Christian events.

The material is repetitive from one newspaper to the next because much of it comes from the Evangelical Press News Service (EPNS) in Minneapolis. EPNS is a syndicated news-gathering service that sends a weekly packet of articles to some 280 Christian media outlets for an annual subscription price of $100. EPNS's weekly packet includes regular news coverage on such topics as abortion-related legislation, election campaigns, and meetings of major Christian Right organizations. By mixing local coverage with EPNS file stories, the regional publications function as everyday newspapers for readers seeking an evangelical spin on the news. The regional papers serve to unify and solidify an evangelical worldview, and this has political implications. Here is just one example.

In February 1995, EPNS reported an incident in which a dozen members of an activist group called Lesbian Avengers entered the Bay Area office of Exodus International. Exodus is the leading antigay counseling ministry. It is well known to evangelical readers as an effort to turn homosexuals away from their "sinful lifestyle." Inside the Exodus office, the Avengers—accompanied by a reporter from a San Francisco gay newspaper—released hundreds of live crickets and waved signs urging God to send a plague on the organization. The incident got little coverage in the local mainstream media. But thanks to EPNS's short dispatch, the story was picked up by many of the regional evangelical newspapers. The story carried a potent message. Exodus executive director Bob Davies was quoted as saying that the incident was "another confirmation that many gays are not interested in tolerance and diversity." Davies warned that the incident was a "foretaste of things to come for all members of the conservative church. The lines are being drawn."[16] Indeed, the protest action of the Lesbian Avengers, regardless of their intent, succeeded in reinforcing in the minds of evangelical readers the view that gay people will break the law and damage private property in order to flaunt their message. The story gave legitimacy to the antigay cause precisely at a time when the Christian Right sought support for its anti–gay rights ballot initiatives. In EPNS's version of events, Exodus was just minding its own business when it was attacked by aggressive lesbians. The story mined the twin themes of "religious persecution" and "gay excess," amplifying an otherwise minor event into a Christian Right parable for a national readership.

The Avenger story typifies the circulation of informational tidbits through the evangelical media. Much of what is published and broadcast is more subtle than the Avenger story, and involves the creation of a general view in which born-again believers can see themselves both as *special* and *protected* from secular influences. The sheer volume of Christian media enables evangelicals to live culturally in a parallel universe alongside secular society. Believers may partake of the secular entertainment and news media to their hearts' content. They can talk sports scores and Hollywood gossip with non-Christian coworkers and still rely on a safety net of information and inspiration coming from their own media institutions.

Sweet Sounds of Success

⮌

The regional newspapers are small-scale projects with circulations each numbering in the tens of thousands. The rest of the evangelical media is big business. Apart from publishing, the major growth industry is contemporary Christian music (CCM). CCM grew out of the youthful Jesus movement of the late 1960s and 1970s, when the goal was simply to make a joyful noise for the Lord. The old church hymns did not capture the spirit of the new converts, so young Christians created their own music by setting born-again lyrics to a rock beat.

By the 1980s, CCM was a phenomenon driven less by the needs of Sunday worshipers and street evangelists and more by the Christian music celebrities who sell millions of dollars' worth of CDs and concert tickets. Singer Amy Grant was the first to gain national fame, but she was soon followed by a long list of superstar solo artists and bands, including Steve Green, Gary Chapman, Michael W. Smith, Ron Kenoly, Petra, DC Talk, and the Newsboys. In 1995, CCM record sales and concert tickets grossed about $1 billion, or one-tenth of the entire $10-billion-a-year music industry.[17] By the late 1990s, with CCM expected to continue to account for 10 to 13% of all music sales, the executives at many secular record labels were rushing to create their own CCM divisions.[18]

The key to CCM's success is the diversity of the music. Gone are the days when "Christian music" meant either gospel singing or Pat Boone in his white, patent-leather shoes crooning happy-snappy tunes about Jesus. CCM artists attract a wide following because they span all the popular musical genres, including country, folk, jazz, heavy metal, grunge, and hip-hop. There is even a Christian reggae band, Christafari, whose members, both black and white, wear their hair in dreadlocks and sing about God as "Jah."[19] What distinguishes Christian music is its lyrics, which stress the saving grace of Jesus and put a Christian spin on "contemporary," controversial themes such as abortion and teenage chastity.

The first wave of CCM was heard mostly at the outdoor gatherings of young self-described "Jesus freaks." Then the recordings began to air on Christian radio stations. Since 1978, the music has had its own trade magazine, simply titled *Contemporary Christian Music,* with ads and articles about all of the latest hot singers and bands. Major Christian record labels include Sparrow and Star Song.[20] The latest recordings are reviewed frequently in popular Christian magazines such as *Charisma,* and the industry even has its own version of the secular Grammy awards, the Dove awards.

About half of all Christian radio stations devote at least part of their broadcast schedule to CCM. A survey by evangelical pollster George Barna found that about 44% of all Christians tune in to CCM some time during a given year.[21] Christian radio is no doubt pivotal in the promotion of CCM record sales. In turn, CCM is a major reason why listeners keep their radios tuned to religious stations. In a 1996 analysis of the growing popularity of CCM, *Religious Broadcasting* magazine reported a survey of CCM radio listeners conducted by a media consultant affiliated with the National Religious Broadcasters. The survey found that listeners to CCM radio use the medium for both entertainment—they like to sing along—and for spiritual uplift, as part of their daily worship routine. CCM radio listeners also expressed strong dissatisfaction with secular radio. They listen to CCM as a way of avoiding secular music, particularly its lyrics. In terms of demographics, the study found that about 65% of regular CCM radio listeners were female and about 35% were male. Age-wise, 73% of listeners were between the ages of twenty-seven and forty-five. Eighty-three percent were Caucasian; 13% were Hispanic; and 2% were African American. Most listeners had some college education; most had middle-class incomes; and most were members of nondenominational or charismatic churches.

Seventy-nine percent identified themselves as politically "conservative," while only 16% self-identified as "moderate" and 3% as "liberal."[22]

Just as secular fans often seek to emulate their favorite music stars, CCM artists conceive of themselves as role models for fellow Christians. Much of their message differs little from that promoted by the secular music business: Buy our CDs. Buy tickets to our concerts. Buy the products we endorse. Copy our styles. Believe that you, too, can get rich in this society if only you try hard enough.

But apart from offering its own version of mainstream consumerism, the CCM industry is also a ministry for preaching Gospel morality. On a regular basis, *Charisma* magazine profiles Christian recording artists and allows them to explain to their readers the point of their music. Some seek to console the broken-hearted. For example, the singers with a group called East to West explain that they come from divorced families; that they found Jesus only after they enrolled in college; and that their songs are about "relat[ing] to Generation Xers who struggle with divorce and forging through an immoral society that often points to the wrong path."[23]

The pages of *Contemporary Christian Music* magazine are full of interviews with handsome industry celebrities, who use their stardom to promote religious themes and the message that they should be listened to because they represent God. For example, in an interview, the young singer Greg Long was asked what he is "required to do" by God, and he answered this way:

> I think it's just required of me to be an example. It's required of me to never let people down. On the same hand, I'm trying to balance that with trying to be Christ-like. That's really my goal because He was always giving, always loving. He was the servant of all and proved it when He gave up even His own life. How much less should I be able to do?[24]

By casting themselves as emissaries of Christ, the CCM artists and their handlers set unrealistic, and presumptuous, expectations for themselves. Yet the marketing of CCM artists emphasizes their moral superiority over run-of-the-mill secular entertainers. Some Christian record companies go so far as to include a "morality clause" in their artists' contracts, thereby allowing the companies to cancel deals if a performer is found to have engaged in adultery. This happened to Michael English after he confessed to having had an affair with a female Christian vocalist. English's company stopped selling his records and forced him to publicly disclose the affair by threatening to hold their own news conference if he did not.[25] Similarly, Sandy Patty, who had been voted Female Vocalist of the Year by the Gospel Music Association for ten years in a row, came under fire when she revealed in an interview with *Christianity Today* magazine that she had been unfaithful to her first husband. Word Records, which had been scheduled to ship Patty's 1995 Christmas album to stores, postponed its release after she revealed her past infidelities.[26] But unlike English, who was forced to reinvent his career by moving to a secular recording company, Patty was treated more generously by the evangelical community and by the CCM industry, which eventually resumed promotion of her music. The difference in treatment was attributed to Patty's more forthright confession and her public pledge to seek counseling from her pastor.[27]

Whereas secular music fans almost expect their idols to misbehave, CCM artists are obliged to play a role well beyond entertainment. It is as if by living out the ideals of the evangelical subculture the CCM artists compensate for the sinfulness in the secular world.

As paragons of virtue, CCM artists are seen as credible purveyors of a range of subtle messages, some as contradictory as those found in secular music. Much of the CCM message revolves around simple praise and worship of God. While some artists stress themes of love and compassion, others promote militancy. One ad for popular male singer Carman's *Righteous Invasion of Truth* album, for example, pictured him in a tough-guy leather aviator jacket, combat boots, and sunglasses poised as if he were about to leap out of an airplane or march into battle.[28] The same month, *Contemporary Christian Music* ran an article on two meek, young Christian housewives who write a regular *Arizona Republic* newspaper column "from a conservative biblical perspective about government, schools, family values and society in general."[29] The same issue of *Contemporary Christian Music* featured a lengthy critique of racism still prevalent within evangelical churches and within the CCM industry itself. The article ended with a checklist of "10 Things You Can Do to Help Erase Racism," including suggestions that Christians get out of their "comfort zone and interact with people of other races," that they "hire qualified minorities for all positions," that they stop repeating racist jokes, and that they register to vote and "elect candidates who promote equality."[30]

To make profit, CCM needs to be all things to all people. Musical diversity and slightly hip political stances can only help CCM attract large audiences, especially the young people who are most likely to buy CDs and concert tickets.

For the record companies, if not for the artists and fans, the bottom line is sales. In 1996, DC Talk, a Christian hip hop group, broke all prior sales records by selling eighty-six thousand units of its new album within one week. Ninety percent of the sales were made in Christian retail stores.[31] On a regular basis, music sales account for about 15% of revenues for Christian bookstores.[32] The vitality of CCM encourages a trend toward greater consolidation of record company ownership, particularly in the hands of gigantic secular corporations. Some of the industry's original artists and executives worry that increasing commercialization will eventually water down the music's Gospel message and fuel the same kind of celebrity worship prevalent among secular music fans.[33]

But for Christians interested in evangelism as well as making money, CCM means new vistas. In 1996, the publisher of *Charisma* magazine, Strang Communications, created a new Sunday-school course for teenagers featuring video footage of the popular Christian rock band the Newsboys.[34] (The name "Newsboys" is a reference to "good news," which is another name for the Gospel.) To help publicize the course, *Charisma* ran a cover story about the Newsboys, six young men from Australia, New Zealand, and the United States, who look no different from any other group of grunge performers. The author of the promotional article delights in describing lead vocalist Peter Furler: "A black tank top hangs from his thick arms and shoulders. The hems of his faded jeans disappear into a scuffed, untied pair of black Doc Marten boots. His half-inch-long spiked hair is dyed light yellow."[35] Furler looks like a rock star from central casting, but he and his comrades are on a mission:

> Like envoys, they take the gospel of Jesus Christ unashamedly into a youth culture that is alienated from the church. But they speak in a language called rock 'n' roll—the voice of raw energy and adrenaline that youth cultures worldwide have listened to since the 1950s.
> The Newsboys sum up their purpose in a lyric from "Shine," one of their best-known songs: "Shine—make 'em wonder what you got."[36]

This is music for young believers who share the musical tastes, if not the secular ideology, of their peers. As CCM evolves, the artists and fans have begun to group themselves into categories of "mainstream" and "alternative." Part of the difference, according to an article in *Christianity Today*, has to do with the degree to which CCM artists stick closely to predictable themes such as devotion to Jesus. "When I was younger," says one Christian alternative blues singer, "I thought that I was supposed to make all of my songs like evangelistic tracts. After a while, you don't want your music to be just propaganda. You want it to stand outside its context."[37] Alternative Christian music purports to reflect the style and sometimes the dark thematic content of popular secular bands such as Pearl Jam.[38] If CCM remains a profitable industry in coming years, it is likely that some of its artists will dilute their evangelistic message. By doing so, they may lose access to explicitly Christian radio stations. But by the same token, they may succeed in filtering subtle religious themes into the secular music world.

In the above-cited survey, CCM listeners indicated that for them the music serves the dual purposes of entertainment and spiritual uplift. There is a more subtle point to this music as well. To the extent that CCM mimics the musical styles of mainstream culture—but with a Christian twist—it keeps believers from becoming thoroughly alienated from normal life. It is much easier to remain part of the evangelical subculture if one does not have to give up one's favorite music. One can blockade an abortion clinic, vote for Pat Robertson, and still play good tapes on the car stereo. CCM enables believers to sustain their religious commitments over the long haul, and have fun, too.

Telling Tales

ﮗ

The 1990s have witnessed a boom in Christian fiction. The most popular books have been novels with strong millenarian and political themes. Among the bestsellers is *Gideon's Torch*, written by Charles Colson and Ellen Vaughn. It is Colson's first novel, and was inspired by the antiabortion movement. The story begins with the assassination of an abortion doctor, on the eve of the inauguration of Whitney Griswold, the newly elected, and thoroughly "proabortion," Republican president of the United States. Griswold's cynicism and lust for power know no bounds. Yet he is politically inept and depends on advice from his chief counsel and old law school buddy, Bernie O'Keefe, who is rapidly destroying himself with alcohol and prescription drugs. Griswold, O'Keefe, and the rest of the administration are eager to contain the rising militancy of the antiabortion movement, even if that means turning the country into a police state. The public has become deathly afraid of street crime and is, therefore, acquiescent to the government's shredding of the Bill of Rights. Among the antiabortion groups under surveillance is a Life Network of twenty cells across the country, with a total membership of four hundred people. One cell meets in the Falls Church, Virginia, home of pastor Daniel Seaton, and this group has learned that the government will soon finish construction of a medical Regeneration Center, which will use the bodies of late-term aborted fetuses to treat AIDs patients (read: homosexuals). Once the new medical facility is complete, the government will encourage women to get pregnant, or to delay their abortions, so that their fetuses can be harvested. So, in the face of this pending horror, Daniel Seaton's brother, Alex, unleashes a bomb that destroys the Regeneration Center. Then Alex and his accomplice die in the ensuing manhunt, and Daniel becomes the scapegoat for Alex's crime because he knew about the plot. Daniel is tried and jailed as an accessory to the crime, and then he is tragically killed by thugs in jail. But the publicity surrounding Daniel's case turns the tide of public opinion against the regeneration centers. The novel ends with members of Congress poised to shut the centers down.

The title *Gideon's Torch* comes from the Old Testament story of the Israelites' many battles with heathen tribes. God orders Gideon to reduce the size of his army so that its final victory will be viewed as a victory by God, not by men. Carrying torches, Gideon's small army charges the enemy camp under cover of darkness. Disoriented, the enemy troops kill each other and flee in panic. In Colson's novel, Gideon's Torch is the name of the Life Network's project to publicly expose the Regeneration Center, because they, like Gideon, expect to win with only small numbers of true believers.

Though *Gideon's Torch* does not appear to have pushed real-life activists in the direction of violence, Colson is aware that his story reads like nonfiction, and that it was released at a time when activists had apparently exhausted legal means of stopping abortion. In an interview with Focus on the Family's *Citizen* magazine, Colson said he got the idea for the book before Paul Hill shot an abortion doctor in Florida, in 1994; before the suicide of Clinton adviser Vince Foster; and before the Oklahoma City bombing of 1995. About his book's uncanny and realistic plot lines, Colson said: "I dread the idea of seeing other elements of the novel come true. This is a prophetic novel in the sense that it warns people of what could happen."[39] Colson said the two messages of *Gideon's Torch* are that "prolifers should not compromise" but that "they can never resort to violence" because "violence doesn't persuade; it hardens." In the same interview, Colson's coauthor Ellen Vaughn stressed that the book is intended to discourage actual violence: "Our primary concern is that some prolife folks may become so frustrated—because they feel marginalized—that they will erupt and use evil means."[40]

As fiction, *Gideon's Torch* is gripping because of its several subplots. In one, Griswold's preppie, female attorney general is eventually converted to Christ by a born-again deputy lawyer. Despite disclaimers by Colson and Vaughn, their message is ambivalent. At one level, they suggest that antiabortion movement violence is wrong because it discredits all prolifers and brings government repression down on them. Protagonist Daniel Seaton, though militant, disavows the use of lethal force. Yet in the Bible, Daniel is a prophet, and what happens in the novel is prophetic in that Seaton's tragic death heralds a sea change in the war against abortion. In the end, like it or not, violence is an integral part of the unfolding events that lead to victory. Violence is a pitfall, but it is part of the prophecy. Read as a sign of the times, *Gideon's Torch* allows the reader to see antiabortion violence as part of God's plan. The novel's realistic details—based, presumably, on Colson's past career as a White House insider—link the religious message to a plausible political story line.

In contrast to Colson's work, the bestselling Christian novels of Frank

Peretti are explicitly designed as fantastic morality plays. A dragon is at the center of Peretti's 1995 novel *The Oath*. The beast is an obvious symbol for Satan. It has been hiding in the northwestern mining town of Hyde River since, over one hundred years earlier, the town's founders massacred scores of their fellow settlers and then signed a blood oath to keep the killings secret in perpetuity. But the days of reckoning begin when wildlife biologist Steve Benson comes to town to investigate the gruesome death of his brother. We soon learn that Cliff Benson was eaten by the dragon after he committed adultery with the wife of Hyde River's corrupt and violent mining boss. While Steve sets out to slay the dragon, a series of townspeople fall prey to the beast, but only after we know they are supernaturally marked for death because they each develop a foul-smelling, slime-oozing sore over their heart. Only after Steve heeds the word of the town's lone, ranting, born-again believer, and converts to Christ, does his own dripping sore vanish. Then Steve's life is miraculously spared.

The Oath is about as subtle as a twelve-gauge shotgun, of which plenty are brandished in the backwoods of Hyde River. Though published, like Colson's novel, by Word Publishing, *The Oath* was written for a broad readership. For this book, Word hired a secular editor to help Peretti make the book appeal to the unconverted. Peretti told *Bookstore Journal* that his bottom-line message is: "Sin's gonna kill you."

> My desire for this book is that God will use it to help people take a careful look inside and let the Lord clean house because if each of us comes to grips with sin in our own lives, repents, and gets right with God, the cumulative effect will be very significant. Change has to happen one heart at a time. The answers to this nation's problems aren't in the ballot box, they're in the human heart.[41]

More than two years after publication, *The Oath* remained near the top of the bestseller lists published by the Christian Booksellers Association. *The Oath* is likely to become a classic, as is Peretti's 1986 first novel, *This Present Darkness*, which I discuss in Chapter 10 in relation to the charismatic practice of *spiritual warfare* or praying for the defeat of demonic spirits. *The Oath* is more mundane. It is an allegory about the deadly results of sin, but it is not as apolitical as Peretti's quote above might suggest. *The Oath* is arguably one of the most reactionary of the popular works of Christian fiction.

Both Tim LaHaye's *Left Behind* and Charles Colson's *Gideon's Torch* preach a message of redemption. *Left Behind* is about the second chance God offers to unbelievers who miss the Rapture; they are free to repent and make their way eventually to heaven. In Colson's book, redemption will come through politics: once people learn the truth about late-term abortion and the medical exploitation of fetal bodies, the citizenry begins what will be a long process of restoring righteousness to the nation. While LaHaye and Colson both condemn secular culture, they offer a way out. They have not given up on humanity.

Peretti's story is much different. The dragon kills the evil town boss Harold Bly, who has been responsible for the deaths of other townspeople. Equally, though, the dragon kills deputy sheriff Tracy Ellis, who tried to save the town and whose only sin was leaving her abusive husband, and subsequently having sex with other men, including the book's hero, Steve. *The Oath* is about vengeance, not the salvation Christ offers indiscriminately to all human beings. The message is political at a subliminal level: any fate that befalls any unbeliever is presented as just retribution. All sin is on a par, even that of the local pastor. He is kind, but he has discouraged his parishioners from believing in the dragon/Satan's existence, and therefore he, too, is marked for death. Other townspeople with normal human failings must die just the same as the murderous Harold Bly.

Concerning fiction, one perennial question is whether a work is popular because it reflects commonly held sentiments or because the work itself shapes or deepens these sentiments. Popular Christian fiction does not become popular in a vacuum; it succeeds thanks to heavy promotion by evangelical print and broadcast outlets. Customers already patronizing Christian retail stores are a ready market for the LaHayes, Colsons, and Perettis. Their books are genuinely fun to read, and beyond that, this literature conveys messages that are highly salient to millions of readers. For conservative Christians, the books reinforce the worldview of people at war with secular liberalism in its many manifestations: abortion, homosexuality, lust, corrupt partisan politics, even the rejection of strict biblical literalism by mainline churches. The novels tell readers sympathetic with the Christian Right that they are justified in seeing evil wherever they look, and that, one way or another, divine judgment will eventually prevail. Readers are right to expect and even welcome harsh treatment of their opponents, who will either turn or burn.

Popular Christian fiction is a genre compatible with participation in and support for the Christian Right. The battle lines are clearly drawn, and the good guys—no matter how few in number—will surely win. Christian fiction plays a role similar to contemporary Christian music. It entertains in a way that reinforces a reader's sense of separation from and superiority to the sinful world while simultaneously keeping the reader connected to secular affairs. If one were to read nothing but the Bible and tracts extolling Christian virtue, one would not feel engaged with the rest of society. Reading about abortion, adultery, and government conspiracies is titillating in its own right. It also keeps one ready to do Christian battle, when opportunity knocks.

Chapter 4

〰

The Long March

The highlight of the Christian Coalition's September 1996 Road to Victory conference was the surprise appearance of presidential candidate Bob Dole. For days, Pat Robertson and Ralph Reed had been trying to convince Dole's handlers that a speech to the Christian Right's largest and most influential organization would boost Dole's flagging campaign. By making the appearance Dole risked looking like a pawn in the Christian Coalition's drive for mainstream respectability. But by declining the invitation, Dole would have thumbed his nose at a constituency the Republicans could not afford to alienate. Support from the Christian Coalition was vital to the Republicans' goal of keeping their majority in Congress. Dole, ever the good soldier, put on a smile and joined a beaming Pat Robertson on stage, where the two men clasped hands in symbolic unity, at the Christian Coalition podium. The crowd of four thousand cheered wildly, and Dole minced no words. "I can't tell you how much your support means to us," he said. "We understand your strength and your potential. I would ask you for your full and complete support."

Dole's speech for the Christian Coalition signified the enduring and central role of the Christian Right two decades after the movement first began organizing for political power. There have been other campaigns and other awkward moments, times when the Republicans have not known whether to solicit or to rebuff the movement's support. In the 1980s, there was a tentative alliance between the movement and the Reagan White House. This was followed in the late 1980s by the TV preacher scandals, and then by the rise of the Christian Coalition and an assortment of Christian Right lobbies and legal outfits. It would be impossible for me to recount every scene in this long-running drama. In this chapter, my goal is to trace some of the major episodes and to show how key organizations have made the Christian Right a force to be reckoned with.

Historical Roots

In *Roads to Dominion,* I detailed the historical antecedents of the contemporary Christian Right, that period between the 1940s and the 1960s when evangelicals were active on two tracks: securing and expanding their access to the nation's broadcast airwaves and fighting what they saw as liberal apostasy coming from the mainline denominational churches. During those years, evangelicals established the National Religious Broadcasters association, which successfully lobbied Congress for a change in the regulations governing TV and radio. The changes were advantageous to those broadcasters who were least shy about raising money on the air and to those, such as Pat Robertson, who were most innovative in their use of the new TV medium. At a time when evangelicals were not yet politically active in a *partisan* way, they were, nevertheless, building media resources that would later become politically vital.[1]

Traditionally, fundamentalist preachers discouraged their parishioners from getting involved in worldly affairs. Many fundamentalists did not vote at all, and if they did, they considered voting a private act, one not worthy of much time spent in church talking about it. That did not mean that evangelicals, more generally, did not think about politics. Simultaneous with the struggle to capture much of the available broadcast time, a number of early Christian Right groups joined in anticommunist campaigns aimed at fellow Christians they viewed as unpatriotic. When Senator Joseph McCarthy and his allies went on their witchhunts for secret communist agents inside the United States, the National Association of Evangelicals encouraged government agents to snag liberal clergy in their net. The liberal churches, by and large, did not fight back when their reputations were sullied by anticommunist Christian Right crusaders. By their overall silence, the liberal churches gave a green light to later Christian Right groups who would make liberalism, both in the churches and in secular institutions, a central target of their hostility.

In *Roads to Dominion* I also analyzed the rise of the nominally secular New Right in the 1970s. I say "nominally" because, while the New Right presented itself organizationally in nonreligious terms, many of the individual leaders of the New Right are highly religious people. (I include here Phyllis Schlafly, Richard Viguerie, Paul Weyrich, and Howard Phillips.) The advent of the New Right gave new life to conservative activists who had labored with limited success in the 1950s and 1960s. For conservatives who previously held little real political clout, the 1964 Barry Goldwater presidential campaign was a milestone. Their candidate lost, but the right wing of the Republican Party succeeded, for the first time, in nominating one of its own. That signal achievement was followed by a new trend in the 1970s.

Corporate donors had long supported candidates. But in the 1970s corporate donors began exerting their influence well before election time, by funding think tanks to do the kind of agenda-setting research and publicity that was not linked with particular candidates. The 1970s saw the formation of the Heritage Foundation and a slew of other policy institutes, plus a new echelon of political action committees intent on electing right-wing Congressional candidates.[2]

The New Right's issue agenda had a triple focus on foreign policy, economics, and traditional morality. After the U.S. defeat in Vietnam, the Right remained stridently anticommunist. Then especially during the Carter administration, the Right pushed for a more aggressive U.S. policy toward the Soviet Union and its clients and sympathizers in the developing countries. Given the corporate backing of New Right organizations, it should be no surprise that tax cuts and business deregulation were also high on the movement's agenda.

The "new" twist for the New Right, though, was a budding alliance between seasoned conservative activists and the evangelical Christians who were just starting to awaken politically. The genius of New Right leaders such as Paul Weyrich and Richard Viguerie was to see that a new focus on issues of morality was the ticket to creating an expanded activist movement, and one that could not be ignored by the Republican Party. New Right leaders helped some of the early Christian Right organizations get started.

Yet the New Right and the Christian Right were never entirely synonymous. The New Right was largely a set of Washington, DC–based interest groups, dependent on large corporate donations for their financial support. The Christian Right groups were tied to prominent members of the clergy and to the religious broadcasting industry. Once the anticommunist projects of the 1980s came to a close, the New Right was effectively eclipsed by the Christian Right, which turned its attention almost exclusively to domestic policy matters, with an ever increasing focus on the state and local levels. The New Right was top heavy and run mostly by professionals. The Christian Right eventually incorporated thousands of amateurs, and it remains more genuinely a social movement. It evolved out of the evangelical subculture, and it has never strayed far from its roots.

The Jesus Movement
✺

The growth of the New Right coincided somewhat with the rise of evangelical Christianity as a cultural phenomenon. Early signs of a coming revival were apparent right after World War II when a young missionary named Billy Graham pioneered the use of televised rallies, preaching to people who were Christians by birth but who had not yet undergone the life-changing "born-again" conversion experience during which believers acknowledge Jesus as their personal savior.

During the 1950s, Graham was the beneficiary of favorable media coverage, particularly from *Time* magazine and the Hearst newspaper chain. The secular media liked Graham because he was anticommunist. Moreover, he raised his voice, but he did not speak in tongues, nor did he engage in any other bizarre antics on stage. Graham was part of a group called Youth for Christ, which brought together young people across denominational lines for Saturday-night rallies featuring guest appearances by World War II veterans and media stars. By 1946, Youth for Christ had sponsored nine hundred rallies and involved about a million young people.[3]

Graham's rallies, first with Youth for Christ and later with his own organization, took him all over the world. His popularity was both the result of and an impetus for the missionary work performed by thousands of American evangelists. Foreign missionary work long predated the rise of the Christian Right, but such activity got a boost during the Cold War years when U.S. influence abroad had strong political overtones. Missionary work is motivated by the drive to convert people who already have their own religions. Much of the post–World War II era missionary work was designed to lift people out of miserable poverty. Missionaries dug wells, built houses, vaccinated people, and taught children. One hesitates to cast aspersions on such humanitarian work, except to note that such projects typically do not address the underlying reasons why so many in the world have nothing while an elite few consume most of the world's resources. At a time when such questions stirred the rise of anticolonial national liberation movements, evangelistic projects like the Billy Graham crusades came with a message in favor of prevailing regimes of authority. Graham's message was explicitly anticommunist, and implicitly supportive of capitalism and all its attendant inequalities.

To more effectively spread the Gospel, in the 1960s evangelical thinkers such as Donald McGavran, C. Peter Wagner, and others promoted a strategy called "church growth," which is still discussed in missionary literature. Church growth is not so much a set of doctrines as a way of thinking about evangelism. The idea is for lay missionaries to become knowledgeable about indigenous cultures so that when they preach to the unconverted, they can appear more relevant.[4]

The idea of adapting a missionary approach to the cultural practices of a target population was useful not just overseas but also in evangelizing the 1960s youth culture. While much of the 1960s generation was deeply committed to progressive politics, there was another, often overlapping, segment of the counterculture that was looking for new kinds of religious experiences. Millions of spiritual seekers gravitated toward Eastern religions. But just as many, if not more, found what they were looking for in what was called "the Jesus movement."

Beginning in the late 1960s, thousands of young people flocked to churches such as Chuck Smith's Calvary Chapel in Orange County, California. Smith's church became known for its mass baptisms of hippies in the Pacific Ocean. Young "Jesus freaks" started a string of coffeehouses and communal homes, from which they hit the streets with Gospel literature and their own visual password: a raised arm with clenched fist and the index finger pointed heavenward, signifying that Jesus Christ is the "one way" to salvation.[5] They held their own versions of the Woodstock gathering, drawing tens of thousands to three- and four-day outdoor revival meetings complete with Jesus rock bands and Bible teaching by charismatic preachers.[6]

What kept the Jesus movement from fading like other fads of the 1960s was the influential role of older, established ministries, including Campus Crusade for Christ, the Navigators, and Intervarsity Christian Fellowship. The Christian World Liberation Front was founded in 1969 in Berkeley, California, by staffers of Campus Crusade for Christ, a group that had been around since the 1950s.[7] Founder Bill Bright, a successful businessman, started Campus Crusade on the University of California at Los Angeles (UCLA) campus in 1951. With the idea of imitating communist recruitment tactics, he urged young Christian converts to form cell groups. Bright self-consciously promoted an image of his ministry as a revolutionary movement. In fact, twenty years after the founding of Campus Crusade, Bright described his staff of three thousand worldwide missionaries as a "conspiracy to overthrow the world."[8] Bright's goal was to recruit young people away from the Left and into a conservative brand of Christianity. Later, between 1976 and 1980, Bright spent one billion dollars on his "Here's Life" campaign; much of the money came from Nelson Bunker Hunt, the infamous Texas silver tycoon. Here's Life involved renting billboards and distributing bumper stickers printed with the phrase "I Found it" above a phone number for the curious to call. If they called they would be evangelized by Campus Crusade phone volunteers. In 1976 alone, Campus Crusade reported that its workers had made 6.5 million personal contacts and that more than half a million people had expressed interest in the ministry.[9]

Unbeknownst to most Christians, by 1976, Bright and a handful of others were also working on a project called Third Century publishers. Their goal was to prompt born-again Christians to become active in politics during the United States' bicentennial anniversary year, and beyond. Third Century published manuals explaining how Christian leaders could begin to recruit people into home study groups, with an eye toward influencing Congressional races.[10]

In 1976, there was little public scrutiny of the emerging Christian Right. But there was great interest in the large numbers of Americans who identified themselves as evangelical or born-again Christians. In 1976, the Gallup Poll found that about a third of all Americans, or about fifty million adults, claimed to have undergone a born-again conversion experience. Gallup also found that about 46% of Protestants and 31% of Catholics believed that the Bible is "to be taken literally, word for word," a doctrine held only by the most conservative Christians. Also, Gallup found that 58% of Protestants, and 38% of Catholics, were evangelical, meaning that they had tried to convert other people to Christ.[11]

This was big news in a society that was supposedly becoming more secular. After the cultural upheaval caused by the social movements of the 1960s, the Vietnam War, and Watergate, millions of Americans were finding inspiration in the certainties of old-time faith. Not all, or even most, of the newly discovered born-again multitudes were politically conservative, but they had the potential to become so, given their conservative theology.

Only time would prove the endurance of the born-again phenomenon. A survey conducted by religion scholars in the late 1980s focused on the baby boomer generation, people born between 1946 and 1963. Of this group, about a third scored as "conservative evangelicals" when they were asked whether they took the Bible literally word for word; whether they accepted the biblical view of creation as opposed to the evolutary view; and whether they agreed that "temptations are the work of the devil." Most of the self-identified born-again evangelicals were moderates, but 13% of the baby boomer sample was labeled as "fundamentalist leaning." This latter group was strongly opposed to homosexuality, abortion, and sexual relations before marriage.[12]

Early on, this segment of the population appeared to be a somewhat cohesive voting bloc. In 1976, President Jimmy Carter, a devout Southern Baptist, did exceptionally well among evangelicals, but he lost that support in 1980 after he refused to back a constitutional ban on abortion. In 1976, at least half of the white born-again Christian vote went to Jimmy Carter; by 1980, that same constituency voted two-to-one in favor of Ronald Reagan.[13] Carter's 1980 defeat actually had little to do with his religion; he was the victim of rising interest rates and his failure to rescue U.S. hostages held in Iran. By 1980, the leaders of the new Christian Right were rallying behind Ronald Reagan. But according to *Washington Post* journalist E. J. Dionne, the evangelical shift away from Carter was not merely the result of what Jerry Falwell and company had to say. "Most of the evangelical conservatives were white Southerners who began voting against the Democrats because of civil rights," Dionne wrote.[14] The Carter administration, like the preceding Nixon and Ford administrations, had authorized federal agencies to investigate racially segregated private schools, on grounds that they were ineligible for tax-exempt status, and this had angered white conservatives.[15]

The switch from Carter to Reagan between 1976 and 1980 showed that the evangelical voting bloc could become decisive in electoral politics. The large chunk of the population that self-identified as born-again could not be considered politically monolithic: there were too many variations across lines of denomination, race, class, region, and party affiliation. That evangelicals were not uniformly wedded to the Republican Party meant that their votes were up for grabs. It meant that the major political currents of the 1970s and 1980s would determine which way a new bloc of evangelical voters would turn as they looked for political leaders to represent them. As it happened, the 1970s offered an advantageous set of circumstances for the birth of a new alliance between the Republican Party and religious conservatives.

A Spark Ignites

∽

The decade of the 1970s was one of major changes. The U.S. war in Indochina polarized the country like nothing else since the Civil War. The civil rights and women's movements signaled massive challenges to a culture and political system based on inequality. The economic prosperity of the decades following World War II gave way to the beginning of a decline in real wages and job security for the working and middle classes. Issues of foreign policy, race, gender, and the economy now mattered to everyone. But for the incipient Christian Right, what inspired the first wave of activists was a series of key events around questions of morality, gender, and family relations.

The 1973 Supreme Court decision legalizing abortion was the single most galvanizing event in the history of the Christian Right. The hierarchy of the Catholic Church mobilized quickly against *Roe v. Wade*. Catholic prolifers formed the National Right to Life Committee which today remains influential. The early antiabortion movement fought to overturn *Roe* through a constitutional amendment. Failing that goal, movement activists debated how best to stop abortion: through restrictive legislation in the states, through acts of civil disobedience, and/or through violence. The antiabortion movement has always been rife with controversies. I have reserved that story for a separate discussion in Chapter 7.

For many Protestant evangelicals who were not previously active, the *Roe* decision was a watershed event. In his 1987 autobiography, Jerry Falwell recalled that during the 1960s civil rights era, he opposed clergy involvement in politics. After *Roe*, he preached against abortion, but then, he wrote, "It soon became apparent that this time preaching would not be enough." The more information he gathered about abortion, the more he "realized that there were other crises facing the nation that required immediate political action from men and women of Christian faith." [16]

For Falwell, one of the crises was the debate over the Equal Rights Amendment (ERA). In 1972, the Senate overwhelmingly passed the amendment, which would have granted women full legal equality. By 1973, thirty out of the necessary thirty-eight state legislatures had ratified the ERA. [17] Then the opposition kicked in. Leading the charge was Phyllis Schlafly, a Catholic, an attorney, and an activist in the anticommunist movement of the 1960s. Schlafly's Stop ERA organization, later renamed the Eagle Forum, created a national network to oppose ratification by the states. Schlafly enjoyed assistance from Senator Sam Ervin (R-NC), the leading opponent of the ERA in Congress. Ervin gave Schlafly his Congressional franking privilege for mailing anti-ERA literature packets to key state legislators. [18]

The Mormon Church, too, joined the fight against the ERA in undecided states. There was no love lost between Mormons and evangelicals, who consider the Church of Latter Day Saints to be an unchristian cult. However, there was no real need for direct collaboration between the two groups. Mostly the Mormon opposition came primarily from church elders, not from parishioners, many of whom supported the ERA. In the end, the Mormon Church was influential in defeating the ERA in Nevada, Florida, Virginia, Georgia, and possibly Illinois and Missouri. [19]

Ultimately, the ERA fell three states short of the thirty-eight required to amend the Constitution. It was an early victory for the Christian Right. The ERA gave opponents of feminism a tangible target. Schlafly used her public visibility to sound the alarm against what she saw as a full-scale "threat" to the traditional family. She claimed the ERA would allow the military to draft women, and that men would shirk their responsibilities to wives and children if women no longer had automatic rights to alimony and child support. [20] She claimed the ERA would make gay marriages legal and prevent a reversal of *Roe v. Wade*. [21] For Schlafly and others, the set of profamily issues was beginning to crystallize into a unified package, with potential for action on many fronts. By 1977, Schlafly claimed she had fifty thousand members in her Eagle Forum. [22]

Also by 1977, the anti–gay rights cause came to the fore. In that year, popular singer Anita Bryant led a successful fight to overturn a Miami antidiscrimination ordinance. Then, in 1978, Bryant joined forces with the sponsors of a California state ballot initiative that would have banned self-identified homosexuals from teaching in the public schools. California's Proposition 6, sponsored by State Representative John Briggs, was defeated at the polls. [23] But sponsors of the initiative used the network they built during the campaign to start Christian Voice, the organization that later pioneered the use of "moral report cards" to rate candidates for office.[24]

It was not surprising that antigay activists targeted public education. Schools are the place where many Christian parents feel their values are most under siege. In the 1970s, as in the 1990s, controversies revolved around curricula and the question of whether government has the prerogative to regulate Christian schools and home schools.

Among the earliest battles was a textbook protest in Kanawha County, West Virginia, in 1974. Alice Moore, a school board member and the wife of a fundamentalist minister, organized parents against a new set of textbooks that they believed were full of "obscene, anti-American, and anti-God" themes. The parents' group gathered over twelve thousand signatures opposing the books, but the school board went ahead and approved them anyway. Then the parents organized a student boycott. Moore's group eventually prevailed, though not before a local minister was convicted for conspiring to bomb a school building.[25]

It was precisely because of conflicts such as the one in West Virginia that many evangelicals pulled their children out of public schools in the 1970s. As the number of private schools increased, so, too, did the number of court cases challenging the way such schools did business. Some of the private Christian schools were established in response to parents' fears about violence, sex education, and the absence of prayer in the public schools. But other Christian academies were formed solely or primarily to evade racial integration. Authors Thomas Edsall and Mary Edsall peg the onset of the Christian Right to a 1969 lawsuit that successfully challenged the federal tax exemptions granted to segregated private schools in Mississippi. The plaintiffs in the Mississippi case won (i.e., the court found that the private school was discriminatory), but the victory was largely symbolic: IRS regulations at the time were too lenient to force the offending school to lose its tax-exempt status. All such schools had to do to continue receiving tax-deductible donations was to formally declare in their charters a policy of nondiscrimination.[26]

That all changed in 1978, when President Carter appointed a new IRS commissioner, Jerome Kurtz. Kurtz proposed that any private schools formed or expanded in the years right after a desegregation order would now have to prove that they were trying to integrate, or else lose their tax-exempt status. Pastors and parents committed to supporting segregated private schools were outraged at what they saw as a threat to their First Amendment rights. If the federal government was not allowed to regulate church membership, they argued, how could it regulate the racial composition of church-related schools?[27] Following Kurtz's proposal, the agency received 126,000 letters of protest, and Kurtz was so alarmed by the threats made in some of the letters that he requested Secret Service protection.[28]

The IRS policy changes caused a severe drop in evangelical support for President Carter. Years later, Richard Viguerie recalled the IRS controversy as "the spark that ignited the religious right's involvement in real politics."[29] In fact, two of the earliest Christian Right organizations, the National Christian Action Coalition and Moral Majority, grew out of networks of fundamentalist churches affiliated with private Christian schools. Republicans, too, recognized the salience of the IRS school regulation issue. In 1979, Congressmembers Bob Dornan of California and John Ashbrook of Ohio won passage of a rider to the IRS appropriation bill preventing enforcement of the new regulations. Then, in 1980, at the Republican Party convention, the writers of the party platform included a sentence vowing that the Reagan presidency would "halt the unconstitutional regulatory vendetta launched by Mr. Carter's IRS Commissioner against independent schools."30 The IRS had been interested in the tax-exemptions claimed by segregated schools since the early 1970s, but it was an expedient issue for the Republicans to pin on the Carter campaign.[31]

Endorsing Reagan

∽

Jerry Falwell and others have often told the story of a May 1979 meeting held in Lynchburg, Virginia. Falwell's friend Robert Billings had organized the National Christian Action Coalition to unify pastors who, like Falwell, were against the proposed new IRS regulations concerning private schools. Billings introduced Falwell to New Right leaders Paul Weyrich, Richard Viguerie, Howard Phillips, and Ed McAteer, and together they hatched the idea of starting an organization called Moral Majority.[32] Each of the men was already running his own organization. Viguerie was in the direct mail fundraising business. Phillips, a recent Jewish convert to Christianity, ran the Conservative Caucus. Weyrich, a devout Catholic, ran the Committee for the Survival of a Free Congress, which held seminars and conducted fundraising for right-wing candidates. McAteer had started the Religious Roundtable, to organize prominent televangelists. Looking toward the 1980 election, Weyrich proposed that if the Republicans could be persuaded to take a firm stance against abortion, that would begin to split the strong Catholic voting bloc within the Democratic Party. The New Right strategists wanted Falwell to pressure the GOP via a new organization of Protestant fundamentalists.

The name "Moral Majority" suggested that most Americans agreed with the newly active Christian Right. This was untrue, of course, but there was no denying the organization's phenomenal early success. By the time of its second anniversary, Moral Majority claimed chapters in all fifty states.

In 1981, the organization spent more than $6 million, mostly on media activities; the *Moral Majority Report* reached more than 840,000 homes; and more than three hundred radio stations broadcast a daily Moral Majority commentary. The organization claimed to have more than four million members. But this was a mailing list figure; a more modest estimate put membership at about four hundred thousand,[33] which was still impressive given the newness of the Christian Right.

The Moral Majority's rapid growth was largely the result of its preexisting leadership. Of the first fifty state leaders, most were pastors of independent Baptist churches. These were men with strong personalities and large followings. Many of these pastors were affiliated with fundamentalist schools, and many also were veterans of local political skirmishes against gay rights and pornography.[34]

Then there was the connection to TV evangelism. Falwell's *Old Time Gospel Hour* gave the Moral Majority a reliable pulpit, and many other Christian broadcasters gave the group all-important name recognition. From Falwell's own 2.5 million member mailing list, a fundraising letter was sent to 250,000 prime donors, and that raised more than $2 million during the first year alone.[35] This was at a time when the Christian Right's organizations were few in number, and it was plausible for a single organization to claim to represent the movement as whole.

Registering voters for the 1980 presidential election was the first goal. In 1980, Moral Majority claimed to have registered four million new voters. More credible estimates placed the figure at about two million.[36] State chapters worked for Congressional candidates and on a consistent set of issues: against gay rights ordinances, for prolife and antipornography legislation, against sex education in the public schools, and against state interference with private Christian schools.[37]

The Christian Right had yet to become a truly grassroots social movement involving tens of thousands of amateur activists. But, in the early 1980s, Moral Majority provided an umbrella under which evangelical ministers—professionals with media and organizing skills—could enter the fray of partisan politics to a degree most had not done before. They were getting organized at a time of general political awakening within the evangelical subculture. Dr. James Dobson had begun the Focus on the Family radio ministry. Pat Robertson's *700 Club* program was becoming increasingly political in content. In 1976, the annual convention of the National Religious Broadcasters brought together, along with the usual media evangelists, a number of political figures who urged Christians to get active.[38] Thereafter, religious broadcasters would continue to play a vital role in the political mobilization of their audiences.

Religious broadcasters were central in two key movement events in 1980. One was the day-long Washington for Jesus rally organized by Pat

Robertson; his friend, John Gimenez, who pastored the Rock Church in Virginia; Bill Bright, of Campus Crusade; and Demos Shakarian, of the Full Gospel Businessmen's Fellowship. Two hundred thousand people came to Washington, DC, for what was then the largest ever political gathering of born-again Christians. They prayed for the moral salvation of the country in an event that was officially nonpartisan.[39]

After Washington for Jesus, in April 1980, Ed McAteer of the Religious Roundtable organized a National Affairs Briefing in Dallas, in August 1980, timed to coincide with the Republican convention. McAteer was a founder of Moral Majority, and the Roundtable was a loose affiliation of politically minded TV evangelists. The "briefing," attended by fifteen thousand people, was more of a revival meeting than a policy conference.[40] The star of the show was candidate Ronald Reagan who, there in Dallas, delivered to the Christian Right one of his most famous lines. "I know you can't endorse me," Reagan said. "But I want you to know that I endorse you."[41] Reagan mustered every ounce of his charm, loaded his speech with biblical imagery, and ran through a litany of political challenges to "traditional values." He indicted government restrictions on "the independence of religious broadcasting" and on proposed IRS regulations to "force all tax-exempt schools—including church schools—to abide by affirmative action orders drawn up by—who else?—IRS bureaucrats." He urged Christians to preserve their blessings by acting on their responsibility to be good citizens. "If you do not speak your mind and cast your ballots, then who will speak and work for the ideals we cherish? Who will vote to protect the American family and respect its interests in the formulations of public policy?"[42]

With his speech, Reagan conveyed to the newly aroused Christian Right the message that he was their man, and that he would turn the White House into God's House. The Dallas speech was a peak experience for Christians who worked throughout 1980 to elect Ronald Reagan. The issues were clear. The Christian Right constituency was aroused and ready to make an impact with the simple act of voting. Key organizations were in place in time for the 1980 election.

Christian Voice was formed in 1978 by Robert Grant, Gary Jarmin, and Colonel Doner. Jarmin was a former disciple of the Korean cult leader Sun Myung Moon. Grant was the leader of a group of California pastors who had backed the 1978 antigay Briggs initiative. After the measure failed, Grant melded his American Christian Cause organization with the antipornography group Citizens for Decency Through Law. To give his group quick legitimacy and name recognition, he recruited sixteen members of Congress to serve on a Christian Voice "Congressional advisory committee." On board were four Republican Senators: Orrin Hatch of Utah (a Mormon), Roger Jepsen of Iowa, James McClure of Idaho, and Gordon Humphrey of New Hampshire.[43] From there, Christian Voice seemed to mushroom. By 1980, the organization claimed a donor base of 187,000 members and a budget of $1.5 million. Its chief activity in 1980 was mailing out literature on behalf of Ronald Reagan.[44]

Christian Voice was the first of the new movement groups to issue "moral report cards" that rated candidates on issues ranging from abortion to Zimbabwe; these cards had a significant impact on political contests because they were distributed in churches the Sunday before an election. Years later, Pat Robertson's Christian Coalition would refine the "report card" technique by calling the leaflets "voter guides" and claiming they implied no direct endorsements. But in the early years Christian Right leaders did not mince words. Moral Majority executive director Bob Billings talked about a "hit list" of liberal candidates his group opposed. Christian Voice spawned a partisan political action committee, the Moral Government Fund, which endorsed Reagan and gave small amounts of money to Republican Congressional candidates.[45]

The moral report cards were an effective, though crude, way to catch the attention of evangelical voters as they left church on the Sunday before elections. Targeted candidates had no time to respond to charges that they had taken "immoral" positions on school prayer, "forced unionization" of teachers, a balanced budget, or aid to the Nicaraguan Contras. The cards suggested that there were "Christian" and "unchristian" positions on all matters great and small, thus reinforcing an us-against-them mentality among new Christian Right voters.

The simple-minded approach paid off in the election of Ronald Reagan. The combined efforts of Moral Majority, Christian Voice, and all the New Right political action committees yielded about two million new voters. Poll data indicated that white fundamentalist voters accounted for two-thirds of Reagan's lead over Jimmy Carter. In general, 17% fewer white Protestants voted for Carter in 1980 than in 1976. Traditionally Democratic southern and border states were won by the Republicans, and for only the second time in U.S. history (Nixon's 1972 election was the first) a plurality of Catholics voted Republican.[46] Beyond the White House, the New Right and the Christian Right took credit for ousting a slate of liberal Senators and Congressmembers who had been in office a long time. These included Senators George McGovern (D-SD), Frank Church (D-ID), Birch Bayh (D-IN) and John Culver (D-IA). Among the new right-wing Senators elected that year were Senators Jeremiah Denton of Alabama, Steve Symms of Idaho, Chuck Grassley of Iowa, Dan Quayle of Indiana, Alfonse D'Amato of New York, and Don Nickles of Oklahoma.[47] The 1980 election was a watershed event because it brought to power a new breed of Republican legislators, people who were more beholden than their predecessors to grassroots right-wing forces back home.

For their part, leaders of the Christian Right were understandably cautious about the legislative implications of the 1980 election results. At the January 1981 convention of the National Religious Broadcasters (NRB), Jerry Falwell urged his brethren to be patient with the new administration's efforts to reinstate public school prayer and to ban abortion. Falwell warned that the damage "caused by secular humanism" could not be repaired in "thirty days." Similarly, Dr. D. James Kennedy of the Coral Ridge Presbyterian Church in Fort Lauderdale told the two thousand NRB conventioneers that secular humanism had become "the established religion of America." Kennedy urged the broadcasters to increase their political involvement because "secular humanists have declared war on Christianity in this country and they are progressing very rapidly."[48]

The concept of "secular humanism" has been a key element of Christian Right thinking since the 1970s. Secular humanism is a catch-all phrase suggesting that the lack of religion is what ails society. In 1980, San Diego pastor Tim LaHaye—who was one of the founders of the Moral Majority and whose wife Beverly LaHaye leads Concerned Women for America—published *The Battle for the Mind*. In this widely circulated book, LaHaye warns readers of a vast humanist conspiracy involving Hollywood movie producers, Unitarian churches, the American Civil Liberties Union (ACLU), the National Organization for Women, the National Association for the Advancement of Colored People (NAACP), and many more. Together, LaHaye claims, these opinion-shapers are out to harm Bible-believing Christians and deny God's sovereignty.

> Simply defined, humanism is man's attempt to solve his problems independently of God. Since moral conditions have become worse and worse in direct proportion to humanism's influence, which has moved our country from a biblically based society to an amoral "democratic" society during the past forty years, one would think that humanists would realize the futility of their position. To the contrary, they treacherously refuse to face the reality of their failures, blaming them instead on traditional religion or ignorance or capitalism or religious superstitions.[49]

After naming the horrors they cause, LaHaye claims that there are only about 275,000 hard-core humanists running amok in the land. They are far outnumbered by sixty million born-again Christians plus a generally moral nonevangelical public.[50] Together, the good people add up to a "moral majority," and all they need to do is to "get involved in the electoral process as faithful citizens, either as candidates ourselves or as workers assisting the right kind of candidates."[51]

The Battle for the Mind ends with a call for Christians to join groups like Moral Majority. LaHaye cleverly links a conspiratorial theory about what ails the nation with a simple prescription for how to fix it. Secular humanism, LaHaye says, haunts the public schools, the Supreme Court, and the television screen. It is threatening because it is everywhere, but it is also vulnerable because it may be attacked everywhere.

The concept of secular humanism gave Christian Right activists, early on, an endless list of targets and a convenient explanation for society's ills. Social problems are not driven by human greed and ignorance but by a lack of faith. The enemy is the unconverted population, and therefore the battle plan is simple: move true believers to the helm of every sphere of life.

The Halls of Congress
⌒

After Reagan's election, the Christian Right turned its attention to Congress, where Republicans controlled the Senate but not the House. As of the late 1970s, the Right had secured only one major victory from the House, the Hyde Amendment, which prohibits federal funding for poor women's abortions. Then, in 1979, a group of New Right Senators, led by Paul Laxalt, the Senator from Nevada and Reagan's 1980 campaign manager, introduced the Family Protection Act. This was an expansive bill with dozens of provisions including the means to restrict abortion and gay rights, water down existing sex discrimination laws, restrict the food stamp program, and give tax advantages to families in which the mother stayed at home.[52] The Family Protection Act was such an octopus that it never made its way out of committees.[53] But the bill's supporters learned a valuable lesson: legislative reforms are best proposed one issue at a time.

However, a more piecemeal approach to legislation brought the Christian Right no victories in Congress during the early 1980s. There were a number of reasons why. Democrats controlled the House, and the Reagan administration was unable to push through legislation *for* school prayer and *against* abortion. Mostly, the White House was preoccupied with its military and economic policy goals. A handful of antiabortion and school prayer bills, put forward by Senators Jesse Helms and Orrin Hatch, simply withered on the vine.[54]

Legislative failure on the social issues might have created a permanent rift between the movement and the Republican Party, but two things prevented that from happening. One was the evolution of the movement toward a more decentralized, grassroots organizational structure, which allows activists to pursue issues at the local level. The other safeguard was the enlistment of Christian Right leaders into the project to keep U.S. military aid flowing to the battlefields of Central America.

Throughout the 1980s, Pat Robertson, Jerry Falwell, the LaHayes, and others in the Christian Right leadership supported right-wing military forces in Central America.[55] This was at a time when the U.S. government backed the death squad governments in El Salvador and Guatemala and the terrorist Contra fighters in Nicaragua. A large movement of progressive North Americans mobilized against U.S. policy. Much of this opposition came from liberal church people acting in solidarity with the priests, nuns, students, and peasants who were being murdered in Central America. Yet most U.S. citizens had little knowledge of what was really going on in the region. Robertson, Falwell, and company helped keep it that way, by using their media channels to spread White House propaganda about a "communist conspiracy" that somehow justified the annihilation of tens of thousands of civilians. When Congress finally got around to investigating some of the illegal arms shipments that came to light during the Iran–Contra scandal of 1987, they were unwilling to explore the myriad ways in which Christian Right figures were helping to keep the Central American wars going. And because they were so eager to collaborate with White House personnel, the leaders of the Christian Right bit their tongues as the administration failed to act on the family values front. Stopping "communism" was the first priority, and it did not matter how much blood and torture were required.

What mattered was keeping alive the alliance between the evangelical camp and the Reagan White House. At the start of the 1984 election season, Reagan made the winter convention of the National Religious Broadcasters one of his first campaign stops.[56] Then at the 1984 GOP convention in Dallas, the Republicans acknowledged their gratitude to the Christian Right by giving the opening invocation slot to Texas TV preacher James Robison. Jerry Falwell delivered the final benediction.[57] Before and after the convention, Tim LaHaye ran a project called the American Coalition for Traditional Values (ACTV). ACTV received a $1 million grant from a White House fundraiser to conduct a voter registration drive that added several hundred thousand new voters to the Republican rolls.[58] These votes were not decisive, given how easily Reagan beat his lackluster 1984 opponent Walter Mondale. It was clear, though, in 1984 that the Christian Right had become a permanent fixture in electoral politics. It was not yet clear which steps the movement would take next.

Inevitably, the early leaders of the Christian Right garnered their share of negative public opinion. Tim LaHaye became the subject of a minor scandal among fellow fundamentalists when it was reported that he had received money from Korean cult leader Sun Myung Moon.[59] Jerry Falwell was a lightning rod for public animosity toward the Christian Right. Falwell came across as smug and self-righteous. The very name of his organization was guaranteed to provoke a popular bumper sticker that read

"The Moral Majority is neither." A series of opinion polls taken in the early 1980s showed that the vast majority of the public had a negative view of Falwell's outfit.[60] In 1986, he changed the name of the organization to Liberty Federation, which did not help matters much, since by then Moral Majority was finding itself upstaged by other movement players. Finally, in 1989, Falwell disbanded the organization altogether. But this was after a full ten years in active duty. While Falwell was busy annoying the general public, he also had built a coast-to-coast network of previously unorganized pastors. And he had contributed to large-scale voter registration drives, thus making it possible for the Christian Right to have a voice in electoral politics.

The Robertson Campaign

⌒

Ronald Reagan's second term had just begun when the *Saturday Evening Post* ran a cover story speculating that Pat Robertson might run for president in 1988. Reporters later wondered if Robertson had been planning a run for the presidency as early as 1981 when he had incorporated the Freedom Council, for the stated purpose of educating *700 Club* viewers about threats to "religious freedom." The Freedom Council was a curious outfit. It was promoted frequently on the *700 Club*, but it did not seem to do much other than to collect names and send out newsletters. Unlike the Christian Coalition, started in 1989 after Robertson's presidential campaign, the Freedom Council was not a grassroots organization with semi-independent state and local affiliates. Instead, Robertson used the Freedom Council to raise money through the one-million-name list of mail donors from his *700 Club* program and, from there, to recruit precinct delegates for the state of Michigan, where the presidential nominating caucuses were held very early in the campaign season.

In 1986, Robertson dissolved the Freedom Council amidst an IRS investigation suggesting violations of tax laws. Without fully or accurately reporting transactions to the IRS, for several years the Christian Broadcasting Network (CBN) poured millions of dollars into the Freedom Council, even though CBN's tax status did not allow it to conduct political activity. The Freedom Council's tax status allowed it to do political work but not on behalf of specific candidates. Yet the Freedom Council recruited candidates to run for seats as Michigan Republican Party precinct delegates, so that they could boost Robertson's chances in the early 1988 Michigan primary.[61]

Michigan was important because the state's unusually early delegate elections—in August 1986—allowed Robertson to launch his campaign before he was legally required to declare himself a candidate. His backers won a plurality of the state's GOP delegate seats. Then, in September 1986, Robertson announced, during a closed-circuit, televised rally for his supporters, that he would declare his candidacy if by 1987 three million voters pledged $100 each to his campaign.[62] During his time of unofficial candidacy, Robertson continued hosting and raising money on the *700 Club*. Ultimately, Robertson was fined $25,000 by the Federal Election Commission for raising campaign funds a year before he officially declared his candidacy.[63]

But for Robertson the fine was just a small part of the cost of doing political business. He was less interested in winning the Republican nomination than in securing a bigger bully pulpit. Robertson won second place in Iowa, a caucus state advantageous to candidates with lots of grassroots supporters. But in the southern states, Robertson fared poorly; for example, he won only 15% of the primary vote in his home state of Virginia.

Much of the problem was Robertson's knack for creating bad press. Loose talk that would have entertained *700 Club* viewers did not fly well on the campaign trail. Robertson said the government should encourage a higher birth rate because the country needed more people to pay future bills and to save "our culture and our values." He declared that no atheists would be allowed to work in his administration. He called for a U.S. military blockade of Libya, and he claimed that Cuba was housing Soviet missiles aimed at the United States.[64] When he accused Vice President George Bush of leaking news of the Jimmy Swaggart sex scandal, Bush called the allegation "crazy,"[65] and the general public was left to wonder how Robertson differed from the rest of the notorious TV evangelists.

No doubt the preacher scandals did Robertson irreparable harm. The 1988 campaign coincided with nearly daily press revelations of the latest twists and turns. The scandals started in January 1987, when Oral Roberts announced that if he did not receive $8 million in donations by March, God would "call him home." Then before anyone could forget the Oral Roberts stunt, Jim and Tammy Bakker's PTL empire began to implode. Under pressure from Jerry Falwell and Jimmy Swaggart, Jim Bakker admitted that years earlier he had cheated on Tammy with a church secretary. Jim resigned from PTL in 1987, and Falwell assumed temporary control of the network. Then Bakker charged Falwell with having plotted a hostile takeover. Because of bad press, Falwell relinquished control, and the network was run for a short while by David Clark, a vice president at Pat Robertson's network. The IRS sought to revoke PTL's tax-exempt status because the Bakkers had, for years, played fast and loose with tax-exempt donations to fund an elaborate theme park. Jim Bakker eventually went to jail as a fall guy for the many PTL executives who were long privy to the financial shenanigans.

In early 1988, while the Bakker scandal simmered and just in time for Robertson's primary races, Jimmy Swaggart appeared on national television, confessed that he had a habit of soliciting prostitutes, and wailed before his family and congregation: "I have sinned against you!" Swaggart had been blackmailed to make the confession by a fellow Assemblies of God preacher who had photographs of Swaggart and prostitutes outside motel rooms.[66]

The TV preacher scandals were treated as serious news stories, though they were best suited for the tabloids. The public was entertained by the sight of hypocrites falling off their pedestals. But relentless scandal coverage created a distorted media impression by suggesting that Oral Roberts, Jim Bakker, and Jimmy Swaggart were stand-ins for the Christian Right as a whole. The image was one of ridiculous scoundrels, not a serious political movement diligently in pursuit of power.

On paper, the 1988 Robertson campaign also looked like a failure. Robertson spent $26 million and arrived at the Republican Party convention in New Orleans with only about 120 delegates. He quickly endorsed George Bush, and was rewarded with a prime-time speaking slot. A polling firm found that a quarter of the delegates at the New Orleans convention were born-again Christians. While most of them were Bush delegates, Robertson claimed that 13% were actually his own campaign workers back in their home states.[67] This was no surprise. During the campaign, it was reported that Robertson campaign workers became the dominant players in several states, including places where Robertson did not do well in primaries.[68] Also during the campaign, Robertson urged his supporters to begin running for local offices themselves.[69] Within the movement, there was a growing sense that it would be fruitful to work toward influencing outcomes at the state and local levels.

The Christian Coalition

∾

The TV preacher scandals and Pat Robertson's abysmal 1988 primary showings made it look to some observers as if the Christian Right had peaked. But the Christian Right was not dead; it was merely changing form. Operation Rescue was drawing large numbers to its abortion clinic blockades. Focus on the Family, as discussed in Chapter 2, was organizing a network of legislative lobbies aimed at state legislatures. The Cold War was coming to an end, and policymakers and activists of all stripes were turning their attention almost entirely toward domestic affairs. The time was right for the formation of a new, grassroots Christian Right organizing project.

That was what Pat Robertson had in mind at the January 1989

inaugural celebration for President George Bush. There he met Ralph Reed and invited the twenty-seven-year-old political campaigner to join him in starting a new organization.[70] Reed was completing his doctorate at Emory University. He was perfect for the job. In his early twenties, he had worked on several Congressional campaigns and had been the director of two successful right-wing student organizations, College Republicans and Students for America. He was a recent convert to the evangelical faith. He was young enough that, unlike Robertson, he had not spent years generating a track record of embarrassing public statements. In fact, early press profiles of Reed usually mentioned his fresh, innocent face. He looked like a choirboy but his role model was the late political consultant Lee Atwater, whom Reed described as "a bare-knuckled, brass tacks practitioner of hard-ball politics."[71]

In 1989, Reed and Robertson began organizing Christian Coalition chapters from the remnants of the Robertson presidential campaign. By early 1990, they announced that the new Christian Coalition had twenty-five thousand members and twelve state chapters.[72] Reed told *Christianity Today* that the Coalition would focus on local politics. "We believe," he said, "that the Christian community in many ways missed the boat in the 1980s by focusing almost entirely on the White House and Congress when most of the issues that concern conservative Catholics and evangelicals are primarily determined in the city councils, school boards, and state legislatures."[73]

The Christian Coalition was able to recruit in large numbers precisely because, by 1990, the movement was already organized at the local level. The first issue of the Coalition's *Christian American* newsletter reported on the work of local chapters. In Virginia, members met with school board officials to lobby against a sex education program. In the Chicago area, they stuffed envelopes and telephoned three thousand people to get out the vote for prolife legislators. In Florida, they held a "political technology" school to train people how to run for office.[74] By the fall of 1990, the Coalition boasted that its members had "spearheaded" the defeat of a gay rights initiative in Broward County, Florida. But the antigay campaign was actually led by a pair of local businessmen who ran their own political action committee.[75] Much of what looked like Christian Coalition organizing was actually the result of independent local activists.[76]

Yet "coalition" was an accurate term for what Reed and Robertson were busy creating. The Christian Coalition gave a more or less unified public face to small groups of activists scattered all over the country. Since 1990, one of the Coalition's regular publications has been the monthly *Religious Rights Watch*. Each issue features six or seven short regional newspaper reports purporting to show that Christians are "under attack" when antiabortion protesters get long sentences or when a public school teaches about homosexuality. Each issue of the *Religious Rights Watch* thanks, by name, the Coalition members who send news clippings for inclusion in the write-ups. Thus, it has been clear that the Coalition enjoys a widespread base of supporters. The sheer volume of reported offenses against "religious rights" suggests a nationwide conspiracy against Christians.

The religious persecution theme has been ubiquitous in Coalition literature. One recruitment advertisement showed a Coalition lapel pin affixed to a tweed suit lapel. The headline read: "If There's Safety in Numbers for Christians, This Is a Safety Pin." Below, the text read:

> Danger! Christian Americans are under siege. Schoolchildren are being threatened and adults jailed for the peaceful practice of God-given rights.
>
> It's time to say, enough. Time to regain a voice in government and raise a righteous standard. When you wear a Christian Coalition lapel pin, you give Evangelicals, pro-family Roman Catholics and other concerned citizens strength in numbers. Strength to speak out in the public arena. To train Christian leaders for social and political action. To protest anti-Christian bias. To represent Christians in courts of law and before legislative bodies.
>
> Now Christians can united behind a grassroots movement that will change the status quo.[77]

Repeatedly, the Coalition has promoted the two-pronged idea that Christians are under siege but that they can easily reclaim their liberty through collective action.

A close reading of the *Christian American,* which went from a newsletter to a newspaper to, eventually, a bimonthly magazine format, reveals the persistence of this theme. There have been endless horror stories, usually with headlines including the words "attack," "assault," or "push" to describe the actions of Democrats, gays or feminist groups. There are also endless articles having to do with the *numbers* of Christian Coalition chapters formed in a given year; the *numbers* of voter guides mailed during an election; the *numbers* of petitions delivered to Congress. The stories tend to be precise, like battle reports: In 1990, the Coalition helped reelect Senator Jesse Helms by distributing 750,000 voter guides and making 30,000 voter contacts "in a non-partisan voter education project."[78] In the fall of 1991, the Coalition delivered to the Senate 50,000 signed petitions backing the confirmation of Supreme Court Justice Clarence Thomas, in what Reed called "one of the largest and most extensive efforts of any group in the nation. . . . It paid off when the chips were down."[79]

Repeated stories on whatever the gays, the abortionists, the feminists, and the teachers' unions are up to lends a hint of paranoia to the Coalition's news reportage. Yet the answer to the fear inspired by aggressive-looking photos of nemeses Hillary Clinton, Joycelyn Elders, Eleanor Smeal, and others of their ilk is to get involved in the nuts-and-bolts of grassroots electoral politics. Collect petitions, make phone calls, hand out voter guides—these small, feasible actions can turn the tide against the liberal conspiracy. From the perspective of Coalition leaders trying to mobilize a following, it makes sense to both raise the level of perceived grievances and to give people the means to surmount their fear of the enemy.

The emphasis on liberal conspirators, combined with the focus on numerical victories, has dovetailed neatly with the Coalition's use of so-called stealth tactics. The 1988 Robertson campaign promoted the use of deception and thus gave critics of the Christian Right the ammunition to charge the movement with routine dishonesty. As early as 1986, during the Republican caucuses in Iowa, an embarrassing Robertson campaign memo surfaced. It encouraged Christian activists to "hide your strength. . .. Don't flaunt your Christianity. . . . Don't come across as a one-issue person. Be perceived as a person interested in the whole spectrum of issues."[80] Such advice was consistent with a view of politics as more of a minefield than a town meeting.

Stealth tactics were responsible for Christian Right victories in a number of elections for city and county offices in 1990. Affiliated candidates ran for all sorts of posts, and sixty were elected, some without ever attending public candidate forums. The secret of victory was to bypass the usual campaign venues. Instead, campaign organizer Steve Baldwin—who several years later won his own seat in the California assembly—generated a large phone list by cross-correlating the membership lists of conservative churches with lists of registered voters. These people were contacted and urged to vote for the profamily slate. Then, on the Sunday before election day, church parking lots were blanketed with slate-endorsement flyers left on car windshields.[81] But victory was short-lived: most of the candidates elected in 1990 were rejected by voters in the next round of elections.

It was the Christian Coalition, though, which elevated the stealth mentality to an art form—again, with the unintended consequence of making the use of sneaky tactics a frequent theme in press coverage of the whole movement. At the Coalition's 1991 Road to Victory conference, Reed talked about his get-out-the-vote project as if it were a job for the Special Forces. His reported statements became the stuff of press folklore after he said: "I want to be invisible. I do guerrilla warfare. I paint my face and travel at night. You don't know it's over until you're in a body bag. You don't know until election night."[82]

The hyperbole spoke volumes about Reed's view of his adversaries, while it also referred to the Coalition's numerical way of thinking about elections. At the same Road to Victory conference, Coalition field director

Guy Rodgers explained the advantage of generally low voter turnout in the United States. Among all eligible voters, only about 60% are registered, and often only half of those who are registered bother to vote. Thus, if only 30% of the eligible electorate votes, the Christian Right can win an election with scarcely more than 15% support. The trick, then, is to use phone surveys to locate the maximum number of "correct" voters in a given district and to make sure they get to the polls—by leafletting their churches and even calling them on election day.[83]

There is nothing mysterious about this labor-intensive approach to voter mobilization. It has, however, raised legal questions, since the Coalition's initial tax status allowed it to do political educational work, but not on behalf of specific candidates, which is part of the reason for a stealth strategy.

Early on, the stealth mentality filtered down to the Coalition's state branches. The 1992 organizing manual of the Pennsylvania Christian Coalition bore hints of stealth thinking throughout. In a section on how to organize within the county committees of the Republican Party, executive director Rick Schenker wrote that the best way to influence the party was simply to elect the majority of people in it:

> Become directly involved in the local Republican Committee yourself so that you are an insider. This way you can get a copy of the local committee rules and a feel for who is in the current Republican Committee. You should never mention the name Christian Coalition in Republican circles. [emphasis in original][84]

Why not mention the name? Because the siege mentality established a pattern by which the Coalition has used the structure of free and fair elections, but with the goal of winning disproportionate representation. In 1993, Reed told *Charisma* magazine that he regretted fostering stealth thinking with his talk about guerrilla warfare.[85] But old habits do not just fade away. At some of the Road to Victory conference sessions in the mid-1990s, grassroots activists talked openly about endorsing candidates and publicly mentioning the name Christian Coalition in Republican circles.[86] However, some of the organization's state branch leaders still talked about getting members to join GOP precinct committees without disclosing their status as members in the Christian Coalition.[87]

Even regarding its membership rolls, the Coalition has played fast and loose with numbers. By 1995, the Coalition claimed it had over 1.5 million members, and the ever-increasing figure was routinely touted as evidence of the Coalition's unquestioned influence. The number was suspicious, though, because "membership" entails a minimum annual dues of $20, and all dues-paying members receive the *Christian American* magazine. At the end of 1995, the *Christian American* reported, in its legally required annual statement of ownership, a paid circulation of about 353,000.[88] Perhaps the Coalition included in its projections several additional family members for each dues-paying subscriber.

By the Numbers

❧

Even a more credible estimate of hundreds of thousands of members makes the Christian Coalition formidable. Most of what the Coalition does is aboveboard. The key to the success of a labor-intensive approach to politics is persistent low voter turnout among the general public.

With grassroots activists in mind, the Coalition's annual Road to Victory conferences run on two tracks. At one level, the conferences are pep rallies for a who's who of Republican leaders. At another level the conferences offer tips on the nuts-and-bolts of organizing. In 1994, for example, the chairperson of the Coalition's South Carolina branch, Roberta Combs, told the conventioneers that she had created a network of Coalition activists in 60% of her state's electoral precincts. "You are in warfare," she said. "Politics equals people. People equals numbers. Numbers equal precincts. Get ten people to start with. Get a map, voter registration lists, church directories, other profamily lists." Combs urged activists to correlate the lists and identify sympathetic voters street by street.[89] The next day, Combs spoke at a briefing session for Coalition chapter leaders, along with Alice Patterson, who was the field director for the Texas Coalition's 134 local chapters. Patterson explained that the Coalition's task was to get a structure in place well ahead of elections or issue controversies. "Concentrate on your county, your cities, your precincts," Patterson advised. "Then whenever the issues come along or candidacies or whatever comes along, you're going to be ready to do that."[90] Both Combs and Patterson stressed that organizing at the precinct level is the key to getting a majority of Christian conservatives elected as delegates to their state Republican parties.

In order to do precinct organizing, the Coalition's national office prepares organizing manuals for chapter leaders. The 1995 Citizen Action manual instructed members to find a local church liaison person, and then persuade this person to get his or her pastor's approval to form a Civic Concerns Committee for voter registration and petition drives. The same manual teaches members that they can become a Christian Coalition Neighborhood Coordinator by taking a list of registered voters in their area, cross-referencing it with local church lists, and then calling people who appear on both sets of lists and asking them to join a chapter or hand out Coalition voter guides. The names and addresses of all the likely prospects are to be sent to chapter and state leaders.

Computer technology makes this kind of machine-building work easier than in the past, but it still requires a great deal of person-to-person contact. It would be impossible, even with an annual budget in excess of $20 million, for the Christian Coalition to pay for the countless hours of recruiting and information gathering done with volunteer labor. Local activists are best suited to speaking with fellow churchgoers living in their own areas, and there is an evangelistic thrust to the search for new supporters.

The 1995 Road to Victory conference was preceded by an afternoon of grassroots lobbying on Capitol Hill. Three hundred Coalition activists from around the country met for a brief session on how to lobby for the Coalition's ten-point Contract with the American Family legislative packet. The Coalition's Washington, DC, lobbying staff gave each activist a folder with printed lists of "talking points" on such issues as banning late-term abortions and abolishing the Department of Education. Also included in each folder were data collection "report cards" to be filled out for each legislator and returned to the Coalition's central office. From there the three hundred activists fanned out and conducted a total of four hundred constituent visits with their Senators and Congressmembers during a two and a half hour shift. This was the way the Coalition members made an impact on their elected officials, and the only thing "stealthy," about it was that it was not reported in the press.[91] Without the political professionals in the Coalition's Washington, DC, offices, the lobbying session could not have been efficiently organized. But without the three hundred activists in town for the weekend at their own expense, the Coalition would not have been able to make its point that afternoon.

Other Lobbies

∽

The Christian Coalition encourages its members to work also within other organizations. Among them, Concerned Women for America (CWA) is highly compatible. CWA was founded in San Diego in 1979 by Beverly LaHaye. She was alarmed by the possssibility of ratification of the Equal Rights Amendment, and she began organizing women into "prayer chapters."

The idea is to get women first to pray about the nation's moral decay and then to become what LaHaye calls "kitchen table lobbyists," performing simple tasks such as phoning and writing government representatives. In 1985, LaHaye and her husband, Tim, relocated to Washington, DC, and

CWA took on a two-tiered organizational structure. It developed a lobbying presence on Capitol Hill while it has also maintained grassroots chapter leaders and "area representatives" all over the country.

Since the early 1990s, CWA has sponsored a daily half-hour radio show, *Beverly LaHaye Live,* which aired on 124 stations by 1996, and on which Mrs. LaHaye frequently promotes the leaders of other organizations. Mostly the program serves an agenda-setting function, with a relentless focus on abortion and homosexuality. In 1996, CWA urged its members to lobby hard for Congressional passage of the Defense of Marriage Act, which allows states to deny the legality of gay marriages. On this project, CWA members led the way in getting a number of state legislatures to pass preemptive laws banning same-sex marriages.[92]

Earlier, in 1991, CWA pulled out all the stops to win the confirmation of Clarence Thomas as a Supreme Court justice. Numerous Christian Right groups lobbied for Thomas. But once his former coworker Anita Hill charged him with sexual harassment, support from a group of conservative women became even more imperative. The Thomas–Hill controversy coincided with the launch of CWA's new daily radio show. *Beverly LaHaye Live* repeatedly broadcast the phone number of the Congressional switchboard, and CWA later reported that the show generated hundreds of pro-Thomas phone calls to Senators. When the hearings began, CWA members gathered outside the Senate hearing room to cheer Thomas as he arrived to testify.

Typically, CWA lobbies on a handful of hot national issues while also allowing "area representatives" in the states to set their own agenda. There has never been a shortage of issues, some of which require intervention by CWA's small team of lawyers. In Maine, for example, during the Hill–Thomas controversy, CWA successfully sued a school district for refusing to allow a local church to use a school cafeteria for a weekend banquet. At the time, the case was one of eight lawsuits filed on behalf of CWA members seeking "equal access" to public facilities.[93]

CWA's *Family Voice* magazine reports monthly on the work of state branches, particularly in the legislatures. In Michigan, CWA members succeeded in getting their legislature to pass an "informed consent" bill requiring women seeking abortions to wait twenty-four hours after reading a pamphlet on the health dangers of abortion.[94] In Massachusetts, CWA members lobbied against a bill to repeal sodomy laws. In Maryland, a CWA activist helped introduce a bill to give parents better access to their children's school records.[95] With a hand in virtually every profamily matter, CWA allows its grassroots activists to gravitate toward issues that concern them most. All the while, CWA's national staff and radio program provide overall guidance and keep far-flung listeners apprised of each other's work.

Apart from Concerned Women for America and the Christian Coalition, the Family Research Council (FRC) is the other leading movement pressure group. When Senator Bob Dole launched his presidential campaign with a summer 1995 blast at Hollywood, he reportedly consulted FRC president Gary Bauer before putting the finishing touches on his speech. When journalists seek commentary on the Republican Party's simmering feuds between prolifers and prochoicers, Bauer's name is at the front of their Rolodexes.[96]

In the mid-1990s, the FRC had a mailing list of more than 250,000, a staff of 70, and an annual budget of $10 million.[97] Bauer was a domestic policy adviser to President Reagan in the 1980s, and served a stint as undersecretary in the Department of Education. In 1988, Bauer left the administration and was adopted by Dr. James Dobson of Focus on the Family. Bauer's FRC became Dobson's Capitol Hill lobbying appendage, until 1992 when the two organizations severed their legal ties so as not to jeopardize Focus's tax-exempt status. The two organizations continue to complement each other. Dobson and Bauer appear together frequently on the radio and at political gatherings. They share mailing lists, and the FRC is a mainstay of information found in Focus's *Citizen* magazine. Bauer knows the ropes of the political establishment, but his influence in Washington, DC, depends on his ties to Focus. Dobson commands the allegiance of millions of radio listeners, so that when Bauer speaks publicly, it is understood that he speaks for a big segment of the evangelical constituency.

Shortly after the new Republican Congressional majority was inaugurated, in 1995, Dobson and Bauer went to Capitol Hill where they cosponsored a breakfast for thirty-four members of Congress, mostly newcomers to Washington. In a letter to FRC supporters, Bauer wrote that "many had tears in their eyes as Dr. Dobson spoke eloquently about the sanctity of life. . . . One after another, the Congressmen made it clear they were counting on FRC to provide them with the research they need on these issues."[98]

At the time, Dobson and Bauer were sharpening their knives for a campaign against Clinton's new nominee for surgeon general of the United States. The FRC had earlier lobbied for the removal of Clinton's first appointee to this post, Dr. Joycelyn Elders. Elders made the irrevocable error of using the word "masturbation" in a public speech about sex education, and she was forced to resign during the ensuing flap. Then Clinton nominated Dr. Henry Foster, an African American obstetrician and gynecologist. The FRC created a media flurry around the fact that Foster was a strong supporter of Planned Parenthood and had himself performed abortions—many more than the White House initially claimed. If that were not enough, the FRC circulated reports that Dr. Foster had not objected when he had served on an Alabama state medical board connected to the infamous Tuskegee Project, which used black men as unknowing subjects in a study of untreated syphilis. Foster denied having known anything about the Tuskegee Project, but the seriousness of the charge turned the tide of public opinion against him.[99] The FRC effectively quashed the nomination of Dr. Foster, and the Clinton administration thereafter chose simply to leave the post of surgeon general vacant.

In its capacity as think tank, the FRC helps to craft the arguments used by Christian Right activists. For example, when Congress debated a "family cap" that would have denied welfare benefits to women who continue to bear "illegitimate" babies, some "profamily" advocates argued that a cap would cause more welfare-dependent women to have abortions. The FRC promoted the contrary view: that a cap on welfare assistance would be good for "the family" because "poor women who are pregnant out of wedlock will forsake the anonymity of the welfare culture and turn to crisis pregnancy groups that will counsel against abortion and discourage further irresponsible behavior."[100] Consistently, the FRC translates, for its constituency, uncharitable policy ideas into the rhetoric of family values.

Material from FRC and newsletters becomes fodder also for the right-wing talk show hosts and sympathetic politicians. Until recently, the Christian Right's organizational infrastructure consisted mostly of media outlets and grassroots lobbies. With growing sophistication, social movements exert themselves through a greater variety of channels. Now central to the Christian Right's organizational loop are a number of legal firms prepared to carry the movement's agenda beyond the airwaves and the voting booths into the courtrooms. There power is contested and policies affecting everyone are yet to be decided.

We'll See You in Court

∾

In 1996, the California Supreme Court ruled against apartment owner Evelyn Smith. She had accepted a security deposit from a couple who wanted to rent from her. But when she learned that the couple were not married, she had refused to rent the unit to them and had returned their deposit. The court ruled that Mrs. Smith was free to believe whatever she liked about unmarried cohabitants, but that she did not have the right to apply her religious views in a discriminatory manner in the housing market. Smith's right to do business had to be balanced with the public's right to obtain housing, regardless of the marital status—or, by extension, sexual orientation—of the renters.[101]

That might have been the end of Evelyn Smith's case. But the Alliance Defense Fund (ADF) came forward, offering to sponsor an appeal to the U.S. Supreme Court. The Smith case is similar to others around the country, where Christians are getting into legal trouble for refusing to do business with homosexuals and other designated sinners. The ADF presents government rulings as a new form of antireligious bigotry. "A positive outcome will set a new legal precedent and bring a halt to this kind of persecution," wrote ADF president Alan Sears in a fundraising letter for the case. "This is both a legal contest and a spiritual battle," he wrote.[102]

Though the Supreme Court was unlikely to hear the Smith case, the ADF vowed to forge ahead. Evelyn Smith would become another symbolic victim of the liberal conspiracy. By publicizing cases like Evelyn Smith's, the ADF is building a financial war chest and a team of lawyers to carry the movement's agenda into the courts. Beginning in the 1960s, African American and feminist lawyers established civil rights law firms with effective legal clout. In the 1990s, the Christian Right began to follow suit.

Thus far, the movement has fostered a number of law firms specializing mostly in First Amendment cases involving abortion protests, homeschooling, and public evangelism. There is the Rutherford Institute, the Christian Legal Society, the Home School Legal Defense Association, the Liberty Counsel, and (biggest of them all) the American Center for Law and Justice, founded by Pat Robertson and headquartered near Robertson's Regent University law school. There are enough cases to keep each of the firms busy in perpetuity.

At the 1994 convention of the National Religious Broadcasters, the ADF announced its formation, not as another law firm but, rather, as a project to coordinate case loads between firms, to recruit and train lawyers, and, most importantly, to bankroll cases. The ADF was founded by some of the biggest names in religious broadcasting: Dr. James Dobson of Focus on the Family, Bill Bright of Campus Crusade for Christ, Gary Bauer of the Family Research Council, Donald Wildmon of the American Family Association, Christian financial adviser Larry Burkett, USA Radio Network executive Marlin Maddoux, and D. James Kennedy of Coral Ridge Ministries. Each of these men has an audience of hundreds of thousands of potential donors. They say their goal, eventually, is to channel more than $26 million annually into legal work against "an unprecedented legislative and judicial assault" on Christians—everything from restrictions on homeschooling to enforcement of antidiscrimination laws in the job market.[103] At the helm of the ADF is Alan Sears, a former federal prosecutor and a specialist in obscenity cases. Under the Reagan administration, Sears directed Attorney General Edwin Meese's Commission on Pornography.

By mid-1995, the ADF claimed victory in two Supreme Court cases. In one, the Court ruled that the government could not force the organizers of a St. Patrick's Day parade in Boston to include gay marchers. In another, the Court ruled that the University of Virginia wrongfully discriminated against a Christian student group by denying them funds for publication of the group's on-campus magazine, *Wide Awake*. As long as the university funded other student newspapers, the Court ruled, the Christian magazine was also eligible for grants from a general pool of student activity funds.[104] Within its first three years in operation, the ADF helped to fund more than one hundred cases, with the goal of winning more than just a few lawsuits. In a newsletter for donors, ADF president Alan Sears explained that every victory would help "build a body of case law that influences and reverberates in many other cases. . . . While we can bring about quick fixes in the voting booth, it is in the courts that we will bring about the type of change that transcends all generations."

It was for that type of change that Pat Robertson, in 1991, founded the American Center for Law and Justice (ACLJ). By 1995, the ACLJ had an annual budget of $8 million[105]—no doubt due largely to frequent promotion, on the *700 Club*, of the firm and its chief counsel and celebrity lawyer, Jay Sekulow.

Sekulow is a Jewish convert to Christianity who, before joining forces with Robertson, ran an Atlanta-based firm called Christian Advocates Serving Evangelism (CASE). In 1987, Sekulow came to national attention when he went before the Supreme Court and successfully argued that Jews for Jesus has the First Amendment right to evangelize in airport terminals. Then Sekulow won another Supreme Court case involving the right of a student-led Bible club to hold meetings in the same public school facilities used by other afterschool clubs. After the Jews for Jesus case, Sekulow became a frequent guest on the nightly *Praise the Lord* talk show, shown on the Trinity Broadcasting Network (TBN). Within a year of his first appearance on TBN, donations to CASE quadrupled.[106]

Sekulow is an aggressive self-promoter. He is the Christian Right's attorney of first resort, especially in cases destined for the Supreme Court. From its inception, the ACLJ has upstaged the older movement law firms, such as the Rutherford Institute, founded in 1982, and the Christian Legal Society, founded in 1975. These firms have worked in relative obscurity for years. But the ACLJ has Sekulow's star power and a built-in donor base, courtesy of the *700 Club* and TBN. Sekulow boasts that he has a "SWAT team of freedom fighters; poised and eager to defend these rights in state and federal courts, and even at meetings of local school boards and city councils."[107]

Sekulow's SWAT teams are drawn mostly to high-profile cases. Randall Terry credited Sekulow with the survival of Operation Rescue during the early 1990s, when judges were issuing harsh sentences and fines.[108] Sekulow argued for Operation Rescue in *Bray v. Alexandria Women's Health Clinic,* a landmark case in which the National Organization for Women sued antiabortion protesters, on the theory that the 1871 Ku Klux Klan Act prohibited Operation Rescue from conspiring to block access to clinics. In 1993, the Supreme Court ruled that the Klan Act did not apply to

Operation Rescue and that opposition to abortion is not a form of discrimination against women per se.[109]

In 1996, the ACLJ joined the fight against same-sex marriage by representing gay rights opponents in Hawaii and by helping to draft the language of Congress's Defense of Marriage Act, which allows states to refuse to recognize gay marriages performed in other states. In 1997, Sekulow predicted there will be hundreds of gay marriage cases around the country in the next few years, and he proposed to fight them by opening ACLJ offices in all fifty states.[110]

The ACLJ has the potential to become, for the Christian Right, what the ACLU is to civil libertarians, though there are differences. The liberal law firms define their task as one of stringent defense of constitutional liberties, which is why the ACLU sometimes represents disreputable clients for the sake of a legal principle. The ACLJ, in contrast, fired one of its own attorneys, Michael Hirsh, who had written a *Regent University Law Review* article justifying the killing of abortion doctors—but only after Hirsh's client Paul Hill actually killed two people at a clinic in 1994.111

This occurred around the same time that the ACLJ was circulating a pamphlet written by its executive director, Keith Fournier, called *Religious Cleansing in the American Republic*. Fournier defined "religious cleansing" as "the current hostility and bigotry toward religion and people of faith that are leading to covert and overt attempts to remove any religious influence in the public arena."[112] At the very least, "religious cleansing" was a tasteless choice of words, coinciding with press reports of the "ethnic cleansing" underway in the former Yugoslavia. Fournier peppered his tract with references to Nazi Germany and claimed that, in the United States in the mid-1990s, restrictions on public prayer and evangelism were on a par with genocidal bloodshed in Eastern Europe.

This sort of hyperbole is not unheard of from organizations dependent on direct mail fundraising. There is also something substantive about the rhetoric of religious persecution. As supporters of the Christian Right increasingly come into conflict with a diverse and secular public, it is inevitable that protesters and proselytizers will find themselves in court fights. They are entitled to qualified legal representation, but it is not true that evangelicals represent a persecuted class of people. They are not denied jobs and housing as racial minorities and homosexuals often are. Nor do they lack political power. On the contrary, it is precisely at a time when the Christian Right enjoys political influence and organizational abundance that the movement is capable of building law firms and sending attorneys to the Supreme Court. Yet in order to justify the flexing of its own legal muscles, the movement needs to portray its members as martyrs to the cause of Christ. The rhetoric of "religious persecution" makes sense, both as a way of enlisting support and as a hedge against public recognition that court cases are often really contests for political power.

As we will see in the next chapter, the ebbs and flows of political conflict require organizations that can stretch without breaking. The Christian Right's most successful players have been those who work collaboratively with existing power brokers yet without fully yielding their independence. In the 1990s, Patrick Buchanan used his two presidential campaigns to stretch the bounds of acceptability within the Republican Party. Buchanan personally took the heat for it and thereby allowed the Christian Coalition to appear moderate and reasonable by comparison. The Coalition has helped to keep the movement from stagnating, in part by continually broadening what is meant by the theme of family values.

Chapter 5

⤳

All Things to All People

Ralph Reed took political pundits by surprise in 1993. At the time Reed's was the most prominent voice of the Christian Right. In the Heritage Foundation's widely read *Policy Review* journal, he published an article titled "Casting a Wider Net," in which he envisioned the Christian Right moving well beyond issues such as abortion and homosexuality, to take on the economic concerns of middle-class families. "The most urgent challenge for pro-family conservatives," Reed wrote,

> is to develop a broader issues agenda. The pro-family movement has limited its effectiveness by concentrating disproportionately on issues such as abortion and homosexuality. These are vital moral issues, and must remain an important part of the message. To win at the ballot box and in the court of public opinion, however, the pro-family movement must speak to the concerns of average voters in the areas of taxes, crime, government waste, health care, and financial security.[1]

Reed's article, excerpted both in the *New York Times* and in the Christian Coalition's own bimonthly newspaper, ended with an invocation from the Apostle Paul who said he had become "all things to all people that I may by all means win some." Reed argued that a broader movement focus on pocketbook issues was the way to "win natural allies" among racial minorities and Catholics. "Building a political agenda around a single issue is a risky proposition," Reed concluded, "because when progress lags on that issue, as it inevitably will, the viability of the entire movement is threatened."[2]

In "Casting a Wider Net," Reed was responding to a number of quandaries the Christian Right faced at that time. The movement's antigay and antiabortion rhetoric had reached a fever pitch. There had been a flurry of antigay state ballot initiatives, and an abortion doctor had been assassinated in Florida. Some pundits blamed President George Bush's 1992 election defeat on the vitriolic speeches delivered by Pat Robertson and Patrick Buchanan at the 1992 GOP convention in Houston, though polling data showed Clinton strategists had correctly read national sentiment with their "It's the economy, stupid" slogan. The inauguration of President Bill Clinton meant that Republicans were (temporarily) suffering from a power deficit, and Reed sought to keep a channel open between the movement and the party. At the same time, as he emphasized in his article, the parental rights movement was on a roll in some parts of the country. In the spring of 1993, in New York City, no less, an unprecedented working alliance came together between members of the Christian Coalition, the Catholic hierarchy, and some parents of color. They ran a slate of candidates, many of whom won, in hotly contested school board elections revolving around the introduction of a gay-positive curriculum in the elementary grades.

Reed's challenge was to figure out how to polish the movement's tarnished reputation while also keeping spirits high and momentum strong at the local level. These two goals seem contradictory. A polished image required a new focus on pedestrian issues such as defeating Clinton's proposed health care reform legislation. The grass roots, though, were burning over homosexuality, "baby killing," and imagined liberal conspiracies in the public schools. On these matters, heated rhetoric is the name of the game. Moreover, it is difficult to arouse large numbers of committed activists without also encouraging excesses. This contradiction continues to perplex the Christian Right. Reed and other movement leaders want to be power brokers in Republican national politics, and they can do so only if they credibly represent a large voting bloc. Amateur activists are much less willing to compromise, particularly on the nonnegotiable question of abortion. Tensions between the professionals and the principled amateurs sometimes threaten to divide the movement. But, as we will see in this chapter, it is precisely this tension that keeps the movement from degenerating, either into a wholly owned Republican subsidiary, or into a ragtag band of protesters with no clout. In discussing this tension, I will begin with the role of presidential candidate Patrick Buchanan. He has been both a team player and an agitator within the Republican Party, and in that respect his campaigns have crystallized some of the dilemmas faced by the Christian Right.

Buchanan's 1992 Campaign

Patrick Buchanan's 1992 and 1996 presidential campaigns drove home some of the perennial rifts on the right, but to the overall benefit of movement activists. For chronology's sake, I address the second Buchanan campaign later in this chapter, in the context of the 1996 elections generally. The two campaigns differed in terms of the issues Buchanan raised each time; of his relationship first to an incumbent president and, then in 1996, to Senate Majority Leader Bob Dole; and of the role played by the Christian Right each time.

When Buchanan first ran in the 1992 primaries, his campaign was not primarily about advocating the wish list of the Christian Right. In 1992, Buchanan had two main targets. One was President George Bush, whom Buchanan and many other conservatives charged with selling out the "Reagan Revolution." Bush had broken his "no new taxes" pledge, and he had offended corporate leaders by signing a Civil Rights Act and an environmental Clean Air Act. Bush's greatest sins, though, were in the foreign affairs realm, which was Buchanan's biggest preoccupation.

Buchanan was the most vocal of a group of rightists who strongly opposed the 1991 Persian Gulf War—not because of the death and destruction suffered by people in Iraq, but because this was a multilateral war, waged by the United States in conjunction with the United Nations. This war had nothing to do with "communism," but instead was about oil and Middle East politics. During the months leading up to the United States-led bombing of Iraq, Buchanan waged a war of words with right-wing war hawks on TV talk shows and on the op-ed pages of leading newspapers. *New York Times* editorialist A. M. Rosenthal charged that Buchanan's newfound isolationism stemmed from his hostility toward U.S. backing of Israel, and was therefore evidence that Buchanan is an anti-Semite.[3]

Buchanan denied the charge of anti-Semitism, and once the killing began in the Gulf in January 1991, he urged his supporters to stifle their dissent and support the bombing of Iraq. The air war ended so quickly that it quieted a simmering debate among people on the Right: after the end of communism, did it still make sense for the United States to intervene militarily where there was no direct threat to American lives?[4] This debate was never fully resolved, both because the Gulf War ended with few U.S. casualties and because the next big foreign policy crises, namely in Haiti and the Balkans, took place under a Democratic administration.

At the start of the 1992 presidential campaign, though, the anti-Semitism charge against Buchanan stuck like glue. Just a few days after Buchanan announced his candidacy in December 1991, William F. Buckley Jr. devoted a full issue of his *National Review* magazine to analysis of anti-Jewish themes in the writings of Buchanan and another vocal Persian Gulf War opponent, writer Joseph Sobran. Buckley accurately distinguished political anti-Zionism from the ethnic bigotry of anti-Semitism, but then concluded that Buchanan and Sobran were guilty on both counts.[5] Buckley is no champion of racial and ethnic diversity in U.S. politics. But the purpose of his article, later published as a book, was to lay to rest the public image that the right wing is anti-Semitic.

Buchanan's 1992 campaign speeches were not usually about the Middle East. Instead, he focused on nationalism, on the direction of U.S. foreign and economic policy within George Bush's "new world order." In the speech announcing his candidacy, Buchanan focused on "the rising economic power of Japan" and "the European superstate." He indicted "the rising drain of wealth and resources to Washington" and "the tax burden on American business." Then he linked economic crisis to the family values agenda.

> When we say we will put America first, we mean also that our Judeo-Christian values are going to be preserved, and our Western heritage is going to be handed down to future generations, not dumped onto some landfill called multiculturalism.
>
> At the root of America's social crisis—be it AIDS, ethnic hatred, crime or the social de-composition of our cities—lies a spiritual crisis. Not in the redistribution of wealth, but in the words of the Old and New Testament will be found not only salvation, but the cure for a society suffering a chronic moral sickness.[6]

Invoking the Bible, Buchanan sounded like his old boss Ronald Reagan—which should not surprise, since Buchanan had been a speechwriter for Reagan. But whereas Pat Robertson's verbal outbursts in 1988 had made him a target for ridicule, Buchanan's bombshells were calculated to grab headlines and make people's hearts pound. In New Hampshire, shortly before the 1992 primary, for example, Buchanan served Christmas dinner at a soup kitchen and then remarked that homeless people should be jailed if they refused to lodge in designated shelters.[7] Then during the southern state primaries, Buchanan went on a radio talk show and called AIDS "nature's retribution for violating the laws of nature."[8]

Buchanan was willing to say what many voters thought. Still, the political establishment was stunned when Buchanan took 37% of the New Hampshire GOP primary vote and proceeded to win 20–30% of the vote in about two dozen other state primary races against the incumbent, President Bush. Some of Buchanan's field directors were veterans of the 1988 Pat Robertson campaign,[9] and yet it was never clear how much of Buchanan's support came from diehard movement activists and how much was simply a protest vote against Bush. Christian Right voters were divided on whether to back Buchanan, and thus send a warning to Bush, or whether to vote for the president, to ensure a strong prolife contingent among delegates at the Houston convention. The quandary revealed that, early on, the leadership of the Christian Coalition sought to make itself indispensable to the elite and powerful. While Buchanan was riding high in the polls, Pat Robertson allowed Bush to mail out a letter of endorsement from the TV preacher. Robertson had endorsed Bush early, during the 1991 Gulf War.[10] In an interview with the secular right-wing newspaper *Human Events*, Buchanan was asked what he thought about Robertson's endorsement of Bush. "I think some folks saw me stealing the conservative movement," Buchanan replied, "and were envious of my ripping a page out of the history books that might have been theirs had they made the race."[11]

It was Buchanan's race, and he did make history. The same *Human Events* newspaper, which functioned as a virtual house organ for Buchanan during the campaign, celebrated Buchanan's success in influencing the Bush camp on several scores. Following Buchanan's lead, the paper noted, Bush called for capital gains tax cuts and a freeze on domestic spending. In response to Buchanan's campaign ads against the National Endowment for the Arts (NEA), Bush fired NEA director John Frohnmayer, whom the Right considered too soft on "obscenity." More substantively, it was Buchanan's unrelenting rhetoric that drove the issue of illegal immigration to the top of the Republican Party's agenda.[12]

Then it was Buchanan who, in the aftermath of the Los Angeles riots, linked immigration to the racially charged indictments of what he called a "barbarian" mob. It was in a May 1992 speech before Jerry Falwell's Liberty University that Buchanan gave a dress rehearsal for the speech he would make later that summer at the Republican convention.

> Friends, make no mistake: what we saw in Los Angeles was evil exultant and triumphant and we no longer saw it as through a glass darkly, but face to face.
>
> In Los Angeles, government failed in its first duty, to protect the property and lives of its citizens. And those who lacked the courage to move against that mob, or to condemn its evil deeds unequivocally, are guilty of moral appeasement. . . .
>
> There is a religious war going on for the soul of America. And just as the Commandments that lay down the law of God have been expelled from our schools, so the lessons of history that undergird these truths are being erased. . . .
>
> The challenge and duty facing this generation, who have the gift of an education rooted in Christian truths and Judeo-Christian values, is to show your countrymen the way to recapture America's culture and our country— from the new barbarism.[13]

The speech was vintage Buchanan. It was familiar in tone and substance to people on the Right, and yet it shocked the nationwide television audience that heard a version of it on the first night of the

Republican convention. The prominence given to Buchanan's speech was rightfully seen as a giant step in the Republicans' lurch toward the family values agenda. Weeks before the convention, Vice President Dan Quayle had sparked a firestorm with a speech that blamed rising urban violence on illegitimate pregnancies, including that of TV character Murphy Brown. Then, at the convention, Buchanan's opening night was followed by prime-time sermons from former drug czar William Bennett, Pat Robertson, and Marilyn Quayle. Robertson charged Bill Clinton with having "a radical plan to destroy the traditional family and transfer many of its functions to the federal government."[14]

It appeared that the Christian Right had simply taken over the Republican Party. An estimated 47% of the delegates were self-described born-again Christians,[15] and over the objections of other Republicans, they secured a party platform demanding a ban on all abortions; opposing civil rights for homosexuals; and calling on the government to stop the sale of pornography and condemn "obscene" art. The platform also endorsed homeschooling and school prayer, and opposed making contraceptives available in public schools.[16] Pat Buchanan was right when he said, in Houston, that there was "a religious war going on for the soul of America."

Bush's November defeat was widely perceived as a casualty of that war. Conventional wisdom blamed Buchanan and Robertson for scaring middle-of-the-road voters away from the Republican Party. There were, of course, many reasons why Bush was unpopular. It was, however, a predicament for the movement to be perceived as a liability. Ralph Reed tried to do damage control. He wrote in the *Christian American* immediately following the election that despite the blame-mongering coming from media pundits, there was "a silver lining in the results for the pro-family movement." The election of Bill Clinton had turned mostly on jobs and the economy, and therefore the family values voters could not have been responsible. Furthermore, Bush was the loser among almost every demographic segment of the electorate. According to a poll commissioned by the Christian Coalition, Bush won only among two categories of voters: people with incomes over $200,000 a year—who were few in number—and evangelical Christians. Fifty-five percent of the 1992 evangelical bloc voted Republican; about 28% of the twenty-four million evangelical voters chose Clinton, and 17% voted for Ross Perot. An impressive 46% of Bush's entire vote came from evangelicals, according to Reed, meaning that the Republicans would have suffered even greater losses without support from the Christian Right.[17]

For the Christian Coalition, the 1992 presidential election, despite Bush's defeat, was a chance to flex its organizational muscles. At the Houston convention, Pat Robertson claimed that three hundred of the two thousand delegates were members of the Christian Coalition.[18] Then shortly before election day, the Coalition distributed some forty million voter guides, mostly through a list of about 246,000 churches.[19] The 1992 voter guide was a sixteen-page tabloid-sized newspaper that rated the presidential and Congressional candidates' positions, pro or con, on six issues: income taxes, abortion, school vouchers, gay rights, government funding of "obscene" art, and a balanced budget amendment.[20] (A discussion of distortions in such voter guides follows below.)

Though they focused on the national races, the voter guides served as useful reminders to get conservative Christians to the polls for local races. It was impossible to calculate the full results of this effort. But in 1992, People for the American Way (PAW) monitored five hundred local races and reported that Christian Right forces won about 40% of them.[21] To assess the results, PAW identified state and local candidates who were either directly involved with what PAW disingenuously calls "radical" Right organizations or who had received an endorsement from such groups, including the Christian Coalition, the National Right to Life Committee, the Eagle Forum, Operation Rescue, the Traditional Values Coalition, and others, differing from state to state. In California, for example, thirteen out of twenty-two Christian Right–backed Congressional candidates were elected, as were sixteen out of twenty-nine candidates for the state assembly.[22]

Many of the winners were mainstream Republican incumbents, and that said something about the Christian Right's electoral strategy. It was partially an effort to infuse the process with new blood, people who would reliably carry the movement's agenda forward. But there was just as much interest in backing status quo politicians who would, despite their inclinations toward compromise, become increasingly hooked on the Christian Right vote. By backing plenty of incumbent Republicans, the movement has protected itself against any credible charges that it is a "radical" force out to fundamentally change the system. When it comes to electoral politics, the Christian Right is a system-supportive movement, intent on legislating its moral policy agenda but without challenging the essence of unequal power and wealth in the United States.

The Christian Right Targets Clinton
ᴄ⌒

On the hot-button family values issues, however, the movement does want to upset the apple cart, and this poses a dilemma for the political establishment. The 1992 elections shocked leaders of both parties and much of the general public. Focus on the Family's *Citizen* magazine reported numerous electoral victories for profamily candidates scattered around the country, particularly in places where Focus's state affiliates have a strong presence.[23] Colorado voters narrowly approved a state ballot measure— overturned by the Supreme Court in 1996—that would have denied equal rights protections to homosexuals. In Iowa, Christian Coalition leader Marlene Elwell, along with others, successfully defeated a state equal rights amendment (ERA).[24] During that fray, it was widely reported, Pat Robertson sent out a fundraising letter calling Iowa's ERA measure part of a larger feminist agenda that encouraged women to "kill their children, practice witchcraft, and become lesbians."[25]

With Clinton in the White House, it was predictable that such rhetoric would continue. At the same time, the movement's leaders needed to cast themselves as Republican team players. The Christian Coalition was in a unique position to negotiate the necessary fervency of the grassroots organizing project with a move toward respectable collaboration with the GOP on national affairs. In part, this involved Pat Robertson taking a back seat to the more politically adept Ralph Reed. Reed's mission became one of striking a softer tone. After 1992, he was both the movement's lightning rod and its standard bearer. At the grassroots level, lesser known organizers were free to be as vituperative as they liked.

Thus the Christian Coalition, and the movement as a whole, evolved into a two-tiered operation. Reed's "Casting a Wider Net" article alluded to this process. The grass roots would continue to agitate locally against perceived outrages such as discussions of homosexuality in the public schools. In the halls of Congress, Reed and company would focus on scoring points for the Republicans. The two tracks are parallel, not at cross-purposes. Indeed, sometimes the two tracks are indistinguishable. The Republicans' first blow against the Clinton administration came in early 1993, when Clinton announced his intention to seek removal of the ban on gay military personnel. Christian Right groups flooded Congress with letters and phone calls against the idea, and Clinton ultimately relented.

For his part, though, Ralph Reed understood that frenzies such as the one over gays in the military are not the mainstay of politics. Shortly after his *Policy Review* article appeared, Reed announced that the Christian Coalition planned to spend at least $100,000 in a mail, phone, and media campaign to defeat Clinton's first proposed federal spending budget.[26] Then, in September 1993, Reed announced the results of a poll the Coalition had commissioned, showing that African American and Latino respondents tend to hold conservative views on social issues including abortion, homosexuality, crime, welfare, and even affirmative action. "We are not going to concede the minority community to the political left any more," Reed said, because "for our movement to realize its full potential, we must reach beyond the white church to embrace the full racial diversity of America and make inroads among traditionally Democratic voters."[27] Reed announced that the Coalition would begin "casting its wider net" by advertising on black- and Latino-owned radio stations and by sending voter guides to nonwhite churches.[28] This new posture was a smart move aimed at dispelling the public image of the Christian Right as both racist and wedded to the Republican Party. It also dovetailed neatly with the broader and more genuine trend of "racial reconciliation" underway in the evangelical church world.

While the Coalition worked to polish its image, there was no letup on organizing, particularly in the form of strident attacks on liberals. Alongside the Family Research Council, Concerned Women for America, and other organizations, the Coalition lobbied the Senate hard against Clinton's nominee for surgeon general, Dr. Joycelyn Elders,[29] and then continued to rail against her after her appointment until she finally resigned at the end of 1994. One *Christian American* article on Elders included an ugly photo that made her look like she was pointing her middle finger at the reader. The article claimed that Elders had an "obsession about condom distribution," and further claimed that while she was director of the Arkansas Health Department, she had "exploited that position to advocate a strident platform of abortion on demand and the promiscuous distribution of condoms through school based health clinics."[30]

The Elders controversy coincided roughly with the Right's full court-press against Clinton's health care reform effort. Mostly the drive was led by Republican legislators, but the Christian Coalition weighed in, too. The Coalition called the campaign against health care reform its "number one legislative priority" for 1994, citing some of the standard objections: that a single-payer insurance system would reduce patients' choice of doctors and services; that small business employers would be unduly burdened; and that such a plan would force taxpayers to subsidize abortions. Reed pledged to spend $1.4 million on a campaign that included radio and newspaper advertisements and the distribution of thirty million postcards to be mailed to members of Congress. The postcard, picturing a doctor vaccinating a child while her mother looks on, said: "Don't Let a Government Bureaucrat in This Picture."[31]

Ultimately, it was partisan politics that sunk Clinton's proposed reforms. The Christian Right truly opposed the Clinton plan, and by joining the campaign against it, the Christian Coalition was able to demonstrate its mainstream support for the Republican agenda. For decades the Right has opposed efforts to create a centralized health care system, not just because the giant insurance companies stand to lose billions of dollars, but also on the grounds that greater government involvement in health care would spell "socialized medicine." In 1993, the Right opposed health care reform because this was the way to deprive the Clinton administration of what otherwise might have been its greatest achievement. The Christian Coalition, at least, took the high road by focusing on legislative lobbying. During Clinton's first two years in office, he suffered attacks from some on the Right that were more scurrilous than any sitting president had ever endured. In 1994, Jeremiah Films, a Christian video company based in southern California, produced *The Clinton Chronicles*, and distributed a hundred thousand copies within four months.[32] Jeremiah Films had previously produced videos mostly against abortion, Mormonism, and New Age spirituality.[33] The anti-Clinton videos were distributed under a front name, Citizens for Honest Government. In 1994, Jerry Falwell and Randall Terry used their TV and radio programs, respectively, to sell *The Clinton Chronicles* and a sequel, *Clinton's Circle of Power.* The videos are based on long interviews with Larry Nichols, a former Arkansas state employee who charges Clinton with having run an elaborate money-laundering and cocaine-smuggling ring while he was governor of Arkansas. Along the way, the videos suggest, Clinton himself became a cocaine addict. He is accused of being personally responsible for a number of suspicious deaths, and of enlisting state troopers to drive him to his adulterous love nests. Paula Jones appears on the videos to repeat her story that Governor Clinton made obscene advances toward her. In 1994, Jones told her tale on Pat Robertson's *700 Club,* and shortly after that, Operation Rescue leader Patrick Mahoney formed a "legal defense fund" to lend her greater publicity in right-wing media venues.[34] Falwell's promotion of the Paula Jones story and the *Clinton Chronicles* video was so relentless that viewers finally complained and a Florida TV station pulled a couple of his programs from the air.[35] But there was cash and political hay to be made with the *Clinton Chronicles,* which is why Randall Terry was still selling the tapes during the 1996 presidential campaign. Terry was determined to paint Clinton as a drug-smuggling, womanizing killer.[36]

As the 1994 midterm Congressional elections approached, the anti-Clinton drumbeat became intolerable for the Democrats. The Clinton camp decided to fight the Republicans not on substantive grounds, but by going after the Christian Right. In June 1994, Vic Fazio (D-CA), chair of the Democratic Congressional Campaign Committee, held a press conference and blasted what he called the "firebreathing Christian radical right." Republicans and movement leaders then called Fazio a religious bigot, and all forty-four Republican Senators signed a letter calling on Clinton to repudiate "Christian bashing." Later that same week, eighty-seven Republican House members called for the resignation of Surgeon General Joycelyn Elders, who had given her own speech denouncing the Christian Right. Clinton responded by doing a phone interview with a St. Louis radio station, during which he indicted right-wing radio and television broadcasters, and named Jerry Falwell and Rush Limbaugh as the source of a "constant, unremitting drumbeat of negativism and cynicism."[37]

Predictably, commentators from the secular Right rallied to defend their evangelical counterparts from the charge that they were "radical."[38] Pollster Richard Wirthlin conducted a survey in 1994, and found that the effort by liberals to characterize the Christian Right as a "radical fringe" of society was futile. Wirthlin reported that 64% of a general sample of respondents were "unfavorably impressed with what was being said about the religious Right."[39]

Democrats simply forfeited their chance to explain to the general public what the alliance between the Christian Right and the Republican Party meant in terms of policies that effect everyone. Such an explanation would have required a serious public discussion of matters such as abortion rights, welfare, rising health insurance costs, declining educational achievements, and the need for campaign finance reform—in other words, the full gamut of political and economic crises facing the country. That was too much for the Democrats and the centrist interest groups that push the "radical right" propaganda theme. It is more expedient to call the Christian Right names than to thoughtfully challenge the movement's agenda.

Republican Voting Guides

～

There was a significant moment at the 1994 Road to Victory conference right before a lunch break. Christian Coalition field director D. J. Gribbin gave a pitch about the Coalition's plan to distribute thirty million voter guides shortly before election day. Gribbin asked those among the crowd of three thousand who wanted to order batches of voter guides for their church or chapter to step into the aisles of the Washington Hilton ballroom where there were boxes full of bulk order forms. The scene became a bit frantic as nearly everyone jammed the aisles and grabbed the forms as if they were worth their weight in gold.

No wonder. Ralph Reed was careful to say that, technically, the voter guides were not endorsements for candidates. But then Chuck Cunningham, the Coalition's director of voter education, explained that conservatives had a chance to win working majorities in both houses of Congress. The voter guides, prepared in three hundred different versions for three hundred regions of the country, would be the "key tool" for achieving that end, Cunningham said, because the voter guides would allow the Coalition to "bypass expensive and biased media" and focus on "issues, not personalities."

Cunningham was right. By election day, the Coalition's get-out-the-vote project, along with those of other groups, yielded an unprecedented turnout by the Christian Right. A group of political scientists who study religious voting blocs concluded that, in 1994, the "Christian Right probably mobilized four million activists and reached 50 million voters—a performance rivaling those of such traditional electoral powerhouses as the gun owners and labor unions."[40] Among the small portion of the eligible electorate that voted in 1994, exit polls indicated that about 25% were white evangelicals. Among this group, 70% voted Republican. White evangelicals were the single largest religious constituency, accounting for 34% of GOP House voters.[41]

Moreover, this voting bloc was decisive, according to the political scientists. Across the board, Congressional candidates backed by the Christian Right won 55% of their campaigns. But among the one hundred and twenty Congressional races where the Christian Right was involved, thirty Republican victories were won by 5% of the vote or less, and these thirty marginal winners were pivotal to the Republicans' capture of the House majority. Also, for the first time ever, about a quarter of the elected first-term representatives were themselves members of evangelical churches, meaning that their numbers had begun to match the proportion of evangelicals among the general public. Finally, the political scientists found that the unprecedented Christian Right voter mobilization was no happenstance but, rather, was the direct result of exactly the kind of organizing done by the Christian Coalition. The 1994 National Election Study poll found that 25% of white evangelicals reported that during the campaign season they were either contacted by a religious group, found political information available at their church, or heard a church leader endorse a candidate or party. The Republican vote was twenty percentage points higher among evangelical churchgoers who were provided with such information, meaning that the movement's grassroots church organizing really did pay off.[42]

While the Democrats gnashed their teeth over the so-called radical right, they might have done better by paying attention to the means through which the Republicans won power. At the Christian Coalition's 1994 Road to Victory conference, speaker after speaker scoffed at the liberals' lame effort to besmirch the movement with the "radical" and "extremist" epithets. Meanwhile, the Coalition's staff was busy compiling voter guides which only later were criticized as serious distortions of candidates' voting records.

For a 1996 book about political corruption, political scientist Larry Sabato and *Wall Street Journal* reporter Glenn Simpson studied about two hundred of the Coalition's 1994 House and Senate election voter guides. They found a consistent pattern of lies and distortions concerning the voting records of Democratic candidates. The voter guides, which were printed as one-page handbills, focused on four to ten issues, captured in a chart using phrases such as: "Balanced Budget Amendment," "Term Limits for Congress," "Homosexuals in the Military," and "Abortion on Demand." Next to each issue, the two candidates were labeled either "Supports" or "Opposes." The voter guides were distributed just a few days before the election, so that Democrats—including many who had never even received the Coalition's candidate questionnaire—had no time to correct distortions.

Concerning a proposed amendment to balance the federal budget, the Coalition simply lied and said that some Democrats opposed the amendment when they had actually voted in favor of it.[43] On some of the voter guides, the Coalition hid its misrepresentation of the truth by printing in small type that the balanced budget amendment rating was based on House roll call vote 62 from March 1994. That vote, however, was about a procedural measure for approving tax increases, and not about the balanced budget amendment at all. Only if voters went and looked up the vote in question would they have seen the distinction. Thus, the rating was deliberately designed to smear candidates as opponents of a balanced budget.[44]

In Illinois, Representative Dan Rostenkowski, chair of the House Ways and Means Committee, was up for reelection, and his reputation was already badly tarnished with charges of corruption. The Christian Coalition finished him off with a voter guide that claimed he supported "Promoting Homosexuality to Schoolchildren." The fine print at the bottom of the page noted the rating was based on House roll call vote number 91. In fact, Rostenskowski had voted for an amendment *prohibiting* the dissemination of "obscene" material on school grounds and barring the use of federal funds for programs that "promoted" homosexuality. Rostenkowski's vote could have been considered "progay" only in the narrow sense that a competing amendment, which was never actually voted on, was even more stringent in barring funding for any program that taught about homosexuality at all. Republican representatives who had voted the same as Rostenkowski did not find a "pro-homosexual" mark on their respective voting guides.[45]

Sabato and Simpson call the voter guides part of a pattern of corruption in U.S. political campaigns. Beyond that, the voter guides have been central in the Christian Coalition's strategy of making itself an indispensable vote-getting machine while keeping church activists fired up about the issues of "abortion on demand," "obscene art," and "homosexuals in the military."

On the heels of the 1994 Republican Congressional sweep, the conservative *Human Events* newspaper credited the movement with making the crucial difference in the party's victory. "The list of House members elected last week with the help of religious conservatives is too long to print here," the paper said, "but how they stood on cultural issues in their successful campaigns is clear: anti-abortion, anti-special gay rights, anti-Department of Education, pro-school prayer, pro-school choice vouchers and pro-home schooling." These were winning issues, and the Republicans knew it. *Human Events* listed just a few of the Christian Right–backed winners of 1994: in the House, Representatives Steve Stockman of Texas, Helen Chenoweth of Idaho, Andrea Seastrand of California, and Jon Christensen of Nebraska; in the Senate, Senators Jim Inhofe of Oklahoma and Rod Grams in Minnesota. The *Human Events* headline captured the movement's role: "Christian Right Helps Work GOP Miracle."

It was well understood that the Christian Right was more than just a vote-getting machine. The movement was on board for the Republicans' full legislative agenda, which Newt Gingrich and others had dubbed "The Contract with America." In his 1996 book *Active Faith,* Ralph Reed tells how he and other unnamed movement leaders cut a deal in 1994 during the drafting of the Contract. Congressmember Dick Armey solicited Reed's advice regarding the Contract. Reed made three recommendations: include a tax cut for families with children, a proposal for parental choice in public schools, and a permanent ban on all taxpayer funding of abortion. But, Reed said, his suggestions were not welcomed. Gingrich wanted the Contract to be signed by all incumbent Republicans in Congress, and therefore ruled that "abortion and other contentious social issues would have to wait."[46] Reed reluctantly agreed to backpedal on abortion and school choice if Gingrich and company would move quickly on the tax cut and agree to work on the social issues after the Republicans' first one hundred days in power.[47] Then, in early 1995, Reed announced that the Christian Coalition would spend a million dollars on a media and grass-roots lobbying campaign for the Contract.[48] Reed wrote candidly in *Active Faith* that his collaboration with Gingrich was about "building up political capital that we could later spend on the social issues."[49] The Christian Right had nothing to lose but much to gain by diverting resources toward a legislative packet that was largely fiscal and procedural in content. If nothing else, Reed wanted to keep Republican movers and shakers beholden to the movement in 1996, when it was expected that prochoice Republicans would try to dilute the party's antiabortion plank.

In the interim, Reed needed "political capital" in the form of support for the Contract with the American Family, which the Christian Coalition unveiled in May 1995. It was a ten-point policy agenda, including a call for the elimination of the Department of Education, a ban on late-term abortions, an end to government funding of the National Endowment for the Arts and the Corporation for Public Broadcasting, and passage of a "religious equality" amendment to protect student-led school prayer. At the press conference announcing the Coalition's Contract, Reed was flanked by House Speaker Newt Gingrich and presidential hopeful Senator Phil Gramm of Texas. Gingrich pledged that the House would vote on restricting abortion and on the "religious equality" amendment. Reed joked that his proposals were "ten suggestions," not "ten commandments."[50] But Gingrich's support was understood as a gesture of gratitude for the Christian Coalition's role in winning Congress for the Republicans. Ultimately, Congress did vote, in late 1995 and again in 1996, to ban the "partial birth" late-term abortion procedure.

Mostly, though, the Contract with the American Family was a symbolic tool. Reed used the Contract to rhetorically link the Christian Coalition's agenda with the Republicans' own Contract with America. Conspicuously absent from the Christian Coalition's legislative blueprint was any mention of gay rights, let alone a forthright call to end all abortions. The Coalition's Contract was part of Reed's public relations strategy of making the Christian Coalition appear respectably mainstream. But by downplaying key issues, Reed incited the ire of rival movement leaders, including Gary Bauer of the Family Research Council. Bauer and presidential candidate Patrick Buchanan criticized the Coalition's Contract for not backing a full-scale human life amendment.[51] Reed's maneuver was clever, though. By taking some heat from less compromising voices, Reed made himself a more palatable power broker with Republican elites. It was advantageous for Reed to allow Bauer, Buchanan and others to appear more strident.

The downside to the Christian Coalition's persistently cozy relationship with the Republicans was that the Federal Elections Commission (FEC), in 1996, finally sued the organization for allegedly illegal campaign contributions, in the form of voter guides and coordination with GOP candidates. The suit stemmed from a 1992 complaint by the Democrats, and yet the suit, too, appeared partisan as it was filed just days before the start of the 1996 Republican convention. Specifically, the FEC charged that the Coalition had broken campaign disclosure laws and exceeded contribution limits by making "in-kind" donations with the voter guides and by coordinating with the National Republican Senatorial Committee to produce and distribute millions of the guides on behalf of Jesse Helms, Oliver North, George Bush, and Newt Gingrich. Naturally, the Coalition vowed to fight the suit, claiming the Coalition's politicking is just a form of good citizenship.[52] Because the Coalition has plenty of money and lawyers, and because of the suit's implications for groups that do similar voting drives, the case is expected to remain tied up in court for several years. In the meantime, the Coalition needs to temper its obvious enthusiasm for Republican candidates, at least until the smoke clears.

The Buchanan Challenge in 1996

ᶜᵃ

On the eve of the 1996 Republican National Convention in San Diego, the place to be was about thirty miles north of the downtown area, at an arts center in Escondido, California. There about one thousand supporters of Patrick Buchanan—and hundreds of journalists—gathered to hear the speech the party would not allow the candidate to deliver from the convention podium. In 1996, as in 1992, Buchanan won several million votes and succeeded in energizing the activist Right. He was a threat to the Republican establishment not because he had ever truly acted against the party's interests, but because he fanned the flames of fear: fear of immigrants and bureaucrats, fear of the increasing globalization of the economy, and, in his 1996 speeches, fear of declining wages and rising unemployment for U.S. workers.

In Escondido, the self-described Buchanan Brigades held a down-home celebration, with beer, barbecue, and a country-western band. Buchanan's campaign manager, his sister Bay, said succinctly that she and her brother were "ecstatic." The week prior to the convention, they, along with Ralph Reed, Gary Bauer, Phyllis Schlafly, and a majority on the GOP platform committee, had succeeded in bolstering the party's antiabortion plank. "We didn't get the nomination," said Bay Buchanan, "but we've captured the heart and soul of the party."

Buchanan's mission that night in Escondido was to mollify those among his supporters who had hoped he would break away from the Republican Party and accept the presidential nomination of the marginal and eccentric U.S. Taxpayers Party. There was never much chance that Buchanan would abandon the Republican Party, the party of his father and of his three political heroes, Barry Goldwater, Richard Nixon, and Ronald Reagan. Amidst the heckling of dozens of people in the crowd who yelled out "U.S. Taxpayers Party," Buchanan stressed two themes. For one, he said, he came to Escondido to declare a truce with presidential nominee Bob Dole and to make sure that the party remained staunchly prolife. He said he could not walk away from the thousands of people who had worked hard to elect him inside the GOP. "Before our eyes and their eyes, this party is becoming a Buchanan party," he said. "Within this party, a new party is being born."

But then Buchanan also said he envisioned a Republican Party that would fight for the poor and dispossessed, though not everywhere, only inside the borders of the United States. "Isn't it time we replace the ethic of corporate greed with a spirit of community and country?," he asked. "If conservatives aren't conserving families and neighborhoods, what is it we're trying to conserve?"

The crowd was enthusiastic while Buchanan told stories of the displaced workers he had met while on the 1996 campaign trail. In Hayfork, California, he met three little girls whose fathers were all out of work because the government had shut down logging in that part of the Northwest. In Louisiana, he met women who were working at a Fruit of the Loom factory for $6 an hour. It was the best job they had ever had, they said, but now the factory was moving to Mexico, where workers work cheaper, and what was going to happen to these women in Louisiana?

Buchanan told the same story and raised the same question a month later in his speech at the annual convention of the Christian Coalition. By never actually articulating who is responsible for the growing economic insecurity of U.S. workers, Buchanan allows his audience to fill in the blank with their own designated culprits. The government, the Mexicans, the environmentalists—they must be responsible for the loss of jobs.

But it was also clear in 1996 that, aside from Green Party nominee Ralph Nader, Buchanan was the only presidential candidate to discuss declining wages and willing to indict corporate greed. In the summer of 1996, *Esquire* magazine published a lengthy interview with Buchanan, conducted by Norman Mailer, who was struck by the seemingly leftist tone of Buchanan's rhetoric of class injustice. In the interview, Buchanan called declining wages "the major social problem of our time."

> We've got to start the income of working men and women rising again, especially those who work with their hands, tools, and machines, many of whom are black and Hispanic and rural white.[53]

Buchanan went on to say that "an affluent society like the United States has a moral obligation to take care of the less fortunate among us now."[54] But his proposed solutions were not about changing the fundamentally exploitative structures of capitalism so much as containing the system within the geographic boundaries of the United States. This is what Buchanan means by "economic nationalism":

> Three ways to do this: One, stop forcing Americans to compete with folks who can work very hard and very well for a lot less—stop illegal immigration into this country cold. Two, I believe you should have a temporary halt to legal immigration. There are twenty million such people here, many of whom work very hard and undercut the wages of working men and women. Three, you have to get rid of these trade deals that force American working men and women into competition with Mexican folks who work for a buck an hour, a buck-fifty an hour, or Chinese who work for twenty-five cents an hour.[55]

There is nothing particularly leftist or progressive about wanting to strengthen a privileged U.S. working class if that means increased misery abroad. But the mere discussion of class conflict was too much for Buchanan's detractors in the corporate press and among some on the Right. On the eve of the 1996 Republican primaries, the *New York Times* published a front-page article to the effect that Buchanan's opposition to "free trade" agreements had brought him "under fire as a left-winger."[56] David Frum of the *Weekly Standard* magazine called Buchanan "America's last leftist," and worried that Buchanan would move Republican voters toward "economic resentment" and away from conservatives' bedrock commitment to unrestrained capitalism.[57]

After Buchanan defeated Bob Dole in the New Hampshire primary, it looked like Buchanan's popularity stemmed from his mixed message of economic nationalism and religious moralism. Buchanan suffered a minor setback when news surfaced that his campaign aide Larry Pratt of Gun Owners of America had appeared at gatherings of white supremacists.[58] Such connections were not entirely unknown among people on the Right. But the flurry of media attention over Pratt raised the specter that Buchanan was a threat to Republican respectability.

After winning the New Hampshire primary and a Republican caucus in Louisiana, Buchanan's primary showings leveled off. He came in second in Iowa and then in most of the southern states, with totals of between 20 and 30% in each primary.[59] Buchanan's mainstay of support came from antiabortion Christians,[60] despite the fact that the leadership of the Christian Coalition was partial to Senator Dole. Officially the Coalition did not endorse a primary candidate, but in key states, such as Iowa and South Carolina, the Coalition's state directors backed Dole.[61]

The pro-Dole stance was not shared uniformly by rank-and-file Christian Coalition members, some of whom hoped Buchanan would accept the nomination of Howard Phillips's U.S. Taxpayers Party (USTP). In the early 1970s, Phillips had worked with Richard Viguerie and Paul Weyrich in the founding of some of the New Right's think tanks and political action committees. Then, in the 1980s, Phillips was a leading apologist for the government of South Africa and for UNITA, the South Africa–backed army that wreaked havoc on Angola. In 1991, Phillips started the USTP after advocating a third-party strategy for many years. In 1991, as in 1996, Phillips sought to lure Buchanan away from the GOP. On the surface, a political matchup seemed plausible: opposition to abortion, gay rights, immigration, and "free" trade topped both the Buchanan the USTP agendas. But between 1991 and 1996 Phillips succeeded in mobilizing no more than a remnant of the patriot movement—a motley crew of John Birchists, old George Wallace enthusiasts, tax protesters, and adherents of the obscure doctrine known as Christian Reconstructionism, which calls for an Old Testament–style theocracy, including the death penalty for abortionists, adulterers, and homosexuals. Phillips himself converted to Christian Reconstructionism in the mid-1970s.[62]

Right after the Republican convention in San Diego, the USTP held its own convention, at which Phillips was selected as the party's presidential candidate. Convention speakers included the previously mentioned Larry Pratt, along with a number of other figures considered beyond the pale by the mainstream of the Christian Right: Operation Rescue founder Randall Terry, militia advocate and antiabortion activist Matthew Trewhella, Christian Reconstructionist author R. J. Rushdoony, and Herbert Titus, who was Phillips's running mate.[63] Titus is the former dean of the law school at Pat Robertson's Regent University. In the early 1990s, at a time when Robertson was seeking academic accreditation for the law school, Titus was forced to resign when he refused to renounce his belief in Christian Reconstructionism.

Buchanan, for his part, did not need to assume the liability of making a public alliance with the most disreputable elements of the Christian Right. It was better to disappoint a few of his supporters and preserve his reputation as a credible media pundit and spokesperson for the antiabortion cause.

Despite his strong rhetoric on the economic front, Buchanan and his campaign manager, sister Bay, astutely chose to direct their energies to the fight over the antiabortion plank in the GOP platform. In the weeks prior to the Republican convention in San Diego, the press reported the touch-and-go conflicts between Buchanan and the Dole camp. Convention choreographers were determined to prevent Buchanan from speaking during a prime time at the convention. Buchanan accepted the non-invitation but promised there would be "no peace in the valley" if Dole selected a prochoice running mate or if the Republicans backed away from the antiabortion plank.[64]

Throughout the spring and summer of 1996, candidate Dole blundered and stumbled over the abortion issue, painting himself, alternately, as a pawn or as a frightened adversary of the Christian Right. At one point, Dole called for the platform to include a "declaration of tolerance" regarding abortion, so as not to alienate the party's prochoice voters. Reed, Dobson, and other movement leaders threatened Dole with a fight during the platform hearings and with a withdrawal of support from the grass roots.[65] After weeks of preconvention wrangling, a grueling several days' worth of platform hearings, and muted calls for a convention floor fight from some of the party's prochoice governors, the Republicans retained their long-standing plank calling for a constitutional human life amendment and legislation to extend Fourteenth Amendment citizenship rights to the unborn. Press coverage of the platform hearings focused on what reporters called the "fearsome foursome": Ralph Reed, Gary Bauer, Phyllis Schlafly, and Bay Buchanan. These four, all influential with prolife delegates and constituents back home, met secretly before the convention and agreed to stick together against any proposed compromise language, such as a statement to the effect that abortion is a matter of individual conscience.[66]

The foursome were successful in keeping prolife delegates on the platform committee united, and in relaying their no-compromise position to the Dole camp and to the press. But it was the activist force behind the foursome that made what they did possible. Beginning in 1990, Schlafly's Republican National Coalition for Life organized to ensure a prolife majority among GOP convention delegates. The Christian Coalition spent part of 1996 training delegates to work as regional coordinators on the convention floor. Had the abortion conflict moved beyond the platform hearings to a full-scale floor fight, Reed and his lieutenants were prepared, via computers and cellular phones, to command teams of uncompromising delegates.[67] Bay Buchanan's trump card was the threat that her brother might refuse to endorse the Dole nomination.

When all was said and done, the convention yielded mixed results for the Christian Right–Republican Party alliance. The antiabortion platform plank was, as in previous years, a symbolic victory. It has yet to translate into a major push by Republican officeholders to ban abortion. Reed boasted that about a third of the delegates in San Diego were associated with the movement.[68] But their presence was downplayed by convention managers. What appeared on television—mostly prime-time speeches by prochoice Republicans—looked very different from the halls of the convention center, where Christian Right delegates wore antiabortion hats and buttons, and crowded around "radio row," a makeshift aisle for broadcasters of right-wing talk shows. It was as if the convention had a split personality: a nondescript face presented for general media consumption masked the prominence, continuing from 1992, of delegates committed to the movement as much as to the party. Christian Right delegates were disciplined enough not to complain loudly about the exclusion of Pat Buchanan and Pat Robertson from the official proceedings. There was a sense that no one wanted to rock the boat, though neither was anyone in the movement terribly excited about Bob Dole's doomed campaign.

Presidential Politics in 1996
ᴄᴏ

The Dole–Kemp ticket drew lukewarm support from the Christian Right. Dole reluctantly agreed to speak at the Christian Coalition's Road to Victory conference in September 1996. By then, the Republicans were desperate to avoid seeing the Dole debacle result in their loss of control in Congress.

As usual, voter turnout—and the disproportionate role of conservative evangelicals in that turnout—was pivotal. A postelection poll conducted by Wirthlin Worldwide showed that 29% of voters in 1996 were born-again Christians who frequently attend church, and that 15% of all voters claimed to be members or supporters of the Christian Coalition. Among this latter group, 67% voted for Dole and 20% voted for Clinton.[69] Another poll indicated that whites identifying themselves as part of the religious right accounted for 17% of all voters. Among this bloc, 65% voted for Dole, and 26% voted for Clinton.[70] That even a sizable minority of the conservative evangelical vote went to Clinton was a surprise, given the Christian Right's relentless organizing against him; given the scandals that plagued the Clinton White House; and given Clinton's support for abortion rights. What the numbers reveal is that the conservative evangelical vote tends to swing reliably to the Republicans, but that this whole bloc of voters cannot be taken for granted. They must be continually courted, and their success at the polls is no foregone conclusion. In 1996, many of the candidates backed by the Christian Right were defeated, as was a parental rights ballot measure in Colorado.[71]

There was more than one way to interpret the Christian Right's 1996 setbacks. In Colorado, the 1992 anti–gay rights Amendment 2 had polarized public opinion. Four years later, liberal forces were better organized, and the general electorate was perhaps better informed in Colorado than in other states about the agenda of the Christian Right.

Gary Bauer of the Family Research Council published an open letter in several right-wing publications, in which he challenged Republicans to heed his explanation of the 1996 race. Clinton won, according to Bauer, "because he swung his party to the right and ran a campaign not from his heart, but with a sleight of hand," and because the Republicans failed to articulate a truly conservative agenda. While Clinton mouthed the rhetoric of "values," Bauer wrote, the Republicans had refused to talk straight with the public about abortion, illegitimate births, family tax relief, preserving traditional marriage, defending U.S. borders from illegal immigration, and whether "Americans have a right to expect that their business leaders will be loyal to them."[72] In essence, Bauer invoked the issues Patrick Buchanan had campaigned on, and then blamed the Republicans for abandoning the cause.

> Bill Clinton did not create the political void into which he stepped. He merely occupied the field his adversaries deserted. Which is why this election loss is particularly hard to take. For the only thing worse than being beaten by an unworthy opponent is being beaten on your own home field.[73]

Bauer tried to persuade the Republican Party to stick with a solid right-wing policy agenda. Similarly, the Christian Coalition's chief lobbyist,

Brian Lopina, announced in early 1997 that the organization would keep pressing for the legislative items in its Contract with the American Family. The Coalition would continue to lobby for a ban on late-term abortions; for a Religious Freedom Amendment to protect public school prayer; for a federal parental rights act to give parents greater clout in court; for laws against gay rights; and for a $500 per child tax credit.[74]

All of the above items were in sync with the goals of the National Right to Life Committee, the Family Research Council, and Concerned Women for America. But beyond the predictable family values agenda, Ralph Reed wanted to take the Christian Coalition in a new direction, one that would confound critics of the Christian Right. Continuing with his idea of "casting a wider net," Reed announced, in early 1997, that the Coalition would expand its outreach to urban black and Latino churches. Calling his plan "the Samaritan Project," Reed outlined a new focus on solving problems in the "inner cities," in a way that would link issues of religious morality with economic needs. Specifically, the Samaritan Project called for legislation to discourage divorce and out-of-wedlock births; to provide federal funds for poor children to attend private schools; to give states financial incentives for reducing youth and gang-related crime; to give taxpayers a $500 tax credit if they volunteer time with an organization that helps the poor; and to give tax incentives to businesses operating in low-income neighborhoods.[75]

Earlier, in 1996, Reed had shown great concern when a rash of arson fires destroyed numerous African American churches in the South. Reed testified on behalf of a Congressional bill to double the criminal penalties for burning a church.[76] The Coalition established a Save Our Churches Fund which in 1996 raised $750,000 to help rebuild twenty-five destroyed churches.[77]

These were laudable gestures. But critics were quick to point out that the Christian Coalition has no track record of working against poverty and racism. It seemed that Reed's minority outreach plan had more to do with public relations than with a newfound concern about injustice. Reed's departure from the Coalition in 1997 caused a short-term decline in revenues. The first thing the Coalition did was to drop formal sponsorship of the Samaritan Project and return to its focus on Congressional lobbying and electing right-wing candidates.[78] Unfettered from the perception that its black director, Reverend Earl Jackson, is just fronting for white sponsors, the Samaritan Project may now more credibly organize among conservative people of color, as well as with white conservative groups other than the Christian Coalition.

The racial reconciliation project is taking place in the churches, outside of electoral politics. Church talk about racial reconciliation focuses on religious charity but only gingerly addresses poverty as a political problem.

As part of the broader racial reconciliation endeavor, the Samaritan Project is an effort to link charity with political organizing. It suggests to the Christian Right's largely white constituency that they can be "their brother's keeper" and reap political advantages at the same time. The Samaritan Project is in sync with the campaign led by the Clinton administration and General Colin Powell to encourage voluntarism as an alternative to government services.

In announcing the new Samaritan Project, Reed dropped a couple of hints about his underlying motives. (This was just a few weeks before he announced his intent to leave the Christian Coalition and start his own consulting firm.) Reed was quoted in the *Washington Post* to the effect that "we're not doing this as Republicans or Democrats. We're doing this as people of faith."[79] In an article for the *Christian American,* Reed said that "we need to replace the welfare state with a culture of caring." The Coalition's chief lobbyist, Brian Lopina, said that "as welfare subsidies are reduced, it's important that private charities receive the support they need to move to the forefront of fighting poverty."[80] These remarks suggested that the Christian Coalition sought to downplay its image as a partisan subsidiary of the GOP.

Not all evangelicals vote Republican. If the Christian Coalition is to remain an election power broker, it would be wise to look for allies among people whose vote must be courted, not taken for granted. On welfare policy, both Republicans and Democrats have been eager to reduce government responsibility for poor people and children. The Clinton administration went along with a Republican plan to gut welfare. This has created an opportunity for some on the Right to demonstrate a humanitarian impulse and to link charity to existing church structures and family values. Even if such charity is benign, it is an inherently conservative idea to make churches the arbiters of the conditions under which poor people may benefit from volunteer work and tax credits.

In the long run, there are some other reasons why an eventual move into the realm of urban affairs and poverty makes sense for the Christian Right. The movement's focus on stopping abortion and gay rights has earned it unending charges of mean-spiritedness and bigotry. Reed's photo opportunities with grateful black ministers rebuilding their churches belied the image of the Christian Right as "extremist." Beyond the public relations realm, liberal organizations have, in many cases, successfully counterorganized against the Christian Right on abortion, gay rights, and school curricula. Even if it is just rhetorical, the Christian Right's professed concern with poverty and racial injustice may redraw the battle lines between the Christian Right and its liberal detractors. How can they argue with a movement that says it wants to help people in dire straits?

The family values theme is largely about maintaining a religiously inspired moral order, one in which husbands and wives, parents and children, know where they fit and behave accordingly. Mostly, the Christian Right's policy concerns are about preserving narrow notions of proper family order against a perceived onslaught from secular society. Crime, illiteracy, and "illegitimacy" are symptoms of this onslaught. It is natural for the Christian Coalition to want to add these social problems to its stable of family matters. The focus on unwed mothers, young hoodlums, and bad neighborhoods is consistent with a rightist worldview that finds pathology in individual behavior while ignoring the social despair that leads so many individuals to make the wrong "choices." Applied to the problems of poverty and racism, the family values refrain blames bad people, not an unjust system.

Chapter 6

∾

Family Matters

On the first day of June in 1996, two hundred thousand demonstrators came to Washington, DC, and marched to the Lincoln Memorial for the Stand for Children rally sponsored by the Children's Defense Fund. It was the largest march for children ever held in the United States, and its theme was a call to reverse society's perilous neglect of children, particularly the growing numbers living in poverty.

The speeches were benign, with little in the way of partisan advocacy. Seemingly, there was little about this rally for children that could rankle the proponents of family values. Yet, in the days leading up to the march, a number of right-wing think tanks turned the event into a minor media controversy. The Heritage Foundation held a press conference to release a report to the effect that the four hundred or so organizational endorsers of the Stand for Children looked like a who's who of federally funded groups. Gary Bauer of the Family Research Council (FRC) complained that the Stand for Children "really stands for big government." He accused Children's Defense Fund president Marian Wright Edelman of inviting to the rally only those groups that advocate large-scale government intervention in the lives of children.[1]

The rally occurred during a campaign season in which both political parties were claiming that they best represented the interests of families. But Marian Wright Edelman's old friend Bill Clinton was poised that season to sign a welfare repeal law that many children's advocates—including Edelman herself—warned would swell the ranks of poor women and youth. Clinton's agenda was to score points with middle-class voters by talking tough about the evils of welfare dependency.

Earlier in the same reelection campaign, Hillary Clinton created her own stir about family values with her book *It Takes a Village,* whose title referred to the African proverb "It takes a village to raise a child." Not to be upstaged in the race for best purveyor of fireside metaphors, conservatives attacked Mrs. Clinton's village theme as a warmed-over recipe for what they considered to be the most illegitimate forms of government economic intervention and social engineering. Taxes, welfare, public schools, legal abortion and access to contraceptives topped the list. Among the many bad reviews for Mrs. Clinton's book, the one in the *Weekly Standard* by columnist P. J. O'Rourke began most succinctly: "The village is Washington. You are the child. There, I've spared you from reading the worst book to come out of the Clinton administration since—let's be fair—whatever the last one was."[2]

But that was not the end of the story: there were many bales of rhetorical hay to be made with the village theme. The Family Research Council promoted Gary Bauer's own bestselling campaign-season book, *Our Hopes, Our Dreams,* with a series of magazine and newspaper advertisements juxtaposing Mrs. Clinton's statement, "There's no such thing as other people's children," with Bauer's retort: "The village can't replace Moms and Dads." Of course, Hillary never said it could or should. But by arguing in favor of a *social* safety net for children, she fanned the fears of those among the Christian Right who believe that the government and the secular culture are colluding to steal from them the hearts and minds of their most prized possessions, their children.

Kay Coles James, an African American woman who served in the Bush administration's Department of Health and Human Services and with the Family Research Council before becoming a dean at Pat Robertson's Regent University, used the village theme to articulate the Right's critique of liberal family policy. In an article for Concerned Women for America's *Family Voice* magazine, James stressed that "the village" no longer really exists because most people have little contact with neighbors, let alone community agencies. The village has been replaced by "town hall," James wrote, and the expanded role of government is destroying whatever village ties still remains. Beyond that, even if the village "exists as a resource" for families, "the village cannot raise a child. Children do not belong to the community. Children belong to the parents who tuck them in at night, wipe away their tears, feed them, and guide them through life."[3]

This assertion of parental *ownership* of children is more than semantic. It cuts right to the heart of what much of the family values debate has been about. Who will *decide* and who will *control* what happens to children, what children and parents can get away with, what spouses can get away with, what pregnant girls and women can and cannot do, what homosexuals can and cannot do? These are all questions of morality wrapped up with questions of power. These old questions are more pressing today because of ongoing changes in the nature of family and gender relations.

The old answers ring less and less certain. The uncertainty fosters finger-pointing and a belief that the family is simply breaking down.

In fact, new forms of "family" are replacing a form that was once prevalent but that now endures mostly in the realms of nostalgia and hope. Sociologist Judith Stacey contrasts what she calls the contemporary *postmodern* family with the *modern* family of the post–World War II era. In 1950, three-fifths of U.S. households consisted of a male wage earner and a full-time female homemaker. Now more than three-fifths of married women with dependent children work in the paid labor force; there are more than twice as many single-mother families as there are families with married, stay-at-home mothers; and, by the mid-1970s, divorce outranked death as the leading cause of the end of marriage.[4] At the end of 1996, the federal government reported that only about one-fourth of all U.S. households consisted of two-parent families with kids.[5]

Stacey concludes, however, that these trends do not represent "an orderly progression of stages of family history." What makes the present-day family most *postmodern* is the fact that "contemporary Western family arrangements are diverse, fluid, and unresolved."[6] Nor for most Americans is this particularly bad news. Stacey cites a 1990 *Newsweek* poll that found, by a ratio of three to one, that people defined the family as "a group of people who love and care for each other" and not necessarily as "a group of people related by blood, marriage, or adoption."[7]

No one denies the recent changes in family composition: the debate is about what the changes mean. Should the changes be accepted and considered as factors for future policymaking, or should the changes be feared and blamed on the government and secular culture? Christian Right activism on the full gamut of family matters can best be understood as an effort to fight change and punish those seen as responsible for it.

Here I do not mean to deny the salience of particular pieces of the family values agenda in their own right. For the Christian Right, abortion, homosexuality, and certain teachings in the public schools are all seen as affronts to morality, irrespective of their impact on the two-parent family structure. For that reason and because such issues have been central to the movement's rise and persistence, I devote separate chapters of this book to the Christian Right's battles over abortion, education, and homosexuality. However, as a prelude to dealing with these top items on the family values agenda, in this chapter I deal with several general themes that recur throughout the profamily movement repertoire.

One is the concept of *parental rights* and the idea that government now threatens parental control of children. As a hedge against this threat, in the late 1990s, Christian Right activists drafted and began an uphill battle lobbying for parental rights legislation at the federal and state levels. Critics of the Christian Right's agenda fear that parental rights legislation will hamstring schools and other agencies charged with training children and protecting them, when necessary, from abusive parents. Nonetheless, parental rights remains a useful rhetorical device in that it reinforces a view of secular institutions as illegitimate.

More impractical than the goal of passing parental rights legislation are calls by the Christian Right to make divorce more cumbersome and, ostensibly, more infrequent. As I will discuss further on in this chapter, the movement's campaign against divorce might be more strident, and more credible, were it not for the phenomenally high divorce rate among evangelicals themselves. Thus, for the Christian Right, divorce is a tricky topic. It is the major cause for the decline of the Ozzie and Harriet–style family, yet attaching great stigma to those who divorce would alienate too many of the movement's own members and supporters.

Similarly, there are risks involved in the way the movement attacks feminism and its supposedly pernicious effect on the traditional family. The Christian Right can safely attack feminist organizations, particularly when they can be linked to "designated evils" such as abortion and gay rights. But because of the reliable role women play within the Christian Right itself, and because of recent undeniable and irreversible changes in women's roles in the family and workplace, the movement has to be subtle in its efforts to cast women as subordinates.

This was less true in the 1970s and 1980s, when the Christian Right waged, and won, a fierce campaign to defeat the Equal Rights Amendment (ERA). The ERA itself was a simple statement about gender equality, but its inclusion as an amendment to the U.S. Constitution would have had wide-ranging effects on all sorts of state and federal laws and eventually on acceptance of gender equality within the culture. The ERA was a rubric under which feminists and antifeminists debated everything from abortion rights to women in combat. The campaign against the ERA was a direct attack on women's rights, an attack that might not work now, nearly twenty years later.

Now direct conflict over gender equality takes a back seat to assertions of *parental rights*. Like the ERA, parental rights is a catchphrase for a range of specific concerns. Broad-based social movements always face the question of whether to work on single or multiple issues. The Christian Right had its first real confrontation with this question in 1979, when a group of Republican Senators introduced the Family Protection Act, an omnibus bill with dozens of provisions intended to restrict abortion and gay rights, blunt sex discrimination laws, and provide tax advantages for families in which the wife stays at home. The bill was so much of a catch-all that it never passed through the phases that would have brought it up for a Congressional vote. Thereafter, Christian Right activists and like-minded legislators promoted the family values agenda one piece at a time and with mixed success. The parental rights project is a new effort to link multiple issues in a single package. Its effect may eventually be measured less in terms of legislative victories than in terms of framing public perceptions about the role of government—some might call it "the Village"—in family life.

Throughout this book, I frequently name groups and individuals working on particular issues. In this chapter, I deal specifically with parts of the family values project not addressed elsewhere. They are connected to each other both as pieces of an ideological whole and as projects that link activists across the movement's many organizations. In this chapter I deal mostly with the concepts underlying the family values project, but it is worth noting how the organizational landscape is laid out. Much of the action in the profamily movement occurs locally and serendipitously, and is reported anecdotally in movement publications. There is no central headquarters where a committee of profamily movement organizers decide exactly who will launch specific campaigns. Organizations such as the Christian Coalition, Focus on the Family, the Family Research Council, and the Home School Legal Defense Association do make decisions based on political expediency and the concerns of their particular constituents. Combined considerations may lead, for example, to proposing a parental rights bill one year or lobbying a state legislature to tighten divorce laws the next year. The national organizations provide local people with advice, information, and sometimes money and lawyers. There is a great deal of networking between leaders and activists from the various groups. Some of it occurs in the world of religious broadcasting. Beverly LaHaye, for one, often hosts guests from groups other than Concerned Women for America (CWA) and then promotes the work of these other organizations through CWA's monthly magazine. An especially compelling story told on one talk show may eventually become part of the movement's collective storytelling, thereby reinforcing activists' awareness of profamily themes and the likelihood that they will act on such themes when opportunity strikes.

Parental Rights

ᢕᢌ

In March 1996, fifty-eight sixth-grade girls were sent to the nurse's office at their public school in East Stroudsburg, Pennsylvania. According to Christian Right groups interested in the case, the girls were ordered to take off their clothes and—without their parents' permission and against their own cries and protests—were subjected to genital exams. The girls were humiliated. Their parents were shocked and outraged, so much so that some filed lawsuits. School officials insisted that the exams were legally appropriate and necessary to detect genital warts. The town became polarized over the incident, which also made national headlines in the conservative press.

Randall Terry, for one, devoted several days of his nationally syndicated radio show to the East Stroudsburg case, even allowing some of the angry parents to broadcast the phone numbers of school personnel. The incident drew attention because it was disturbing in its own right and also because of its timing. That same spring, momentum was building for parental rights legislation in the form of a Congressional bill, a ballot measure in Colorado, and proposed laws in twenty-nine states.

For years, Christian Right law firms and media outlets have publicized cases in which parents allege their rights have been violated by schools and social service agencies. Most of the school cases involve sex education, condom distribution, and abortion counseling. Homeschooling parents frequently allege unlawful inquiries about whether they neglect or abuse their children. In 1994, Senator Charles Grassley of Iowa asked attorney Michael Farris to draft legislation that would strengthen the legal hand of parents to exclusively direct the education, religion, health care, and discipline of their children.[8] Farris now heads the Home School Legal Defense Association, and previously directed the legal arm of Concerned Women for America. Farris has fought for many years for parents' rights to homeschool their children with no government interference. Now he and others argue that if parents have a right to exempt their children from public schools, then parents also have a right to block whatever might happen to children in the public schools—or anywhere else, for that matter.

While Farris drafted the first Congressional bill on parental rights, the Virginia-based group Of the People began organizing activists to introduce parental rights amendments to their state constitutions. The language suggested by Of the People is a simple assertion of the already legally recognized "right of parents to direct the upbringing and education of their children." While Of the People concentrated on state legislatures, and eventually helped introduce legislation in about two dozen states, in 1995, on the federal level, Senator Grassley joined forces with newly elected Representative Steve Largent (R-OK). Grassley and Largent jointly introduced the Parental Rights and Responsibilities Act, which would prohibit any federal, state, or local government from "interfering with or usurping the right of a parent to govern the upbringing of a child," unless there is a "compelling interest" such as abuse or neglect.[9] The federal bill quickly won dozens of cosponsors in the House and Senate, but as of early 1998, it had yet to move through the legislative pipeline.

On the surface, parental rights legislation seems innocuous. In theory, few would oppose the right of parents to direct their children's upbringing and education. Politically, however, parental rights legislation is no easy sell. In 1996, activists in Colorado tried and failed to win passage of a ballot initiative that would have amended the state constitution with a statement strengthening parental rights. Opponents of the initiative, including civil libertarians, successfully made the case that a parental rights amendment would endanger children by making them the property of their parents, including criminally abusive ones. Opponents also argued that a parental rights amendment would disrupt public schools and some adoption procedures, and would threaten the reproductive rights of minors.[10] Proponents vowed that they would try again. But to the extent that voters link initiatives such as the one in Colorado with the political ambitions of the Christian Right, public support for parental rights is no sure bet.

By the same token, however, politicians eager to court the Christian Right may find parental rights a useful theme. Almost any discussion of parental rights legislation is accompanied by a litany of horror stories—mostly gleaned from school districts where parents have clashed with the educational establishment. Included in a legislative packet sent to inquirers from Representative Largent's office in 1996 was a list of parents' major grievances: condom distribution against parental consent; laws requiring teacher certification for homeschool parents; intrusive values clarification tests and surveys; legal challenges when parents ground minors as a method of discipline; sexually explicit curricula; health care provided without parental consent; and prohibitions on parents' viewing of scholastic tests.[11] Next came a memorandum entitled "Why Do We Need the Parental Rights and Responsibilities Act?" which begins with the story of the sixth-grade girls in East Stroudsburg, Pennsylvania, and then discusses a docket of recent lawsuits in which parents were battling the courts. For example, in Massachusetts, the state's Supreme Court denied that parents had the right to exempt their son from an in-class presentation by "Hot, Sexy, and Safer Productions," in which the boy allegedly was told to lick a condom. In Washington State, the Supreme Court ruled that it was not a violation of parents' rights to remove an eighth-grade girl from her home because she objected when her parents grounded her for smoking marijuana and sleeping with her boyfriend. In Texas, parents were denied the right to preview a mandatory test that they feared would ask students objectionable questions about their religious beliefs. The parents won a lawsuit in a lower court, but the Texas Education Agency pursued the case further with an appeal.[12]

The stories of cases such as these are collected and retold by parental rights activists and like-minded politicians as evidence that the courts and school bureaucrats are out of control—and that parental rights legislation would give parents more clout in court. The casual observer cannot evaluate the validity of each case and each ruling. Nor can one tell whether some of the cases that land in court do so precisely because they *are* aberrations from the norm. Instead, the sheer volume of anecdotes paints the picture that schools and child protection agencies seek to disempower parents, and that parents are truly at a legal disadvantage when they confront an arm of the secular state.

Thus, for profamily advocates, the parental rights project is not only legally necessary, it is also ideologically attractive. The parental rights project, whether successful or not in the U.S. Congress or the state legislatures, is part of a broader effort, led by the Christian Right, to undermine the public legitimacy of secular schools and government agencies. Liberal supporters of the prevailing U.S. political system often characterize such activity as an "attack" on noble government bureaucracies—as if there is no real need for reform. In truth, public schools and government agencies are flawed, but not as seriously as the Christian Right asserts. The movement mixes real or perceived grievances with a large dose of political expediency. The litany of "atrocities" committed by schools and courts then fuels and justifies aggressive activism from the Christian Right.

Added to the galvanizing effect of fear-inspiring stories is a fundamental philosophical difference between parental rights advocates and secular institutions. Supporters of the government agencies charged with training and protecting children take the Hillary Clinton approach. They view children as the collective responsibility of the whole society, even if that means that some kids and parents will object to the program. In contrast, parental rights advocates see children as the unique possessions and responsibilities of father–mother teams, even though that means inevitable conflict with the secular establishment.

The parental rights project is much more than the sum of its court cases and Congressional bills. It is about two conflicting paradigms. Who will control what happens to children? They are everyone's concern, but they are also a political football in battles over family values. In lamenting the demise of the family, Christian conservatives identify two major culprits: the government and secular culture. Parental rights advocates feel threatened by both.

The Way It Should Be

ഇ

In the midst of the parental rights project, Michael Farris—father of nine, president of the Home School Legal Defense Association, drafter and promoter of parental rights legislation—had time to write a novel. *Anonymous Tip*, published in 1996, is a page-turner that captures, better than any political tract or legal brief, some of the biggest fears and quandaries of the profamily movement.

The story begins when Gwen Landis's alcoholic, good-for-nothing ex-husband Gordon makes an anonymous call to Child Protective Services (CPS). Gwen is a gorgeous woman who works as a nurse. Gordon is mad that Gwen will not take him back, so he falsely claims that Gwen has been beating their four-year-old daughter, Casey, with a stick. Despite no actual evidence of abuse, CPS bureaucrats Donna Corliss and Rita Coballo make an unannounced visit to Gwen Landis's home. When she refuses them entry, they decide to make her pay for her resistance. They return a few days later with a police escort. They forcibly strip-search Casey and then falsely report seeing bruises on Casey's body. They take the false report to court and succeed in getting Casey placed temporarily in a foster home pending psychological examinations of both mother and child. By this time, Gwen's father has hired an attorney. But the lawyer is incompetent and loses round one of the case. Worse, he solicits Gwen to have sex with him in lieu of paying fees. Gwen runs from his office crying and bumps into Peter Barron in the parking lot. Barron is an attorney, too. He takes Gwen to lunch, hears her tale, offers to represent her on a $25-a-month basis, and assures her that he has no lecherous intent because he is a born-again Christian.

The romantic tension between Peter and Gwen builds as he works on the case. Peter is enthralled by Gwen's beauty, and she begins to see him as her knight in shining armor. The CPS bureaucrats enlist a sleazy psychologist whom they have been paying to lie to the court in child abuse cases. Peter Barron suspects foul play. He hires another psychologist to testify, and wins Casey's release. Gwen and Peter's next move is to sue CPS for traumatizing Casey and for falsely reporting bruises on Casey's rear end.

Gwen starts attending services at Peter's evangelical church and weekly Bible classes with the wife of Peter's best friend's. Peter agonizes over his growing love for Gwen. Other Christians interpret Scripture differently, but Peter long ago made a vow to God that he would never marry a woman who had been divorced for the wrong reasons. Gordon is a deadbeat but he did not commit adultery and therefore Gwen should not have divorced him. It would be adulterous for Peter to marry Gwen—unless Gordon dies. Otherwise Peter would be breaking his commitment to God just because he finds Gwen irresistible. Peter prays and studies other Christian views on marrying divorcées. He tells Gwen about his quandary and promises that within a few weeks he will either have a change of heart or he will stop stringing her along.

Peter loses the first round of his federal civil rights suit against CPS. But the Supreme Court agrees to hear an appeal. Just when Peter has finally decided that he cannot violate his principles and marry Gwen, the by now insanely jealous ex-husband Gordon gets drunk and has a fatal car accident. Gwen is now, according to Scripture, a widow. Peter is free to marry her and adopt Casey. While the newlyweds are on their honeymoon in Hawaii, the Supreme Court rules in their favor.

At one level *Anonymous Tip* is about the nightmare of dealing with an unaccountable government agency, and about ultimate victory for the righteous. Farris uses his legal expertise to create a seemingly realistic picture of how the child protection bureaucracy works. The bureaucrats care only about winning a battle of wits with an uncooperative mother and her smart-mouthed lawyer. The subtext here is that many cases of child abuse may be as fraudulent as the one Gwen is charged with. Why, then, should one believe the mainstream media and their reports about the high frequency of child abuse? What really matters is the trampling of parental rights. The bureaucrats want to secure their jobs, their power, and their fat budgets. Their greed is counterposed to the heart-wrenching travails of a scared preschooler, her beautiful and vulnerable mother, and her morally unflinching lawyer–suitor. Peter is a fine lawyer but he is an even better caregiver and servant of God.

The novel is more than a legal potboiler. It is about duty to God, which is intimately linked to finding the biblically correct kind of family. Like the project of legislating parental rights, *Anonymous Tip* is about securing a proper order between husbands and wives, parents and children. The novel is written mostly from the perspective of the male character Peter, but the story is every bit as much about women's roles. Gwen's problems stem from not having a husband to help her raise her child. Sure, she left Gordon for a plausible reason: he refused to get a job and support Casey. But according to the Bible, Gwen should have stayed in her marriage, despite the damage to herself. Once Gordon makes the false report and the bureaucrats predictably lie and cheat, Gwen and Casey need to be rescued. Peter wins Gwen's court battles. But his real manly role lies in winning Gwen's soul for Christ, and then winning her body, heart, and progeny in marriage.

Happily Ever After

∾

The draw for *Anonymous Tip* is a plot about a phony child abuse case. Then, once hooked, Farris tweaks his Bible-believing readers with the provocative topic of divorce. For the Christian Right, divorce is a hot potato. It is the leading factor in the breakup of the two-parent family. Yet divorce is so rampant that to stigmatize it by making it a political issue would be to risk alienating a sizable chunk of the population, including many evangelicals.

Despite all the talk about traditional family values, born-again Christians have just as poor a track record as everyone else in the United States when it comes to marriage. In 1996, the evangelical polling firm led by George Barna released a study that compared a born-again Christian sample with a random sample of adult Americans. *The Barna Report* found that one out of every four adults (24%) who has been married has experienced a divorce, and that born-again Christians are slightly more likely (27%) than non-Christians to get divorced. Among those who describe themselves as Christian "fundamentalists," 30% have experienced divorce. Moreover, among the Christian believers who have been divorced, 87% did so *after* they converted to Christ, meaning that their religion is no safeguard against marital breakup.[13]

Barna offered no explanation for the somewhat higher divorce rate among people presumably more opposed to it. One might speculate that born-again Christians may be less likely to live together before marriage, and that they may have more idealistic and/or rigid expectations about marriage. In any case, they hold no moral high ground on the divorce question, and yet the drive to save the traditional family requires some sort of response. There are two approaches within the Christian Right and the broader evangelical subculture. One, the legal route, is to try to make a divorce more difficult to obtain. The other, more affirmative approach is to promote ideas about what sustains a successful marriage.

A recent issue of the Heritage Foundation's *Policy Review* magazine featured short essays by well-known profamily "experts" who were asked the question "Can Government Save the Family?" Congressmember Steve Largent (R-OK), Michigan Governor John Engler, former Vice President Dan Quayle, and Christian Right leaders James Dobson, D. James Kennedy, Paul Weyrich, and Kay Coles James all ranked the elimination of no-fault divorce laws high on the agenda of what government should do to protect families.[14]

No-fault divorce laws were enacted in all fifty states in the 1970s and 1980s with the idea of reducing bitter court proceedings and making it easier for abused women, in particular, to get a divorce. Under the old fault-based system, the courts would grant a divorce only if one spouse was found guilty of adultery or cruelty. Judges had the discretionary power to deny a divorce if both parties were at fault or if the innocent party did not want the divorce. Obviously, the ease of obtaining a divorce under no-fault divorce laws is but one of the factors in the more than one million divorces in the United States each year.[15] But it is in the realm of law that ambitious politicians can score the most points with profamily constituents. As of 1996, modifications of no-fault divorce law were under consideration in about twenty state legislatures. Proposals include making divorce more difficult by requiring proof of physical abuse, substance abuse, adultery, or desertion; and, in cases involving children, by requiring parents to receive counseling on the negative effects of divorce.[16] It is ironic that such proposals originate from conservative legislators and activists, who often say they want government to stay out of people's personal lives. In truth, profamily forces want government to selectively intervene on behalf of their biblical view of proper moral conduct.

When not trying to use government to enforce family values, the evangelical movement concentrates on preaching to the converted about what makes a marriage stick. For example, much of the literature and speech making in the Promise Keepers (PK) movement is about how to strengthen the bonds of marriage. To give credit where credit is due, PK stresses that husbands need to become better communicators and companions for their wives and children—though always with the idea that men are the leaders and final arbiters of any household decision. No doubt, the popularity of PK stems in large part from the high rate of divorce among born-again Christians. Many men in the evangelical community want to keep their marriages intact. They come to PK already believing that their religion has the answers for how to organize their families.

There is plenty of advice to be found. From evangelical media outlets come both practical advice on how to negotiate relationships and an underlying perspective on the proper hierarchical relationship between husbands and wives. The practical and the theoretical are entwined. For practical advice, Focus on the Family is the single most important resource. Every month at least several of the daily Focus radio broadcasts are devoted to interviews with Christian marriage counselors and authors of the latest how-to books. The broadcasts tie in with related articles in the monthly Focus on the Family magazine, which the organization sends to about two million listeners. There are cute articles, such as the one directed at wives about "Living with a Messie," which advises making sure the home is always well organized and easy to clean up quickly.[17] There are more serious articles too, for example, on how to be a better listener, how to forgive one's spouse after a fight, and how to accept basic character flaws in one's spouse.

The message is one of commitment. Despite the reality of high divorce rates, conservative ideology insists that marriage is forever. It is not about fleeting feelings of satisfaction or dissatisfaction, any more than faith in God means one will always have a nice day. In an article on why divorce is rampant, a writer for Concerned Women for America's Family Voice magazine stresses that while most Americans want to be married, "few understand that true love is willing to give up personal expectations and take on personal responsibilities. . . . True love is grounded in commitment that surpasses emotional impulses."[18]

In a marriage based on biblical models, the partners know their place. This point is stressed over and over in evangelical literature. It is not that men are permitted to be brutal tyrants but that wives need to "submit" to their husbands, just as both partners submit to Christ. Whenever the topic comes up, the key Bible passage quoted is from the fifth chapter of the Book of Ephesians: "Wives, submit to your husbands as to the Lord. For the husband is the head of the wife as Christ is the head of the church." The same chapter goes on to say that husbands are to love their wives just as Christ loves the church, implying that husbands wield authority in exchange for the sacrifices they make for their wives. All of this can easily be seen as a green light for men to order their wives around. No doubt, many men do, but such behavior is becoming harder to justify. Because female submission is a controversial topic, writers for the popular evangelical press frequently try the semantic maneuver of claiming that a submissive wife is still an equal partner. A version of the submission teaching published in *Charisma* magazine is worth quoting here at length:

> The Bible makes it clear that the husband is the head of the home, and the wife is to submit to him. But how does this work? With the circulation of feminist ideas in the church and so many abuses of "male dominance," most women flinch at the mention of the word *submission*.
> The popular perception is that to submit to your husband is to accept an inferior status. Therefore, when a wife submits, she is declaring herself to be lower than her husband, less intelligent and not as capable as he is. . . .
> The popular perception of a husband's authority as head of the home is one of absolute dictatorship without intelligent reason or compassion attached to it. . . .
> But these popular perceptions are not based on God's word.
> The Word of God commands the husband to love his wife aggressively and sacrificially. While he does have final authority in the home, he serves those he leads. Jesus set the precedent when He washed the disciples' feet and declared that the highest in command is the one who is the greatest servant.
> When a woman understands what God is requiring when He asks her to submit to her husband—and she obeys—she will reach a new level of personal freedom.
> Although the husband is head of the home, he is not superior to his wife. Although the wife submits to his final word, she is not inferior to her husband. They are equals.[19]

The *Charisma* article proceeds to offer as a proper role model for Christian women the biblical figure Sarah, wife of Abraham. In Genesis, even after God ordains that Sarah will be the matriarch and queen of the Israelites, she remains subservient to Abraham and calls him her "lord." Her power derives from knowing her place, which makes sense within an ancient religious hierarchy. But what does such hierarchy have to do with the organization of daily activities in a modern household? The reference above to Christ as servant of his disciples only emphasizes the point:

Christ—or the husband—is loving and sacrificial, but he is also the king of kings. Anything that challenges the sovereignty of God—or the male—is sacrilegious.

Within a worldview that conflates spiritual hierarchy with mundane family arrangements, anything that threatens the traditional family order is not just misguided but downright evil. Divorce is an act of nonsubmission; it therefore must have disastrous repercussions, and must be opposed. Remarriage and the formation of blended families are inevitable and probably preferable to single parenting, but the undefiled traditional family is superior.

Feminism on Demand

ᘓᘐ

Virtually all of the Christian Right's organizations are preoccupied with the subject of proper relations between men and women. More than the rest, Concerned Women for America (CWA) has a mandate to represent godly women who are politically active, yes, but unalterably opposed to feminism as they see it. As an organization, part of CWA's function is to explain for its members why feminism is a threat to the family.

In one sweeping article, CWA magazine editor Rosaline Bush blames the decline of the traditional family generally on the culture's failure to obey God and specifically on feminism.

> At Creation, God designed the family as the foundation of civilization. And for those who followed His directions, He provided a guarantee against structural damage and collapse. God's guidelines are that:
> Each family member must worship God only, trusting in Him for guidance and protection.
> A husband and wife must be monogamous, loving each other unconditionally.
> Children must be treasured, protected, and taught to live by God's laws.[20]

From there, Bush writes a history tracing the destruction of the traditional family. During World War II, fathers went off to war. Mothers went to work and later many returned only reluctantly to the job of raising children. Then the 1960s brought sexual license and a youth rebellion against authority.

> And divorce ran rampant as individuals chased after their dreams of self-fulfillment through sex and drugs. Feminists pushed women's rights above and beyond their concern for family solidarity. And the family began to lose its identity.[21]

Everything is connected to everything else: divorce, drugs, women's rights, television as a surrogate babysitter, the increase of sexually explicit themes on television, the rise in teenage promiscuity, the promotion of sexual content in the public schools, teenage pregnancy, and abortion. "The drug scene, the criminal explosion, the wanton disregard for human life, and rampant promiscuity are devastating manifestations of a culture whose moral foundation has cracked."[22]

It all adds up. The morass is about a breakdown of order, and feminists pushing rights are at the center of the chaos. In religious terms, feminism is the ultimate form of nonsubmission to male authority. Culturally, feminism is linked to all manner of "antifamily" policies. That is why, in the 1970s and 1980s, Phyllis Schlafly and others fought tooth and nail against the Equal Rights Amendment. In the 1990s, though, things have changed. Even on the Right, it is no longer politically correct to make direct attacks on women's equality. Men and women are *different*, indeed. They have different roles to play. But one does not read or hear arguments from the Right that women *should* be paid less than men for the same work or—with the exception of work in the military—that women *should* be denied career options. Even the speakers and writers for the Promise Keepers movement are careful not to overtly cast women as second-class citizens.

The Christian Right's rhetorical attacks on feminism are directed not at the basic feminist principle of equality but rather at a caricature of feminism as a movement of man-hating, power-mongering ideologues who do not really represent most women anyway. This is a subtle point, one often lost on critics who think that the Christian Right is monolithically and virulently misogynistic—and, therefore, why would any woman in her right mind be active within the movement? It is precisely because women are among the leaders in the Christian Right that the antifeminist theme is so carefully crafted.

Aside from well-known figures such as Phyllis Schlafly and Beverly LaHaye, who head their own organizations, women also direct some of the Christian Coalition's most successful state branches and many of the local chapters. Though they don't enjoy the kind of fanfare accorded to the big-name religious broadcasters, it is women who run the crisis pregnancy centers and who head the local campaigns against sex education in the schools and objectionable library books. Women are less likely to run for office, but they probably conduct proportionately more of the nuts-and-bolts grassroots activity. No doubt, activist women in the Christian Right get less credit than they deserve. But within the movement a wholesale denigration of women's abilities simply does not happen, nor would it make sense.

Instead, the Christian Right's discourse on feminism paints a contrast between good, family-minded Christian women and pushy, narrow-minded feminists. In order to make the distinction clear, the propaganda focuses on how "extreme" the feminist agenda secretly is. One typical series of articles on organized feminism published by Concerned Women for America accused feminists of seeking to abolish marriage and destroy the role of women as homemakers, and of promoting sexual promiscuity, especially of the lesbian kind.[23] The rhetorical trick here is to find a quotation or a news report from or about one feminist personality and then extrapolate to indict the entire movement. For example, (1) NOW president Patricia Ireland had a lesbian lover, and (2) feminists generally endorse gay rights; therefore, (3) the movement is "promoting" homosexual perversion.

In 1995, the United Nations convened a World Conference on Women in Beijing, China. Delegates from more than 170 nations met to discuss a range of problems plaguing women and children, including poverty, disease, warfare, and political repression—all of which are linked in some way to more explicitly sexual issues such as abortion and contraception, homosexuality, and women's relationships with men. From the United States, most of the participating nongovernmental organizations were liberal, though not particularly progressive, feminist and population control groups. To hear it from the Christian Right, though, the Beijing conference was part of an international conspiracy to destroy traditional families by reinventing the definition of gender. Both Concerned Women for America (CWA) and Focus on the Family sent observer delegations to China and organized letter-writing campaigns for their members to protest taxpayer funding of the official U.S. delegation. In their respective publications and broadcasts, both CWA and Focus treated the Beijing conference as if it were an atrocity on a par with the real bloodshed then underway in the Balkans and central Africa.

Dr. James Dobson devoted two of his eight-page monthly letters to radio listeners to polemics over the conference. A month before the event began, Dobson called it "the most radical, atheistic and anti-family crusade in the history of the world." Below a warning that "portions of this letter are not suitable for children," Dobson outlined the "breathtaking wickedness" embedded in the preconference documents drafted by "a virtual who's who of radical feminists," led by "that veteran sexist warrior, Bella Abzug."

> At the heart of the draft document is enormous hostility to the institution of the family. Marriage is seen as the root of all evil for women, and hence, it will be largely ignored in the deliberations. Everything related to traditional male and female relationships is despised. Men are seen as oppressors and exploiters whom women should regard as lifelong enemies. . . .
> What is being proposed is a new way of looking at human sexuality. The notion that babies come into the world as male or female based on the size

and shape of their genitalia is anathema. Sexual identification, they say, is something society imposes on children and then expects them to play out in their behavior ever after. . . .

In other words, the only biological differences between men and women are relatively insignificant, external features....Taking that concept to its illogical conclusion, the radicals want to dissolve the traditional roles of mothers and fathers. They also hope to eliminate such terms as *wife, husband, son, daughter, sister, brother, manhood, womanhood, masculine* and *feminine*. These references to sexual identity are being replaced with gender-neutral terms, such as *parent, spouse, child* and *sibling*. The ultimate goal of those who drafted the document, although they tried to hide it, is a plan to get rid of traditional sexuality in order to destroy patriarchy.[24] [emphasis in original]

No wonder there was cause for alarm. In practice, according to Dobson, the threat to patriarchy took form at the Beijing conference when women organized themselves into workshops

focused on redesigning the family, reordering the way males and females interrelate, promoting "reproductive rights for women," distributing condoms and safe-sex nonsense to kids, propagating "homosexual and lesbian rights," weakening parental authority, undermining "patriarchal" religious teachings and spreading feminist ideology to every nation on earth.[25]

Some feminists may think that their goal is to enhance the economic and political status of women. But for Dobson, LaHaye, and their constituents, the themes of these atrocious workshops—whether they dominated the conference or not—are evidence of a bold plan by feminists to reinvent the fundamental structure of God's creation. If the threat to patriarchy is as great as Dobson fears, then one must channel one's outrage into political activism.

If God's social order is as threatened as many evangelical Christians think it is, political activism is necessary but not sufficient. The normal means of effecting political outcomes are accompanied and strengthened by the cumulative power of small, individual actions. Thus, some of the evangelical movement's most popular projects are those that seem the most futile. True Love Waits, for instance, is a project that combines the themes of parental rights, support for marriage, and opposition to abortion and sex education. First initiated by Southern Baptists but supported by a range of evangelical churches plus Catholics, True Love Waits sponsors rallies at which teenagers pledge to remain virgins until marriage. (Those who are not virgins can join, too, if they pledge to never engage in premarital sex again.[26]) An article for a midwestern evangelical newspaper described how the whole family was inspired when thirteen-year-old Rebecca asked her parents to give her a True Love Waits covenant ring, symbolizing the commitment she has made to God, her church, her youth group, her parents, and her future husband to "remain sexually pure" until marriage.[27] The Promise Keepers' *New Man* magazine advertises a special pendant (available in gold or silver) for fathers to give to their daughters. It is a locked heart. He keeps the key as a reminder to "keep your daughter in constant prayer as you await her wedding day—when you will pass the key to the patient man she now calls *husband*."[28]

In the chapters that follow, I take up the Christian Right's chief concerns in the realms of gender and family matters: abortion, gay rights, and education. All of these issues are heated because they are about sex. But it would be reductionist to say, except perhaps about homosexuality, that sexual fear is the sole driving force in the movement's activism on these issues. Abortion politics is about who will decide what is life and what is murder. School battles are about who will control the hearts and minds of children. Gender is never absent from these debates. If one cannot be certain of clear, wide boundaries between male and female, how can there ever again be any reliable social order?

Chapter 7

෨

As If It Were Murder

Midweek during the 1996 Republican National Convention in San Diego, prolife delegates and their friends celebrated with what they called a "whale of a party" at the Sea World marine theme park, home to the famous killer whale, Shamu. Billed as "the most exciting social event of convention week," the party was hosted by the Republican National Coalition for Life (NCL), which Phyllis Schlafly had founded in 1990 for the purpose of electing a majority of prolife delegates in as many states as possible. In 1992 and again in 1996, NCL kept the Republicans' antiabortion platform plank intact, despite the skillful efforts of the party's pro-choice wing. Under a festively decorated canopy, the prolife conventioneers ate a barbecue buffet lunch and listened to short speeches from their movement's leading lights: Patrick Buchanan, Gary Bauer, Ralph Reed, Pat Robertson, and Beverly LaHaye. A gray-haired and grinning Jerry Falwell sat in the crowd. The Christian Broadcasting Network was on hand to tape the whole affair for television. A minor scuffle broke out when comedian Al Franken, of the Comedy Central cable TV channel, mingled among the tables with his own video crew and asked the guests sarcastic questions such as why, if they were so "prolife," were they eating dead animals?

The most vivid moment came at the end of the party, after the crowd sang the final chorus of "God Bless America." Robert Dornan, the fiery, nine-term Congressmember from nearby Orange County, California, jumped up onto the stage, announced that it was Phyllis Schlafly's seventy-second birthday, and demanded that she dance a waltz with him before the band packed up. Mrs. Schlafly gracefully obliged, and as they danced, the smiling conventioneers knew their moment had arrived. Bob Dornan did not know that a few short weeks later he would be unceremoniously defeated by a young, female, Hispanic Democrat from his traditionally conservative district. But then the waltz symbolized the enduring marriage between reliable antiabortion legislators like Dornan and stalwarts like Phyllis Schlafly, who has been a Republican delegate at almost every convention since 1956. However even working together, the politicians and the activists have been unable to outlaw abortion. They have, instead, built around the issue a fractious movement, one that cannot be mollified and will not go away.

Outside the Republicans' convention center in downtown San Diego stood a few dozen members of Operation Rescue (OR) holding giant-sized photos of blood-drenched fetus heads. Among the diehard picketers I met Norma McCorvey, once the plaintiff in *Roe v. Wade,* now a converted Christian and traveling demonstrator with OR. She and her friends were handing conventioneers a pamphlet charging Christians in the Republican Party with "selling their birthright for a mess of pottage." (The reference, from Genesis, is to Esau, who is so hungry that, in exchange for a bowl of lentils offered by his younger brother, Jacob, he sells his favored status as Isaac's first son.) Similarly, OR charged, Ralph Reed and others in the Christian Right are so hungry for power and party unity that they sold out their prolife principles by backing Bob Dole.

Inside the convention hall, and for the benefit of the television cameras, hundreds of prolife delegates were wearing white hats, provided by Phyllis Schlafly's group, stamped with the words "The Life of the Party." Inside and outside the halls of power, the contradictions remain rife. The party has no life without its antiabortion activist contingent, and yet the party will not do what it would take to end abortion.

Without the unifying and galvanizing drive to end legal abortion, the Christian Right would not have become a social movement formidable enough to swing elections. Certainly, opposition to gay rights and secular humanism in the public schools would have fostered their share of skirmishes. However, on such issues alone, the movement would have floundered and withered. What has given the Christian Right its marching orders is the clarion call that "abortion is murder."

Unlike issues of taxes, school curricula, Pentagon spending, or any other public policy matter, abortion is a question around which there can be no true compromise. One is either in favor of *choice,* meaning that each woman does what her own conscience dictates, or one is against *murder,* meaning that it is incumbent upon government to ban the practice altogether. The all-or-nothing nature of the abortion issue itself has drawn the boundaries between the opposing camps, while giving antiabortionists a clear and broad mandate for action. They will stop government funding for poor women's abortions. They will elect candidates who will back prolife judges. They will place their own bodies between clinics and women seeking abortions. And if all else fails, some conclude, they will take the law into their own hands and prevent abortions by whatever means necessary.

For more than twenty years, prolifers have debated with each other about the best means to stop abortion. The goal is unquestioned. But the politics surrounding the drive to end abortion make for shifting strategies and, often, opportunistic alliances with politicians. It is the unyielding quality of the abortion conflict that has solidified the Christian Right into a voting bloc that Republicans cannot ignore. Yet precisely because most of the U.S. public remains at least nominally prochoice, it is dangerous for politicians to ally themselves too closely with the antiabortion cause. The perpetual jockeying for power—both by activists eager to stop abortion and by politicians eager to court them—is repellent to some prolife activists, and that has caused perennial internal conflicts for the Christian Right. Each election cycle highlights the dilemma: Should prolifers vote for the lesser-of-two-evils candidate, or should they fight abortion through media campaigns and protest tactics? Curiously, the antiabortion movement's internal struggles have never caused a fatal rupture for the Christian Right. Instead, debate has strengthened the movement by pushing activists to work on many fronts.

Making Abortion Political

⌇

The 1980 presidential campaign and subsequent election of Ronald Reagan was a milestone for antiabortion activists. They had faith that their leader would fight strenuously to end abortion, but he would eventually disappoint them. During the campaign Reagan made a point of courting the evangelical and Catholic vote. He told a gathering of ministers in Dallas that he would base his presidency on traditional values, and he sent a congratulatory message to the June 1980 convention of the National Right to Life Committee.[1]

But once elected, Reagan and his administration focused almost exclusively on foreign and economic policy. A number of Senators and Congressmembers introduced antiabortion legislation, and prolifers watched, at first patiently, for signs of commitment from the Reagan White House. In 1981, Senator Orrin Hatch (R-UT) sponsored a constitutional amendment that would have nullified the 1973 *Roe v. Wade* Supreme Court decision, and Senator Jesse Helms (R-NC) introduced a "human life bill" to ban taxpayer-funded abortions and to remove the power of federal courts to overturn state antiabortion laws. Prolife activists bickered over which of the Senate bills they should support. The Catholic bishops endorsed Hatch's broad goal of overturning *Roe*. But seasoned New Right activists viewed the Hatch amendment as impractical because it required an impossible two-thirds majority vote in Congress. This was years before the Republicans would capture a majority in both the House and the Senate. In the early 1980s, neither Senator Hatch nor Senator Helms was able to bring his bills to the floor of the Senate for a vote.[2] Still, their efforts kept the prolife movement temporarily hopeful that the Reagan Republicans were in their corner. Movement leaders praised White House assistants for lobbying on behalf of the Helms bill.[3]

However, the defeat of the Hatch and Helms bills was followed by precious little antiabortion action either from the Senate or from the White House. Prolifers felt betrayed and more than a bit frustrated. Ten years after *Roe v. Wade* legalized abortion, virtually nothing had been accomplished. In 1973, just weeks after the *Roe* ruling, Senator James Buckley (brother of *National Review* publisher William F. Buckley Jr.) had introduced the first constitutional amendment to outlaw abortion,[4] but to no avail. The National Conference of Catholic Bishops had mobilized parishioners to begin lobbying against abortion, and Catholic activists started the National Right to Life Committee, which would eventually become a lobby with major influence.[5] New Right political action committees took up the abortion issue throughout the 1970s, but there was always a divergence of opinion over which course to take: the principled stand (total victory now and nothing less) or the pragmatic approach (compromise principles today to win incremental victories tomorrow). All sought a constitutional amendment to ban abortion. But the National Right to Life Committee was willing to allow exceptions to save the life of a mother, while the National Pro-Life Political Action Committee (NPL-PAC) and the Life Amendment Political Action Committee (LAPAC) would not tolerate any exceptions. Paul and Judie Brown of LAPAC wanted to fight abortion by joining multi-issue coalitions with other New Right groups, which they did. New Right strategist Paul Weyrich recruited the Browns to attend weekly meetings with a network of 120 right-wing organizations.[6] (The Browns later changed the name of their PAC to the American Life Lobby, which remains one of the leading antiabortion groups in the late 1990s.) New Right leaders were hopeful that the abortion issue had such emotional salience that it would lead people to become involved in a wide range of issues.

That may have happened. By the early 1980s, the Christian Right was, indeed, active in battles against everything from objectionable textbooks in elementary schools to helping fight "communism" in Central America. Nevertheless, stopping abortion has always been the movement's single most important goal. And because of the frustration associated with stopping abortion through legislative means, the "radical" wing of the antiabortion movement has always been more committed to direct action.

Armed for Life

〜

At first the ammunition was mostly psychological. Outside clinics, antiabortionists armed themselves with picket signs covered with pictures of bloody fetuses. Picketing and shouting at women entering the clinics proved mostly futile, so it was inevitable that some frustrated picketers would turn toward violence. The first bombing took place in 1982.[7] By 1984, dozens of clinics had been bombed, almost always at night, when no clinic personnel were present. The Reagan administration finally admitted that the bombings were acts of terrorism, but only after vocal pressure from women's and civil liberties groups.[8] The FBI was reluctant to investigate the attacks, claiming the bombings were not really acts of terrorism because they were not attacks on the government.[9] This was at a time when, under the rubric of fighting "terrorism," the United States was backing anticommunist proxy wars around the world. Yet potentially deadly attacks on private property inside the United States were not seen as cause for alarm by the top law enforcement officials of the United States. The government claimed that the bombings were the work of isolated individuals, not an organized conspiracy, despite the fact that some of the perpetrators arrested were known figures within the antiabortion movement.[10]

Critics of government inaction charged that seemingly civil leaders of the antiabortion movement were, in fact, fomenting the climate of violence. Veteran activist Joseph Scheidler of the Pro-Life Action League in Chicago mailed instructions to hundreds of antiabortion groups around the country on how to dog 1984 Democratic presidential candidate Walter Mondale and his running mate Geraldine Ferraro at every one of their campaign stops.[11] This was harassment but still within legal bounds. Next, though, Scheidler published what would become a manual for activists bent on guerrilla tactics of disruption. In Closed: 99 Ways to Stop Abortion, Scheidler instructed activists how to do everything from jamming clinic answering machines to employing detectives to dig up dirt about abortion doctors.[12] Indeed, it was Scheidler who introduced the strategy of targeting individual doctors, thus stimulating a mindset that led later to assassinations.

Scheidler was also credited with inspiring the formation of Operation Rescue (OR), in 1987. While Scheidler was quoted to the effect that "to admonish prolifers not to bomb clinics would be an insult to the prolife movement," he was also among the first to pioneer the use of the clinic blockade.[13] Here was a way to channel the growing militancy of the antiabortion movement while ensuring lots of publicity, the disruption of clinics, and, initially, no serious legal consequences for protesters. Neither legal picketing nor clinic bombings had stopped abortion or galvanized broad support for the cause. OR clinic blockades were the next step in the movement's effort to turn the tide. OR leader Randall Terry was fond of exhorting demonstrators that "if those who know abortion is murder would begin acting like it is murder, we could close down every abortion clinic in the United States."[14] He was right in a sense. Clinic blockades enabled activists to put their bodies where their rhetoric was and to experience their own power to shut down clinics, even if only for a day or two.

For several years, beginning during the 1988 presidential campaign season, OR blockades were well attended. The use of civil disobedience was a big departure for the Christian Right, and it was controversial because evangelicals are taught to obey authority. Not since the 1960s antiwar movement had thousands of people gone to jail in civil disobedience protests. OR was a major media story because this time the protesters were not particularly young or rowdy. Most were average middle-aged churchgoers no longer content to just vote and write letters, as the established prolife organizations suggested they do.

Randall Terry reportedly was inspired to start OR after hearing about clinic blockades from Joseph Scheidler in 1986.[15] Terry was then in his late twenties. He was a used car salesman and a graduate of the pentecostal Elim Bible Institute in upstate New York. He had already spent several years picketing abortion clinics during his lunch hour, and in 1984 he and his wife had opened a crisis pregnancy center. Then, in 1986, Terry and six others were arrested after locking themselves inside a Binghamton, New York, clinic. Terry spent ten days in jail, and from then on he was hooked on the idea of doing "rescues" in cities across the United States.[16] *Roe v. Wade* might remain the law of the land, but if women could not physically get into a clinic, then the legality of abortion would become moot.

Terry's personal style may have had something to do with his ability to mobilize a following. He is fond of calling his fellow prolifers "sister" and "brother" or "dude." He peppers his exhortations with 1960s-sounding phrases like "hey man" and "right on." And unlike the more established prolife leaders, Terry is not at all squeamish about calling abortion "child killing" and labeling fellow Christians who disagree with his tactics as outright "enemies" of the prolife movement. His single-minded focus on shutting down clinics resonated with prolifers who were tired of mincing words and waiting for action from politicians. Between May and December 1988, Randall Terry claimed that eleven thousand activists participated in clinic "rescues," and Terry attributed the high turnout in part to the endorsements of prominent Christian Right leaders whom he listed in one of his newsletters. Among them were Cardinal John J. O'Connor, D. James Kennedy, Jerry Falwell, Pat Robertson, James Dobson, Gary North, and Beverly LaHaye.[17] These were not leaders who had themselves engaged in civil disobedience but they gave OR favorable promotion in Christian media outlets. Concerned Women for America president Beverly LaHaye endorsed the rescue movement unequivocally. "I think every prolife person should attend one of these [rescues]," she said. "This experience brings you face to face with how strong your convictions are."[18] Jerry Falwell went further, giving OR a $10,000 donation, and joining Terry's troops at a protest in Atlanta.[19]

OR was riding high in 1988 and 1989. The rescues were frequently reported on Pat Robertson's TV network and Dr. James Dobson's radio show. For people tuned in to the Christian Right media, there must have been a palpable sense that, through civil disobedience, this time the prolife movement would truly be able to stop abortion. Randall Terry and other OR leaders kept morale high by sending their supporters a slew of newsletters and pamphlets, ticking off numbers of arrests at each blockade, and celebrating the numbers of women and "children" prevented from the "hell of abortion." In September 1988, Randall Terry announced that "child killing" was down by 20% at one abortion "mill," and that a local crisis pregnancy center had seen a 50% increase in clients seeking adoption not abortion—all to the credit of OR protests. Terry also noted that 80% of the eight hundred people who had been arrested by that time were first-time participants in civil disobedience. "They are going to their homes around the country with a vision and zeal for rescue," he wrote.[20] And, said Terry, there were collateral benefits to the long, hot days spent in jail, especially during a summer and fall 1988 spate of "rescues" in the city of Atlanta.

> The jail experience has been a blessing for hundreds! Over thirty-five inmates have received Christ! Powerful prayer meetings and preaching fill the cell blocks. The system has tried to get tough on our people (by intimidation, long processing, mixing us with general population, etc.), but the effect has been tremendous on our people. Satan never learns. The more God's people are affected, the stronger they become.
>
> The Atlanta pro-life community is blossoming. A handful of dedicated activists is growing into a mighty force for life.[21]

It was a community linked by the appeal of the civil disobedience tactic. During OR's heyday between 1988 and 1990, the numbers of clinic bombings and arson attacks dropped precipitously, as did the incidents of peaceful picketing.[22] It was as if the "rescues" offered an alternative both to outright violence and to milder forms of protest.

Terry and others believed that the strength of their convictions and the use of graphic rhetoric and imagery would sway an unconvinced public toward the prolife side. Like any good street protest movement, OR used theatrical props, including at times a chemically preserved aborted fetus, which they dared the secular media to describe and photograph.[23] This was strong stuff, even for the already converted, and in OR's literature, Terry seemed to want to continually justify OR tactics by stressing the biblical basis for asking Christians to break the law. In essence, Terry said, there were two reasons to "defy civil authority: (1) to save someone's life, and (2) to remain faithful to God." Both of these reasons required much more than routine political pressure. Terry invoked the long historical precedent of using civil disobedience to effect profound social change:

> The birth of America, the end of slavery, women's voting rights, repeal of prohibition, the civil rights movement, the anti-Vietnam war movement, and the feminist movement all testify to one truth: whether for good or bad, political change comes after a group of Americans bring enough tension in the nation and pressure on politicians that the laws are changed. Politicians see the light after they feel the heat!
>
> The truth is, we don't stand a chance of ending this holocaust without righteous social upheaval occurring across the country that "inspires" politicians to amend the Constitution. Right now they have no reason to. The status quo is peaceful. But even if one percent of the evangelical and Catholic community (about 800,000 people) would take their own rhetoric seriously ("Abortion is murder!") and start acting like children are being killed, things would change. By doing *massive* rescues, we could create the tension needed to turn the tide. When government officials have to choose between jailing tens of thousands of good, decent citizens, or making child killing illegal again, they will choose the latter, partly because there are no jails big enough to hold us if we move together in large numbers![24]

Terry's analysis that change happens through social upheaval was an accurate reading of history. But he miscalculated by thinking that OR could, in fact, galvanize the kind of critical mass he envisioned. There were obstacles to the kind of massive, continuing blockades OR leaders hoped for. One deterrent was the rising fines and increasingly long jail sentences imposed on OR demonstrators. But even during the period of OR's greatest support and apparent success, there was dissension among the evangelical ranks over OR's rising militancy.

Among the most vocal critics was Earl Paulk, pastor of the ten-thousand-member Chapel Hill Harvester Church in Atlanta. Paulk's church had, for years, sponsored a home for unmarried mothers, and Paulk feared that Terry's confrontational tactics showed a lack of compassion toward women in crisis pregnancies. Moreover, in a guest editorial for the *Atlanta Journal and Constitution,* Paulk questioned the very idea of using civil disobedience tactics to challenge the morality of abortion. "Moral law and civil law are not synonymous," wrote Paulk. "The individual, the family and the church legislate moral law. Civil law legislates secular law. This is true separation of church and state."[25]

Another critic, Southern Baptist Convention leader Charles Stanley, argued that the unleashing of law-breaking protest tactics might lead to tragic and counterproductive violence down the road. "Where does it stop?," Stanley asked. "If blocking an entrance is permitted, then why not physical restraint . . . or even destruction of those who are performing the procedure . . . ? Anarchy and chaos will ultimately result."[26]

Reverend Stanley was prescient. The eventual decline in the frequency and size of OR demonstrations would, by the 1990s, lead a small number of "rescue" veterans to begin to advocate the "justifiable" murder of abortion doctors. Terry's attitude, initially, was that whatever stopped "child killing" was a righteous act. But other prolifers were not so fixed on the idea of shutting down clinics that they could not foresee the negative fallout from OR tactics. Their skepticism no doubt kept many rank-and-file evangelicals from joining up with OR and ensuring its continued growth and longevity.

Dr. James Dobson of Focus on the Family was an early endorser of civil disobedience. But even so, a 1989 Focus on the Family *Citizen* magazine article raised pointed questions about OR's legitimacy. *Citizen* writer Tom Hess asked why in the city of Los Angeles, home to scores of prolife churches, OR's 1989 Easter clinic blockades had attracted fewer than one thousand demonstrators. Hess interviewed some of OR's critics and found a pattern of objections. Dallas Theological Seminary professor Norman Geisler claimed that OR had no biblical authority to break the law as long as the government was not compelling Christians themselves to "do evil." Bible teacher Bill Gothard compared OR to the French Revolution, which began with civil disobedience but eventually involved great bloodshed. Evangelical journalist Gretchen Passantino was concerned about Randall Terry's arrogance in dealing with secular reporters. At one OR press conference, Terry brought with him an aborted fetus inside a small coffin and told reporters to "ask the dead baby your questions."[27] To all of the critiques, Terry answered simply that years' worth of sidewalk counseling, lobbying, and education had yielded nothing but "more dead babies." But he added that the rescue movement had invigorated the legal wing of the antiabortion movement and that, ultimately, all kinds of activity were essential.[28]

Restricting Access

⚭

Terry was probably correct in claiming that the "rescuers" inspired an acceleration of other forms of antiabortion activity. Beginning in the mid-1980s, following disappointment with the lack of action from the Reagan administration, prolifers shifted their focus to the state legislatures. If they could not win an outright ban on abortion through a constitutional amendment, they believed that their next best bet was to restrict access to abortion through legislation state by state. The goal of OR was to prevent access at the site where abortions are performed. Meanwhile, the more legislatively minded activists began to sponsor restrictive laws such as those requiring parental consent for females under the age of eighteen.

One package of restrictive state laws was eventually challenged all the way up to the Supreme Court which, in 1989, ruled that states could restrict access to abortion in certain circumstances without threatening the essential constitutionality of *Roe v. Wade.* In this case, *Webster v. Reproductive Health Services,* the Supreme Court upheld a restrictive law, enacted in Missouri in 1986, that barred public employees from performing or assisting in abortions not necessary to save a woman's life; denied the use of public buildings for performing abortions; and required doctors to perform tests to determine whether the fetus, twenty weeks after conception, could survive outside the womb.[29] All of these provisions were intended to make a woman think longer before proceeding and to penalize her if she chose abortion.

The *Webster* decision did not overturn the constitutional right of a woman to obtain an abortion, but it paved the way for prolife activists to make that right increasingly less of a reality. Despite their campaign rhetoric, the Reagan–Bush administrations had done virtually nothing to push a constitutional amendment to ban abortion. *Webster* underscored the wisdom of a prolife strategy geared toward state legislatures rather than toward national Republican leaders. By the late 1980s, the Christian Right had already turned its focus toward electing sympathetic officeholders at the state and local levels. Brian Johnston, leader of the California branch of the National Right to Life Committee, concluded that "what is perhaps most significant about the *Webster* decision . . . is the growing realization that state legislators do make a difference. The persons you elect to the state Senate and Assembly will now take stands that are more than ideological; they soon will determine if babies live or die."[30]

Webster coincided with efforts to restrict abortion access in a number of states. In Louisiana, the state legislature voted to enforce an old statute banning abortion under any circumstances. (A court order prevented its implementation.[31]) The governors of Florida and Texas both proposed restrictive laws similar to those upheld in Missouri. Idaho's state legislature approved a ban with few exceptions, but when prochoicers threatened to organize a boycott of Idaho potatoes, the ban was vetoed by Idaho's governor. Between the time of the *Webster* decision and the end of 1991, some six hundred restrictive antiabortion bills were introduced in forty-four states. Of these, only twelve passed, but abortion rights are in greatest jeopardy in states where prolifers have succeeded in electing both supportive governors and state legislators.[32] Since *Webster,* antiabortion activists have succeeded in tightening restrictions on abortion access more and more each year. By 1997, most state legislatures supported some form of restrictive legislation. Nearly one-quarter of the states enforce three or more restrictions, including mandatory twenty-four-hour waiting periods between requesting and having an abortion, mandatory counseling, parental consent or notification, Medicaid funding restrictions for low-income women, bans on insurance coverage for abortion, and prohibitions on the use of public facilities for abortions.[33]

The restrictive approach to reducing the numbers of abortions did not, in the immediate aftermath of *Webster,* phase the militant civil disobedience activists in OR. They were not particularly interested in playing compromise politics with state legislators. However, the large clinic blockades of 1988 and 1989, coinciding as they did with the *Webster* decision and other visible legal threats to abortion rights, caused a resurgence of prochoice activism. Prochoicers were justifiably frightened by the gains of the anti-abortion movement, and they used various means to fight back. One strategy was to mobilize prochoicers to defend the clinics, by getting to the buildings ahead of OR and often in greater numbers. Another strategy, pursued by the National Organization for Women (NOW), was to sue OR for monetary damages. In 1990, the U.S. attorney's office in New York seized OR's bank accounts and financial information after OR refused to pay a $50,000 judgment to NOW.[34] This was after the jail sentences and fines imposed on OR demonstrators had already begun to mount to the point that fewer and fewer prolifers were willing to risk arrest.[35]

Also by then, though, OR was branching out into a far-flung network of roving demonstrators. Terry closed the Binghamton, New York, office. The national headquarters moved to the friendlier political climate of South Carolina and stopped soliciting funds that could end up in the hands of suing plaintiffs.

During OR's heyday, the press typically focused on Randall Terry, though there were other "rescue" movement leaders scattered all over the country: Joseph Foreman, Pat Mahoney, Keith Tucci, Flip Benham, and Jeff White—to name a few. As OR was forced to become a more decentralized organization, some of these leaders stayed with OR while others developed their own followings and tactical specialties. One spin-off organization, the Lambs of Christ, was a nomadic Catholic group whose members, when arrested, refused to give their names or pay bail, preferring instead to serve long jail sentences.[36] In 1990, Pat Mahoney started the Christian Defense Coalition in Washington, DC, through which he recruited prolife attorneys to defend protesters.[37] Joseph Foreman cofounded, with Matthew Trewhella, an OR splinter group based in Milwaukee called Missionaries to the Preborn, which conducted clinic blockades, harassed doctors and clinic escorts, and later got involved in recruiting for the U.S. Taxpayers Party.[38] The Missionaries also had a subsidiary project, Prisoners of Christ, through which they raised funds for jailed antiabortionists, including people who had used and/or endorsed violence.

One of the activists with Prisoners of Christ, Gary McCullough, called himself a "media consultant" for Paul Hill during the time when Hill was advocating "justifiable homicide" against abortion doctors.[39] Prior to shooting an abortion doctor himself in 1994, Hill was in legal trouble for relentlessly harassing clinics in Florida. His attorney Michael Hirsh had been the director of OR in Atlanta during OR's summer wave of protests outside the 1988 Democratic Party national convention. Later Hirsh was trained as an attorney at Pat Robertson's Regent University law school and worked for the American Center for Law and Justice. But in 1994, he was dismissed during a controversy over a Regent law journal article he wrote in which he defended the killing of abortion doctors.[40] Around the same time, Matthew Trewhella had become increasingly enamored with violence. In 1994, an undercover reporter for Planned Parenthood videotaped Trewhella speaking at the Wisconsin state meeting of the U.S. Taxpayers Party, calling for the formation of armed militias.[41] OR's more violent cadre were no longer restrained by the hope that civil disobedience would end abortion.

As the years went by, the "rescue" movement was taken over by people with less patience and more militancy. There were fewer of them but they posed a greater danger. The numbers of violent attacks on clinics and abortion personnel rose and declined with shifting political circumstances. For example, during the period between 1991 and 1993, the numbers of blockades fell to about 170, from a total of more than 400 between 1988 and 1990, and during that same 1991–1993 period, there was an increase in incidents of property damage, hate mail, and harassing phone calls.[42] The year 1993, following the election of prochoice President Bill Clinton, marked the peak of violence, which followed by a gradual decline between 1994 and 1996, after Congress passed legislation making clinic violence a federal crime.[43]

No Place to Hide

∾

The decline in open acts of civil disobedience and the rise in more aggressive attacks on clinics coincided with the end of the Reagan–Bush era and the election of President Bill Clinton. In 1992, the Christian Right was mostly focused on defeating Clinton at the polls. Randall Terry and others were right in step with other prolifers on this score. Terry circulated a pamphlet titled, "To vote for Bill Clinton is to sin against God," in which he called Clinton a "neo-pagan" who "promotes rebellion against the Ten Commandments" because he "endorses same sex unions . . . advocates giving our junior-high students condoms . . . promotes child killing . . . supports placing our women in combat . . . endorses children divorcing their parents." Many Christians, Terry wrote, were tempted to vote for Clinton because he promised to fix the economy. But Terry concluded that "if Bill Clinton is elected, he will help destroy three centuries of Christianity in America."[44]

The panic with which many in the Christian Right viewed the incoming Clinton administration was then reinforced by Clinton's prompt fulfillment of campaign promises he had made to prochoice voters. During his first few days in office, Clinton signed executive orders reversing several of the Bush administration's restrictions on abortion access.[45] Clinton strongly backed the Freedom of Access to Clinic Entrances Act, which passed through Congress in 1993 and made clinic violence a federal crime. For prolifers, the prospects of banning abortion through legislative channels at the federal level looked increasingly dim. The worst nightmares of Randall Terry and other prolifers appeared to be coming true.

It was during the transition period between the Bush and Clinton administrations that the declining numbers of active OR participants developed No Place to Hide (NPH), a campaign aimed specifically at abortion doctors. Though most of the advocates of this campaign would later publicly disavow violence, NPH was a pivotal juncture in the eventual development of a call for the "justifiable" killing of abortion doctors. One can imagine that it was while spending long hours together in jails and outside clinics that "rescuers" came up with the idea of attacking doctors directly. Leaders of NPH instructed activists to identify and confirm which local doctors were performing abortions, and then to create and display Wild West–style "wanted posters" complete with the doctor's photo, home and work addresses and phone numbers, and estimates of the numbers of "killings" the doctor had committed. Activists were instructed to contact the doctors directly by phone and mail, and to concentrate picketing at the homes and offices of doctors for a period of one to two months.[46]

In interviews about NPH, Randall Terry told the press that "the doctor is the weak link." With abortion doctors available in fewer and fewer U.S. counties—many had been driven out of the practice by the stigma and terror of frequent clinic protests—and with medical schools training fewer doctors to perform abortions, Terry argued, the harassment of remaining doctors could put a stop to the practice. Joseph Scheidler said that the targeting of doctors was expedient because clinic blockades required a continuing supply of demonstrators willing to risk arrest.[47] By the early 1990s, there were not enough protesters to shut down clinics on anything but a very infrequent basis.

The campaigns against doctors, not buildings, required fewer troops using stronger ammunition. NPH was a reckless group. Whereas OR's clinic blockades focused on the singular act of using one's body to prevent patients from entering a building, NPH set no bounds on appropriate action and encouraged an "anything goes" mentality. The "wanted posters" made the conflict highly personal. Righteous prolife vigilantes now gave themselves a license to stop doctors, with real names and faces, dead in their tracks.

That is exactly what happened. Two decades after the antiabortion movement began using heated rhetoric about "baby killers" and a nationwide "holocaust," someone finally pulled the trigger. On March 10, 1993, during an otherwise routine protest outside a Pensacola, Florida, abortion clinic, Michael Griffin calmly fired three bullets into the back of Dr. David Gunn and then turned himself over to a police officer on the scene. Dr. Gunn died several hours later. His murder marked a turning point for the antiabortion movement. Out of the woodwork emerged a small group of activists who defended the killing, calling it "justifiable homicide," because Dr. Gunn was a repeat offender of the "crime" of abortion and was about to do it again that day.

Now for the first time, since other strategies had failed, some antiabortionists were willing to go all the way to stop abortion. Griffin's deed inspired others. In August 1993, Rachelle "Shelley" Shannon, an Oregon activist, traveled to Kansas and tried to kill a doctor there. Less than a year later, back in Pensacola, Paul Hill shot and killed a doctor and a clinic escort. Then, at the end of 1994, a deranged young man named John Salvi went on a shooting spree and killed two women who were working at two different abortion clinics in Massachusetts. He was later convicted of murder and committed suicide in prison.

The killings caused a split over the justifiable homicide position among groups once affiliated with OR. At a time when most of the Christian Right was focused on a broad repertoire of issues, relying heavily on an electoral strategy and enjoying a growing sense of power within the Republican Party, the more militant, "direct action" activists were increasingly left out in the cold. Not surprisingly, some felt the need to justify the violent actions of their comrades. But their rhetoric about justifiable homicide discredited the prolife movement as a whole and fractured the shrinking network of activists committed to civil disobedience protest.

The assassination of Dr. David Gunn prompted some antiabortion activists to reconsider the consequences of their own militancy. Michael Griffin was a relative newcomer to the movement. But in the month prior to the killing, Griffin had come under the tutelage of John Burt, an ex-Klansman who was a regional director of Rescue America (RA), one of the most aggressive of the direct action groups.[48] Dr. Gunn had been the subject of a long campaign of harassment and surveillance by RA, a group similar to OR in its use of clinic blockades and its participation in NPH. One of RA's "wanted" posters described Gunn as "armed and dangerous."[49] Griffin took that message literally and killed him.

Antiabortion leaders now had a quandary on their hands: how to respond publicly to the killing without acknowledging their own role in fomenting violence. Comments made by antiabortion leaders immediately after the killing revealed the lines of division within the movement. Randall Terry called the shooting an "inappropriate repulsive act" and said he grieved for the Gunn family just as he grieved for the thousands of babies Gunn had aborted. Spokespersons for the National Right to Life Committee were less equivocal in condemning the violence. But RA president Don Treshman refused to condemn the killing, saying instead that while he thought Gunn's death was unfortunate, "the fact is that a number of mothers would have been put at risk today, and over a dozen babies would have died at his hands." Joseph Foreman, then leader of a group called Missionaries to the Preborn, said that the killing of Gunn would be more condemnable had not five to ten "human beings who were scheduled for execution" been spared.[50]

In the weeks following the shooting, divisions began to sharpen between those who condoned and those who condemned Griffin's deed. The monthly *Life Advocate* magazine, published by the direct action group Advocates for Life Ministries in Portland, Oregon, became the central venue for an activist debate on the use of lethal force. Not surprisingly, groups more involved with legislative lobbying than with civil disobedience protest had the easiest time condemning the violence. *Life Advocate* published a column by American Life League president Judie Brown, one of the senior leaders of the movement's legislative lobbying wing. She urged prolifers to agree that "truth is the only weapon that will win the battle to stop the killing of innocent children. It is not my role, nor is it the role of any person to judge another human being, much less violently take his life."[51] In contrast, spokespersons for direct action groups were ambivalent about the use of force. Joseph Foreman of Missionaries to the Preborn sought to blame the escalation of violence on the Clinton administration's support for federal legislation to protect clinics from obstruction by antiabortion blockaders. "I've been saying for years that if the government insists on suppressing normal and time-honored dissent through injunctions, it turns the field over to the rock-throwers, the bombers and the assassins," Foreman said.[52] Steven J. Pruner, a clinic picketer from California, wrote in a May 1993 article for *Life Advocate* that he could not condemn Griffin's act. "Either Christians take up non-violent intervention en masse to effectively stop the murder of unborn children," Pruner wrote, "or we may be forced to accept the use of lethal force by a few 'brave' individuals."[53]

In the summer of 1993, as the debate about violence simmered, OR proceeded to organize a City of Refuge campaign of clinic blockades around the country. But in the wake of the Gunn killing, the City of Refuge campaign attracted far fewer participants than previous national demonstrations.[54] Meanwhile, in June 1993, the antiabortion movement faction least averse to violence held a national conference in Oklahoma. There activists debated the legitimacy of using lethal force against abortion doctors. *Life Advocate* magazine publisher Andrew Burnett said that the killing of Gunn had caused him to rethink his earlier opposition to the use of force. "Over the last few months I have been compelled to change my mind about an issue that I had never been really willing to think about," Burnett said. "I'm not sure that we can really say that 'Abortion is Murder,' and at the same time react in horror when a person who is about to murder someone else is not able to do that anymore because of whatever means was necessary to stop that person."[55] Not only did Burnett introduce the defense-of-necessity argument, but he raised the stakes further by charging that the prolife movement itself had been the "greatest defenders of abortion clinics in the last decade," because prolifers had been too concerned about what others would think of them if they truly tried to stop abortion.[56]

In effect, Griffin's action forced out into the open a "by any means necessary" argument among activists who had become weary of endless demonstrations, none of which had resulted in an end to abortion. Griffin's pending murder trial, and the media spotlight already aimed at the direct action wing of the movement, provided the context for the expression of a "justifiable homicide" defense of Griffin. The man ready to lead the charge was Reverend Paul Hill, also from Pensacola, Florida. Hill was an Orthodox Presbyterian minister who had been removed from his pastorate for espousing the use of force.[57] Within days of Griffin's killing of Dr. Gunn, Hill publicly defended Griffin before a nationwide TV audience on the *Phil Donahue Show*. Then, in the summer of 1993, Hill organized a "Defensive Action" media campaign for Griffin. As part of the campaign, Hill drafted a statement calling for Griffin to be acquitted on the grounds that lethal force is "justifiable provided it was carried out for the purpose of defending the lives of unborn children." Within the next few months, Hill circulated his statement in several versions. It was eventually endorsed by more than two dozen "rescue" movement leaders, including Andrew Burnett; Cathy Ramey and Paul deParrie, of *Life Advocate*; Dave Leach, publisher of the *Prayer and Action News* in Des Moines; and representatives of Missionaries to the Preborn and other aggressive protest groups. Conspicuously absent among the signers of Hill's statement were any remaining national leaders of OR. They were unwilling to take the rap for defending violence. Hill and several writers with *Life Advocate* magazine published a series of position papers arguing a biblical basis for justifiable homicide. Hill circulated a sixteen-page treatise, "Was the Killing of Dr. Gunn Just?," through his Pensacola, Florida, post office box.[58] One version of this position paper was published in *Life Advocate* magazine in August 1993. Citing selected verses of Scripture, including the commandment to "Love your neighbor as yourself," Hill argued that Christians were obliged to "take all action necessary to protect innocent life," even if the use of force is against the law. In fact, Hill raised justifiable homicide as an explicit challenge to the state's defense of abortion doctors.

> There is no question that deadly force should be used to protect innocent life. The question is, *whose life is innocent*—those who kill our children or the children who are being killed? The government believes those who kill our children should be protected. We believe the unborn should be protected. The question then for us is, should we protect innocent life from harm if the government forbids us to do so?
>
> The Golden Rule clearly and irrefutably answers the question in this way: 'Therefore whatever you want others to do for you, do so for them; for this is the Law and the Prophets,' Matthew 7:12.[59]

Thus Hill answered the question about how a "prolifer" could endorse killing; the answer lies in making a careful distinction between "innocent" versus "guilty" victims. But beyond the most salient argument about defending "innocent" life, Hill advocated the use of lethal force as a form of *collective atonement*, as a means to appease the wrath of God and to prevent an entire society from being punished for the sin of abortion. Here it is worth quoting at length from one of Hill's manifestos.

> In addition to defending the innocent from a brutal death, there are other reasons for using force in the abortion controversy. One of these reasons is found in Numbers 35:33. "So you shall not pollute the land in which you are; for blood pollutes the land and no expiation can be made for the land for the blood that is shed on it, except by the blood of him who shed it." Numbers 25 makes a similar point through the example of Phinehas.
>
> Phinehas violently took the lives of two immoral persons in order to turn God's wrath away from the people. Numbers 25 tells us that the Israelites were playing the harlot with Moabite women. God's wrath in the form of a plague, therefore, turned against the people. As a result of the sins committed, Moses and the judges were weeping before the Tabernacle. As Moses and the leaders looked on, Zimri, the son of Salu, brazenly brought a Moabite woman named Cozbi by the weeping leaders. He led her past them and into a tent for immoral purposes. When a priest named Phinehas realized what was happening, he was

filled with zealous jealousy. He then followed them to the tent and checked the plague by driving a spear through them both. The startling truth is that this act was not done by a civil leader or after due legal process. Yet, this zealous act by an individual "made atonement for the sons of Israel." Though sin had fanned god's righteous anger to a searing blaze, the shedding of guilty blood had cooled the flame and saved the people from destruction. . . .

Are there any heinous sins being committed today that could again fan the flames of God's righteous anger to the scorching point? Is there any need in today's world for men of the stamp of Phinehas? If any similar zeal be found among us today, occasion to exercise it will not be lacking.[60]

No doubt Paul Hill conceived of himself as a modern-day Phinehas, obliged to defend Michael Griffin and later to kill an abortion doctor himself as a means to save society from punishment for collective sin. Yet it was this aspect of Hill's justifiable homicide argument that was least likely to win support from fellow antiabortionists, even those who might have endorsed his "protection of innocent life" argument.

Among those to whom Hill sent copies of his manifestos was Dr. Gary North, a well-known Christian author and a leading promoter of Christian Reconstructionism. This doctrine advocates the reinstatement of an Old Testament code of moral law within contemporary society. Such a code would include the death penalty for abortionists, adulterers, sodomites, and other severe "sinners." Hill had been ordained in the Orthodox Presbyterian Church.[61] (Distinct from the better known, liberal Presbyterian Church U.S.A. denomination, the Orthodox Presbyterian Church is conservative and Calvinist in orientation; some of its ministers and lay members subscribe to Reconstructionism.) Gary North also comes from an Orthodox Presbyterian background, and Hill may have expected North to lend legitimacy to his Phinehas priest argument for justifiable homicide. But North did just the opposite. In 1994, North published a pamphlet, *Lone Gunners for Jesus: Letters to Paul J. Hill,* in which he blasted Hill for thinking he could justify killing doctors by using a story from the time of Moses. Though North agreed that abortion is murder, he argued that Hill had no authorization to kill a "murderer," because he was not, by any stretch of the imagination, a Mosaic priest. Hill had, in fact, been excommunicated from his own church.[62]

At one level, North was splitting hairs because he acknowledged that individual believers could be authorized to "kill someone who was committing a moral infraction so great that it would have brought blood guiltiness on the entire community."[63] North's point, though, was that Hill's "autonomous act has placed in jeopardy the lives of perhaps millions of unborn infants, either because of a potential political backlash . . . that will extend the present abortion laws or because of the speeding up of the introduction of abortifacients."[64] North circulated his pamphlet among fellow Reconstructionists in an effort to protect the prolife movement from Hill's reckless application of Old Testament passages. In effect, North threw down a gauntlet, saying that killing doctors could not be justified if the executioners were merely self-appointed Phinehas priests operating outside the boundaries of a Christian theocracy.

Despite North's condemnation of Hill, what was up for debate was the role of Christian citizens within a secular state that condones and even facilitates what North, Hill, and others all consider to be infanticide. Hill's call for a Phinehas priesthood ready to purge the land of sinners was echoed in a toned-down version of the justifiable homicide argument in *A Time to Kill*, a book by Lutheran minister Michael Bray. Bray served prison time for the destruction of seven abortion clinics in the Washington, DC, area, and he was a signer of Hill's Defensive Action petitions. *A Time to Kill* was published and circulated by Advocates for Life Ministries in Portland, Oregon, the same outfit that published the monthly *Life Advocate* magazine.

In the book, Bray goes back and forth between two arguments. The first is that capital punishment is sanctioned by the Bible. He argues that the state is responsible for punishing perpetrators of capital crimes. But because the state is now in the business of helping doctors get away with murder, believers are justified in carrying out their own extrajudicial executions. Bray's second argument is the "defense of necessity," which was Paul Hill's first justification. Individual prolifers have the right, if not the duty, to get up in the morning and do whatever they can to prevent doctors from killing unborn children that day. In his book, Bray stresses the idea that to be prolife is not to be a pacifist. Anyone who says otherwise, including top leaders of OR, are not truly committed to the belief in the personhood of the unborn fetus.

Yet Bray hedges at the end of his book by writing that when he is interviewed about the latest clinic bombing or the shooting of a doctor, he "discriminate[s] between defending the justice of forceful intervention and advocating the same."[65] Bray acknowledges that his rhetoric might seem disingenuous. But there is more to it than that. To *advocate* force, Bray writes, places Christian prolifers in jeopardy because such advocacy makes them de facto opponents of the government and of the existing social order. There is no telling what price might be exacted for such opposition. Yet Bray goes on:

> There is a bit of irony here. The use of force for the purpose of saving innocent lives is arguably much less rebellious than the public stridency expressed in the sit-ins. The fellow who shoots the abortionist or demolishes his slaughter house doesn't necessarily make any public statement to the government. He does not

even address the government. His deed is directed exclusively toward the evil he intends to eradicate; and the children he intends to save. His action suggests that he will not tolerate child killing; his view of government is unknown. On the contrary, those who block doors spend most of their "rescue" efforts face to face with the governing authorities. After a few minutes of sitting by a street in front of a door, he spends hours being arrested, processing through the local police precinct; he spends a day or two in the court room, a few minutes writing a check to the government, and perhaps a few days, weeks, months or years in prison. Throughout the process, he is expressing his opposition—albeit respectfully—to the government's unjust prosecution of himself. He voices his objection to baby killing and politely defies the authorities by sitting and remaining seated in forbidden places.[66]

Bray does not resolve the question of whether individual acts of violence or collective acts of civil disobedience are more provocatively antigovernment. His point is that beyond the deeds of a Michael Griffin or a Paul Hill, the advocacy of justifiable homicide raises the stakes for an entire submovement headed toward an all-out confrontation with a seemingly all-powerful government.

For most of the direct action wing of the antiabortion movement, even those inclined toward clinic vandalism and harassment of clinic personnel, advocacy of outright killing is more rhetorical than tactical. The small number of justifiable homicide apologists have strained their relationships with fellow prolifers. Few of these apologists would actually act on the call to "defend" unborn babies with lethal force. Short of doing as Michael Griffin and Paul Hill have done, continued advocacy seems to serve other purposes, namely, to maintain a sort of sectarian ideological cohesion among the small number of people who endorse justifiable homicide. Through the late 1990s, *Life Advocate* magazine and the *Prayer and Action* newsletter continue to publish articles debating the use of violence. Through selected editorials and news coverage of the prolife movement at large, they also continue to mark boundaries between those willing to condone violence and the rest of the movement, which is deemed insufficiently committed to the cause. *Life Advocate* and *Prayer and Action* function as sort of an underground press for those attracted in some way to the justifiable homicide view. Numerous articles reiterate the arguments in favor of lethal force. In 1996, for example, *Prayer and Action* published instructions from an "Army of God" manual on how to bomb buildings using homemade explosives,[67] and in subsequent issues, editor Dave Leach defended his publication from critics who charged him with inciting violence. There have been frequent articles on the "persecution" of activists who were questioned by federal authorities during a government investigation into possible conspiracies organized by violent prolifers. There also have been frequent editorials against Christian Right spokespersons, including leaders of OR, who publicly disavow violence. *Life Advocate* has editorialized against prolifers who focus on legislative work, particularly those who lobby for a Congressional ban on late-term abortions. Consistently, the apologists for justifiable homicide have refused to endorse campaigns not aimed at eradicating abortion in one fell swoop. That uncompromising stance leaves the tiny proviolence faction on the sidelines of its own movement, which is where its members seem to want to stay.

Partial-Birth Abortion
⌒

One of the workshops at the Christian Coalition's 1996 Road to Victory conference was billed as a session on "new strategies for protecting the unborn." The only new strategy discussed was the effort to ban so-called partial-birth, late-term abortions. All the speakers agreed that "partial birth" abortions are relatively rare. Prochoice advocates know that the procedure is performed only in cases of severe fetal abnormality and in order to safeguard a woman's ability to survive delivery and possibly have more children.[68] But Douglas Johnson, the legislative director for the National Right to Life Committee (NRLC), explained why prolifers decided to focus on this particular type of abortion. Publicity about "partial birth" is useful, he said, in cutting through the public's "screens of denial" about the violence of abortion. Beginning in 1995, the NRLC lobbied for a ban on partial-birth abortions by publishing newspaper advertisements with intentionally graphic drawings of how the procedure occurs. At a time in gestation when a healthy fetus would be large enough to survive premature delivery, the doctor pulls the baby, legs first, out of the mother, leaving only the head inside. The doctor then "jams scissors" into the baby's skull, makes a hole in its head, and with a suction catheter sucks the baby's brains out before finally removing the head. What could be more grisly? How many politicians on the fence about abortion rights could be swayed by grotesque imagery?

At the Christian Coalition workshop, Representative Charles Canady (R-FL) spoke about introducing the first Congressional bill to ban partial-birth abortions in 1995. Canady said his bill never would have passed without the lobbying efforts of the NRLC and the Christian Coalition. In November 1995, the House of Representatives voted overwhelmingly for a bill banning partial-birth abortions. It was the first time in the more than two decades since *Roe v. Wade* that Congress voted directly to ban a type of abortion. The Senate then voted to ban the procedure except to save the life of the mother, and the bill was sent back to the House for adoption of the amended language on exceptions. By early 1996, the presidential campaign season was in full gear. Clinton vetoed the partial-birth bill when it came up again in the spring. Republican supporters of the bill then tried unsuccessfully to make it a defining campaign issue, but they were unable to marshal enough votes to override Clinton's veto.[69] The override, which came up for a vote in the fall of 1996, was a longshot, as it would have required a two-thirds majority vote in both the Senate and the House. That election season, candidate Bob Dole was drowning, and the rest of the Republicans were trying just to keep their heads above water. There was little incentive for them to risk losing moderate, prochoice voters by making partial birth their top, vocal priority.

After Clinton's reelection, though, Republicans took up the issue again. In early 1997, the House voted for a ban on the late-term procedure, by a margin wide enough to override a Clinton veto. Then the Senate passed a similar bill, but not by a veto-proof margin.[70] Toward the end of 1997, the House voted again for a ban. Clinton vetoed the bill, and Senate Republicans appeared unable to muster enough votes for an override.[71]

Antiabortionists were heartened, shortly before the House vote, by the admission of a leading abortion rights advocate that he had lied about partial-birth abortions during the 1996 debate. Ron Fitzsimmons of the National Coalition of Abortion Providers admitted that he had earlier lied when claiming that partial-birth procedures are very rare and done only in cases of severe fetal abnormality or danger to a mother's health.[72] Antiabortionists looked to the long-term possibility of banning late-term abortions, if not first in Congress, then in the states; by 1997, legislative bans were under consideration in twenty-eight states.[73] At the Congressional level, the late-term abortion issue remained stalemated. But it was useful for legislators who could keep telling their constituents back home that they were working hard on the matter, one way or another.

Rescuing Women

◦◦

Outside of the legislative arena, other prolife activists have entrenched themselves for the long project of making abortion, if not illegal, at least less publicly acceptable. In the effort to ban "partial birth," circulation of pictures of dead babies is intended to increase the stigma surrounding abortion. A more benign but no less ambitious project underway is the one to rescue women and unborn babies through crisis pregnancy centers (CPCs), now numbering about three thousand around the country.

CPCs first became popular in the 1980s. They quickly earned a bad reputation for trying to deceive the public about their true intent. That was because several dozen centers sponsored by the St. Louis–based Pearson

Foundation deliberately posed—and advertised in telephone directories—as abortion referral services. The scheme was to lure a woman in to take a free pregnancy test, and if her test result proved to be positive, to then give her a lecture on the health hazards of abortion.[74] A spate of negative press coverage and several lawsuits resulted in most CPCs agreeing to advertise themselves as "abortion alternatives" in a separate section of the yellow pages from abortion clinics.

Today the typical CPC advertises that it offers pregnancy tests, legal and medical advice, infant and maternity clothes, and adoption information, but *not* abortions or abortion referrals.[75] Most of the CPCs are staffed by one paid employee and a dozen or two volunteers. Some CPCs are housed within churches. About one-third of the estimated three thousand CPCs are represented by two umbrella organizations, the Protestant-oriented Christian Action Council (CAC) and the Catholic-oriented Birthright.[76] To help provide coordination, Focus on the Family has a Crisis Pregnancy Center Ministry through which Focus sends the CPCs, free of charge, literature on fetal development and tapes of relevant Focus radio shows.[77] There is no reliable data on how many women visit CPCs—though a *Christianity Today* reporter once estimated seven hundred thousand to one million women annually—let alone how many who visit decide not to have an abortion.[78]

To make the CPCs more professional, to prevent centers from unscrupulous dealings with the public, and to increase the likelihood that women will choose not to have abortions, many of the CPCs have begun to network more closely with one another. In the early 1990s, the CAC—which is incorporated as a lobby—spawned Care Net to provide conferences and how-to guides for the volunteer staff of more than 450 CPCs.[79] Along the same lines, Thomas Glessner, formerly with the CAC, directs the National Institute of Family and Life Advocates (NIFLA), which coordinates legal advice for the CPCs. NIFLA helps CPCs become licensed medical facilities, both to avoid lawsuits and to use technology as a means to persuade women not to abort. Many of the CPCs do little more than offer pregnant women used clothing and nursery items and, because CPCs now advertise that they will not make abortion referrals, therefore attract mostly women intending to have babies, not abortions. Glessner's goal is to change the clientele for CPCs by offering ultrasound and other on-site medical services that he believes will lead women to choose not to abort. Glessner explained his idea in a newspaper interview: "When she views her baby on the sonogram, and asks what the pulsing is on the screen, and the doctor says, 'Well, that's the baby's heart,' you see her whole mind-set turn around. Modern technology is on our side."[80]

While it is patronizing to suggest that women need a machine or a doctor to tell them that pregnancy will lead to childbirth, the approach here is to use persuasion, not coercion, and to see women, to some degree, as decisionmaking agents. While part of the antiabortion movement has moved in the direction of demonizing anyone who performs or has an abortion, the organizers of CPCs seem more resigned to the fact that abortion is and will remain a widespread practice.

With increased professionalization, the CPCs are moving toward more of a medical model—a term Glessner uses—than a model that casts women as criminals and sinners. The CPC staff and volunteers still want to see abortion outlawed, but they know that goal is not foreseeable. For one of its magazine articles on CPCs, Focus on the Family interviewed three women active with CPCs. Frederica Mathewes-Green, a leading writer on the subject, stressed the growth potential for CPC activism, given that most churches that proclaim themselves prolife have not yet gotten involved. "You may feel frustrated because you cannot pass the Human Life Amendment tomorrow, but what you can do tomorrow is volunteer at your CPC and comfort a woman who is in need," said Mathewes-Green, who also believes she can find common ground with prochoice people regarding what she calls "post-abortion healing."[81] To her credit, Mathewes-Green strongly advocates that CPCs move beyond the goal of "saving" babies to making adoption a practical alternative for women who truly would like to go that route.[82]

Closely linked to the CPC view of women as morally receptive, decisionmaking agents is the idea of women as *victims*: of abortion doctors, of bad information, of pressure from husbands and boyfriends. Some of the CPC activists are women who themselves once had an abortion, and they are more willing than the rest of the prolife movement to acknowledge how widespread abortion is among Christians. Mathewes-Green cites the figure, based on a survey by the Alan Guttmacher Institute, that one out of every six women having an abortion considers herself to be a born-again Christian.[83] In an article on postabortive depression and regret, *Charisma* magazine suggested that 25% of the women sitting in churches on any given Sunday have had an abortion.[84] The guilt and regret such women feel is no doubt genuine, but it is also exacerbated by the constant condemnation from within the evangelical subculture. A number of organizations, including Care Net, Heartbeat International, and the National Office of Post-Abortion Reconciliation and Healing, are working to develop CPCs into places where women can come for counseling and support groups *after* they have had abortions.[85]

It is hard to achieve emotional healing after undergoing an abortion when one's fellow believers—and much of the political establishment—keep insisting that abortion is murder. The CPCs may help some women make a *choice* that is best for them, and this is the personal angle of the antiabortion project. But the personal is also political. The broader effect of rescuing individual women and babies is to hold the antiabortion crusade in abeyance at a time when the legislative battle is at a standstill. By keeping the antiabortion flame burning, the prolife movement ensures its own longevity and guarantees that abortion will remain an unyielding axis of political conflict.

Chapter 8

∽

The Antigay Agenda

According to the Christian Right, homosexuals want to make promotion of homosexuality and all forms of sexual perversion a mandatory part of the curriculum at all levels of public education. They want to legalize any kind of sex between adults and young children. They enjoy disproportionately high salaries, take more vacations than the average American, and wield undue influence at all levels of government, media, and the corporate sector. Some of them deliberately go out and spread the AIDS virus. Most of them engage in violent and disgusting sexual practices, dangerous to their own health.

Above all, they want everyone else to see, know about, and condone their vile acts. "Radical homosexuals in America today," wrote Concerned Women for America president Beverly LaHaye in a 1991 fundraising letter, "DO NOT want to be simply left alone. Instead, they have *a hidden agenda* to legally force you and every other American to accept their depraved 'lifestyle.' . . . Parents across America have told me that they fear homosexuals want to *own* their kids' minds, bodies and souls."[1]

During the 1990s, the Christian Right's vilification of homosexuals reached an all-time high. In recent times, gays and lesbians have been subjected to a relentless barrage of scurrilous attacks. Nor have the antigay campaigns been merely rhetorical. Hateful words about gays and lesbians have been crafted in service to the goal of forestalling the extension of full legal rights and protections to one of the last groups of citizens for whom discrimination is still sanctioned by law. In picking on a group of people for whom the general public often shows little sympathy, organizers of the Christian Right find a profitable target, a symbol for the putative liberal attack on the traditional family.

The 1990s antigay campaigns, despite their mixed results, have been well suited to the Christian Right's own organizational makeup. Ballot initiatives have been fought at the local level by the movement's energetic grassroots forces. Congressmembers were lobbied against lifting the ban on openly gay military personnel. Some candidates for public office have chosen to take cheap shots at opponents deemed insufficiently homophobic. There is plenty of money to be made in the production of antigay videos and literature. And as we will see in this chapter, all the while, the Christian Right professes its ability to rehabilitate homosexuals through dubious psychological counseling ministries.

The antigay agenda was born in the 1970s, shared the stage with other Christian Right preoccupations in the 1980s, and rose to prominence again in the 1990s. In 1977, the Dade County, Florida, board of commissioners passed an ordinance protecting gays and lesbians from discrimination in housing, employment, and public accommodations. From a liberal point of view, this act was progressive; homosexuality then was hardly the openly discussed topic it is today. The gay rights movement was still in its infancy; it had been born in 1969, in New York City, when police made a routine raid on a gay bar, the Stonewall Inn, and the patrons fought back, for the first time. The Dade County ordinance might not have made national headlines if it weren't for the backlash it provoked. Singer Anita Bryant was then a spokesperson for the Florida orange juice industry—TV ads had her grinning and telling everyone that "a day without orange juice is like a day without sunshine." Bryant was also a born-again Christian and a friend of Phyllis Schlafly who was, in 1977, organizing against the Equal Rights Ammendment (ERA). Bryant launched a ballot initiative to repeal the Dade County ordinance, and it passed by a wide margin. Bryant's campaign was a wake-up call for gay rights advocates who, in the late 1970s, succeeded in passing antidiscrimination ordinances in a handful of cities. Without skipping a beat, one of Anita Bryant's allies, California state senator John Briggs, placed on his state's 1978 ballot an initiative that would have allowed public school boards to ban openly gay teachers. The Briggs initiative was defeated, but some of its key backers, including Reverend Louis Sheldon of the Traditional Values Coalition, would remain committed to the anti–gay rights mission.

By 1980, national Christian Right organizations were focused on electing Ronald Reagan to the presidency. As governor of California, Reagan had opposed the Briggs initiative,[2] but by 1980 he was eager to court the likes of Jerry Falwell and others for whom homosexuality is an abomination. In 1981, thinking he could score points with the Christian Right, Reagan appointed Dr. C. Everett Koop as surgeon general of the United States. Koop was a well-known evangelical and an opponent of abortion rights. But he also took seriously his role as public physician, and in the face of the AIDS epidemic, Koop defended the need for federal funding of sexually instructive AIDS education in the schools.[3] Koop and other responsible policymakers were opposed time and again by homophobic lawmakers—led by Senator Jesse Helms. Helms sponsored a series of unsuccessful antigay bills to ban federal funding for everything from AIDS education to sex surveys that included questions about homosexuality, on the grounds that such funding is tantamount to "promoting" homosexuality.[4]

The AIDS epidemic put questions about homosexual "behavior" on the national radar screen. Initially, AIDS was considered a "gay disease," and that perception coincided with the growing strength and coordination of Christian Right organizations. AIDS inspired a cottage industry in the publication of antigay propaganda. Paul Cameron, whom I discuss in more depth later in this chapter, issued pamphlets charging homosexuals with deliberately spreading the virus. While the AIDS epidemic devastated the gay community and fanned the flames of homophobia, gay activists knew they had to organize to secure their civil rights. During the 1980s, numerous city councils and a few state legislatures passed antidiscrimination laws. The Christian Right was then, in the 1980s, broadly focused on issues ranging from stopping abortion to raising support for anticommunist forces in Central America. By the end of the 1980s, it was clear that homosexuals were gaining increasing political representation and public acceptance. With the end of the Cold War and the stalemate nature of the abortion conflict, leaders of the Christian Right needed new issues to galvanize their followers. The brouhaha over federal funding for "obscene" art fit the bill, but the opportunities for action on this front were limited to lobbying Congress. Anti–gay rights ballot initiatives were expedient because they fostered the Christian Right's shift toward a grassroots orientation and allowed activists to fight as if they were the victims of aggressive homosexuals pursuing "special rights." In reality, the local and state initiative campaigns were not entirely of the grass roots and spontaneous. Leaders from national organizations served as advisers to some of the local players who were new to politics.[5] It was the combination of old experience with the new furor over "special rights" that made the antigay agenda a viable project for the Christian Right in the early 1990s. Then, in 1996, the Supreme Court ruled discriminatory ballot initiatives unconstitutional, leaving antigay organizers focused on fighting same-sex marriage and continuing to circulate bigoted propaganda. At each phase of the Christian Right's history, the activists most preoccupied with homosexuality have adjusted to shifting possibilities for action.

Special Rights and Videotape

✑

In the effort to thwart the expansion of gay civil rights in the 1990s, one early milestone was the furor that ensued in 1993 when the newly inaugurated Clinton administration announced its intention to lift the ban on openly gay military personnel. Emerging seemingly out of nowhere, Ty and Jeannette Beeson of the Antelope Valley Springs of Life church in Lancaster, California, suddenly made headlines with their nationwide promotion of *The Gay Agenda,* a twenty-minute video featuring scenes from gay pride marches and interviews with antigay doctors, all to the effect that gays threaten social stability. *The Gay Agenda* made its debut during the 1992 anti–gay rights ballot initiative campaigns in Oregon and Colorado, discussed below. But soon after the controversy over gays in the military broke out, Pat Robertson broadcast *The Gay Agenda* for the one million viewers of his *700 Club* program.[6] Antigay military officers showed *The Gay Agenda* at prayer breakfasts and Bible-study meetings.[7] The film was an effective piece of propaganda in the campaign, led by Christian broadcasters in early 1993, to flood Congress with phone calls against the lifting of the ban.[8] Under pressure from the Christian Right and from top military brass, Clinton ultimately reneged on his promise to lift the ban.

The Christian Right and many military leaders were deathly afraid that inclusion of homosexual GIs would threaten the health and sexual well-being of those charged with defending the republic. Dr. D. James Kennedy of Coral Ridge Ministries in Florida outlined his fears of the gays-in-the-military threat in a 1993 fundraising letter sent to supporters in 1993:

> Honorable and decent men and women of the military should never be forced to shower, share latrines, and bunker with homosexuals who find them *sexually attractive.* Not to mention the devastating effect this would have on the *morale* of our troops.
>
> Further, military leaders know there's no pure blood supply during time of war. During a medical emergency, blood is often obtained from the soldier closest to the injured victim.
>
> *What if the blood-giver has AIDS?* There's no way to find out on the battlefield. . . .
>
> Honestly . . . would you want your son, daughter, or grandchild sharing a shower, foxhole, *or blood with a homosexual?* [emphasis in original][9]

It is, of course, irrational to fear that diseased GIs will be sent into combat or that homosexuals will seduce heterosexuals and convert them into homosexuals. The goal of Kennedy's exemplary piece of direct mail was to bypass what could have been a civil national debate on military policy by, instead, going straight for the jugular vein.

Only slightly less visceral has been the "no special rights" theme used in antigay ballot initiative campaigns. Beginning in the 1980s, scores of cities and more than a dozen states passed ordinances and bills to protect gays and lesbians from housing and employment discrimination, the stated goal being to extend existing laws against racial and gender discrimination.

Yet the Christian Right attacks gay rights protections as a form of "special rights" and as part of a grand plot to force straight America to accept homosexual sex acts as being morally neutral and/or as "natural" as heterosexual sex acts. The idea is to cast civil rights as a limited pie: if one group gets more rights, it can only be at the expense of another group's rights. In reality, the extension of civil rights to homosexual citizens would reinforce the fundamental principle that everyone should have equal rights. But rather than admit that their goal is to actively deprive gay citizens of legal remedies for the acts of discrimination they endure, Christian Right organizers claim that gays are out to get something on top of what everyone else deserves. The "special rights" theme relies on the argument that sexual orientation is not, in fact, the basis for widespread discrimination and that gays simply want to win "legitimacy" for their deviant behavior by putting it on a par with immutable characteristics such as skin color or ethnicity.

After the success of *The Gay Agenda* video, Louis Sheldon's Traditional Values Coalition, in conjunction with Jeremiah Films, produced *Gay Rights, Special Rights,* a forty-minute video aimed explicitly at conservative people of color. This video begins with footage of Dr. Martin Luther King Jr.'s famous 1963 March on Washington. It then moves quickly into a tedious mix of footage of gay rights marches, with scenes of gay people kissing and taking their clothes off, intercut with shots of young children's angelic faces and interviews with "experts" on how the extension of legal protections to gay people would diminish hard-won civil rights for people of color. In 1993, fifty thousand copies of this video were sold through churches and Christian bookstores, and it was also used successfully by antigay activists in Cincinnati during a campaign to rally support for the repeal of a local gay rights ordinance.[10]

With the "no special rights" theme, antigay organizers strike several chords at once. They offer multiple messages for their multiple audiences. For conservative people of color, the message is that gay rights diminish the value of legitimate protections against racism. For advantaged whites who are weary of one group after another demanding rights—African Americans, women, the disabled, criminal defendants, now gays—the message is: "Enough is enough. One's lifestyle should not entitle one to special treatment by the rest of us." For the broadest possible audience, "no special rights" is a device to shift discourse away from moralistic jargon about sin and sodomy. The general public is averse to making a religious creed the arbiter of public policy. In a democracy, everyone agrees that no one should get "special rights." Gay rights supporters are placed in a defensive mode, forced to persuade a largely homophobic public that, despite their sexual "deviance," when it comes to legal rights, they are as all-American as apple pie.[11]

The "no special rights" theme was crafted specifically for ballot measures aimed at preempting state and local gay rights laws. Its utility is lessened now that such ballot initiatives have been ruled unconstitutional by the Supreme Court. The theme will recur, though, in any legal challenge to discrimination against gays, as in the coming conflicts over gay marriage.

Ballot Measures

ᴄᴧᴐ

In May 1996, the Supreme Court struck down Colorado's Amendment 2, on the basis that homosexuals cannot constitutionally be singled out for exemption from rights that apply to everyone else, particularly protection from discrimination in housing, employment, and access to public accommodations. The Court's ruling sounded a death knell for what was, up until that point, the Christian Right's chief means of organizing against gay rights—and against increasing public acceptance of gay and lesbian people. Will Perkins, a leader of Colorado for Family Values, which sponsored Amendment 2, called the Court ruling "a truly chilling day for people of conscience across America." "Those forces," he said, "bent on forcing a deviant life style down the throats of the American people have moved a long step forward in making government their pet bully."[12]

Ballot measures to preempt or overturn local gay rights ordinances were, for several years, among the Christian Right's chief projects. The strategy first gained hold in Oregon, in 1988. There the governor had issued an order prohibiting employment discrimination based on sexual orientation in the executive branch of the state government. The then little known Oregon Citizens Alliance (OCA) had been unsuccessful at running a candidate for U.S. Senate and promoting a ballot measure to end Medicaid funding for abortion. An antigay campaign was just what the OCA needed to remain a player in Oregon politics. While Portland is considered a bastion of liberalism, people in the rural parts of the state tend to be more religious and conservative. They proved receptive to the idea that gay rights equals "special rights," and before gay rights proponents knew what they were up against, in 1988 OCA placed on the state ballot a measure to repeal the governor's order. It passed handily.[13]

On a roll, the OCA next drafted Measure 9, the Abnormal Behaviors Initiative, timed for the 1992 election season. With this proposed amendment to Oregon's constitution, OCA went way beyond blocking "special rights." The first draft of the measure lumped homosexuality together with bestiality and necrophilia. The final draft language of the measure banned state protections or funding for "promotion" of homosexuality, pedophilia, sadism, and masochism—as if the latter three predilections are linked somehow to gay civil rights. OCA raised the specter that allowing a gay group to meet in a public library is somehow akin to promoting violence and child abuse. OCA succeeded in polarizing Oregon voters, and the circulation of vicious antigay propaganda had the effect of increasing the incidents of death threats against and violent attacks on gay people.[14] Ultimately, Measure 9 was defeated by 57% to 43%, largely because of heavy turnout in liberal, populous Portland. But in twenty-one out of thirty-six counties, the measure passed. All told, more than half a million Oregon voters approved the idea of using a constitutional amendment to condemn homosexuality as a perversion.[15]

Meanwhile, in Colorado, the "no special rights" project was a bit less vulgar but no less vigorous. There the anti–gay rights ballot campaign began after the Denver city council, in 1990, approved an ordinance banning discrimination based on sexual orientation in housing, employment, and public accommodations. The following year, the city council in Colorado Springs considered doing the same thing. But by then numerous evangelical groups had established headquarters in Colorado Springs. They organized successfully and prevented the city council from adding sexual orientation to the city bylaws as a category protected from discrimination. That victory for the local Christian Right inspired the formation of Colorado for Family Values (CFW), which set out to preempt any new local gay rights laws with an amendment to the state constitution. CFV drew financial support from Will Perkins, a Colorado Springs Chrysler dealer, and from Bill Armstrong, who had just retired as the state's U.S. Senator. Armstrong's good reputation in Colorado made it unlikely that the state's Republican leadership would step across party lines and ally themselves with progay rights forces.[16] For the 1992 election, the antigay activists crafted Amendment 2 strictly in terms of "no special rights," without resorting to crude language about homosexual "perversion." CFV focused on the idea that "real" minorities would lose ground if the definition of minority status were broadened to include sexual orientation. Compared with the higher rhetorical volume around Oregon's Measure 9, the somewhat more subtle approach of CFV was a factor in the passage of Amendment 2, by 53% to 47%.[17]

CFV was founded by two local men, Kevin Tebedo and Tony Marco. CFV succeeded, in part, thanks to assistance from a national movement already in place. CFV's original board of advisers included activists from local outposts of the Traditional Values Coalition, Focus on the Family, Concerned Women for America, and the Eagle Forum.[18] The National Legal Foundation, a Virginia-based Christian law firm founded by Pat Robertson but no longer affiliated with him, helped CFV formulate the ballot language for Amendment 2. The National Legal Foundation advised CFV to use the "no special rights" slogan in campaign materials for Amendment 2, but not in the legal formulation of the initiative.[19] "Special rights" was a conscious propaganda theme, recognized by Christian Right strategists as something that would arouse voters.

Amendment 2 was swiftly challenged in court; it was ruled unconstitutional by a Colorado judge in 1993 and by the U.S. Supreme Court in 1996. But before the unconstitutionality of such matters was decided by the Court, Amendment 2 inspired several local ballot campaigns to ban gay rights protections. In Cincinnati, in 1993, Citizens for Community Values, led by Phil Burress, sponsored a successful ballot measure that repealed the city's antidiscrimination ordinance. Then, in 1994, after the Austin, Texas, city council approved domestic partnership benefits for city employees, a local Baptist preacher organized a ballot measure that quickly led to repeal of the ordinance.[20] The Oregon Citizens Alliance spawned the formation of counterpart groups in Idaho, Nevada, and Washington State. In these states as well as in several others, Christian Right activists tried, with mixed success, to qualify anti–gay rights initiatives for their ballots.

Thus, during the mid-1990s, gay rights activists were kept on a permanent state of alert defending the gay community from anti–gay rights measures. Fighting the Christian Right's initiatives cost energy, time, and money, and kept countless progressive activists from moving forward on other issues.

Moreover, the Christian Right's years of antigay organizing created a climate that contributed to increasing incidents of harassment and violence against gay people. Reported incidents have included everything from death threats to the removal of gay-positive books from public libraries and schools. Beginning in 1993, the lobbying group People for the American Way released an annual report, *Hostile Climate,* documenting antigay incidents state by state. Some were ludicrous, such as the time when the parent of a California kindergartner protested the classroom viewing of *Sesame Street* because characters Bert and Ernie lived together and were therefore "promoting" homosexuality. Most of the incidents have been far more consequential: expulsion of Baptist churches by their denominations for allowing gay and lesbian parishioners; violent attacks on gay and lesbian high school students; defeat of a Texas state bill that would have stiffened penalties for hate crimes based on sexual orientation; and routine appeals to city councils and county commissions to prevent or repeal gay rights ordinances.[22]

Not all of the attacks come from identifiable members of Christian Right organizations. But by making a priority of the antigay agenda, the movement has forestalled the day when gays and lesbians can expect to be treated with common decency and as full citizens.

Going Straight

∽

At evangelical and Christian Right gatherings, one often finds pamphlets for local affiliates of Exodus International, the California-based umbrella group for some two hundred counseling ministries intent on converting homosexuals out of their "lifestyle." The implication is not that some of the churchgoers themselves might be gay, but, rather, that there is help available for their gay loved ones. The other message is that Christians who are fighting vigorously to stop gay rights are still righteous because while they hate the "sin," they love the "sinner." For evangelical Christians, redemption from sin is always just around the corner. In fact, there is a tradition, particularly among pentecostals, of recounting the depths to which one had sunk before finding the Lord and turning away from drugs, violence, and all manner of perversion. Talk shows on the evangelical broadcasting networks often feature riveting testimonies of conversion from wretchedness to righteousness. The deeper a sinner sinks, the more amazing the grace that saves him or her.

Given this mindset, it is no wonder the ex-gay counseling project has been so popular. There is no telling how many lesbians and gays have been counseled to truly repent for their homosexual feelings and behavior. There may be many homosexuals (so stigmatized by the widespread homophobia that is fanned by the Christian Right) who would choose to go "straight" through therapy if they could. There is a debate as to whether homosexuality is genetic or chosen, or a little of both. The American Psychiatric Association has found no scientific basis for the idea that gays can be counseled out of their sexual orientation.[23] But, some "ex-gays" claim that this is exactly what happened to them when they converted to Christ, and they then decided to set themselves apart as role models for other gays and lesbians.

In 1995, two gay reporters working independently in different parts of the country each went undercover into one of Exodus' ex-gay ministries. Both men were told by their Exodus counselors to immerse themselves in a full-time regimen of Christian activities—nonstop group therapy sessions, Bible studies, and church services—as if by keeping themselves busy they could push "sin" out of their lives. Both reporters found counselors eager to probe their life stories for evidence that childhood hurts and failed relationships were responsible for their sexual deviance—as if gay people suffer more than heterosexuals from child abuse and later hardships.[24]

No doubt, some ex-gays truly believe they have been "saved" from homosexuality. Their belief then bolsters the claims of ex-gay counselors that homosexuality is a sin that only Christ can heal. In 1994, as the opposition to gay rights remained at the top of the Christian Right's political agenda, Focus on the Family drove this point home with a magazine cover story on ex-gay Christians.

One who gave her testimony was Jamie Breedlove. She had first "fallen into" homosexuality following the tragic death of the young man she had hoped to marry, when she had an affair with her Bible college roommate. Jamie remained a Christian, though she went from one lesbian liaison to another. Her parents were crushed, and their devastation caused her to struggle with the question of whether she would be kept out of heaven because of her sin. Finally, she met her future husband. He knew she was a lesbian, but he still wanted to date her. Jamie married Ben and gave up her "sinful lifestyle." Together, they started His Heart North, a Colorado ministry for homosexuals seeking change and for people with AIDS. The magazine photo of their smiling faces, along with those of their two cute children, serves as evidence that Jamie has truly been saved.[25]

The point of Jamie's testimony and similar stories recounted in the evangelical press is to preach one, and only one, path to personal happiness. Left unexamined are questions of what "lifestyle" Jamie might have chosen had she not been stigmatized by her own parents and by a religious dogma that would bar her from heaven. Might she have avoided years' worth of painful guilt, started another kind of family, and still, also, become a helpful counselor? The happy ending of Jamie's story is all well and good. But her story tells us that "straight" is the only way to go, thereby reinforcing the prerogative of Christians working to deprive gays and lesbians of the right to live and tell a different kind of story.

Queer Experts
∽

Happy-ending ex-gay stories, irrespective of the sincerity of those who tell them, are used by the Christian Right in tandem with even cruder and more aggressive forms of propaganda. The ex-gay stories were regular features of the *Lambda Report on Homosexuality,* published during the 1990s by Peter LaBarbera, first in newsletter form, later as a tabloid newspaper. LaBarbera began his activist career as a writer for Reed Irvine's Accuracy in Media, became a reporter for the conservative *Washington Times,* worked as a freelance reporter based in Nicaragua, and then served as the editor of Concerned Women for America's *Family Voice* magazine. He eventually became captivated by the ins and outs of homosexuality and hooked up with Ty and Jeannette Beeson, producers of the *Gay Agenda* video. The Beesons initially bankrolled LaBarbera's *Lambda Report,* though it was LaBarbera who did all of the reporting on what homosexuals "really do."[26] To gather data, LaBarbera scoured the gay press and frequented gay bookstores and public events, always on the lookout for new dirt about the evil doings of gay people. Among his most startling exposés, LaBarbera reported that the United Nations had granted consultative status to the International Lesbian and Gay Association which included, among its member groups, the North American Man/Boy Love Association. Then, for months, LaBarbera touted this tidbit as evidence that the mainstream gay movement condones pedophilia.[27] And if that was not enough, LaBarbera attended a Leather Pride conference—coinciding with the 1994 twenty-fifth-anniversary Stonewall celebrations in New York City—and there he found a director of the National Gay and Lesbian Task Force speaking on a panel entitled "Creating the Leather Agenda."[28] Interspersed with LaBarbera's investigative reporting were graphic descriptions of shocking gay "lifestyle" practices, with a particular emphasis on anal intercourse. For a readership gripped with lurid fascination, LaBarbera portrayed gay people as uniformly consumed by perversion. The only exceptions were the former homosexuals, featured in almost every issue of the *Lambda Report,* who had been counseled by Exodus International's ex-gay ministries and who were now on the road to recovery. By including the ex-gay stories, LaBarbera seemed to want to soften the impression that he was simply obsessed with gay sex acts.

LaBarbera is one of a handful of antigay activists whose "expertise" circulates widely within the Christian Right. Among other "experts," the best known is Paul Cameron, a former psychology instructor who founded the Family Research Institute in 1987, as a vehicle to circulate antigay propaganda. In the early 1980s, Cameron ran the Institute for the Scientific Investigation of Sexuality, which did little but publish outrageous antigay pamphlets, distributed widely at Christian Right gatherings. In one pamphlet, *Medical Aspects of Homosexuality,* Cameron claims that "of all the vices, only homosexuality constitutes a conspiracy against society," and that "homosexual habits pose a much greater threat to public health than smoking." That, he claims, is because homosexuals' sexual habits involve "extensive unsanitary contacts with excrement"; thus gays have much higher rates of all sorts of infectious diseases, not even counting AIDS. Homosexuals, according to Cameron, spread diseases by shaking hands with strangers and by using public restrooms.[29] After Cameron claimed in other pamphlets that gays are disproportionately responsible for child molestation and other violent crimes, the American Psychological Association investigated him, found that he misrepresented research, and expelled him from the Association in 1983.[30]

But by then the AIDS epidemic had given Cameron an expanded audience for his fear-mongering pseudoscience. In the early to mid-1980s, much of the public knew little about how AIDS was actually transmitted. Cameron exploited public fears and called for a quarantine of gay people regardless of their health status.³¹ At one point, Cameron was hired as a consultant to California Congressmember William Dannemeyer while he served on the House Energy and Commerce Subcommittee which had jurisdiction over the funding of AIDS research. Upon Cameron's advice, Dannemeyer proposed a national ban on blood donations by gay men, including monogamous gay men.³²

Still, Cameron has never been considered too far beyond the pale to be forced out of Christian Right circles. In fact, at the 1994 Christian Coalition Road to Victory conference, Cameron was on hand selling copies of his book *The Gay Nineties,* which he published at the height of the gays-in-the-military controversy. In the book, Cameron reiterates some of his earlier claims: that a majority of gays eat feces during sex; that they account for an unusual number of society's serial killers; and that some AIDS sufferers deliberately go out and infect others with the disease.³³ Cameron's antigay writings are shockingly vulgar—just the sort of material that fuels a deep, irrational hatred of lesbians and gays among those who take his writings seriously.

One of the central themes in the propaganda arsenal is the notion that homosexuals wield disproportional political power. They are to be feared and envied. They are conspiratorial and successful because they enjoy the backing of the liberal establishment. Paradoxically, while people in the Christian Right amass political influence within the Republican Party, they at the same time project that quest for power onto their gay enemies.

Two prominent antigay groups have promoted the theme of excessive gay political power through fictional accounts of the "gay agenda." During the months when Colorado's Amendment 2 was under legal challenge, its sponsor, Colorado for Family Values, added to its monthly newsletter serialized excerpts from an unpublished novel, *Colorado 1998,* in which homosexuals take control of the government and exact revenge against Bible-believing Christians. In one vignette, four-year-old Heather is taken from her family and placed in foster care after her teachers identify her as a problem child "being home schooled in a right-wing homophobic home." When Heather's mother refuses to comply with a family court order to undergo a Queer Sensitivity Services training session, the child is told she will never see her parents again.³⁴

Conspiracies by gay and progay government officials is also the theme of *The Lambda Conspiracy,* a novel published by the otherwise reputable Moody Press. In this tale, a cabal of gay male New Agers secretly control the White House and plot the assassination of a Christian U.S. Senator while he is speaking at an evangelical broadcasters' convention. The hero is a young TV journalist who tries to expose the assassination plot. Along the way, he becomes a born-again Christian and falls in love with an attractive young woman. Spenser Hughes, author of the *The Lambda Conspiracy,* was a featured guest at a supposedly factual 1994 Washington,

DC, briefing on the "gay agenda" conducted by Louis Sheldon's Traditional Values Coalition, which sold the book through its newsletter.[35]

Among antigay propagandists, the line between fact and fiction is virtually nonexistent. Many evangelicals assume that the secular press hides the truth about homosexuality, thus giving greater credibility to authors who abuse respectable science and history and whose goal is to paint homosexuals in as horrible a light as possible. One subtext of antigay literature is the charge that secular scholarship and media accounts are fraudulent. Thus, the more far-fetched the antigay stories become, the more compelling they are, as with the 1995 book *The Pink Swastika: Homosexuality in the Nazi Party.* Coauthored by Oregon Citizens Alliance (OCA) leader Scott Lively, the book was originally marketed through OCA's own mailing list and later by other movement groups. In the preface, coauthor Kevin E. Abrams explains the book's purpose:

> *The Pink Swastika* is a response to the "gay political agenda" and its strategy of portraying homosexuals as victims of societal and Nazi persecution. Although some homosexuals, and many of those who were framed with trumped-up charges of homosexuality, suffered and died at the hands of the Nazis, for gay apologists to portray themselves as historical victims of Nazi persecution, on par with the Jewish people, is a gross distortion of history, perhaps equal to denying the Holocaust itself.[36]

From there Lively and Abrams weave a bizarre tale to the effect that homosexuality was at the very core of Nazism, and that homosexuals were not, in fact, among the groups targeted by the Nazis for extermination. Much of the book revolves around dubious comparisons between present-day gay rights activists and the old Nazi Brownshirts. The message is that the contemporary gay rights movement harkens back to Nazism and should therefore be viewed with the requisite fear and loathing.

The Pink Swastika was self-published and has not appeared to enjoy wide circulation. It is disreputable, but nevertheless intended to disallow gay rights supporters from making rhetorical connections with other targets of bigotry. In that regard, it is similar to the *Gay Rights, Special Rights* video with its theme that people of color have no good reason to ally themselves with gay rights advocates.

Unholy Matrimony

ᏆᏯ

"Adam and Eve, not Adam and Steve." The slogan is popular on right-wing call-in shows and on protest signs at gay rights marches. It captures the essence of what the Christian Right fears about homosexuals: that their unions, by definition, threaten biblical order and traditional gender relations.

Building on the networks established during years of anti–gay rights organizing, the Christian Right prepared to fight gay marriage on many fronts. In 1996, the Cincinnati office of Phil Burress's Citizens for Community Values became the headquarters for the National Campaign to Protect Marriage. Its first steering committee consisted of leaders from the American Family Association, Colorado for Family Values, the Traditional Values Coalition, the Family Research Council, and Concerned Women for America. By May 1996, the campaign had a contact person in almost all fifty states, and had drafted a proposed "marriage protection resolution" to be introduced in each state as needed. The creators of the successful *Gay Agenda* video produced another one titled *The Ultimate Target of the Gay Agenda: Same Sex Marriage,* which was promoted and sold by all of the participating organizations.[37] The 1996 video consists of interviews with a series of antigay activists, all to the effect that gay marriage is an oxymoron, but that if its legalized and normalized, this would mean an end to the norm of heterosexual monogamy.

The start of the 1996 Republican primary season coincided with the specter that same-sex marriage was about to be ruled legal in the state of Hawaii. Eager to exploit the antigay agenda for all it was worth, an ad hoc group called the National Campaign to Protect Marriage organized a rally in Des Moines the weekend before Iowa's primary vote, and challenged all the GOP candidates to sign a pledge opposing same-sex marriage. Candidates Bob Dole, Steve Forbes, and Lamar Alexander complied. Candidates Patrick Buchanan, Alan Keyes, and Phil Gramm made personal appearances at the rally,[38] which was duly aired on C-SPAN. It was the first time that an explicitly anti–gay rights rally was also a major presidential campaign stop.

From there the Christian Right hoped to make gay marriage the hottest issue in the presidential campaign of 1996. It would have been had not President Clinton endorsed the so-called Defense of Marriage Act (DOMA) which was crafted by Republican legislators and moved quickly through Congress during the campaign season. DOMA defined marriage as a relationship between one man and one woman and gave states the right to recognize or not recognize same-sex marriages performed in other states. While DOMA won overwhelming support in both the House and the Senate in the summer of 1996, by then several dozen state legislatures had already passed or were considering their own bills to ban same-sex marriage.[39]

Quick and expedient action from legislators temporarily headed off a firestorm from the Christian Right and prevented the gay marriage issue from dominating the 1996 elections. But DOMA and the bills in the state legislatures only forestalled a national controversy over gay marriage, and leaders of the Christian Right knew this. In December 1996, a circuit court judge ruled that in Hawaii there was no "compelling state interest" in denying marriage licenses to three gay couples who had sued the state for the right to marry five years earlier.[40] The circuit court judge's ruling was appealed to the Hawaii Supreme Court; as of this writing, the case has not yet been decided.

At the Christian Coalition's 1996 Road to Victory conference, attorney Jay Sekulow announced that the American Center for Law and Justice (ACLJ) planned to open a legal office in all fifty states by the year 2000, specifically to fight gay marriage. In Hawaii, the ACLJ represented eight state legislators who opposed the circuit court judge's pro–gay rights ruling. Sekulow called the fight against gay marriage "the greatest challenge" of his career. Sekulow anticipated hundreds of lawsuits involving gay couples married in Hawaii and then attempting to gain legal recognition of their marriages in other states.[41]

For the ACLJ and the rest of the antigay apparatus, the fight against gay marriage is a cloud with a silver lining. They know they might lose but they can build big war chests and big reputations in the process. Ideologically, the gay marriage issue crystallizes the Christian Right's fears about the role of government in facilitating any kind of alternative to the traditional family—and a breakdown of firm sex roles. In a newsletter promoting the DOMA bill in the spring of 1996, Gary Bauer of the Family Research Council summarized the threat:

> Now, a tiny segment of a tiny fraction of the population—the homosexual activist community—is on the verge of radically redefining marriage and family. If they succeed, all distinctions based on sex may fall, and the worst aspects of the rejected Equal Rights Amendment will be imposed. Homosexuals will gain the "right" to adopt children; school children will be taught that homosexual sex is the equivalent of marital love between husband and wife; businesses will be forced to subsidize homosexual relationships; churches will be pushed outside the civil law; and government power will be wielded against anyone who holds the biblical view of homosexuality.[42]

Beyond the legal implications of gay marriage in terms of tax, insurance, adoption, and employment policies, Will Perkins of Colorado for Family Values emphasizes that

> the best argument against granting legal status to homosexual "marriage" is that it would affirm homosexuality to an extent we never have before. Do we really want to vote to give homosexuality society's "Badge of Approval"?

Once society affirms homosexual "marriage," how will we refuse them the rest of their agenda? How do we deny them minority status, or affirmative curricula in the schools?[43]

From the standpoint of evangelical Christianity, as Charles Colson explained in one of his *Christianity Today* magazine columns, gay marriage threatens "the public good" because "accepting homosexuals privately is not the same thing as normalizing homosexuality by granting homosexuals a legal right to the public institution of marriage."[44] Colson is bothered not so much by what homosexuals do behind closed doors but by the idea that society would remold "the fundamental social institution by which we unite our lives in family and kinship relationships." Tampering with this "objective moral order," Colson argues,

assumes that the universe is malleable and that individuals create their own truths, their own values. Sexuality has no intrinsic purpose, it is merely an opportunity for pleasure, intimacy, and reproduction. Family structure is as pliable as Play-Doh, and virtually any form is acceptable.[45]

Here Colson takes the rhetorical high ground, casting his opposition to gay marriage in philosophical terms about order and enduring truths. Others, less lofty, have been more willing to articulate their visceral fears about gay sexuality. In the same ACLJ newsletter in which Jay Sekulow pledged to fight gay marriage in the courts, ACLJ executive director Keith Fournier reacted this way:

Homosexual living arrangements under the guise of marriage are not only sterile, incapable, and insufficient, they are destructive to the very fabric of our society. The strategy to inculturate active homosexual practice into our society as a favored institution is synonymous with injecting a cancer into a healthy body. Homosexual marriage directly attacks the family which is the most vital cell in society. The family is the first government, the first church, and the first school. We must not allow this vital cell, the rock upon which society is built, to be inculturated with a perversion that will destroy it, and with it the future of our children and grandchildren.[46]

The cancer image, at the most obvious level, is an allusion to gays as carriers of AIDs. Metaphorically, if not literally, Fournier reveals his fears about bodily pollution and invasion. What starts out slow—just a few cells—cannot coexist with a healthy body, which will eventually be destroyed. Left unsaid are thoughts about what a healthy body must do to arrest a spreading cancer.

Why Homophobia?

Keith Fournier's cancer metaphor is startling not least of all because of who he is. The ACLJ was founded by Pat Robertson but it is a respectable law firm, and Fournier is an educated man. That people with brains and good table manners would publicly liken homosexuality to cancer speaks volumes about the resonance of antigay sentiment.

At the organizational level, the antigay agenda suits the Christian Right's needs to raise money and to keep activists in motion. That a new group now demands "special rights" can be used to mobilize latent resentment toward women and racial minority groups, who have been fighting for an expansion of their rights for decades. People within the Christian Right can congratulate themselves as righteous underdogs, now besieged by a government acting on behalf of a supposedly privileged sexual minority.

All of these factors make the antigay agenda work as a political project, but they do not explain the mystery of homophobia. One can only read as tea leaves the antigay writings of Christian Right leaders and speculate as to why homophobia has such holding power on them. Some of the drive is, as Gary Bauer indicates, about losing a grip on inviolable gender roles or, as Charles Colson puts it, about a malleable universe where individuals create their own truths. In a gay marriage, who is on top? Who submits? Who decides who will submit? Acceptance of homosexuality, as one possible type of relationship among many, is a logical extension of the feminist idea that gender norms are socially constructed, not written on stone tablets. Variability in family relations means that the behavior and thoughts of men and women—especially women—cannot be tightly controlled by central authority.

The unhidden presence of homosexuals in public space—in media, politics, walking down the street—means that everyone has to acknowledge that there are choices to be made about sex roles and sexual practices, or that sex exists at all. Sex is frightening because it means losing control. It means opening a floodgate. If one changes one's mind about sexual propriety, the world might turn upside down.

Chapter 9

∽

By the Book

In early 1994, nine months before the Republicans won control of Congress, the Christian Right went into high gear. A Democratic Congressmember tried to amend an education bill (H.R. 6) with a requirement that homeschool teachers (in most cases, parents) be state-certified in all subjects they teach. At the time, most states required no more than a high school diploma for homeschool teachers; thus state certification would have put most of these parent teachers out of business. Within days of the vote on the bill, Michael Farris of the Home School Legal Defense Association had mobilized his organization's thirty-seven thousand member families through phone- and fax-tree networks. Farris and other homeschooling leaders had appeared on two nationally syndicated Christian talk radio shows, Dr. James Dobson's *Focus on the Family* and Marlin Maddoux's *Point of View,* to denounce the proposed amendment. Together Farris, Dobson, and Maddoux called for an urgent Congressional lobbying blitz. Homeschool supporters jammed the Capitol Hill switchboard with nearly one million phone calls in a few days. By the time H.R. 6 came to a vote, the sponsor of the amendment, Representative George Miller (D-CA), was the only House member willing to vote for it.[1]

For homeschool families and their supporters, the vote was a tangible display of their numerical strength. At stake was their belief in parents' rights to educate children without state interference. For thousands of evangelical parents, homeschooling is an institution that lies outside the grasp of either the government or the secular culture. This is not to say that homeschooling is not political. Anything that involves the ideological training of children is inherently and profoundly political. In fact, were it not for the tens of thousands of families who have simply withdrawn from public education, the Christian Right's school board battles would be more frequent and more fierce than they are. When parents choose homeschooling, they make a political statement about the public schools and about their unwillingness to allow their children to come into close contact with people of diverse viewpoints. Thus, the practice of homeschooling is at one end of a continuum that includes efforts to eliminate objectionable school books, as well as all other objectionable forms of ideological material, to which children might be exposed.

In the 1990s, school board elections and fights over public school curricula boosted the Christian Right, even though it lost many skirmishes. School board races and education controversies suit the movement's local grassroots organizational structure, allowing many concerned parents to channel their fears about sex education and homosexuality into bite-sized projects. School battles are central to the parental rights campaign. In school board conflicts, the Christian Right enjoys an advantage over its liberal opponents: the former's partisans are preorganized thanks to church membership and can be mobilized via local Christian radio stations. Liberal opponents often find themselves playing catch-up.

On the educational front, evangelicals spread their energies widely, in part because they see the purported evils of public education as a broad, multifaceted threat and in part because their education projects connect well with other long-standing preoccupations: against homosexuality and "obscenity," for example. Some of the theoreticians of homeschooling view the practice as a means to raise up a new generation, one committed to the values of its elders and ready to do battle with the secular world.

In recent years, some hotly contested public school battles have made national headlines, thus alerting people otherwise unaware of the Christian Right's influence. But, much of what happens in the world of homeschooling is unknown outside the evangelical subculture. Homeschoolers are a driving force behind parental rights legislation. The parental rights project is about strengthening the legal prerogatives of families in the face of real and perceived threats by government agencies. It is, theoretically, about reducing the power of government.

But practically speaking, and in what looks like a paradox, the Christian Right also seeks to restrict the free flow of media images to children. Under the banner of family values, innumerable battles have been fought over materials available to children in public schools and libraries. Critics charge "censorship," and yet members of the Christian Right claim that all they want is to protect young minds.

Censorship, in its purest form, means a government ban on designated ideas and images. But, in a capitalist system, censorship is mostly a question of who stands to profit from the types of information and entertainment "freely" circulated. In the early 1990s, the Christian Right made, literally, a federal case over government funding of controversial artists, resulting in the reduction of such funding and a chilling effect on grant applicants. Less evidently successful are the ongoing pressure campaigns against the commercial sponsors of insufficiently chaste and wholesome TV shows, campaigns led by the American Family Association (AFA). For AFA, violence is much less objectionable than sex. The focus on foul language and sexual innuendo leaves unchallenged the more pervasive messages of our daily dose of commercial media: buy stuff, stay smiling and mentally unchallenged, and buy more stuff. The Christian Right is unfazed by excessive consumerism and, instead, objects to agenda-setting by the corporate media only when sympathetic TV characters are portrayed as gay, divorced, or sexually promiscuous.

This chapter looks at how the Christian Right carries out an array of educational projects, broadly defined to include textbooks and other ideological products such as art and mass media. What is the connection between homeschooling and a boycott against the commercial sponsors of a network TV show? Some strategies are more successful than others. But whether the Christian Right builds alternative institutions or assails mainstream culture, the goal is always the same. The various projects are not at cross-purposes. The goal is to narrow the range of acceptable ideas and images in an attempt to bolster traditional lines of authority: between men and women, between parents and children, between saints and sinners.

Homeschooling

⌒

Exact figures on the numbers of homeschooled students are difficult to determine. Michael Farris of the Home School Legal Defense Association uses the figure of between 700,000 and 1,000,000 homeschooled students. In 1994, the Department of Education estimated between 248,500 and 353,500 homeschooled students. By 1997, now using data collected in 1995, the Department of Education estimated the numbers at between 500,000 and 750,000. The numbers represent between 1 and 2% of the total school-aged population and between 10 and 20% of the privately schooled population. The increase between 1994 and 1997 is due both to better surveying by government agencies and to real growth in the practice of homeschooling.[2] Farris's more generous estimate may be due to his inclusion of students who, though officially enrolled in private Christian academies, spend part of their school week studying at home.

Most homeschooled students are from highly religious families. They are more than twice as likely as the general population to attend church; about one-third belong to evangelical or pentecostal churches.[3] Parents' reasons for opting out of public education include concerns about overcrowded classrooms, poor instruction, violence and drugs, sex education, and the lack of religious instruction. The average homeschool family includes three children, more than the national average. For families with large numbers of children, homeschooling is more cost-effective than private education.[4]

Consistently, studies of homeschooled students show them to be high achievers on standardized academic performance tests. On reading, language, and math tests for grades kindergarten through high school, homeschooled students rank between the 70th and 80th percentiles, meaning that they score well above national averages.[5] This should come as no surprise. In the public schools classrooms are often overcrowded, with thirty or more students who are taught as a group, while homeschooling allows for close supervision and individualized instruction. Homeschool researcher Dr. Brian Ray synthesized several studies of homeschool families and found that the average homeschool parent has attended or graduated from college. Homeschool families, as of 1990, earned incomes about the same or somewhat lower than the average family in the United States.[6] Most homeschooled children are formally instructed for three to four hours per day, with an emphasis on reading, math, and science, and with a lot of extracurricular time devoted to church youth group activities, sports, music lessons, and the like. One evangelical magazine profile of homeschooling noted that homeschooling families often get together one day a week for field trips. One charismatic church in California had so many homeschool families that it established a weekly "enrichment day" for special parent-led classes in drama, music, art, and typing.[7]

Particularly for large families, the success of homeschooling relies on the good organizational skills of the primary teacher, who is almost always the mother. To teach the basics, parents can rely on a mountain of textbooks, flash cards, maps, games, and workbooks produced by about a dozen leading Christian publishers. Among the largest producer of homeschool materials is A-Beka School Services, the publishing arm of Pensacola Christian College in Florida. As of the mid-1990s, A-Beka sold textbook sets for 680,000 students annually (this number includes private school students as well as homeschool students). A-Beka's catalog begins with the advisory that its editorial department "has rejected the humanistic philosophy and methods of the progressive educators and has turned to original sources and the writings of true scholars. Of course, the most original source is always the Word of God, which is the only foundation for true scholarship in any area of human endeavor."[8] The A-Beka curriculum for grades K–12 includes Bible study, history, math, science/health, and language skills, with age-appropriate materials for each subject, and with an emphasis on curricular conformity to biblical principles and conservative politics. A-Beka's tenth-grade biology set, for example, called "God's Living

Creation," is advertised as "truly non-evolutionary in philosophy, spirit, and sequence of study."[9] Parents are assured that the high school government text is "written from the standpoint of Biblical Christianity and political and economic conservatism. . . . The concepts of private property, free enterprise, profit and capital, and limited government are clearly presented."[10]

To get a sense of the kind of "true scholars" writing for the homeschool market, one need only peruse a couple of the history textbooks for elementary grades. The A-Beka books emphasize memorization of key dates and facts, such as the names of our Founding Fathers, prominent missionaries, and industrialists. Designed for fourth graders, *The History of Our United States* is appalling in its treatment of Native Americans and African Americans. Toward Native Americans, the book's stance is one of lies, omissions, and religious bigotry. Here is an excerpt:

> Before the Europeans began exploring America, each Indian tribe took care of all its own needs. They had not yet learned to trade with other tribes and because of this, they were often very poor.
>
> The Indians were isolated from the gospel and had never seen the Scriptures. Each tribe made its own religion. Some worshiped idols. Some worshiped the sun and moon.
>
> When the white men began to explore and settle America, the Indians' way of life slowly changed. They began to trade furs and food for strong iron pots and shiny copper kettles. . . .
>
> As the white men built more homes and killed more game animals, there was less meat for the Indians to eat. Indians were forced to farm more by planting crops to grow food. This improved their way of life. . . .
>
> The biggest change of all came when the Indians heard about the one true God. The Indians had been locked into a system of false religion. They had no Bible to read, and they often offered prayers and sacrifices to the "god of the sky," the "god of the forest," the "god of the river," and many other false gods.[11]

Further on, the chapter on the Civil War explains the conflict as a "quarrel," like a family quarrel, between the North and the South. The problem started because the northern states, plus England and France, wanted cotton and tobacco, which could only be grown in the South:

> Because the world wanted these two crops, the Southern planters happily grew them.
>
> The Southern planters bought more land as their crops sold more. The purpose of buying more land was to plant more cotton and tobacco. But who could take care of such large fields? The Southern planter could never hire enough people to get his work done, and so he turned to buying slaves.
>
> Slaves easily learned how to pick cotton and tobacco. The Southern

weather was warm and the slaves stayed healthy. There was no need of factories in the South, for cotton and tobacco made the South rich.[12]

The line about how the planters "could never hire enough people" is repeated in A-Beka's sixth-grade history text, *New World History and Geography in Christian Perspective*. This book also emphasizes religion in a chapter on "How the Native Americans Lived."

> Indians have a long heritage that goes all the way back to our first parents, Adam and Eve. Like all people everywhere, the Indians were made in the image of God and after Adam's fall inherited fallen human natures. All are in need of Christ as their Savior. The best friends of the Indians have been missionaries, including Christian Indians who have taken the gospel message to their own people. . . .
>   Rather than worshiping the God who made the mountains, plains, valleys, rivers, oceans, people, animals, and all else, the Indians worshiped imaginary spirits that they said lived in the mountains, the trees, the water, the animals, and the plants around them. This false spirit worship caused the Indians to live in fear of nature rather than to conquer nature, as God told man to do (see Gen. 1:29). Their false religion kept them from working together to build up the wonderful land in which they lived.[13]

From there, the chapters on specific tribes of Indians are presented region by region, interspersed with discussions of the flora and fauna found in different parts of North and South America.

At best, the Indians are treated as part of the scenery, for the A-Beka history books assume white, Christian supremacy as an ideological given. These days, the reputable textbook companies have abandoned such openly bigoted material, if only because the publishers have to sell their stock to large school districts, where political sensibilities are too polite for crude racism. Yet thousands of Christian children use the A-Beka series in private schools and for home study. These children may, indeed, excel on exams testing reading, writing, and math skills. One can only wonder, though, how graduates of the right-wing homeschooling world will score in the real world of learning, and how they will treat people of diverse races.

Learning the Rules

⌒

Thanks to teaching materials published by A-Beka, and also by Bob Jones University, the Christian Liberty Academy Satellite Schools (CLASS), and other companies, there is no shortage of how-to information for homeschool parents. The Oregon-based bimonthly magazine *Teaching Home* is chock-full of articles on motivational teaching techniques, and ads for the latest books, videos, computers, and lab equipment. Each issue features a special section on how to teach specific topics: math, phonics, classical literature, art, music, and the like. Each issue also features a cover photo and story about a homeschool family, almost always with four or more cute smiling children, a gainfully employed father, and a contented stay-at-home mother. The repetitive stories reinforce not just the wisdom of homeschooling but also the virtues of managing an orderly traditional family and a life of service to fellow Christians through volunteer work in the local church.

Teaching Home moves seamlessly, page by page, from mundane tips on how to remove crayon stains to suggestions on how to influence the political process. It is precisely the linkage of the personal and the political that makes keeping up with the latest legislative battles accessible to moms who might otherwise be more preoccupied with wiping the peanut butter from a toddler's face. It is impossible to know how many Christian homeschool parents make political activism part of their regular routine. However, key proponents of homeschooling write to the effect that the decision to educate one's own children is a political act.

One of the most popular books advocating homeschooling is *The Right Choice* by Home School Legal Defense Association (HSLDA) attorney Christopher Klicka. The book is a compendium of the academic, moral, and philosophical crises plaguing the public schools. Academically, Klicka claims that "public school history books are filled with pro-Communist propaganda."[14] Philosophically, the danger lies in the humanist underpinnings of public education.[15] Klicka acknowledges that homeschooling is practiced by parents of all religious and political persuasions, including many holdovers from the 1960s hippie subculture. But he urges Christian parents to stay away from homeschoolers who are not also born-again Christians.[16]

For Christian homeschoolers, the project is far more encompassing than teaching the three Rs. Each issue of *Teaching Home* magazine includes a section full of legal and political updates. There are state-by-state reports on legal challenges to parental autonomy, and there are regular updates on the status of parental rights legislation in Congress and in the state legislatures. Christopher Klicka of the HSLDA directs a division of the organization called the National Center for Home Education (NCHE). In 1996, the NCHE proposed and then lobbied for a Congressional bill to eliminate the federal government's role in education by cutting $60 billion from education programs. Klicka and Farris were unable to convene any Congressmembers or Senators to sponsor their bill, called the Restoring Local Schools Act. The bill died in committee at the end of 1996, when

Congress voted to fund the Department of Education to an even greater extent than requested by the Clinton administration.[17] Farris and Klicka are likely to reintroduce a similar bill in the future, and they are hardly alone in their desire to eliminate all federal funding for public education. It is a goal shared by Concerned Women for America and the Family Research Council. Elimination of the Department of Education was part of the Christian Coalition's 1995 legislative agenda, the Contract with the American Family.[18]

Teaching Home magazine gives parents information about issues plus how-to suggestions for activism. There are frequent articles such as "How to Get Students Involved in the Election Process" with tips on writing letters, interviewing candidates, and walking precincts.[19] An article on "Getting Out the Vote" discussed the do's and don'ts of registering voters at church. It also reminded parents that since only about half of all eligible voters are registered, and only about half of these registered voters go to the polls, the impact of "principled, informed, and spiritually discerning voters" can be great.[20]

In every issue of the magazine, Michael Farris gives readers a political update. In his 1994 columns he congratulated homeschoolers for their successful grassroots lobbying blitz to defeat H.R. 6, the Congressional amendment that would have required state certification of all home teachers. The victory was the result of quick action, Farris wrote, made possible because by 1994 the HSLDA had already spent a decade building a "federal response network":

> If we had been required to spend a long time explaining to the home-school community why teacher certification was a bad idea, we would have been dead in the water. . . .
> Tens of millions of people were concerned about homosexuals in the military. Similar numbers of people held strong views about NAFTA [Norh American Free Trade Agreement]. Every American was directly affected by the Clinton budget and tax increases. Yet according to some congressmen, many congressional offices received more calls on H.R. 6 than on these other three issues combined. . . .
> On Capitol Hill there is now a standing joke: "If you want to defeat a bill on providing foreign aid, call it The Foreign Aid and Home Schooling Regulation Act."[21]

Farris proceeded to identify what he sees as the proper limits for legislative lobbying from the organized homeschool movement. He said he would deploy his network of homeschool family lobbyists only on issues directly involving homeschooling, parental rights, and religious liberty. But he also said he had to "confess" that he "long[s] for the day freedom-loving Americans, affronted by the continual erosion of their liberties in other arenas, demonstrate the same degree of seriousness displayed by home schoolers."[22]

It is, indeed, with the same degree of seriousness, that Christian homeschoolers articulate a vision of proper gender and family roles that is inescapably political. Articles in *Teaching Home* magazine reinforce the idea that, though the mother may do most of the daytime teaching, the father is the headmaster and the final arbiter in the home. In a special issue of the magazine on government and political action, the lead article was about "The Father's Role in Teaching Government." It was written by Douglas Phillips, who works with Michael Farris and Christopher Klicka at the National Center for Home Education. According to Phillips, the father has three responsibilities as family leader. The first is to preserve the "religious" liberty to "worship God, to make personal medical decisions, to be an independent businessman, or to own private property." The second charge is "defending the home against legislative threats" by "promot[ing] public policies which respect the sanctity of the home." The father's third role is to teach the children about God and "about the nature of the civil government which God has placed over them."[23]

In the philosophy of Christian homeschoolers, there are no clear boundaries between the realms of religious expression, family order, and political activism—though the last is ostensibly defensive in nature. Homeschooling is an ideological practice where religion, family, and politics all come together.

The means for teaching this ideology is through the repetition of stories. Like evangelicals generally, the homeschoolers love to share testimonies of how God rewards the faithful. Every issue of *Teaching Home* begins with a story told by the family featured on the magazine's cover. Almost invariably these families are white, with middle-aged parents of modest means, and four or more children.

One 1996 cover story that stood out from the rest was written by Andy and Besty (née Bradick) Barth, two newlyweds who look barely old enough to drive, though they are in their twenties. They begin by thanking God for having had parents who did not allow them to date haphazardly but who, instead, arranged their courtship for them. The parental Barths live in Vermont and the parental Bradricks in Washington State. Both are homeschool families. The two families attended a homeschool convention in 1994, where the parents met but the two youngsters did not even notice each other. Several months later, Andy's father called Betsy's father and asked him to consider a courtship arrangement between their two offspring. The families met several more times. Only after Betsy's parents "were completely at peace with this being possibly God's will for their daughter" did they ask Betsy to pray about it. Both families had fax machines, which Andy and Betsy used to correspond. "It was so good," Andy writes, "to be under authority during our entire courtship and to be able to seek our parents' counsel in all the decisions we made." When the young couple wed, their fathers performed the wedding ceremony. Andy concludes by advising young people who are seeking a life partner to "place yourself totally under your parents' authority."[24]

The story is presented as the "normal" way that young people should meet and pair off. It reflects the belief that parents should decide whom their children will marry. At a homeschooling conference in California, Michael Farris outlined his view that parents should not allow their teenage children to date, but should allow them to court. The difference between dating and courtship is that dating is a frivolous form of male–female socializing, while courtship is a nonfrivolous form where the primary goal is to determine if a pair will make compatible marriage partners. Needless to say, no physical interaction is allowed during courtship, and the court-ship must be strictly approved and strictly supervised by both sets of parents.[25]

This degree of obedience to parental authority is virtually unheard of in contemporary mainstream American culture. But within the fundamentalist homeschooling subculture, obedience is the surest sign of one's faith in God. Were Christian homeschoolers living in isolated communities like the Amish, then parentally arranged courtship and marriage would not seem so incongruous; but the homeschoolers combine an isolationist mentality with living also in a diverse, modern society. The Christian homeschoolers want to nurture their children within an environment protected from government regulation and "worldly" cultural influences. But that is not all they want. They also want to have a say in how and even whether government educates everyone else's children. They want to involve themselves on the full range of family values issues. Their goal is a biblically ordered hierarchical society in which men and women, parents and children, rich and poor, believers and heathens—all know their place. Homeschooling is the means to practice orderly living in the smallest unit of social organization, the family. Homeschool families can point to their children's high test scores as evidence of the academic virtues of home education. But the ultimate proof in the pudding of homeschooling is whether the finished product, a young adult, will adhere to traditional lines of authority—and reproduce a new generation of true believers.

Boards of Education

∽

Homeschooling is popular but it is feasible only for the most stalwart and financially secure two-parent families. It is not an option for everyone sympathetic to the Christian Right. As long as most of the country's school-age children attend public schools, the schools themselves will remain a contested battleground. Apart from skirmishes over abortion, the movement's participation in school board elections has, in recent years, brought the Christian Right the greatest national media attention. In New York City, in 1993, the Christian Coalition won majorities in a few of the city's several dozen districts by joining forces with the Catholic diocese in a campaign against a gay-positive, multicultural curriculum program called "Children of the Rainbow."[26] In a suburb of San Diego, California, the Vista school board became polarized beginning in 1992 when a three-member Christian Right majority was elected to sit on the five-member board. During the two years the Christian Right activists served before being voted out of office in 1994, they used their power to vote for the teaching of creationism and a religiously oriented sex education program promoting abstinence. They also voted to refuse government funding for a breakfast program for poor children.[27] Around the same time, a Christian Right majority won control of the Lake County, Florida, school district for one term. While in charge in Lake County, Christian Right school board members voted to require that the district's multicultural curriculum teach that the United States' form of government, its capitalist economic system, and its "other basic values" make it "superior to other foreign or historic cultures."[28]

In Lake County, the Christian Right school board majority failed to win reelection in 1994. Despite the controversies, Ralph Reed proclaimed school board fights as necessary elements of Christian Right activism. "Instead of focusing on winning the White House," Reed told the *Human Events* newspaper, "we're developing a farm team of future officeholders by running people for school boards, city councils and state legislatures."[29] School board fights are training grounds for candidates and potential office holders, which is why the Christian Coalition has sponsored a series of seminars for school board candidates.[30]

It is hard to assess the impact of school board races nationwide. A campaign here and a textbook controversy there make national headlines while most of the grassroots activism—which takes place in small cities and suburban towns off the beaten path—is reported only in local media outlets. Moreover, much if not most of the activism involves parents pressuring existing school boards, not running for office themselves. But, obviously, countless campaigns at the school board level involving large numbers of dedicated though often initially amateurish, parent activists must have an effect on U.S. society—if only of transforming many amateur activists into seasoned veterans. For these moral and social conservatives, there is no shortage of objectionable things going on down at the local public school. There are unending chances to take on the "education establishment" in small, curriculum-sized pieces.

Focus on the Family's monthly *Citizen* magazine keeps track of local school board campaigns and reports regularly on parents who have influenced school board decisions. Most of the controversies are about sex education programs, particularly those that do not emphasize abstinence or that present homosexuality as an acceptable practice. Here are just a few examples from the ranks of people Focus on the Family calls "hometown heroes."

Susie Roberts of Issaquah, Washington (population 7,786), is a mother of three and a long-time volunteer in the public schools. She was asked to preview AIDS education videos under consideration by the State of Washington. She was appalled that the videos did not promote abstinence, and then took action. She wrote letters to school officials and sent them one of Focus on the Family's own abstinence-based videos. Then she organized other mothers in her church to pray for her success. Their efforts paid off when the local school board voted to approve the use of abstinence-based videos in their curriculum.[31]

Tim and Delores Cripes, grain farmers from Argos, Indiana (population 1,642), similarly took matters into their own hands when their eighth-grade daughter was exposed to a public school sex education textbook that included material on homosexuality, pornography, "graphic descriptions of the sexual experience, and only a couple of sentences devoted to abstinence." The Cripeses tried unsuccessfully to pressure the school board to remove the textbook, and then decided to remove their daughter from the sex ed class. They convinced other parents to follow their example, and then they started an alternative, afterschool sex ed class, using an abstinence-based program approved by the Christian Right.[32]

Barb Anderson of Champlin, Minnesota (population 16,849), helped form Taxpayers for Excellence in Education after learning that her nephew would be exposed to a sex education course called "Values and Choices," which presented homosexuality as normal. Anderson and other parents were initially unsuccessful in getting their school board to drop the course. But after a four-year struggle, Anderson's group won a major victory when the school board voted to delete homosexual organizations from teachers' resource lists, and to promote marriage and abstinence in sex ed courses.[33]

In Merrimack, New Hampshire, parents opposed to a Planned Parenthood sex education pamphlet organized to elect a conservative majority to the school board, which then voted to disallow the distribution of Planned Parenthood materials in district schools. About a year later, the same board voted to prohibit schools from providing "any program or activity that has either the purpose or effect of encouraging or supporting homosexuality as a positive lifestyle alternative."[34] Presumably this meant anything other than a derogatory presentation of homosexuality.

Consistently, the fear of sexually explicit lesson plans is what galvanizes school board activists more than any other aspect of public instruction. Parents claim a legitimate right to determine the course of their children's upbringing. The focus on sex education is connected to a view that the state, represented by the public school bureaucracy, has intruded into the most intimate realms of private decisionmaking. These parents, though, are motivated not only to safeguard their own children from unacceptable ideas, but also to make sure that nobody else's kids have access to such information. The Christian Right press reports successful efforts and downplays resistance from liberal-minded parents and school board officials. But each small victory strengthens the morale of Christian Right activists and emboldens them to make new forays against secular institutions.

Teaching Fear

∽

In part, this is because of successful networking between small, local groups and well-heeled national organizations. Focus on the Family's *Citizen* magazine, as well as other media outlets, publish success stories to inspire other would-be activists. The National Association of Christian Educators (NACE), also known as Citizens for Excellence in Education (CEE), serves as a clearinghouse for activists around the country. NACE/CEE was founded in 1983 by Dr. Robert L. Simonds, a former minister and math teacher who wrote a widely circulated booklet, *How to Elect Christians to Public Office*. In the mid-1990s, Simonds claimed to have organized 1,550 chapters and to have helped elect almost five thousand school board members nationwide.[35] There is no way to verify Simonds's figures. In recent years, he has claimed simply to have "over 100,000 parents involved" in his work, with "CEE parent chapters. . . . active in over 1,500 communities."[36] To be "involved" may mean nothing more than being on a mailing list. Simonds preaches to the choir but, for those interested in starting a CEE chapter, he provides reams of literature about objectionable books and trends in the public schools. From there, local chapters choose their own battles.

For example, a CEE chapter in San Antonio, Texas, tried to ban *Little Red Riding Hood* from the school library because the grandmother in the story drinks wine. A chapter in Illinois persuaded its school board to include use of the Book of Genesis in science classes.[37] In his monthly newsletters, Simonds reports for parents the goings-on at particular school boards. Again, his unsubstantiated claims of success are designed to raise the morale of his troops. For example, at the end of 1995, he claimed that CEE had helped elect "over 10,000 parents" in the previous year's elections alone, and he called "our victory in public schools" the "single most important victory for God's church in this century!"[38]

If anything, Simonds's organization plays an agenda-setting role within the Christian Right by alerting supporters to the latest objectionable trends in public education. Along with Phyllis Schlafly and Beverly LaHaye, Simonds was among the first to sound the alarm on a vague but ominous sounding school trend called "Outcome Based Education (OBE)."[39] OBE-inspired curriculum plans have been adopted by a number of states in their efforts to reform public education. OBE is, indeed, controversial, but some Christian activist parents portray it as a conspiracy for "remaking your children through radical educational reform" and for "dumbing down America's schools."[40] Philosophically, OBE is intended as a departure from the conventional focus on how much classroom time is spent on particular subjects, with letter grades assigned based on performance on quantifiable tests. With OBE, the idea is for students to demonstrate mastery or successful "outcomes" with particular tasks, not necessarily linked to a child's official grade level. OBE is controversial not just because it suggests that children differ in the amount of time they need to learn reading and math, but also because OBE greatly expands the range of desirable academic "outcomes." OBE advocates argue that children need to learn more than basic reading, writing, and arithmetic. According to OBE theorist William Spady, children also need to learn more ill-defined skills such as "critical thinking, effective communication, technological applications, and complex problem solving."[41]

Regarding OBE, parents have multiple concerns. If successful mastery of tasks is to replace letter grades, will not the standards simply be lowered so that all children can pass through the system? More ominously for many parents, OBE opens up a Pandora's box as to what is meant by "critical thinking" and "communication." In Minnesota, for instance, one of the proposed outcomes was for children to "understand diversity and the interdependence of people."[42] That goal sounds noble, but will teachers and school officials begin giving students ideological litmus tests with a particular political bent? At a time when most parents are concerned over whether the public schools have adequate resources to teach children basic skills, OBE raises the fear threshold to a new level. Will children learn spelling and arithmetic, or will their teachers focus on teaching the latest trends in self-esteem and values clarification education?

These are valid concerns, but Christian Right organizers have used them to rally support for broader attacks on public education. Eagle Forum, Concerned Women for America, CEE, and other organizations have sent reams of scare-mongering literature to their constituents, claiming that public school officials are deliberately creating an educational system that parents will not understand; that the growing number of computers in classrooms will be used to build intelligence files on children and parents; and that the schools are politically motivated to indoctrinate children with anti-Christian, anti-American values.[43]

Throughout the 1990s, the Christian Right has used OBE as a catch-all term for all of the real and perceived evils of the public education system. Having aroused parental fears through relentless discussion of OBE over religious broadcasting stations, Christian Right organizers are in the cat-bird's seat when any local controversy arises.

A 1994 controversy in California illustrates how quickly parental outrage can rise and fall. The case in point revolved around the California Learning Assessment System (CLAS) test, which was then administered to public school students in the fourth, fifth, eighth, and tenth grades. The furor began when Beverly Sheldon of the Traditional Values Coalition went before a state board of education committee and protested the test's use of a reading comprehension question based on "Roselily," a story by author Alice Walker. Sheldon claimed the story was "antireligious" because the main character questions marriage and religion. Rather than offend the Traditional Values Coalition, state educators removed the Alice Walker story from subsequent tests, touching off a public outcry over censorship.[44]

The highly publicized incident then became a green light for Christian Right organizers eager to assail the CLAS test altogether. Leaders of the Capitol Resource Institute, a state policy think tank affiliated with Focus on the Family, made scores of appearances on Christian radio stations urging parents to lobby their state legislators against CLAS.[45] The southern California–based United States Justice Foundation threatened to sue California school districts if they continued to administer CLAS, on the grounds that it violated California Education Code prohibitions against questioning students about "personal beliefs or practices in sex, family life, morality and religion."[46] The Rutherford Institute, a national Christian Right legal firm with a branch in Sacramento, sued several school districts on behalf of groups of Christian parents clamoring to have their children exempted from taking the CLAS test.[47]

After months of protest, in the summer of 1994, the state scheduled a day for public viewing of the CLAS tests at several dozen sites in California. In the entire San Francisco Bay Area, only a half dozen individuals appeared at the offices where the tests were available.[48] It was apparently more exciting to rail against the test than to see its actual contents. But the end result of the controversy was the loss of an exam highly regarded by educators because it tested reading and writing skills through complex essay questions. Several months after the furor died down, Governor Pete Wilson vetoed a bill that would have reformed but preserved the exam, thus leaving the state's schools, at least temporarily, without a valuable diagnostic tool for measuring student achievement.[49]

Library Dangers

∽

Rather than face the wrath of the Christian Right in California, state officials acquiesced to a pressure campaign fueled by people not particularly concerned with the actual content of the objectionable materials. Somehow the *idea* of the state asking children questions about touchy subjects was enough to make some parents' heads spin. The CLAS controversy was a case of censorship flying under cover of parental rights.

Other school and library pressure campaigns also use the defense of children as a rationale for restricting access to printed matter, especially about sex. School and library campaigns are ideally suited to the Christian Right's grassroots style of organizing. There is enough work to keep anyone who wants to run their own organization occupied.

Karen Jo Gounaud was an ordinary housewife living in Springfield, Virginia. In 1993, she began complaining to her local library because it served as a distribution site for a free gay newspaper, the *Washington Blade*. Gounaud was appalled that children could easily pick up copies of the *Blade*. She attended a Christian Coalition organizing seminar and began talking about the library at her church. She joined a group of several hundred Fairfax County activists who mailed out thousands of leaflets to local residents. They eventually pressured the county board of supervisors to vote to restrict free distribution of the *Blade*.[50] Next, in 1994, Gounaud pressured the library board to remove from shelves a history book on the gay and lesbian movement. She then persuaded library officials to order more than one hundred copies of books with antigay themes.[51] For her efforts, Gounaud became well known in Christian Right circles, and was a frequent guest on Christian radio stations.

In 1995, Gounaud joined forces with Ohio antigay activist Phil Burress. They gathered fifty people from eleven states for a meeting in Cincinnati to start a new organization called Family Friendly Libraries (FFL).[52] Their goal is to challenge the fifty-seven-thousand-member American Library Association (ALA), which frequently intervenes when libraries are targeted by censorship groups.[53] In a Focus on the Family *Citizen* article that praised Gounaud and her project, she said the goal of FFL is to "empower people at the local level . . . to determine what is done with their tax money and how their children are influenced by the materials that [libraries] purchase."[54] Specifically, Gounaud recommends electing local Christian activists to library boards; getting libraries to sever their ties with the ALA; and reversing library policies that prevent parents from knowing what books their children check out.[55] Fighting the availability of progay literature continues to be a central focus for Karen Jo Gounaud. In one paranoid-sounding summary of her group's efforts against the ALA, Gounaud claimed that progay activists are "using libraries to target child and teenage readers with new books that celebrate homosexuality while belittling or erasing images of traditional marriage and of a committed mother and father as a standard for families."[56]

Now, several years after she founded FFL, Gounaud says that her group is small and her achievements modest, and she claims that she spends most of her time mailing information to people about "sexually inappropriate material" in schools and libraries. In one of her occasional newsletters, Gounaud discusses FFL's drive to ensure that libraries offering Internet access prevent minors from viewing pornography on-line.[57] Under the rubric of protecting children, Gounaud next plans to lobby state legislatures for laws giving parents access to their children's public library borrowing records. Thus far, FFL has won such parental access in Michigan and in one Maryland county.[58]

In Gounaud's world, children, including teenagers, do not have a right to privacy. For Gounaud and others in the Christian Right, libraries, like public schools, are tangible symbols of "immorality" backed by taxpayer money—and therefore amenable to public pressure. Libraries are close to home. They belong to neighborhoods, and it seems that they should reflect the values of local residents. But Gounaud and others like her have their work cut out for them, as libraries are also widely seen by the public as First Amendment safe havens. They ought to be above the fray of any group's narrow agenda. This makes libraries difficult but perpetually challenging targets for the would-be arbiters of public morality.

Watching Indecency
⌒

Along with the projects of pressuring schools and libraries, a project to end government funding of art proved irresistible to cultural warriors for a number of years. Beginning in 1989, the National Endowment for the Arts (NEA), which used to fund a wide array of artistic projects, came under fire. The American Family Association, the Christian Coalition, Concerned Women for America, Eagle Forum, and Focus on the Family combined to wage a grassroots lobbying campaign against NEA funding of two controversial photographers, Andres Serrano and Robert Mapplethorpe. Donald Wildmon of the American Family Association circulated a letter to Congress, the major media outlets, and Christian lobbying organizations, to the effect that Andres Serrano's *Piss Christ,* an exhibition piece consisting of a crucifix immersed in urine, fit a pattern of "bias and bigotry against Christians."[59] Senators Alfonse D'Amato (R-NY) and Jesse Helms (R-NC) responded by denouncing the NEA on the Senate floor in the spring of 1989. In the House, Representative Richard Armey (R-TX) led one hundred of his colleagues in an open letter criticizing the NEA for its funding of a Mapplethorpe exhibit. Then, in 1990, Congress imposed an "indecency" restriction on NEA grant applicants. The restriction was later challenged in a lawsuit brought by four artists who sued NEA, charging political bias in denying them grants.[60] Since the early 1990s, Congress has gradually reduced the NEA's budget. In 1995, Senator Helms succeeded in adding to a budget bill language that could prohibit grants to artists who "denigrate the adherents to a particular religion" or whose work could be construed as sexually explicit.[61]

The conflict over federal arts funding set a tone for local jurisdictions. In 1993, in Cobb County, Georgia, part of Newt Gingrich's Congressional district, county commissioners passed a resolution condemning the "gay lifestyle" and banning the funding of any activities that went against "community standards." Later, the same commission voted to cut off all funding to the arts, thereby leaving local theaters and museums to fend for themselves.[62] This was exactly what Christian Right organizers hoped to achieve. They argue that the government has no role to play in supporting artistic endeavors of any type: let the "free market" determine which arts projects are funded and which are not. They oppose the idea that the arts have an inherent value and that they ought to be made more accessible to people of modest incomes. The Christian Right views federally funded art not as a social good, but rather as a threat to those who uphold Christian values.

For Christian Right organizers, there has been no downside to the fight against federally funded art. The fight offers another chance to mobilize old supporters and to enlist new ones with reminders about government outrages. During the initial round of the NEA controversy, Pat Robertson's newly formed Christian Coalition used the NEA issue to reap a windfall of public attention. In 1990, several years before the Coalition had grown powerful enough to become indispensable to the Republican Party, the organization spent $200,000 on an anti-NEA advertisement in USA Today in an effort to use the using the arts controversy to enlist new members.[63]

In taking on the NEA, Robertson took advantage of the years of ground work done by Donald Wildmon, a career warrior against "obscenity" in the arts and media. For years, Wildmon's American Family Association—based in Tupelo, Mississippi, the birthplace of Elvis Presley—has led efforts to force convenience stores to stop selling softcore pornography and to stifle "indecent" television programs by boycotting advertisers.

Wildmon got his start in political activism in 1977 when, as a Methodist minister, he asked his congregation to do without television for a week to protest sex and violence over the airwaves. From there, Wildmon founded the National Federation for Decency, later renamed the American

Family Association (AFA). In 1978, Wildmon organized his first boycott, threatening to picket Sears Roebuck if Sears continued to sponsor *Three's Company, Charlie's Angels,* and *All in the Family.*[64] In 1980, Wildmon teamed up with Jerry Falwell. They started the Coalition for Better Television which, with help from direct mail specialist Richard Viguerie, soon claimed a network of two hundred organizations representing a total of three million members.[65] Like other movement leaders, Wildmon plays the numbers game. He always claims large numbers of supporters, even if most take no action beyond opening his direct mail appeals.

Wildmon's numbers, however, are impressive. By 1993, AFA enjoyed an annual budget of $11 million, and a mailing list of 1.2 million, including 170,000 churches receiving the monthly *AFA Journal.*[66] Thanks to these impressive numbers, Wildmon is able to throw his weight around. He claimed credit when, under pressure, Pepsi canceled a $5 million advertising campaign featuring Madonna; when the Southland Corporation decided to remove *Playboy* and *Penthouse* magazines from 7-Eleven stores; when the Public Broadcasting System terminated its successful but progay TV series *Tales of the City*; and when profits for the Kmart corporation dropped following an AFA boycott over the sale of softcore porn magazines through Kmart's subsidiary Waldenbooks.[67]

One of Wildmon's best known campaigns was the drive to force ABC to cancel the primetime TV series *NYPD Blue.* The show has been popular precisely because it has an adult combination of violent and risqué content. Wildmon's intent, if he could not get the show canceled outright, was to punish the network for airing it. By urging his supporters to boycott *NYPD Blue*'s advertisers, Wildmon tried to force ABC's total advertising revenues down. "The name of the game is money. That's their god," Wildmon told the evangelical *World* magazine.[68] In 1994, Wildmon estimated that AFA's campaign against *NYPD Blue* had cost ABC more than $20 million, and he proudly reported that fifty-nine of ABC's affiliate stations had refused to carry the show.[69] AFA's method is to send its members preprinted postcards which they are urged to mail to local affiliates and corporate advertisers. AFA's monthly mailings always include lists of consumer products to be boycotted.

But *NYPD Blue* was no unique target. A regular feature of the *AFA Journal* is a monthly "Action Index" of objectionable primetime programs. Pages of entries document the offenses, give addresses and phone numbers of corporate sponsors, and list products to be shunned. AFA staff must spend an inordinate amount of time watching and summarizing network shows. Here is part of one month's entry for the popular TV situation comedy *Friends.* In the examples below, the code "H" stands for "promotes homosexual agenda," "P" stands for profanity (the number after "P" indicates the number of times profanity is used in the program).

Friends H P9
   NBC 10/26/95 — In this repeat episode, Ross's ex-wife Carol, who left him because she decided she's a lesbian, comes back to tell Ross she's pregnant. She and her new lesbian lover want Ross to play a part in their child's life. God's name is used in vain about once every 2.5 minutes. . . .

November 2 H P4
   Ross's friends Joey and Chandler babysit little Ben, but leave him on the bus in order to try to pick up women. There are numerous homosexual and condom jokes.
   Advertiser: Procter & Gamble[70]

If one is inclined to ignore network television—for religious or other reasons—one can still keep apprised of it through the *AFA Journal*, which also provides an annual list of the "AFA Dirty Dozen: The 12 Top Sponsors of Prime-Time Filth." At the end of 1996, the list included the following corporations: Sony, Upjohn, Schering-Plough, Hyundai, Merrill Lynch, Pfizer, MCI, Toyota, Echo Star, American Honda Motor, Slimfast Foods, and the Warner-Lambert Company. The previous year's "Dirty Dozen" were Visa, Anheuser-Busch, Sara Lee, Toyota, MasterCard, Paramount Communications, Maybelline, Adolph Coors, MCI Communications, Bristol-Myers Squibb, Unilever, and Coca-Cola.[71] Together, these companies produce hundreds of consumer items. If an ardent AFA supporter were to boycott Kmart, Coors beer, most brand-name processed foods, cosmetics, soaps, and cleaning supplies, he or she would have a severely limited list of "approved" consumer goods to purchase without fear of subsidizing what AFA calls "prime-time filth."
   No doubt, most AFA supporters are selective in choosing which products they will boycott. The sponsors of media "perversion" are so numerous as to suggest a wholesale secular attack on Christians, and there is no easy way for the aggrieved to fight back. By casting its net to include as Christianity's "enemy" much, if not most, of the corporate world, AFA risks reinforcing its image as a bunch of cranks. Wildmon can claim credit for damaging a network's advertising revenues or getting certain bookstores to stop selling pornographic magazines. But he cannot buck the bottom-line profit motive that drives corporate media.
   What he does have at his disposal is a permanent band of supporters (total numbers, unknown) who are ready to be deployed against the latest media atrocities. Wildmon was once quoted to the effect that obscenity, per se, was more a symptom than a cause of what ails society. "What we are up against is not just dirty words and dirty pictures," Wildmon said.

   It is a philosophy of life which seeks to remove the influence of Christians and Christianity from our society. Pornography is not the disease, but merely a visible symptom. It springs from a moral cancer in our society, and it will lead us to destruction if we are unable to stop it.[72]

The intense emotions provoked by the "obscenity" issue, and AFA's frequent high-profile jousts with major media, have prompted political leaders to score points by fighting "indecency." In June 1995, as he was preparing his bid for the White House, Senator Bob Dole went to Hollywood and delivered one of his most memorable speeches: a broadside against the "nightmares of depravity" emanating from the entertainment industry. Dole singled out a series of violent movies and the Time Warner media conglomerate, purveyors of rap records with obscene lyrics. "We must hold Hollywood and the entire entertainment industry accountable for putting profit ahead of common decency," Dole said, as if the industry is ever motivated by anything but profit. The next day former education secretary and drug czar William Bennett, already immersed in his own campaign against violent and obscene rap lyrics, sent letters to Time Warner board members asking them to stop distributing so-called gangsta rap.[73]

At the time, Dole's rhetorical attack on Hollywood was widely perceived as a pitch for support from the Christian Right, and it worked. At the September 1995 Christian Coalition conference, Dole—all talk and no action—was, nevertheless, applauded for his blast at Hollywood.[74]

Dole's remarks, timed to coincide with a Congressional vote to eliminate the National Endowment for the Arts by the end of the 1990s and Republican calls to gut the Public Broadcasting System,[75] raised the specter of outright government censorship in a way that Donald Wildmon's boycott campaigns never have. Wildmon claims he is not in the business of censorship; he is just using the power of the boycott to apply pressure where pressure is due. "Networks can show what they want to show. Advertisers can sponsor what they want to sponsor. And the consumer can buy what he wants to buy," Wildmon said.[76]

Since censorship, strictly speaking, means prior restraint by government agents, Wildmon is technically accurate when he says he is not a censor. But because our entertainment and news are increasingly produced and distributed by large media corporations, the question of government censorship is largely a moot point. More important questions revolve around how corporate media perceive and respond to well-organized Christian Right activists. Censorship in the United States is mostly a matter of silencing dissident voices, not by government edict, but through the power of corporations to stifle or ignore what they deem unprofitable. Progressive spokespeople and their ideas are kept out of the mass media spotlight because they contradict the capitalist imperative to keep consumers content with the status quo.

Dueling Censures

❧

Pervasive, corporate-driven censorship is not on the radar screen of the centrist interest groups that try to cast the likes of Donald Wildmon and Pat Robertson as the preeminent threats to freedom of speech. People for the American Way (PAW), for example, publishes reports on the Christian Right's efforts to ban materials from classrooms and libraries. However, PAW is typically not critical of the corporate stranglehold on ideas and information. PAW effectively denies the existence of the most far-reaching and consequential forms of censorship by directing public attention to the efforts of people with little power compared to that of the media giants.

This is not meant to defend Christian Right campaigns to ban books and broadcasts, but rather to place such efforts in context. Members of the profamily movement make repeated efforts to narrow the range of publicly accessible facts and ideas. More often than not, their rationale is to "protect" children, which is why most of the efforts are aimed at getting school officials and librarians to remove books.

PAW publishes an annual report, *Attacks on the Freedom to Learn*, which includes hundreds of incidents, listed state by state. Typical incidents involve parents going to the school and demanding to have a particular book removed from a library or classroom. Among books frequently targeted, according to PAW, are Alvin Schwartz's *Scary Stories to Tell in the Dark*, Maya Angelou's *I Know Why the Caged Bird Sings*, and John Steinbeck's *Of Mice and Men*.[77] PAW gets valuable press coverage for its annual reports on would-be parental censors. This has caused Christian Right groups to counterattack with their own statements to the press. Concerned Women for America has called PAW's reports "an attempt to further entrench their position in the culture war."[78]

Supporting such an assertion, in 1996, a former PAW staff researcher published an exposé on how the organization exaggerates the threat of censorship for its own self-aggrandizement. Assuming that most journalists will report without fact-checking on "research" that seems reliable and exhaustive, PAW produces a lengthy document and includes, under the rubric of censorship, parental complaints that never go beyond a statement made to a school librarian. Most complaints to schools and libraries do not result in the actual banning of a book. Nor does the number of reported complaints fluctuate wildly from year to year.[79] PAW banks on the fact that most reporters for the corporate press dislike the Christian Right and are not inclined to suspect the movement's critics.

Apart from PAW's disingenuous way of reporting on censorship, Gary Bauer of the Family Research Council disputes PAW's entire notion of what constitutes censorship.

When a government restricts what its citizens can read—that's censorship. But when parents have input on what local officials do in the schools—that's democracy.

Obviously not every school and every library can have every book in existence. The question is will schools and libraries listen to parents or will they listen to People for the American Way? The real story here is the breakdown of democracy. How many times a day does a school board or a school library ignore parents who are merely trying to have input into the education of their children? Who are the real extremists?[80]

Bauer's reasoning is flawed because PAW, despite its inflated statistics, does not dispute the rights of parents to prevent their own children from taking out a particular library book. At issue are cases where parents want to make materials off-limits to *all* students.

The sticking point is whether parents have the right to protest when their child cannot simply ignore a particular book, that is, when he or she is part of a captive audience. Textbooks are contested because they are adopted wholesale for entire school districts. Among numerous textbooks that have come under fire, the *Impressions* reading series inspired a particularly strong panic among Christian Right groups.

In September 1990, Focus on the Family's *Citizen* magazine published a cover story, "Nightmarish Textbooks Await Your Kids." The article charged that the *Impressions* series was promoting witchcraft and the occult because some of the fictional stories were about sorcerers and monsters— exactly the kind of stuff most kids love to read about. The *Citizen* concluded with a "What You Can Do" box urging parents to write protest letters to the publishers, Harcourt Brace Jovanovich, and to their state education departments.[81] Reportedly, the publisher received more than eight hundred protest letters. Other national organizations, including Donald Wildmon's American Family Foundation, the Christian Coalition, and Citizens for Excellence in Education, alerted their members to protest the *Impressions* series, too. From there local groups began protests within their school districts, most of which decided to retain the series.[82] According to Focus on the Family, parents did succeed in getting the states of Georgia, North Carolina, and Mississippi to reject the *Impressions* series.[83] In California, the American Family Association backed a group of parents who tried to get a federal court injunction against the use of thirty-four stories and exercises in the *Impressions* books. Their suit alleged that because a lesson plan suggested that children could write make-believe magic spells after reading one of the stories, that the publisher was, effectively, promoting Wicca, which is an officially recognized, tax-exempt religion.[84] This was quite a leap of logic but it was certainly a revealing one. Parents feared that *Impressions* was part of a conspiracy to convert their kids to paganism—or, at least, to promote unchristian themes for young imaginations.

No End in Sight
∽

With most of its efforts the Christian Right fails to eliminate objectionable books outright. But there is no way to measure the extent to which publishers preemptively self-censor themselves in order to head off the hassle of an organized protest. Similarly, school districts in many parts of the country have a built-in incentive to choose the least risky sex education materials, instead of programs that would give students the most straightforward information.

Between parents inspired by the Christian Right and public schools charged with educating children, the struggle over acceptable ideas is intractable. Outcomes are determined largely by the degree to which all parents in a given locale get involved. Conservative evangelical parents ought to have a say in what happens to their children, but not to the exclusion of other parents' voices.

For activists in the Christian Right, the battles over school books, public art, and mass media are appealing regardless of whether the activists win or lose the power to draw the lines of acceptability. For three decades, the Christian Right has been unable to reinstate school prayer in the public schools. Nor does the idea of abolishing the Department of Education fly with most budget-cutting Republicans. Conservative evangelicals can do little to fight growing secularism in society as a whole. But they can attack it in manageable pieces, one textbook and one situation comedy at a time. Whether or not "bad" books or "bad" art will truly damage the psyches of children, there is something else at play in the drive to impose boundaries on what can be seen and heard—particularly at taxpayers' expense. What is at stake for people in the Christian Right is the chance to flex their political muscles; to satisfy themselves with the superiority of their own ways of thinking; and to deprive secular institutions, such as public education, of some of their long-held legitimacy.

Chapter 10

∾

The End Is Near

*F*atigue is a common problem for members of any social movement. Activists who achieve few of their goals are likely to suffer burnout. But by periodically expanding or changing its issue focus, a movement may compensate for its lack of achievement. To sustain its members, a successful social movement must provide them with a long-term vision and a sense that, despite long odds, someday victory will be theirs. What keeps the Christian Right in motion, despite obstacles and constant setbacks, is the dual nature of the movement. It is a narrowly focused political force but one that swims in the hospitable pool of a big evangelical subculture. Despite their defeat in a particular election or their failure to successfully challenge a local school board's policy, people in the Christian Right take solace in believing that God is on their side and that they or their successors will eventually prevail.

In general, the evangelical church world provides its adherents with an ideology well suited to the ups and downs of political conflict. Indeed, some of the most controversial practices within the evangelical subculture actually enable people to better sustain long-term commitment. Some of these practices can be distractions from thinking and acting politically. But even a good distraction can reenergize the faithful for the battles ahead. In this chapter I look at some recurring ideas, activities, and controversies that may at first sight seem to have little bearing on pragmatic politics but that do help to explain how the Christian Right sustains its fervor.

Millennial Thinking
∾

A willingness to sacrifice and a sense of inevitable victory are both integral to the Christian faith. Among true believers, both feelings are likely to intensify as the year 2000 arrives. On the issue of when Christ might return to reign in person over the entire earth, evangelicals hold a wide variety of opinions. Some, like Tim LaHaye, think the beginning of the end is just around the corner. Others believe that Christ will return only after they prepare the way by establishing a theocratic kingdom on earth. Still others look to the coming millennium simply as a time when unbelievers will become more receptive to the Gospel message.

Media missionary Pat Robertson was already at the forefront of the religious broadcasting industry when he beckoned the new millennium with his first novel, *The End of the Age*. Published in 1995, the book quickly rose to the top of the Christian Booksellers Association charts, though it was poorly written compared to other bestsellers, such as the novels of Frank Peretti and Charles Colson. Robertson's *The End of the Age* begins in the year 2000, when a huge meteor hits the southern California coast, setting off a series of worldwide tidal waves and nuclear meltdowns, killing half a billion people, and dooming everyone else to subservience under a demonic dictator who seizes control of the U.S. government. From their base camp in New Mexico, a small group of Bible-believing Christians uses satellite TV and radio transmissions to coordinate Christian resistance to Satanic government agents. Finally, the Rapture begins and the faithful are transported into heaven to spend eternity with Christ.

Throughout, the plot is thickened with gems from the mind of Pat Robertson. After the president of the United States commits suicide while on national television (out of remorse for not warning the country about the meteor), the Hillary Clinton–like wife of the drunk and degenerate vice president moves into action. She is a bisexual and a dabbler in New Age religion and feminism. She conspires with a foreign billionaire named Tarriq Haddad who arranges the assassination of her husband and the ascent to the presidency of one Mark Beaulieu. Beaulieu is the Antichrist, who has been possessed by the Hindu god Shiva ever since he served in the Peace Corps in India. Shiva, it turns out, is Satan, as are all non-Christian deities, which makes evangelization of the non–Western world all the more imperative before the year 2000.

The necessity of evangelism is the intended message of Robertson's book. In an interview with *Charisma* magazine, Robertson said he wrote *The End of the Age* not because he personally has any idea when the end will come, but because he believes the world is moving inevitably toward two major spiritual events, "worldwide evangelization and revival of epic proportions" and "world judgment." Robertson cites as evidence "an increase of progressively severe warnings and judgments of God—things like the earthquakes, tornadoes, floods and heat waves we've recently experienced." The message of the book, Robertson says, is that Christians have only a short time to "take the gospel to the world." He wants "readers to be seized with the sense of absolute urgency."[1]

Urgency is *the* theme in millennial thinking. Most evangelicals have long since abandoned the possibility of predicting an exact date for the Rapture. But a few preachers and authors still mine the esoteric and symbolic Book of Revelation looking for clues. What I call the "hard millennialists" try to link current events in world politics to a timetable for Christ's return. But the date-setters are outnumbered by those I call "soft millennialists." These believers heed the New Testament warning that "no man can know the day or the hour" of Christ's return (Mt. 24:36). Instead of predicting dates, they look at objectionable trends in society and see them as signs of difficult times ahead.

There are political overtones to both hard and soft millennialism. The handful of date-setters have been criticized by fellow evangelicals for making the evangelical community look foolish when they announce specific dates for Christ's return, dates that pass without incident. Moreover, hard millennialism has the effect of turning believers away from long-term political activism. That is why the majority of evangelical preachers teach their flocks a double message: as an individual, be prepared now, for the Final Day could be at hand; and as members of the Christian community, take a longer view, and work to spread Christ's message, for the Kingdom may be a long way off. Hard millennialism tends to foster a conspiratorial reading of political events: the misdeeds of world leaders are read as signs that they are doing the bidding of the Antichrist. Soft millennialism is more consistent with on-the-ground evangelism, which requires a willingness to deal with people of foreign cultures, though always with the goal of converting them to Christianity. In the 1990s, intensified millennial thinking has prompted an increase in missionary interest toward third world countries. The drive to win the world for Christ reveals the unwillingness of evangelicals to coexist gracefully with people of different, though no less authentic, cultures.

In the Last Days

✤

Robertson's 1995 book was probably best appreciated by evangelical believers steeped in eschatology, the study of the "end-times." One cornerstone of the Christian Gospel is the belief that Christ will eventually return to earth. Yet there has always been great controversy over when (and how) this event will take place. Most modern U.S. evangelicals believe in "premillennial dispensationalism." According to this view, God has divided human history into several ages, or "dispensations." We are in the final dispensation, which will end when Christ returns to reign over the earth. At some point, there will be a Rapture, during which all truly born-again Christians will ascend into heaven with Jesus. Some premillennialists believe that the Rapture will inaugurate a seven-year "Tribulation," a time when humankind will suffer a series of wars, famines, and natural disasters. Others—apparently including novelist Pat Robertson—believe that the Rapture will occur midway through the Tribulation. The most pessimistic believers expect that the Rapture will occur after the Tribulation, and that the faithful will have to endure suffering alongside the unbelievers. In any case, the Rapture will be tied closely to Armageddon, an all-out war between the forces of good and evil. Ultimately, the righteous will prevail, and their victory will herald the beginning of Christ's new millennial kingdom.[2]

A small proportion of conservative Christians adhere to a postmillennial eschatology. These are advocates of Reconstructionism, or "dominion theology," who believe that they must establish a theocracy on earth before Christ will return.[3] Among the much larger camp of premillennialists— which includes Baptist and charismatic/pentecostal subgroups—there has been heated debate about when the end-times will begin. Many of the conflicting interpretations revolve around political and military events in the Middle East. The establishment of the state of Israel, in 1948, was seen by many as the beginning of the generation that would witness Christ's return. The 1967 Six Day War, during which Israel seized all of Jerusalem and the West Bank, was interpreted by many as another sign that the end was near.

Prophecy writer Hal Lindsey's bestseller *The Late Great Planet Earth*, which has sold more than fifteen million copies since it was published in 1970, popularized premillennial eschatology for lay evangelical audiences. The book is a pastiche of Bible quotes and intimations that Armageddon will begin with a Soviet nuclear strike on Israel. Throughout the late 1970s and 1980s—the period of Cold War retrenchment and heightened public fears about nuclear war—Lindsey was a frequent guest on Trinity Broadcasting Network TV talk shows. Claiming to be privy to inside tips from military experts, he would interpret current events as signs that the end was near. Though he never set a precise end-times date, Lindsey's millennialism was "hard" in that he used real-world events as signs of an impending final battle. Only God's people would be "raptured," and thus spared from a fiery holocaust, but in the meantime, Lindsey promoted the 1980s U.S. nuclear buildup and massive U.S. military aid to Israel.

Lindsey's success inspired others to add to the popular genre of hard millennial books. Christian bookstores continue to stock special "prophecy" sections with titles by Lindsey, Jack van Impe, David Webber, John Walvoord, and others. Walvoord's 1974 "classic," *Armageddon, Oil, and the Middle East Crisis,* was reprinted in 1990 and became a bestseller for a second time, selling one million copies.[4] Walvoord, chancellor of the premillennialist Dallas Theological Seminary, was careful not to claim that the Persian Gulf War itself signaled the beginning of the end. His point was that biblical prophecy indicates that the Middle East will be "the battleground for the road to Armageddon and the second coming of Christ," and that "with world attention on the Middle East . . . the major components of the end time are in place."[5]

Walvoord, Lindsey, and most of their colleagues refrain from the kind of precise date-setting that would damage their credibility—and future sales of their next books. This is not the case with a couple of end-times date-setters who enjoyed brief notoriety on the evangelical media circuit. In 1987, Edgar Whisenant, a retired engineer and amateur Bible student, published *88 Reasons Why the Rapture Will Be in 1988.* Using an idiosyncratic set of calculations extrapolated from events mentioned in the New Testament, Whisenant predicted that the Rapture would occur between September 11 and September 13, 1988. By the time those dates had come and gone, he had sold 4.5 million copies of his booklets, and then he audaciously sold thousands more of subsequent tracts.[6]

Similarly, in 1992, Harold Camping, a once-respected broadcaster with the shortwave Family Radio ministry, began predicting that the world would end in September 1994. Using what many other Bible scholars considered a tortured reading of dates and numerical clues in the Bible, Camping claimed that the Tribulation actually began in 1988.[7] Camping's critics were particularly concerned when his book *1994* became a bestseller. Throughout 1994, the southern California–based Christian Research Institute, which monitors "heretical" Christian groups and broadcasts the nationally syndicated weekday *Bible Answer Man* radio program, targeted Harold Camping for criticism. Radio host Hank Hanegraaff took particular issue with Camping's claim that after September 6, 1994, no new believers could be converted. Hanegraaff and other critics indicted the date-setters for encouraging fatalism, and thereby abandoning the Christian mandate to go out and make new disciples.[8]

Most evangelicals hold to a soft millennialism, to the effect that because the timing of Christ's return cannot be known but is nevertheless imminent, proselytization of the "unsaved" is always urgent. Especially within the milieu of charismatic Christians—who believe that the ability to prophesy, the ability to heal, and other "gifts of the Holy Spirit" or "charismata" are as real today as during Christ's lifetime—the most popular preachers emphasize the approaching year 2000 as an impetus to escalate evangelism. In a book summarizing the teachings of leading charismatic figures, including Oral Roberts, Kenneth Copeland, Kenneth Hagin, Lester Sumrall, Marilyn Hickey, Jack Hayford, and Benny Hinn, pastor James Horvath concludes that most view the year 2000 not as the definitive "end-time" but rather as a "target date" for the goal of preaching the Gospel to the whole world. "We must not retreat from society; we must advance," Horvath wrote. "As the end of time draws closer, the body of Christ is to be actively involved in every arena—economically, socially and politically."[9]

Yet many premillennialists are, in fact, tempted to withdraw from society, if only by focusing rhetorically on divisions between the "saved" and "unsaved." That division is a major theme in Pat Robertson's novel and in other popular books published recently. One of these, *Left Behind*, by Peter and Patti Lalonde, was written putatively for readers who would witness "the disappearance of millions of people from the earth" during the Rapture.[10] The Lalondes' book (which bears the same title as the Tim LaHaye novel I discussed in Chapter 3) is a how-to effort to help these poor souls figure out what had happened to their saved loved ones and how they, too, may—better late than never—repent and still get into heaven.

Again, there are political overtones to both the hard and soft versions of premillennial eschatology. The harder theories tend to promote a sort of siege mentality. Lindsey and his cohorts read every Middle East peace negotiation, and every shift in the balance of forces between the global superpowers, as a sign that Christians should hunker down and wait to be raptured. This brand of millennialism might be a comfort to the sizable minority of the U.S. population who do believe the end is near. A 1993 *Time* magazine/CNN poll found that 20% of a general U.S. sample responded "Yes" to the question "Will the second coming of Jesus Christ occur sometime around the year 2000?"[11] A 1994 poll by *U.S. News and World Report* found that 59% of a national sample believed the world would come to an end. Twelve percent thought the end would come in a few years; 21% thought the end would come within a few decades. Forty-four percent of the same sample said that they believed the Bible literally, that there would be a Battle of Armageddon and a Rapture of the church.[12]

Clearly, the prophecy writers have a large potential market for their theories and books. But their popularity is matched by the prominence of soft premillennial leaders who urge a more involved, proactive response to the uncertainty over Christ's return. For the political activists of the Christian Right, it is far more expedient to promote the idea of Christians getting involved in all spheres of life than to suggest that they fatalistically sit tight waiting for the Rapture. The heroes in Pat Robertson's *The End of the Age* are able to rally Christian resistance to the Antichrist only because they spent the last years of the twentieth century amassing the technological know-how to preach the Gospel. Robertson's book is intended as a wake-up call to Bible believers: Know that secular political institutions are controlled by demonic conspirators, but take advantage of existing freedoms to harvest as many souls as possible before it is too late.

Windows of Opportunity

∽

Toward that end, and spurred by the approaching celebration of Christ's two thousandth birthday, evangelicals have made the 1990s a time of renewed commitment to the global mission fields. In the 1980s, U.S. evangelicals saw the world as a battleground on which the United States was fighting "communism" from Central America to the Philippines. With the fall of the "communist" menace, and with technology making the world increasingly smaller, the next great task is to convert the whole world to Christ. The major obstacles to this goal are the non-Christian religions indigenous to foreign cultures. Global evangelization, therefore, will require cooperation between U.S. evangelicals and their counterparts abroad.

In May 1995, four thousand evangelists from nearly two hundred countries met in South Korea for a nine-day Global Consultation on World Evangelism to devise strategies on how to spread the Christian Gospel to every corner of the earth before the year 2000. The event was billed as the broadest gathering of evangelicals in Christian history,[13] but it was just one event in a larger effort called the A.D. 2000 and Beyond movement.

Founded in 1990, and with headquarters in Colorado Springs, Colorado, A.D. 2000 and Beyond is a clearinghouse for a number of projects geared toward massive worldwide evangelism in the year 2000—and thereafter. The group intends to continue its work well after the dawn of the new millennium—its literature contains no suggestions that the world is about to end. The plan is to establish an international network of evangelical churches for every ethnic and religious group by the year 2000 as a birthday gift for Christ. Among the A.D. 2000 plans are two called "Praying Through the 10/40 Window" and the "Joshua Project." The 10/40 Window plan targets the overwhelming majority of the non-Christian "people groups" living in parts of the world located between ten and forty degrees north of the equator. This span of the planet includes much of Africa, all of the Middle East, all of India, and most of Asia—in other words, the most heavily populated part of the world, where people practice Islam, Hinduism, Buddhism, and other indigenous religions.[14]

Praying Through the Window is a project organized by evangelical leaders, including Christian Broadcasting Network chairperson Michael Little and theology professor C. Peter Wagner. Publicized through evangelical media outlets, Praying Through the Window involves convincing churches and individual Christians who are not otherwise active in missionary work to choose one of the one hundred "gateway cities" in the 10/40 Window region as the object of their prayers for a successful evangelical revival in that area. The "gateway cities" include Cairo, Istanbul, Baghdad, Tehran, Delhi, Bangkok, Beijing, and Tokyo.[15] In 1993, A.D. 2000 reported that over twenty million Christians from one hundred and five countries prayed for sixty-two nations in the 10/40 Window.[16] The subsequent campaign focused on praying for "gateway cities," those with populations in excess of one million; areas representing the "spiritual, political, and economic centers in their respective countries"; and areas that were also "the centers of Islam, Buddhism, Hinduism, Shintoism, Sikhism, and Taoism—religions which dominate this unreached region and hinder the growth of Christianity."[17]

Complementing Praying through the Window is the Joshua Project, launched in December 1995, when Christians from seventy-seven countries met in Colorado Springs to start a five-year plan to establish churches among "1,700 peoples whom mission leaders have agreed are most in need of a church planting effort."[18] The idea is to search out the ethnoreligious groups least touched already by the Christian Gospel and to match these "people groups" with local churches willing to pray for them and/or to sponsor a church among them.[19] Critics of the A.D. 2000 projects note that the 10/40 Window emphasis is trendy and has the potential to divert attention and resources away from more accessible mission fields. One critic has suggested that the emphasis on praying for "unreached people groups" might lead to a neglect of personal evangelism.[20]

There is no evidence that the A.D. 2000 prayer project is a detriment to more traditional, on-the-ground forms of evangelism. What has been evident within the evangelical subculture is a surge in the popularity of "spiritual mapping." This concept involves researching the demographics and history of a given geographic area, and then identifying the particular social problems and "territorial spirits" associated with that area. One of the advocates of "spiritual mapping" is Pastor Bob Beckett of the Dwelling Place Family Church in Hemet, California. He has mapped significant sites in his community, including the location of intertribal Indian warfare and the location of a failed water company drilling effort that has drained the water supply for native people in the area. Beckett uses the mapping information he acquires to encourage prayer and repentance by local Christians. He has claimed effective evangelism of Native Americans and other people in the areas he once "mapped" as spiritually difficult.[21] Beckett's approach to spiritual mapping is somewhat controversial because it suggests that evangelists focus on demonic spirits. Nevertheless, spiritual mapping has had the support of a number of groups active within the A.D.

2000 movement[22] because it resonates with A.D. 2000's focus on particular "people groups" and "gateway cities" as centers of non-Christian belief, that is, centers still under the sway of Satan.

Spiritual mapping is part of a broader charismatic practice called *spiritual warfare*, which involves praying for God to "intercede" to tear down "Satanic strongholds" that exist everywhere, from a believer's personal life to the highest echelons of political decisionmaking. The concept of spiritual warfare is based on a New Testament passage (Eph. 6:12), which says that believers "wrestle not against flesh and blood, but against principalities, against powers, against the rulers of the darkness of this world, against spiritual wickedness in high places." This verse is frequently invoked by charismatics, who take it to mean that their battle against evil is primarily a war of prayer.

More than an esoteric practice, spiritual warfare is a psychological mindset through which believers focus their attention on specific outcomes: winning a loved one to Christ, electing candidates to office, opening a foreign country to missionaries. Secular observers may doubt the efficacy of prayer, but there is something affecting about large groups of people acting together and trying to change the world through prayer. Within Christian Right political circles, people are usually asked first to pray about a problem before they make suggestions about tactics or decide on a plan of action. Praying about a situation tends to give believers a stake in seeing their prayers answered, and encourages them to make their prayers come true by actually doing something.

The evangelical media of the 1990s has devoted considerable attention to foreign missionary work. The popular magazine *Charisma* frequently publishes stories chronicling evangelistic efforts abroad. Coverage typically has a political angle. In 1995, for example, *Charisma*'s cover story, "The Holy Spirit around the World," began with an article about Haiti, where U.S. troops had recently been deployed to restore order. The article focused on Christian challenges to Haitian voodoo. But the article's title was "An Invasion of Mercy in the Caribbean," and it featured a full-page photo of a smiling U.S. soldier holding a smiling Haitian boy. So the article also carried a not-so-subtle political message: "I was saved by the U.S. military."[23] The Haiti story was accompanied by one on the spread of Christianity in North Korea, titled "Penetrating Stalin's Last Stronghold," and another on Colombia, titled "Revival behind Enemy Lines."[24] Consistently, *Charisma* covers evangelism in hot spots such as the Middle East, the Philippines, Brazil, and elsewhere, always with a slant suggesting that Christianity is the antidote to crime, disorder, and political dissent.

Despite the renewed interest in praying for the spread of Christianity overseas, the mission field remains fairly static. Generally, missions-minded U.S. evangelicals prefer to support native-born converts, who can more easily and inexpensively evangelize their compatriots, rather than putting expensive U.S. mission teams in the field. World Vision, one of the largest of the international mission agencies, has a southern California–based research division, the Mission Advanced Research and Communications Center (MARC), which compiles handbooks on worldwide evangelistic efforts and demographic facts about "unreached people groups," numbering some five hundred in the 1990s. In terms of numbers of missionaries sent abroad, for both short and long durations, the top-ranking U.S. groups are the Southern Baptist Convention, the Wycliffe Bible Translators, the New Tribes Mission, the Assemblies of God denomination, the Churches of Christ denomination, and Youth with a Mission.[25] Some one hundred groups supported about 50,500 missionaries in the field in 1988.[26]

MARC's most recent handbook notes that between 1988 and 1992, the total number of missionaries sent by U.S. and Canadian organizations actually *decreased*, reversing many years' worth of steady growth. However, MARC found increases in U.S. missions' financial support and training for national workers evangelizing in their home countries, as well as an increase in short-term missionary projects led by nondenominational groups.[27] The MARC report lamented the fact that only about 1.2% of foreign missionary funding was devoted to reaching the 1.2 billion people living in the least evangelized parts of the world.[28] The most heavily evangelized parts of the globe remain those already most hospitable to intrusions by North Americans: Latin America, Western Europe, and a handful of countries in Africa and the South Pacific.[29] Despite the rhetoric from groups affiliated with the A.D. 2000 project about "praying through the window," few tangible resources have been directed to the least evangelized areas.

Winning the World

❧

This gap between the rhetoric about reaching "unreached people groups" and the reality of a fairly static foreign mission field raises questions about the future politics of evangelical millennialism. The A.D. 2000 project correctly identifies a dearth of Christian missionary work in those parts of the world where people practice Islam, Hinduism, and Buddhism. But there is no sense on the part of the A.D. 2000 missionaries that they ought to simply cede parts of the world as places where people have their own religions. On the contrary, as the year 2000 approaches, evangelicals remain convinced of their prerogative to convert people of other religions. But the resistance and hostility to Christianity in much of the 10/40 Window area make actually going there a difficult prospect. Thus, the evangelical focus on spiritual warfare—unless, around the time of the new millennium, U.S. Christians actually increase their physical outreach to "unreached people groups."

That raises the specter of Christians coming into conflict with authorities in "unreached" countries. In 1996, anticipating increased problems for missionaries abroad, the National Association of Evangelicals (NAE) adopted a Statement of Conscience on "worldwide religious persecution" of Christians. The NAE urged the Clinton administration to appoint a special adviser for religious liberty and to cut foreign aid to countries that persecuted Christians. Also in 1996, a Congressional committee on human rights held a hearing on alleged abuse of Christians abroad and heard testimonies on incidents of harassment by governments in China, Cuba, North Korea, Vietnam, and the Islamic nations.[30] Neither the NAE nor the various missionary agencies expressed any concern about well-known and large-scale human rights abuses in countries where the greatest numbers of U.S. missionaries were sent: Indonesia, Brazil, and Colombia, for example. Instead, the possibility loomed that U.S. evangelicals might at some point challenge the prerogatives of U.S. foreign policymakers over countries deemed hostile to Christian missionaries. In response to lobbying by the NAE, the Senate passed a resolution condemning abuses of Christians around the world. In the fall of 1996, the Clinton administration quietly formed a State Department advisory committee on religious freedom. Twenty prominent religious leaders and scholars were invited to submit recommendations on how the U.S. government should respond to foreign governments that have jailed, tortured, and killed Christian missionaries (and adherents of other religions, too).[31]

In many parts of the world, religious persecution is a matter of life and death. Among U.S. evangelicals, the soft millennial project of converting people of other faiths keeps attention focused on international affairs, but in a very narrow way. The NAE is not particularly concerned about the uneven distribution of wealth in most parts of the world, though some missionaries see life-threatening poverty as an impediment to the spread of the Gospel. Evangelical Christians tend to view the rest of the world's religions as Satanic strongholds—not as the expression of culture by other people with an equal right to live and worship as they please.

Charismatic Controversies

✊

A wave of revival began in 1994, inside a tiny charismatic church near the Toronto airport. From around the world, thousands flocked to witness and experience it for themselves. They prayed, fell on the floor, shook, sobbed, roared like animals, and laughed uncontrollably, often into the wee hours of the morning. This form of revivalism is called "holy laughter." Many evangelicals believe that the Vineyard Christian Fellowship in Toronto is a place where God seeks to infuse people with a fresh reminder of the power of the Holy Spirit. Pastors visit, stay for a few days, and then carry the "Toronto Blessing," as it is called, back to their home congregations. As churches around the country become sites for ever more bizarre forms of worship, the charismatic subculture currently has on its hands yet another in a series of controversies over applied theology and proper relationships between leaders and disciples.

In the late 1990s, holy laughter and its assorted manifestations have become a source of divisiveness among charismatics. In the 1980s, charismatics wrangled among themselves over an authoritarian form of church management known as "shepherding" and over the self-appointed Word of Faith preachers who teach that Christians will be healed and grow rich if only they pray hard enough. Underlying the controversies is the belief in spiritual warfare: Christians are engaged in a supernatural battle with all the forces of evil, here on earth and in the invisible realms. In large part, the charismatic controversies are about how Christians should live their lives spiritually and in relation to fellow believers. What is politically relevant about spiritual warfare is the extent to which religious belief and behavior—like the content of Christian entertainment media—promote an ideology of combativeness toward the rest of society.

The holy laughter phenomenon originated with the ministry of Rodney Howard-Browne, a South African pentecostal minister who immigrated to the United States in the late 1980s. In 1993, Howard-Browne was invited to conduct services at pentecostal preacher Karl Strader's Carpenter's Home Church in Lakeland, Florida. Howard-Browne walked the church aisles, called on people to stand, and performed on them an act called "slaying in the spirit." In this act, a pastor puts his hand on the forehead of a believer, pushes, and causes the believer to fall backward onto the floor—or into the arms of a "catcher"—in an altered state of consciousness in which the believer feels filled with the Holy Spirit. To this standard technique, Howard-Browne added something new: he encouraged the faithful to let loose with raucous laughter. Word of the laughing going on at Home Church spread, and its membership skyrocketed. Howard-Browne began to receive invitations to replicate the phenomenon at other churches around the country. When asked what he was doing, he said, "I'm just the Holy Ghost bartender. I just serve the new wine and invite them to drink."[32]

Rodney Howard-Browne became a celebrity in charismatic circles. *Charisma* magazine published a cover story about him. Trinity Broadcasting Network aired many hours' worth of Howard-Browne's videotaped laughing services, so that viewers could see exactly how ordinary-looking churchgoers look when they land on the floor and laugh hysterically. The

TV images served as a form of role-modeling for others who would eventually experience the Toronto Blessing.

Randy Clark, of the Vineyard church in St. Louis, Missouri, was one of the first pastors to be heavily influenced by Rodney Howard-Browne. The Vineyard is an association of several hundred nondenominational but charismatic churches. The first of the Vineyard churches was founded by the late John Wimber in Anaheim, California, in the wake of the 1960s Jesus movement. Wimber was an ardent promoter of what he called "Signs and Wonders," the belief that modern-day Christians could and should experience the kinds of supernatural "gifts of the spirit" granted to Christ's original disciples and described in the second chapter of the New Testament Book of Acts.[33] The best known "gift" is the ability to speak in tongues, a phenomenon whereby Christians utter strings of apparently unintelligible syllables, which they believe can be interpreted by fellow born-again Christians who have had a secondary conversion experience known as "baptism of the Holy Spirit." Other gifts include the ability to heal and the ability to deliver prophetic messages about the future.

Tongues, healing, and the deliverance of prophetic messages have been fairly standard practices in charismatic churches since the original Pentecostal revival meetings of the early 1900s. But for those who believe that the Holy Spirit continues to grant supernatural gifts, some new sign of divine grace was long overdue, particularly now that we are moving toward the millennium. In early 1994, while Randy Clark was preaching with John Arnott of the Vineyard church in Toronto, the laughing phenomenon took hold during a series of all-night revival meetings. Word spread that the Toronto Airport Vineyard was a place to experience an unusual blessing. By the end of 1994, some seventy-five thousand believers from all over the world had made pilgrimages to the Toronto Vineyard. Soon, though, mere uncontrolled laughing was tame stuff. The behavioral repertoire has now expanded, much to the chagrin of critics such as Hank Hanegraaff, who hosts the daily *Bible Answer Man* radio program, sponsored by the Christian Research Institute (CRI). As president of CRI, Hanegraaff has attended Vineyard church services during which people writhe on the floor and bark like dogs. He routinely calls such phenomena a "counterfeit revival." The CRI was founded in the 1950s to combat the evangelistic efforts of the Mormons, Jehovah's Witnesses, and other Christian-style "cults." But in recent years, its radio call-in show has frequently focused on controversies within the evangelical world, particularly end-time date-setting, fraudulent faith healers, and holy laughter. On the air and in his 1997 book, *Counterfeit Revival,* Hanegraaff charges that holy laughter, at the very least, involves psychological manipulation of believers looking for a quick, wild experience. At worst, Hanegraaff believes, the laughing, barking, and generally uncontrolled carrying on is evidence of an altered state of consciousness that may open practitioners to "demonic" influence.

Some of Hanegraaff's fellow evangelical heresy hunters dislike his confrontational style.[34] But the ongoing controversy concerning holy laughter led John Wimber, in early 1996, to sever his ties with the Toronto Vineyard church, on the grounds that the "blessing" had drifted too far out of the bounds of scriptural teaching.[35]

Nevertheless, holy laughter has enjoyed overall favorable treatment by the charismatic media. A laudatory article appeared in the Christian Coalition's otherwise politically focused newspaper.[36] Pat Robertson himself effectively endorsed holy laughter by hosting Rodney Howard-Browne at a Christian Broadcasting Network "Signs and Wonders" conference in 1995.[37]

Holy laughter and related behaviors have set a new pattern for what is acceptable and expected in charismatic churches, and have also set off a controversy that is likely to continue brewing for years. In many respects, the holy laughter controversy revives themes associated with an earlier controversy involving "Word of Faith" preachers. Some of the same charismatic leaders who now support holy laughter, including Oral Roberts, his son, Richard Roberts, and Kenneth Hagin of the Rhema Bible Training Center in Tulsa, are also Word of Faith preachers. These preachers (who enjoy heavy media exposure on the Trinity Broadcasting Network) teach that if Christians suffer physical or financial problems, it is because they are not praying adequately. Conversely, they teach that if one prays in the right way, one will achieve health and wealth. Those who preach what is known as "the prosperity message" are popular because they tell people what they want to hear.

In between his blasts at holy laughter and date-setting, Hank Hanegraaff uses his *Bible Answer Man* radio program to detail the latest antics of the Word of Faith preachers. But the problem, for Hanegraaff, is not just a handful of preachers who offer a perverted version of Christ's message. It is the fact that untold thousands of Christians are feasting on a diet of what Hanegraaff calls "fast food Christianity," to the effect that with prayer they can simply "name and claim" any sort of healing or financial windfall they desire. This faith message is promulgated in the syndicated preacher shows on Trinity Broadcasting Network (TBN) and through dozens of books and tapes sold by the most popular of the Word of Faith teachers. Oral Roberts, Kenneth Hagin, Kenneth Copeland, Benny Hinn, Frederick Price, John Avanzini, Robert Tilton, Marilyn Hickey, Charles Capps, and Jerry Savelle are the best known. They are all frequent guests of TBN president Paul Crouch, and they enjoy frequent promotion on the pages of *Charisma* magazine.

In his 1993 bestselling book *Christianity and Crisis*, Hanegraaff called the Word of Faith preachers a bunch of cultists who rely on the New Age notion that one's own mind has the power to change the course of events.[38] Hanegraaff considers this idea decidedly unchristian. At best, he argues, Word of Faith preachers encourage a spirit of greed and a lack of appreciation for one's lot in life. At worst, they are scam artists, particularly in the realm of faith healing.

During his revival crusades, preacher Benny Hinn brings sick people up on stage and "slays them in the spirit," knocking them into the arms of an usher while he commands them to believe they are healed. I find it disheartening to watch while Hinn holds young children in his arms and tells their desperate, gullible parents that their tumors or other serious health problems are now a thing of the past. What are these families to think when the doctor tells them otherwise? That their child is still sick because they lacked faith in the power of the Holy Spirit? The faith healings, like Rodney Howard-Browne's holy laughter sessions, are highly visual and therefore ideally suited to TV evangelism. Such activities are exciting to watch. But they also encourage a cult of personality around top-ranking celebrity preachers.

In the late 1980s, three highly publicized scandals permanently demolished the reputations of TV preachers Jim Bakker, Oral Roberts, and Jimmy Swaggart. These men betrayed the trust of their viewers and donors. Less well known is another preacher scandal, one that involved a group of charismatic leaders who fostered a style of pastoring known as "shepherding."[39] Following the heyday of the youthful Jesus movement, many young converts were eager to make their faith a twenty-four-hour-a-day commitment, and they looked to some of the older pentecostal ministers who were similarly eager to shepherd people full-time in every aspect of their lives. The problem began in the early 1970s, when a group of ministers who called themselves the "Fort Lauderdale Five" created a "covenant relationship," which they likened to marriage, and took on the task of overseeing each other's personal and spiritual lives. All of their disciples, too, were implicated in this net. The preachers taught that they were in total authority and that their disciples needed to "submit" themselves to the elders, lest they stray from the faith, do harm to their own spiritual growth, and lose their ability to win new converts. Shepherding was established with a pyramid structure. The top leaders appointed lieutenants to control small churches which were, in turn, organized into cell groups. The tightly knit, hierarchial organization made it feasible for participating pastors to monitor people's daily behavior. Shepherding caught on with other preachers as quickly as abuses set in. The shepherds claimed the right to tell followers whom to marry, how husbands were to treat their wives, how families were to spend their money, and much more. This was a drastic departure from the way pastors typically related to parishioners. Yet shepherding flourished in the charismatic subculture, with little public criticism from more responsible evangelical leaders. Eventually, however, beginning in the 1980s, numerous members of shepherding churches defected. They told stories reminiscent of those told by people who had joined the various non-Christian cults rampant during the 1970s and 1980s. Ex-members of shepherding churches reported feeling humiliated by their loss of personal sovereignty. Many also believed that by leaving the churches, they could no longer be Christians.[40]

At their peak of power the Fort Lauderdale Five—Bob Mumford, Derek Prince, Don Basham, Charles Simpson, and Ern Baxter—controlled a network of churches representing an estimated 150,000 followers. By the 1980s, though, the abuses were so obvious and the defections so massive that the shepherds began to dismantle their network. In late 1989, Bob Mumford publicly apologized for the abuses at a meeting of charismatic pastors.[41] By then Don Basham had died, and Prince and Baxter had gone their separate ways. But Charles Simpson continued to claim that shepherding helped people be good Christians; as of 1990, he continued to oversee a network of ten thousand people in 150 churches.[42]

Shepherding took its greatest toll on people's personal lives, but the submovement was also politically right-wing. Some of the top leaders and lieutenants were active in the 1980s in the Coalition on Revival (COR), founded by Jay Grimstead as a forum to unite evangelical ministers who disagreed with each other on millennial theology and for the purpose of drafting a series of position papers on how Christians should and could "take dominion" in all spheres of social life, including education, economics, law, and the entertainment media.

For a number of years, COR was home to advocates of an esoteric, noncharismatic strain of Christianity called Reconstructionism. This brand of theology is rooted in Calvinist teachings. Its leading proponent is Rousas John Rushdoony, who was born in 1916 and who founded the Chalcedon Foundation in California in the mid-1960s. Rushdoony was strongly influenced by Westminster Theological Seminary professor Cornelius Van Til, a Dutch theologian who emphasized the Bible's inerrant authority and the irreconcilability between believers and unbelievers. Rushdoony, his estranged son-in-law, Gary North, and a handful of other authors have issued a stream of books and journals promoting the postmillennial view that Christ will return only after Christians establish the Kingdom of God on earth. In the meantime, the Reconstructionists advocate a total reorganization of contemporary Western society to conform to the laws of the Old Testament. Rushdoony goes so far as to say, in his major manifesto *The Institutes of Biblical Law*, that a wide range of sins should be punishable by death. These include murder, adultery, incest, homosexuality, witchcraft, unrepentant juvenile delinquency, and even blasphemy.[43]

Because he is so far out of step with most people in the Christian Right, Rushdoony has a limited, though loyal, following. A conference held in April 1996 to honor his eightieth birthday was attended by some two hundred people from around the country. Among the speakers was Herbert Titus, the former dean of Pat Robertson's Regent University law school. Titus had been forced to resign precisely because he adhered to Rushdoony's Reconstructionism. Also on hand was Howard Phillips, founder of the U.S. Taxpayers Party. Phillips is a Jew who converted to Christianity and later to Reconstructionism after reading Rushdoony's work. In 1992 and again in 1996, Phillips made an unsuccessful effort to get Patrick Buchanan to run for president as the U.S. Taxpayers Party candidate.[44]

The Reconstructionists are at the extreme end of a worldview unalterably opposed to secular, liberal society. Hard-core Reconstructionists oppose even most of the evangelical movement, which they see as too compromising, too enamored with spiritual experience, and insufficiently grounded in the mandates of the Bible. It is true that many charismatics stress experience over Scripture study. But holy laughter, faith healing, and contemporary Christian music are popular precisely because they gave people emotional experiences, not more grist for the mind.

Invisible Trenches

ᵔ

The excitement of experience dovetails neatly with the idea of *spiritual warfare*, which was greatly popularized through Frank Peretti's first novel, *This Present Darkness*. Peretti is the son of an Assemblies of God pastor and a minister himself. As a young Christian he became convinced that the New Age movement is the most serious threat to Christianity. He wrote his novel to convey this message.[45] *This Present Darkness* is about a group of New Age conspirators, including one disguised as a psychology professor, operating inside a respectable church, who try to take over a small town in middle America. Throughout the story, the visible action that takes place in the town coincides with a supernatural battle between demonic forces led by Satan's deputy, Rafar, and a band of angels led by a good spirit named Tal. The demons and angels fight battles between themselves while they also guide and foil the actions of the people in the town. *This Present Darkness* makes the point that Christians can be victorious if, through what Peretti calls "intercessory" prayer, they call on angelic forces and God Almighty to rout demons from territories under attack by Satan.

Peretti's version of spiritual warfare is presented as fiction, but many charismatic leaders take the phenomenon literally. *Charisma* magazine publishes frequent articles on the role of spiritual warfare in successful church building and missionary outreach. A number of organizations are dedicated to organizing "prayer warriors." The best known of these is called Generals of Intercession, founded in 1985 by Cindy Jacobs. She works closely with the A.D. 2000 and Beyond project, and she appears frequently at missionary conferences where she teaches people to pray that nations targeted for evangelism will become receptive to missionaries. Jacobs's writings are full of warfare rhetoric. She told *Charisma* magazine that "churches have not been effective in winning nations for Christ because Christians have lacked a military-style prayer strategy."[46] She is aggressive about praying against demons, yet she is also a leader in the drive for racial reconciliation (a topic I discuss in the next chapter).

In 1994, Generals of Intercession, in collaboration with A.D. 2000, sponsored a conference called "Healing America's Wounds." The conference focused explicitly on "prayer for healing the deep wounds and scars done by the white man to the Indians," and for "re-entry of blacks into America as people of covenant and not slaves."[47] With a notion of collective and generational sin, Jacobs called on conference attendees to repent for the sins of racism and slavery and to pray for God to heal the land. In her *G.I. News*, Jacobs explained her view of the impact of such prayer.

> One important result is that it stops Satan's legal right to blind people's eyes to the Gospel. The prayer seemingly drains the anger off the people and makes them less resistant to the Gospel. Hardened hearts suddenly become receptive to the Gospel. Also, people who were not at the meeting hear what has been said and are able to forgive those who committed racial sins against them. Others have been physically healed as a result of being in a prayer meeting where repentance for the sins against their people has been made.[48]

Advocates of spiritual warfare claim to oppose New Age teachings, and yet the above description is consistent with New Age beliefs about the healing power of prayer.

There are differences, however. New Age spirituality focuses on positive, angelic spiritual entities. (Traditional witchcraft denies even the existence of Satan.) Christian spiritual warriors link their prayer battles to evangelism. One of *Charisma* magazine's numerous articles on spiritual warfare reported amazing stories of how missionaries used prayer to break Satan's grip on a geographical area previously resistant to evangelism. There is no way to verify such reports that prayer warfare is subsequently followed by membership growth in churches. But the article urges prayer warriors to be strategic about identifying demonic influence in their cities. A sidebar urged Christians to monitor their neighborhoods for trends designated as "Satanic," such as increased racial tensions, greater influence of homosexuals, and higher teenage suicide rates, and to ask themselves: "What do these trends reveal about the nature of the unseen realm over the city?"[49]

The term "spiritual warfare" is a rhetorical flourish but it also suggests the real mindset of "prayer warriors." They believe themselves to be not just in disagreement with unbelievers but engaged in actual combat with them. They see common social problems and political conflicts as events orchestrated by none other than Satan who, though ferociously powerful, can be defeated by fervent prayer and the "intercession" of godly forces. Prayer alone is not always enough to defeat Satan. If, for example, homosexuals or abortion rights advocates are becoming too powerful, prayer warfare is called for. But the success of prayer will be most evident if other actions are taken. Prayer gives legitimacy to more mundane forms of warfare, such as running for office, circulating politically slanted literature and videos, and forming crisis pregnancy centers and antigay counseling ministries. No matter how aggressive such efforts are, they are justified because Christians are at war with the enemies of God.

Spiritual warfare is a constant theme in the evangelical entertainment media and in the worship practices of charismatics, in particular. In stories such as Frank Peretti's novel *This Present Darkness*, it is exciting to read about battles between clearly delineated good guys and bad guys—with wings. Psychologically, spiritual warfare makes matters, religious and political, more simple. There is an obvious right and there is an obvious wrong. It is right for those who are wrong to suffer and lose.

Some of the partisans in the great battle between good and evil are easily identified. They are bad sinners arrayed against good, profamily people. But, as we will see in the next chapter, on matters of race and gender in the evangelical subculture, the battle lines are not always fixed nor easy to discern. This is all the more reason why prayer warfare and the advice of pastoral leaders are necessary to separate the wheat from the chaff.

Chapter 11

✌

Coming to Terms

Typically, from the liberal perspective, the Christian Right is seen as a reactive force. Particularly on the issues of abortion rights, gay rights, and sexually liberal media and educational content, the Christian Right wants to roll back changes created largely through the efforts of the movement's opponents. As for the rest of what goes on within the evangelical subculture, much of it may seem politically irrelevant to liberals. What difference does it make what happens at a Sunday morning charismatic church service? But some of the trends underway in the evangelical world stem directly from changes underway within the secular political culture. And these evangelicals trends, in turn, have (or will have) an effect on secular culture. Evangelicals are part of mainstream society. Like everyone else, they must accommodate themselves to at least some of the irreversible social changes of the last few decades. Racial and gender issues have had a significant impact on the evangelical world. Typically, liberals want to dismiss the idea that conservative Christians could be anything but intransigent on such matters. In reality, evangelicals are addressing the impact of racism on U.S. society and the role of men in a culture where feminism has taken root.

In this chapter I look at the project of *racial reconciliation* underway both in the evangelical world and in the political work of the Christian Coalition. Here I also address the Promise Keepers phenomenon. At the most obvious level, Promise Keepers is an organization that sponsors heavily attended weekend worship rallies for men. I argue that Promise Keepers is popular not because it rehashes old-fashioned theories of male domination but, rather, because it does not. Promise Keepers is working hard to bridge the racial divide between white and black men already converted to Christ. Mostly, though, the Promise Keepers project is about preserving traditional gender roles and distinctions between men and women, albeit without the excesses of crude sexism. Even the most conservative evangelical males can no longer view or treat women as they did in the 1950s. Promise Keepers is not so much a knee-jerk reaction to feminism as it is an effort to help Christian men retain their sense of male supremacy, now couched as "leadership," while they struggle to keep their marriages and families from falling apart. By looking at how the evangelical subculture treats matters of race and gender, one can see the dynamic nature of movement ideology. What was true twenty years ago is no longer true, and one can safely predict that the Christian Right will continue to evolve in its framing of social hierarchies, its definitions of what is acceptable and what is not.

Racial Reconciliation

∾

It was a scene straight out of the New Testament. At an interracial gathering of Pentecostal ministers held in Memphis in October 1994, the leaders of long-segregated denominations took turns washing each other's feet, as Jesus once did for his disciples. It was a powerful display of racial healing and forgiveness, symbolic of a genuine trend underway in the evangelical subculture. At the Memphis meeting, the Pentecostal Fellowship of North America, representing twenty-one white denominations, broke with seventy years of racial segregation and formed a new body, the Pentecostal–Charismatic Churches of North America, with an executive committee of six black and six white ministers representing ten million denominational pentecostals. (Another five million North American pentecostals belong to unaffiliated churches.) The new body represents large denominations, including the Assemblies of God, the International Church of the Foursquare Gospel, and the African American Church of God in Christ.[1]

The birth of this new interracial group brought pentecostalism back to its historical roots in the early part of the twentieth century. In 1906, a religious revival broke out at a church on Azusa Street in Los Angeles. Led by an African American preacher named William Joseph Seymour—whose parents had been slaves in Louisiana—black, white, and Mexican believers danced together and shouted for joy night after night. They prayed in a strange language consisting of seemingly unintelligible syllables. They called their prayer language "speaking in tongues," and they called themselves "pentecostals," after the term "Pentecost" from the second chapter of the New Testament Book of Acts. In this passage, Christ has long since been crucified, and the first generation of disciples gather in Jerusalem to celebrate the Jewish holiday of Pentecost. They are visited by the Holy

Spirit. Their heads are magically crowned with flames or "tongues" of fire, and though they have come from many nations, they suddenly understand each other's languages. They recognize their newfound understanding as the fulfillment of the Old Testament prophecy that "in the last days," before the return of the Messiah, all believers will receive the gift of prophecy and the ability to interpret unknown tongues.

In the Book of Acts, the pentecostals are a flock from many nations. Thus, the multicultural character of the early-twentieth-century Azusa Street revival was consistent with the original New Testament story. The Azusa Street revival soon spread to other parts of the country. The flamboyant worship style, including prayer in tongues, caught on among church leaders who were looking for a sign that the last days were imminent, that Christ would soon return. But as the pentecostal movement grew, it also splintered into innumerable factions. White pentecostals were eager to lead their own churches, and they followed the racist norms of the time by starting their own all-white denominations.[2] Race quickly became the dividing line in the pentecostal subculture, as it was in the evangelical subculture, the greater Protestant subculture, indeed, in U.S. culture as a whole.

Earlier, in the mid-nineteenth century, the Baptist Church in the United States split into two branches, an antislavery northern church and the proslavery Southern Baptist Convention. After the Civil War, the Southern Baptist Convention still held to its prewar views regarding white racial superiority. Consequently, following the end of slavery, most black Baptists formed their own denominations. In 1995, leaders of the Southern Baptist Convention celebrated the 150th anniversary of their denomination with what many considered a long overdue public apology for the church's history of racism. The public statement marked a slow trend toward integration within the denomination, if not within individual churches. As of 1995, there were almost two thousand recently formed black Southern Baptist churches.[3]

While it remains to be seen whether rank-and-file congregations will begin to exhibit true color blindness, public calls for racial reconciliation emanating from the white pentecostal and Baptist leadership reflect a new mood among white evangelicals. Most political observers are skeptical about the sincerity of white conservative Christian leaders. The national climate of racial intolerance gives little cause for optimism.

Most troubling, the year 1996 saw a rash of burnings of African American churches in the South. These acts of arson were reminiscent of Ku Klux Klan attacks on black churches during the civil rights movement era. Indeed, at least some of the 1990s perpetrators are known supporters of white hate groups. Most of the crimes have gone unsolved by law enforcement agencies, but with each new act of church destruction, religious figures and groups around the country pledge their support.

Among the most visible supporters of vandalized black churches has been Ralph Reed of the Christian Coalition. In 1996, Reed offered a $25,000 reward for information leading to the arrests of the arsonists.[4] At a Congressional hearing on a bill to double the criminal penalties for burning a church, Reed testified to the effect that the Christian Coalition hopes to make amends for the movement's past neglect of civil rights issues. "It is a painful truth that the white evangelical church was not only on the sidelines but on the wrong side of the most central struggle for social justice in this century," Reed said. "So we come with broken hearts, a repentant spirit and ready hands to fight this senseless violence." In July 1996, the Coalition organized a Racial Reconciliation Sunday and urged the hundred thousand churches on its mailing list to take up a collection to help rebuild damaged black churches.[5]

African American civil rights spokespersons have not been favorably impressed. The Reverend Joseph Lowery of the Southern Christian Leadership Conference accused Reed of "trying to exploit the situation."[6] Jesse Jackson complained that it was the Christian Coalition that "contributed to the race baiting that goes on in this country," and he refused to give credence to Reed's apology. "We must be aware of those who set the climate for racial storm and we must not let them hand out umbrellas," Jackson said.[7] Reed's pronouncements did smack of opportunism, coming as they did during an election season when the Christian Coalition was organizing the distribution of millions of voter guides for the benefit of right-wing candidates.

In the 1990s, Christian Right leaders have looked on conservative people of color as an untapped source of new voters and new allies. In 1991, for example, the Reverend Louis Sheldon of the Traditional Values Coalition mobilized African American pastors to lobby for the confirmation of Supreme Court nominee Clarence Thomas. Other prominent conservatives of color have served as useful advocates for state ballot measures to deny civil rights protections for gays and lesbians. Some people of color strongly oppose affirmative action policies and also hold conservative views on other social policy issues.

In the fall of 1993, the Christian Coalition released the results of a poll it had commissioned showing that large percentages of African Americans and Latinos oppose abortion, gay rights, welfare, and affirmative action. The validity of this poll data is dubious, but its purpose is clear. Reed pledged that his movement would no longer "concede the minority community to the political left," and he announced that the Christian Coalition would begin recruiting from within black and Latino churches.[8]

Around the same time, the Coalition began to feature black and Latino speakers at its annual Road to Victory conference.

The tactic is a form of blatant tokenism, but it is also a move with potential to grow beyond mere symbolism. The Republican Party wants to appeal to middle-class voters across racial lines, and the Democratic Party has become an increasingly unreliable champion of civil rights. In that vacuum, and especially with the use of controversial social issues, the Christian Right has a double agenda. One is to put behind it the movement's long-held (and rightly so) reputation for bigotry. The other is to tap a previously neglected base of potential new supporters, African Americans who share with whites of the Christian Right strong church affiliations and religious commitments. Reed is right when he calls it a mistake to concede the minority community to the Left, by which he means the Democratic Party.

It is hard to imagine the Christian Right becoming a racially integrated social movement, let alone one committed to true racial equality. The *political* project of cross-racial recruitment is likely to sink or swim to the extent that the evangelical *culture* continues to encourage racial reconciliation. By making the treatment of racial harmony a commonplace theme in the churches and in the alternative evangelical media, the promoters of racial reconciliation are sowing the seeds of a future political alignment based more on perceived interests and shared moral values, and less predictably on racial identity.

Expanding the Mission Field
∽

Political strategists like Ralph Reed naturally see racial reconciliation as a chance to make political alliances. For evangelical clergy who want to break the color line, there are political considerations, to be sure. Racial reconciliation has the potential to reshape church bodies, which are small political and fiscal entities in their own right. Breaking racial barriers may allow ambitious church leaders to broaden their constituencies and their influence. They may express this goal in terms of reaching new souls for Christ, but there are more secular interests at play as well.

Charisma magazine, for example, is a steady promoter of themes of racial reconciliation. The magazine has a circulation in the hundreds of thousands and an interest in appealing as broadly as possible to charismatic Christians of all colors. "Charismatic" is a self-descriptive term used by late-twentieth-century pentecostals who pray in tongues and, by so doing, feel they have received a secondary "baptism of the Holy Spirit," secondary in that it follows their initial born-again conversion experience. Decades after the pentecostal Azusa Street revival of the early 1900s, a new charismatic renewal started, beginning in the 1960s, among previously staid churches, even among some Roman Catholics.[9] For the sophisticated, the term *pentecostal* calls to mind images of hillbillies rolling in the aisles of run-down storefront churches. The *charismatic* label is more respectable and reflects the spread of emotion-driven worship practices into more middle-class churches. *Charisma* magazine, launched in the mid-1970s, caters both to the old-fashioned pentecostals and to a new group of charismatic churches, including many that emerged from the Jesus movement. (Among the new charismatics are the Vineyard churches discussed in the previous chapter.)

 Charisma is full of advertisements for revival meetings around the country. By the early 1990s, there were noticeably more announcements for gatherings headed by black preachers. Increasingly, the events feature interracial teams of well-known preachers. In a 1993 cover story, "Healing the Rift between the Races," *Charisma* praised some of the new, large, racially mixed charismatic churches, including John Meares's Evangel Temple in Washington, DC; Rod Parsley's World Harvest Church in Columbus, Ohio; Benny Hinn's Orlando Christian Center; Dick Bernal's Jubilee Christian Center in San Jose, California; and Joseph Garlington's Covenant Church in Pittsburgh. The cover photo was a close-up of a smiling black child's face pressed cheek-to-cheek to a smiling white child's face. Inside, though, the article lamented the fact that most charismatic churches have a long way to go to such a degree of racial integration. Many major denominations, such as the Assemblies of God, still have extremely segregated churches. African American pastors are often reluctant to join new interdenominational associations, which are led by historically white denominations.[10] Nevertheless, the lack of racial diversity is now on the minds of evangelicals, not as a fact of nature, but as a social problem to be fixed.

 Since 1993 *Charisma* has frequently discussed the subject of racial reconciliation, both in editorials and in news reports on interracial gatherings. *Charisma* is also a venue for some religious theorizing about the sources of and solutions for racism within the churches. One particularly notable article was written by C. Peter Wagner, a professor of church growth at the Fuller Theological Seminary in Pasadena, California. Wagner is also a coordinator of the A.D. 2000 and Beyond project. He is a leading promoter of the use of spiritual warfare as a means to make "unreached" territories more receptive to missionaries. In his *Charisma* article, Wagner links evangelism to a new term he coined, *identificational repentance*. Christians, Wagner argues, know that they need divine forgiveness for the personal sin in their lives. True repentance requires, first, that one confess one's sins. Then one must take action to repair the damage done by one's sinning in the past and promise not to sin and cause such damage again. Paralleling the individual process, Wagner writes, "nations can and do sin corporately." Therefore, nations, too, must confess their sins and take redemptive action. Wagner's argument is worth quoting at length:

> The principle sin of my nation is clearly racism. The corporate sins that have established this spiritual stronghold are clear. The broadest and most pervasive sin was committed in bringing Africans to our shores as slaves—human merchandise to be bought, sold and used for any conceivable purpose to satisfy the desires of their white masters.
>
> Beyond this, however, is an even deeper root of national iniquity; the horrendous way white Americans treated their hosts in this land, the American Indians. . . .
>
> Why should we be concerned about the sins committed by our ancestors? . . . The answer derives from the spiritual principle that iniquity passes from generation to generation. . . . Technically speaking, *sin* can be understood as the initial act and *iniquity* as the effect the sin has exercised on subsequent generations. . . .
>
> Time alone does not heal national iniquities. In fact, if the sin is not remitted, the iniquity oftentimes becomes worse in successive generations.
>
> But the cycle can be stopped by corporate repentance. The only ones who can confess the sin and put it under the blood of Jesus are those who are alive today. Even though they did not commit the sin themselves, they can choose to *identify* with it, thus the term "identificational repentance." . . .
>
> When we remit the corporate sins of a nation by the blood of Jesus Christ, we effectively remove a foothold that Satan has used to keep populations in spiritual darkness. By actively applying the truth that "the weapons of our warfare are not carnal, but mighty through God to the pulling down of strong holds" (2 Cor. 10:4, KJV), the glory of Christ is able to shine through, and the kingdom of God can come in power.[11]

Wagner proceeded to invite Christians to join with A.D. 2000 in a 1996 prayer campaign called "Heal the Land." The major event was to be a walk by thousands of Christians who would retrace the routes of the medieval crusaders, all the while praying for repentance for the sins committed centuries ago by Christians against Muslims and Jews. Wagner urged U.S. Christians to pray in repentance for slavery and for the slaughter of Native Americans, and he urged Europeans to pray for the sins of World War II.[12]

Ultimately, Wagner's goal with "identificational repentance" is to facilitate evangelism, and thus build God's Kingdom on earth. Wagner's call for collective repentance is a departure from a more widespread approach, which is to see racism as a matter of individual prejudice. He, at least, has a recognition that racism is a historical process, and that entire groups of people have been both victims and beneficiaries of this most virulent social sin. This approach is a stark departure from the way in which many on the Right have wanted to frame racism: as a lack of interpersonal consideration, now on its way out. Wagner's article appeared during an election season in which the Right, as well as many liberals, claimed that affirmative action policies are unjust, either because society has already reached the goal of racial fairness and/or because today's individuals should not have to pay for the discriminatory actions of past generations.

Secular society is immersed in a debate: is racism mostly about insensitive individual behavior, or is it primarily about entrenched institutional hierarchies, in which jobs, education, and other social goods are unequally distributed along racial lines? The debate has profound implications for the direction of government policy. Will society as a whole seek to thwart future racial injustice by, effectively, "repenting" for the racism of the past? The debate within secular society is heated in a way it is not among evangelicals who are focused on reforming their own institutions, for their own sake and for the purpose of making a better appeal to an "unsaved," racially diverse world.

There are always connections between personal behavior and political culture. Therefore, it was highly significant when *Charisma* magazine published a favorable article on interracial marriage.[13] In a profile of several successful interracial marriages, *Charisma* signaled that evangelical calls for racial reconciliation were sincere.

This sincerity will not necessarily translate into a radical critique of a racist social order. But given the long history of segregation in the United States and the intense fears surrounding the old taboo of interracial marriage, there is something phenomenal about the racial reconciliation project underway in the evangelical subculture. Just as Ralph Reed said he would no longer concede people of color to the liberal wing of the political establishment, it is best for secular advocates of racial equality to neither concede nor dismiss the changing racial dynamics among conservatives.

Similarly, it is best not to dismiss the ways in which shifting attitudes about social hierarchies may have the effect of reducing some forms of inequality while strengthening others. Specifically, the racial reconciliation project is always framed by evangelicals in the context of bolstering the traditional family. Interracial Christian marriage is "good" because it is heterosexual marriage between fellow believers in Christ. It may be problematic to raise children within a still racist society, but interracial marriage does not tamper with the norm of male dominance in the household, nor does it address, at all, economic disparities between different types of families. Progressive critics of racism emphasize that class, race, and gender inequalities have a way of mutually reinforcing each other, and therefore all must be confronted as variant forms of injustice deserving equal attention. For conservative evangelicals, however, racial reconciliation involves downplaying class boundaries while reinforcing other boundaries: between believers and the "unsaved," and between men and women. The former is a boundary between the evangelical subculture and the rest of society. The latter has to do with how evangelicals cope with changing gender relations in the secular world, as well as within their idealized traditional family.

Making Promises

‿

For liberals in the late 1990s, almost nothing inspires fear and trembling like the spectacle of a Promise Keepers (PK) rally. In 1996, the organization held twenty-two weekend events in sports stadiums around the country, with a total attendance of about one million men. For newspaper photographers and TV news crews, the rallies offer irresistible pictures: men in all shapes and sizes huddled in small groups, singing, embracing, weeping and wailing for God to restore their manhood and help them deal with their messed-up lives. At first view, PK looks like a Christian men's encounter group with corny music. A second, deeper view reveals a right-wing political force in the making. The sight of all those men releasing all that emotion is scary to some. Men gathered en masse to hear and cheer speeches about the importance of families, the central role of marriage, and male personal responsibility must somehow mean that the "promise" these guys aim to keep is an old-fashioned promise to keep women obedient and unequal.

Beneath the surface, though, the messages emanating from the PK are both more subtle and more complex than a mere regurgitation of male supremacy. PK calls for racial reconciliation, for strengthening marriages, and for more frequent and more committed churchgoing. Like any good social movement, PK draws its adherents by the thousands because it meets their personal needs, religious, social, and political. Promise Keepers is compelling because it addresses—albeit in narrow ways—society's racial tensions, the battle of the sexes, and psychological problems such as dealing with guilt and self-control. Just as sports appeal to men on a number of levels, PK attracts for multiple reasons.

PK is a place to go. It is both a series of events and an evolving mindset about how faithful, Christian men are supposed to think and act. An outsider can report on what happens at a PK rally, but an outside observer can only speculate about what such gatherings mean to participants, let alone how and why the PK project may be changing men's minds about gender and race.

PK began as a simple idea. In 1990, Bill McCartney, who was then coach of the University of Colorado football team, was driving with a friend to a meeting of the Fellowship of Christian Athletes when the two hit on the idea of filling a sports stadium with Christian men. They held their first gathering at the University of Colorado, in 1991, and attracted 4,200 men. By 1994, they were holding gatherings in seven cities and attracting 250,000 men. By 1996, PK had a staff of more than four hundred and an annual budget in excess of $115 million.[14]

In 1997, PK brought hundreds of thousands of men to Washington, DC, for a one-day "Stand in the Gap" rally that seemed to mimic the "Million Man March" for black men led by Louis Farrakhan. Weeks before the Stand in the Gap rally, there was a flurry of press coverage, mostly favorable, toward Promise Keepers, though the National Organization for Women (NOW) and other critics used the scheduled rally as a news hook to charge PK with wanting to roll back women's rights.[15] Coach McCartney used Stand in the Gap to launch two new PK projects. He announced that PK would begin to organize stadium events internationally, and he called for large gatherings of Christian men to assemble on the steps of every U.S. state capitol on January 1, 2000, to "bear witness that the giant of racism is dead in the church of Jesus Christ."[16] Within the United States, PK announced that over the next two years it would hold thirty-seven free-of-charge stadium gatherings, nine of these exclusively for male and female pastors.[17] As with any social movement organization, PK needs to continually reinvigorate itself with new possibilities for recruitment and new means of attracting old members.

The standard PK rally takes place in a venue familiar to most men: the local sports stadium, where the men can eat hot dogs and wear T-shirts and baseball hats. A typical three-day rally begins on a Friday night with the men chanting, "We love Jesus, yes we do. We love Jesus. How about you?" The opening night features a concert and prayer. The Saturday and Sunday schedule is packed with popular Christian musical bands and speakers well known from Christian TV and radio. Many men come with their church groups and sit together wearing matching T-shirts.[18] Except for its all-male aspect, a PK rally differs little from a traditional evangelical tent revival. The addition of contemporary Christian music is reminiscent of the big Jesus movement camp meetings that were popular in the 1970s.

The rallies are carefully orchestrated. Between the sermons and the music, there are interludes of raucous singing and moments where men are allowed to break down and cry out in repentance for their sins. The stadium venue is saturated with hypermasculine energy, so that even the most macho man can cry at a PK weekend event. For men who rarely—if ever—express strong emotion, a PK rally may be a uniquely cathartic and mind-altering experience.

The men come to have a good time and to get excited about becoming better men. Each year the rallies have a slightly different theme. In 1995, the theme was "Raise the Standard," and the focus was on obedience to the Bible. In 1996, the theme was "Break Down the Walls," with an explicit emphasis on interracial healing. The most consistent theme is commitment: commitment to God, to wife, and to family. PK's founding text and mission statement is *Seven Promises of a Promise Keeper,* a collection of essays on each of the seven promises. A Promise Keeper commits to: (1) "honoring Jesus" and obeying the Bible; (2) "pursuing vital relationships with a few other men to help him keep his promises"; (3) "practicing spiritual, moral, ethical and sexual purity"; (4) "building strong marriages and families"; (5) "supporting the mission of his church and praying for his pastor"; (6) "reaching beyond any racial and denominational barriers to demonstrate the power of biblical unity"; and (7) obeying Jesus' Great Commandment to love God and one's neighbor and the Great Commission to evangelize the world.

The theme of racial reconciliation is constant at PK events and in the group's literature. At one level, the project of racial reconciliation is a sincere effort by many white evangelicals to make amends for past injustices. But for PK, the cross-racial message is also a way of bolstering one sort of unity as the means for highlighting other divisions: namely, the gender divide and the line between born-again Christians and everyone else. By promoting interracial unity, the organization preempts the charge that it is just another bunch of "angry white men" at odds with women and minorities.

The focus on race is also a means to implicitly raise the issue of class inequality without having to deal with it head on. When black preachers speak at PK rallies about the problems of gangs and violence in the "inner cities," everyone knows they are talking about racial and class deprivation, but in that very remote, very American way of not fully coming to terms with injustice.

Still, by making racial reconciliation central to its mission, PK has to comply with its own rhetoric, to some extent. The solution, not unlike the way secular society handles racism, is to focus on individual mobility and individual prejudices. At the end of 1996, PK, in a very "politically correct" sort of way, established a reconciliation division with a national manager to recruit new people from each major racial group. PK announced that its 437-member staff would now better reflect the ethnic makeup of the United States, with 30% minorities: 16% African American, 13% Hispanic, and 1% Native American.[19] Obviously, PK's leadership hopes that a racially diverse staff will translate into a more racially diverse audience for PK gatherings. This numbers approach makes sense in terms of networking with minority churches. Also, with greater racial diversity, the substance of the PK message might change over time.

Already PK has been willing to address some historically taboo racial matters. In 1997, PK's *New Man* magazine published a cover story on interracial marriage, featuring photos of black baseball player Bobby Meecham and his white wife. The gist of the article was that interracial marriage reflects positively the racial mix of Christ's own followers.[20] *New Man* editor Edward Gilbreath said the goal of the article was not to promote or glamorize interracial marriage but rather to treat it as one aspect of the ongoing racial reconciliation project.[21] The article received favorable letters to the editor.

More controversial was an interview *New Man* published around the same time with Raleigh Washington, the African American pastor appointed to head PK's racial reconciliation division. In the interview, Washington said that white Americans "don't have a clue about the depth of oppression that is still felt and still happening throughout America." He called on "white Christians to take responsibility for the racial sins of the past," but he also said that "people of color must understand, however, that whites cannot make a change unless their repentance is responded to with genuine forgiveness and love."[22] Washington's talk about collective responsibility drew some strong reactions from *New Man* readers. Washington responded by reiterating his point that "while we may not have personally committed the specific sins of our ancestors, we often reap the benefits—or hardships—of those injustices and participate in the society resulting from those wrongs."[23]

Most of the letters to the editor concerning Washington's interview were not favorable. One reader wrote that "the vast majority of white men in my generation who love Christ have no problem with race relations until men of color blame us for past societal problems." Another wrote that he was

> disappointed that in our secular world, people of color wish to be recognized as different and seek recompense for the sins of our fathers. Washington brings this same secular belief into the Christian world—and just when I thought we were beyond that.[24]

Candidly, one letter writer conveyed his ambivalence over the question of his own responsibility.

> I heard Pastor Washington speak at the Los Angeles Promise Keepers meeting. I must admit, the more I listened to his message, the madder I got. I told myself, This message is not for me. I'm not prejudiced.
>
> Still, I could not get beyond my irritation, so I stopped and prayed that God would help me. He then showed me the ill feelings I had been harboring towards my brothers of color for many years. At the conclusion of Washing-

ton's message, which I realized really was for me, I felt I needed to apologize
to my brothers of color. . . .

I pray daily for God's will to be done in this area of reconciliation and
for the strength to let it begin with me.[25]

Here we have a vivid example—from one man's testimony—of how
the PK experience can change men's attitudes. Given the large numbers and
the varied reasons why men may join PK, it is impossible to know how
selectively the men internalize the messages they take in. Some of the
thematic material is contradictory, which may be precisely why it is so
attractive. The Promise Keepers, like other men, seem to be in a state of
flux on questions of gender and race. The weekend rallies and *New Man*
magazine—which had a circulation of about three hundred thousand by
the end of 1996—are places where PK's ideas about gender and race are
evolving, even while they remain confused.

Leaders and Servants

∾

The premier issue of *New Man* magazine, published in the summer of
1994, began with an editorial, "How to Be a Real Man." In it editor Brian
Peterson pointed to the popularity of "post-sensitive" men such as Rush
Limbaugh, Howard Stern, and Jerry Seinfeld. Peterson concluded that
American culture gives men no clear role models:

Now men are *really confused*. The "Sensitive Man" of the '70s and '80s gave
way to Robert Bly's "Wild Man" of the early '90s. And now we have the
Post-sensitive Man—who is nothing more than a modern-day version of the
'50s man, but too young to remember the shortcomings of men in that decade.
    The bottom line: Men are caught in a vicious cycle, searching for
happiness and fulfillment in the wrong places.
    The Sensitive Man, the Wild Man, the Macho Man, the Feminized Man,
and yes, even the Post-sensitive Man will ultimately be disappointed.
    In the end only one type of man will be truly fulfilled—the Godly Man.
Read about him in the Bible. It tells men there's only one perfect role model.
His name is Jesus Christ.[26]

In fact, the Promise Keepers often refer to Christ as their role model,
not just spiritually but also in terms of gender relations. At a press
conference before one California PK rally, Coach Bill McCartney was asked
about his constant references to "male leadership." He finessed the implication that he means male domination by saying he uses the term "leadership" synonymously with "servanthood." Christ led by serving his disciples.

Therefore, Promise Keepers need to go home and become "servants" for their wives and kids. The rhetoric of leading and serving at the same time is similar to the Christian Right's semantic game that women can be submissive and yet equal to their husbands (and other men). By dodging and weaving around "leadership" and "servanthood," PK may encourage men to take more responsibility in the home. But the role model, Christ, is still the King of kings.

An excerpt from *The Seven Promises of a Promise Keeper* is revealing. Regarding the third promise, to practice "spiritual, moral, ethical and sexual purity," an African American pastor named Tony Evans wrote that America is "losing its families" primarily because of the "feminization of the American male."

> When I say *feminization,* I am not talking about sexual preference. I'm trying to describe a misunderstanding that has produced a nation of "sissified" men who abdicate their roles as spiritually pure leaders, thus forcing women to fill the vacuum.[27]

Here leadership is in contrast with the feminine. Evans uses old-fashioned name calling to remind men that it is bad to be like women. No doubt, that is what many men want to hear from PK. They are in charge, end of story.

Touching Feelings

ↄ๏

But it is not really the end of the story. Even while the PK project gives license to male domination, it softens the blow in order to salvage the essence of sexism and traditional family values.

As I noted earlier, evangelical Christians have a slightly higher rate of divorce than Americans generally. PK is most overtly concerned with marriage, and much of PK's thematic content is aimed at teaching men how to stay happily hitched. *New Man* magazine devotes sizable space to articles by psychologists and marriage counselors. One typical article warned men that the leading cause of divorce is wives' feeling that their husbands ignore them.[28] The same issue included an article, "Best Friends Once Again," instructing men at various stages of life about how to keep a good relationship going. In this and many other articles the emphasis is on encouraging men to become better talkers and better listeners.

To do both, they need to get past some of their ingrained male tendencies. *New Man* offers instruction in the basics of popular psychology, though always grounded in references to the Bible. One particularly cogent and clever article is titled "The Power of Anger." It begins with the idea that anger can be constructive as a motive for change. It then advises that men do not need to give up anger; they just need to learn to recognize the physical and mental "warning signs" of anger looming out of control. Most tellingly, after assuring men that anger is okay, the article gingerly lets men in on the secret that anger is often a "secondary emotion caused by the primary emotions of fear, hurt or frustration."

> Many men associate fear with vulnerability and weakness and find it more comfortable to express anger than fear. When you are angry and aren't sure why, ask yourself, "Is there something that I'm afraid of that could be triggering my anger?" . . .
>
> What are some healthy ways for you to respond to anger? First, if it involves someone else, determine whom you need to talk to, the best time to talk, and how to best communicate your feelings.
>
> A good rule of thumb is to deal with a problem as soon as you become aware of it and have had time to choose how you can best express your feelings.[29]

Feelings? There is no way to know how many of New Man's readers take to heart the advice about dealing with their emotions. But what is going on within the PK milieu is the construction of new models for how "real men" ought to think and act. This is profound, and it accounts, no doubt, for the popularity of PK among evangelical women. By 1996, evangelical women had formed several organizations aimed at mimicking PK by holding conferences and publishing literature on how to be "Godly women." Groups called Promise Reapers, Heritage Keepers, Suitable Helpers, and Chosen Women promote the idea that men and women have fundamentally different, though equally important, roles to play in keeping the family intact.[30]

At the PK weekend rallies, a contingent of women work as volunteers. They direct traffic around the stadiums and staff literature booths in the exhibit areas. The women watch and listen to the rallies from TV monitors inside the booth areas. One female journalist who reported on a PK rally for an evangelical newspaper wrote that she was touched by PK's goal of creating better husbands and fathers. "To know there were men who want to better fulfill their God-given roles as leaders of the home, the nation, and the church fills me with gratitude and, yes, a sense of security," she concluded.[31]

Another woman who worked as a volunteer at a PK rally in Pittsburgh wrote of her mixed feelings about an all-male event.

> Promise Keepers must deal more realistically with sexism. Without women speaking for themselves any discussion of this painful subject will always lack authenticity and impact. . . .

Just as I have defended women's fellowship groups based upon the special needs of women in society, I can now appreciate the need for men's fellowship groups based upon the special needs of men. I saw that with sexual tension gone from their lives for just a few hours men could concentrate on something more important. But single sex gatherings must only be a step toward a goal, and that goal is the unity of all believers in Christ.[32]

This female writer then suggests that PK ought to consider including some women speakers, but she notes that "the most often commented upon aspect of Promise Keepers is the outpouring of emotion by those attending."

It is not surprising that when men need to learn to express some emotion other than anger, they would feel most comfortable in a sports stadium with a football coach leading them forward. Seeing the men stand with their arms around each other, I thought again about the need for men to have a safe place to express emotion. . . .

When men are allowed to display affection for each other that is not immediately tagged homosexual, perhaps then they can begin to relate to their sisters in Christ in a non-sexual way.[33]

The issue of sexual "purity," which means control, is a central theme in PK. The rallies allow men to give rein to emotional expression within the safely masculine environment of the sports arena. But losing control of one's sexuality remains a major preoccupation for these men. Frequently, articles in the *New Man* magazine warn men of the dangers of losing control by reading or viewing pornography, by indulging in fantasies about women other than their wives, and by masturbating.

An article in the magazine's premier issue, "Escape the Sexual Trap," tells men that "Satan is alive and well" and may take the form of "attractive females who will call you a wimp if you shy away from having sex with them."[34] The article advises avoiding temptation by warding off sexual thoughts with the repetition of Bible verses.

What's tempting? Playboy magazines in a barber shop? There they sit on the reading table inviting you to pick them up. Refuse to bite. The video rental store? Stay away from the "mature themes" section. . . .

The moment a wrong thought enters my mind (Is there anyone not subject to sexual images?), I bring it into "captivity" and lay it at the feet of Jesus Christ.[35]

Another article by a Christian psychology professor titled "Sex under Control" assures readers that "most Christian men face a lifelong struggle controlling their sexuality." He notes that the use of pornography, sexual fantasies, and masturbation are particularly difficult to avoid. Masturbation with one's wife present is okay, according to the Christian psychologist, but if practiced alone, it may lead a man to "neglect sex in the marriage," and wives may feel "punished" by this neglect.[36] The problem with masturbation is that it is "habit-forming and it invites the sins of lust and fantasy," as does exposure to pornography. According to the article, 15.5% of married Christian men and nearly 7% of clergy are addicted to pornography.[37] The psychologist warns that even "more pervasive than pornography is how men use sexual fantasies to boost their sexual experiences." The problem here is that fantasies are "a violation against women" and "fantasies later seek real fulfillment." To get control of lust and fantasy, the psychologist suggests that men throw out all pornography, find someone to talk to confidentially about sex, and train themselves to look at and think of women in nonsexual ways.[38]

This advice might help men treat women more humanely. But if a born-again guy did not already feel guilty before exposing himself to PK, he could not avoid feeling so afterward. Archaic attitudes about sex set the Promise Keepers far afield from the secular culture and make it inevitable that PK men will have to struggle to repress their responses to ubiquitous sexual imagery. For Christian men already committed to the ideal of repressing sexual thoughts, PK may help them achieve their goal. One reader thanked *New Man* magazine for an article on male sexuality that, he said, "strongly hit home."

> I have always been physically faithful to my wife—but not so mentally. For many years masturbation and fantasies of other women was [sic] the basis of my sexual life. After reading your magazine, I realize that many other Christian men struggle with this. I ask for your help to take us to the next step.[39]

The "next step" seems to be to practice denying one's illicit thoughts about sex. Men can feel guilty about continuing to think about sex, or they can deny that they do so. Psychologists have much to say about sexual repression. The political relevance is that repression establishes a norm by which one is habitually at the mercy of external authority. One need not act on all of one's thoughts. But by denying one's thoughts and feelings, one may become increasingly dependent on the thoughts and directives of others.

Winning Converts

∽

As of this writing, the mass draw of PK seems more personal than political. But once men come to feel their lives profoundly impacted by PK, they may be more receptive to the political leanings of PK leaders. Bill McCartney downplays his politics, though he has spoken at gatherings of Operation Rescue, and he supported Colorado's anti–gay rights Amendment 2.[40] At a typical PK stadium event, the exhibit hall includes literature booths for Focus on the Family and the Family Research Council.[41] Men convinced that their own traditional families are under siege may very well want to increase their political acumen. PK is a conveyor belt from the private world of discontent to the public battleground of gender politics.

The church is a powerful mediator between the personal and the political. Men (almost exclusively) pastor evangelical churches, but men are underrepresented in the pews. PK is partly about getting men to attend church more regularly. It is also about training evangelical men to become better at proselytizing their unconverted friends. In an article for *New Man* magazine, evangelical pollster George Barna summarized some of his survey data on why men are, by a range of ten to twenty percentage points, less likely than women to attend church, read their Bibles, pray, and volunteer in churches. "Most men require that churches provide practical, tangible solutions to the difficult problems they face," Barna wrote. "Our studies show these men are less anxious to learn spiritual principles than they are to discover how to 'make life work.' "[42] Barna and other evangelical strategists are concerned about recent data showing overall declines among men in church attendance, Bible reading, volunteering, and donating money at church. Barna advises the Promise Keepers to win over their unsaved friends not with church lingo about getting "washed in the blood" of Jesus but rather with conversation that is "simple, accessible, practical and personal."

> Your friends don't want Theology 101 or Church 201. They want Personal Finance 201, Family Stability 301 and Life Purpose 401. When you can relate your Christianity to the issues they are battling, then they will have "ears to hear."[43]

This emphasis on a problem-solving message is what gives PK its greatest potential. During the 1970s heyday of the Jesus movement, young converts focused on their spiritual connection to Jesus. Their language was about getting "convicted" and "walking with the Lord." Now, in the 1990s, the rhetoric is more relational and more pragmatic: it is about saving marriages and parental responsibilities.

PK's mass weekend rallies may appear extraordinary to secular TV audiences, but the stadium events are part of a long evangelical tradition of holding big outdoor gatherings. "Tent revivals" drew crowds long before the advent of religious broadcasting and the growth of large urban churches. In the 1970s, the Jesus movement grew out of mass rallies and

Christian rock concerts, some of which went on for days. As an event series, PK is popular because it is the latest twist on the tent revival tradition.

The New Man
∾

In its 1997 conference brochure, PK explains why it is for men only. It exists to "fill a void in Christian resources" by addressing men's issues specifically. PK's stated goal is "to deepen the commitment of men to respect and honor women."[44] Respect and honor are certainly preferable to overt condescension. But they are the closest PK men can come to treating women equitably. Overall, PK is an attempt by evangelical men to create a new male model: one still based on masculine "leadership" but one that must also come to terms with the irrevocable gains of feminism. That the PK men waffle about "leadership" and "servanthood" while they work on improving communication with their wives is a sign that the feminist principle of equality has crept into even the staunchest bastions of sexism. Even the most recalcitrant men can no longer get away with what they once did. Talk about racial reconciliation and the focus on interpersonal psychology are a collective means of asserting that Christian men are basically good, that they are trying to help each other and themselves.

Within the evangelical subculture, ideas about race and gender are intertwined. Ideological and organizational work to achieve a modicum of racial equity has the effect, whether intentional or not, of preserving sexism, albeit a kinder, gentler sexism. By looking like they are color blind, the Promise Keepers cannot be accused of wanting to protect privilege for rich, white men only. Concern about social problems related to poverty is subsumed under rhetoric by preachers of color about the "inner cities" and "underclass" violence. No one has to take any action to alleviate urban poverty. That is not the mission of PK anyway. There is no "eighth promise" about making sure that one's fellow citizens have adequate food and shelter. Despite its pretenses of diversity, PK is a mostly white, middle-class movement for men concerned about the private realms of the church, the Little League, and the bedroom. To the extent that any of these sanctuaries are seen as threatened by secular, liberal culture and public policy, then the Promise Keepers have a duty to get involved in politics.

In family matters the essential biblical view is hierarchy, not equality. Yet even within the evangelical subculture, gender relations are subject to change. Secular society is moving, albeit at a snail's pace, away from the dominator model and toward a partnership model of male–female relations. Evangelical women cannot be expected to tolerate the 1950s prototype of "father knows best," nor do evangelical men necessarily want to remain as emotionally alienated as conservative social conditioning leads many men to be. Despite resistance, the feminist project of gender equality has exerted a permanent influence even on die-hard sexists. Though the Promise Keepers may be nostalgic for a male-dominated world, they cannot reverse the tide. The Promise Keepers project is a stopgap measure. It aims to preserve an essentially male supremacist ideology and family structure, although it is also willing to polish some of the roughest edges smooth.

Chapter 12

∽

Conclusion

There was something almost inevitable about Ralph Reed's announcement, in the spring of 1997, that he planned to resign as executive director of the Christian Coalition in order to start his own political consulting firm. Reed said he wanted to move beyond his role as spokesperson for the family values agenda to play a more direct role in winning elections.

It was inevitable that the Christian Coalition would eventually cramp Reed's style. In 1996, the Federal Election Commission (FEC) sued the Coalition for alleged violations of election laws dating back to 1992, including in-kind contributions for Republican candidates. The Coalition's tax status allows it to fund "political education" projects, but not to channel money to particular candidates. The suit, still not resolved as of early 1998, put a damper on the Christian Coalition's overt politicking for Republicans in 1996, but did not stop the organization's generic get-out-the-vote efforts. Among likely outcomes in the FEC suit, the Coalition may be assessed for back taxes, may be fined for violating election laws, and may in the future be subject to the campaign disclosure requirements applied to political action committees (PACs).

As for Reed, the consummate operative, he obviously does not want to retreat from partisan electioneering, during the 1998 Congressional races, or thereafter. Unhampered, Reed plays to win. In his new role, he will no longer be just a broker between the Christian Right and the Republican Party. He will play a more proactive role in helping to craft campaigns before they start.

Other seasoned Christian Right activists are likely to do the same. With much less fanfare, but also in 1997, Gary Bauer of the Family Research Council became the chairperson of a new PAC called Campaign for Working Families. Its stated purpose is "to help elect pro-life, pro-family, pro-free enterprise candidates." In 1996, its executive director was a financial aide to presidential candidate Patrick Buchanan.[1]

As for the Christian Coalition, Reed's departure spells a change of course but no end to its influence. From 1991 through 1996, the Coalition held an annual Road to Victory conference, first in Virginia Beach and then in Washington, DC. Republican presidential candidates made it a point to speak at the conferences, as did Newt Gingrich and other Republicans solicitous of the movement's support. In 1997, the Coalition moved its Road to Victory conference to Atlanta, Reed's hometown. The Coalition treated Reed to a farewell dinner, and welcomed incoming president Don Hodel. Perhaps because the conference took place outside the Washington, DC, area, the 1997 Road to Victory gathering received far less press coverage than in previous years. But Pat Robertson reportedly told a private meeting of one hundred Christian Coalition leaders in Atlanta that they need to forge a united effort behind a single conservative presidential candidate in the year 2000. "We have absolutely no effectiveness when the primary comes. None whatsoever. Because we have split our votes among four or five people and the other guy wins," Robertson said.[2] Robertson did not sound gun-shy about playing partisan politics. There was no reason to expect any letup in electioneering from the organized Christian Right.

When the FEC initiated its suit, Reed said that he was "totally confident" that "the courts will affirm that people of faith have every right to be involved as citizens and voters."[3] Of course, no one disputes the right of religious people to be involved in politics. Reed's statement reflects the common habit among people in the Christian Right of suggesting "religious persecution" whenever their political tactics are challenged. As I have discussed throughout this book, the religious persecution theme is perennially useful though rarely honest.

Ambiguity about whether the Christian Right is a political or a religious force—I believe it is both—is precisely what allows the movement to endure setbacks in the political arena. When political victories are few or when there is little visible political activity to sustain the movement's momentum, the Christian Right falls back on its stock concerns with private virtue and vice. The May–June 1997 issue of the Christian Coalition's magazine, for example, had little to offer in the way of action alerts or victory reports. The cover story was about a woman who survived the trauma of rape and now, with her husband, runs a counseling ministry for fellow rape survivors. Another article was about improving one's marriage in the second half of life. These are important matters. As an organization, the Christian Coalition survives by catering to a full range of its constituents' needs and interests. Were the organization, and the broader movement, focused solely on achieving tangible goals, members would soon come to feel like cogs in a wheel.

238 ~ NOT BY POLITICS ALONE

Not that there are no contradictions in the panoply of concerns one finds addressed by the Christian Right, and especially by large organizations such as the Christian Coalition and Focus on the Family. The same issue of the Coalition's magazine, *Christian American,* included an advertisement for a new book by Peter and Patti Lalonde called *The Edge of Time: The Final Countdown Has Begun.* The Lalondes cohost a weekly TV show in which they review recent news events and link them to quotations from the Bible, in an effort to prove that Jesus will soon return. Their latest book identifies "a united world, a global police force and a one-world economy" as part of "Satan's master plan for Earth's last days." The book bears no explicit endorsement from the Christian Coalition but the publisher, Harvest House, understands that readers of the *Christian American* are likely buyers of the book.

A few pages later the Christian Coalition advertised its own Visa credit card, with which members can earn frequent flyer miles for themselves and make a small donation to the Christian Coalition every time they use it to pay for something. One cannot help imagining someone reading the Lalondes' book about the coming Rapture purchased, perhaps, with a Christian Coalition credit card issued by the Visa division of the Satanic international banking conspiracy.

Yet this sort of cognitive dissonance, oddly enough, has never been a hindrance to the forward march of the Christian Right. Now that we are on the cusp of the new millennium, we might wonder about the political effects of stepped-up end-times thinking. Logically, we might expect a retreat by people who hope—or suspect—that the year 2000 will see Christ come to rescue believers before all hell breaks loose on earth. Why bother running for office if the end is near? Yet less than two years before 2000, there has been no big push among respectable evangelicals to set a precise date for Christ's Second Coming. Who wants to be wrong? It is more expedient to take a wait-and-see attitude: the good Christian should be ready for the Rapture if and when it happens, but ready, too, to "take dominion" and create God's kingdom here and now.

What end-times thinking and the profamily issues package have in common is that both are part of a mindset that allows members of the Christian Right to set themselves apart from the rest of society. They have "better values" and, to boot, they are on their way to heaven, sooner or later. They are superior to the rest of us sinners, and yet they are also experiencing "religious persecution."

Thanks to its sense of collective martyrdom, the Christian Right will surely continue to engage in conflict with the secular political culture. Although I do not know exactly what issues will crop up in the next few years, I can still foresee parts of the movement's coming agenda. No doubt the Christian Right will continue to lobby for legislative bans on partial-birth abortions in Congress and in the state legislatures. Because this type of late-term abortion is relatively rare, Democrats may want to compromise and agree to bans that allow exceptions in cases where a woman's health is surely jeopardized. At both the federal and state levels, the Christian Right will seek to enact parental rights bills to strengthen the legal clout of parents in disputes regarding their children. Here, too, there is little reason for Democrats to fight hard against bills that seem reasonable on the surface. Local skirmishes over textbooks and sex education are likely to continue. On gay rights, the next front will be same-sex marriage. Antigay activists will use the Defense of Marriage Act, passed by Congress in 1996, to fight legal recognition of gay marriages in the states.

All of these issues are tailor-made for grassroots activism and for grandstanding by ambitious politicians. All of these issues are also piecemeal answers to circumstances the Christian Right, alone, can do little about. For example, despite clinic violence and dozens of state laws restricting access to abortion, the right to have an abortion if one so chooses remains constitutionally protected, most people remain prochoice, and women will continue to have abortions. The Christian Right has been relegated to trying to roll back abortion rights in bits and pieces.

Advocates of gay civil rights have a long way to go to secure full legal equality. Yet already there are significant changes underway in the popular media, which increasingly presents homosexuality in an acceptable light. Movies that portray gay people sympathetically, even positively, are proliferating. The ABC sitcom *Ellen* had a likeable lesbian as its lead character, and protests from Jerry Falwell, Donald Wildmon, and others in the Christian Right had little effect on the show's popularity. Past a certain point, the promotion of grotesque bigotry has a tendency to backfire.

In the field of public education, the possibilities for the Christian Right are similarly mixed. Teachers and school superintendents are not about to kowtow to every disgruntled Christian Right parent, though they may acquiesce to some parental demands. For the Right, the greatest opportunities lie in opening their own private schools and, they hope, eventually winning federal funding through voucher programs whereby parents choose their own schools. Christian Right activism in the schools is part of a much broader, ongoing societal quandary: in a democracy, are all children entitled to a common base of knowledge and experience, or is every family supposed to fend for itself and refuse to associate with neighbors of a different stripe?

On the family values front, the Christian Right continually has to march uphill to do battle with secular society. However, the perpetual motion of the Christian Right makes it, for the foreseeable future, an entrenched fixture in electoral politics. Republicans ignore the movement at their own peril. In 1998, the leading organizations of the Christian Right need to flex their muscles and show that they can again swing Congressional elections for the Republicans, as they did in 1994. Unfortunately, the narrow logic of the two-party system will likely hold. In 1998, the GOP will need the movement vote to defeat Democrats in the House and Senate. The Christian Right will need to demonstrate its utility in order to have a credible voice in the selection of a GOP presidential candidate in the year 2000. No doubt, some Republicans will try, as they did in 1996, to dampen the power of the Christian Right in 1998 and in 2000. But the lesson from the last few election cycles has been that well-organized minority voting blocs can usually play the numbers game to their own advantage. Of course, the game is currently rigged to exclude genuine opponents of the existing system. To break the logjam of the Republican–Christian Right alliance, not to mention corporate domination of the entire electoral process, progressives would have to come close to matching the steady, mass mobilization of the grassroots Right. As of 1998, there is no sign of a coming revival on the Left—but that is a subject for another book and another author.

For more than two decades, the Christian Right has made continuing inroads within the Republican Party alongside continuing demands on elected officials to do the movement's bidding. We ought to expect more of the same in the near future. The likes of Ralph Reed, Gary Bauer, James Dobson, Beverly LaHaye, Mike Farris, Donald Wildmon, and Judie Brown—and scores of others with less name recognition—have built careers and multi-million-dollar organizations around the pursuit of power. Were they simply entrepreneurs, they might easily move on to other pastures. But they are accountable to and dependent upon thousands of supporters. Together, leaders and followers are on a godly mission, a mission that they will not give up lightly. A taste of power is enticing, but one taste is never enough. For the morally righteous, especially, victory appears always to lie just around the corner.

❧

While the Christian Right has not accomplished—and probably cannot accomplish—most of its family values agenda, the movement is strengthened by currents underway within the evangelical subculture. Some of these, as I discussed in Chapter 10, have to do with maintaining commitment and solidarity internally, within the movement. In this book, I have highlighted the Promise Keepers and racial reconciliation projects because I think they represent innovative changes with serious political implications. Evangelicals, like others in our society, are grappling with questions of racial and gender equality. It is facile to dismiss evangelical responses to racism and sexism as mere tokenism or as just another part of a backlash against civil rights. As I have stressed, I do not see anything progressive about Promise Keepers or racially integrated church bodies, though the latter is a good and long overdue idea.

What I do see changing is the potential base of support for the Christian Right as well as the nature of the movement's concerns. Gender and race figure into the equation differently. On both scores, though, it does no good for progressive critics to repeat, as part of a litany, that the Right is simply racist and sexist. It is true that the Christian Right wants to preserve male dominance, though now they term patriarchy "leader- ship." But calling the Promise Keepers a bunch of misogynists is unfair and will ring increasingly hollow as the years go by and the organization proves itself to be teaching men to "respect and honor" women. If anything, PK should be challenged to live up to all of its talk about male responsibility. Let's call PK to account: to take on, for example, the deadbeat dads who pay no child support or the male bosses who harass women in the workplace. Now that PK has begun to open conservative men's minds about racial injustice, it is not impossible that PK, with its goal of molding a "new man," may surprise critics by addressing some of the excesses of male irresponsibility.

My point, on matters of both race and gender, is that by loosening old boundaries, conservative evangelicals are in the process of creating for themselves a new kind of social movement. Critics will be left in the dust if they fail to see the changes afoot. Racial reconciliation is a direct challenge to the old tradition of bigotry within right-wing circles. Today, the most active efforts at racial integration are underway within conserva- tive denominations, not within the liberal churches. Organized political liberalism, in the form of the Democratic Party, is bankrupt when it comes to claiming any moral high ground on race matters. This is a problem not just because many people of color may start to vote Republican—or not vote at all. It will be a problem for progressives, in the future, to link appeals for racial and class justice if leaders of the Christian Right succeed in becoming credible spokespersons for the downtrodden.

Both Promise Keepers and the evangelical racial reconciliation projects have emerged at a particularly disadvantageous time for progressives. There are all sorts of notions circulating: that feminism has failed; that bad mothers are solely responsible for turning out bad kids; that government funding for social services is counterproductive. These ideas are as fraudu- lent and reactionary as they are popular, in lieu of more humane responses to social dysfunction. We are undergoing a monumental historical retreat from the premise that government ought to protect its weakest citizens from the ravages of the powerful and greedy. The dismantling of the welfare state is accompanied by the idea that civil society must and can make up the difference, this despite the fact that within our culture of crass individualism there are relatively few private, voluntary associations able to meet people's basic needs. Into the vacuum comes the likes of the Christian Coalition and its ally, the Samaritan Project, targeting the "inner cities" and the "underclass," both terms code names for poor people of color. In the new millennium will we return to the days when the Salvation Army gave soup to people willing to sit still for a sermon? Because the social safety net is being ripped to shreds, the Christian Right has new opportunities to link humanitarian assistance to its brand of evangelism.

To the extent that the Christian Right repents for its racist past, the movement may win credibility on other issues: from moves to privatize the public schools with vouchers to draconian prison policies to a relaxation of labor and environmental laws. I cannot make specific predictions, but there is, conceivably, a "biblically correct" view on everything under the sun. One can foresee a time when someone like Dr. James Dobson or Gary Bauer may function as a voice of moral authority and political pressure, on a par with Jesse Jackson or AFL-CIO president John Sweeney. The long-term entrenchment of the Christian Right means that its leaders— however eccentric they still may seem to liberal critics—have won a great measure of legitimacy.

There are some lessons to be learned here. Under the best of circumstances a social movement must cope with defeats and disappointments. The Christian Right has recovered from its many losses because the movement works on numerous issues with multiple strategies and multiple types of organizations. Most visibly, on the abortion front, the direct action groups reached a peak and then fractured into debates about violence while the legislative lobbies keep pressing for new restrictions. Promoters of prayer in the public schools introduce Congressional bills on a cyclical basis, but between tries they work on something else. Where there is a will, there is a way.

With equal doses of religious zeal and political know-how, the Christian Right has fastened itself to the wheels of power and policymaking. In the long run, the tenacity of a social movement may count as much as the moral appeal of its arguments. Of course, endurance is more likely for a movement flush with money, microphones, and the receptive ears of politicians. Still, a successful social movement is one that keeps its membership feeling useful and focused on tangible goals. This is easier for movements intent on reforming, not radically restructuring, the existing system. It may be easier for a political faction linked also to a religious subculture. One wields the sword most gallantly from behind a shield of faith. I say this not to suggest that political success accrues only to religious groups. It is necessary, however, as the Christian Right has learned, to counterpose the realities one rejects with a plan for action and a steady vision of a better future.

Notes

Notes to Chapter 1

1. Tom Hess, "1990s: The Civil War Decade," *Citizen*, Jan. 1990.
2. Thomas C. Atwood, "Through a Glass Darkly," *Policy Review*, Fall 1990, pp. 45, 52.
3. Throughout this book, I use terms such as *family values, prolife*, and *profamily* without quotation marks, but not because such terms have a single and transparent meaning; they do not. Such terms are part of the rhetorical arsenal of the movement under study. Often the terms are used hypocritically. However, I have chosen not to clutter the text with excess quotation marks, and I assume the reader will decode the connotations of frequently used movement slogans.
4. John D. Woodbridge, "Culture War Casualties," *Christianity Today*, March 6, 1995, pp. 20–26.
5. James Dobson, "Why I Use 'Fighting Words,' " *Christianity Today*, June 19, 1995, p. 28.
6. James M. Penning and Corwin Smidt, "What Coalition?," *Christian Century*, Jan. 15, 1997, p. 37. This was a poll conducted by the Wirthlin Worldwide organization. The same Wirthlin poll indicated that 15% of all voters identified themselves as members or supporters of the Christian Coalition, and that among these, 67% voted for Dole and 20% for Clinton.
7. Ibid.
8. Pat Robertson, quoted in Joseph L. Conn, "Mutiny on the Right," *Church and State*, Dec. 1996, p. 4.
9. "Christian Group Vows to Exert More Influence on the GOP," *New York Times*, Nov. 7, 1996.
10. On the theory and case studies linking these three sets of factors, see esp. Doug McAdam, John D. McCarthy, and Mayer N. Zald, eds., *Comparative Perspectives on Social Movements: Political Opportunities, Mobilizing Structures, and Cultural Framings* (New York: Cambridge University Press, 1996).

11. John Lofland, *Social Movement Organizations: Guide to Research on Insurgent Realities* (New York: Aldine de Gruyter, 1996), p. 1.
12. See esp. Stephanie Coontz, *The Way We Never Were: American Families and the Nostalgia Trap* (New York: Basic Books, 1992).
13. Pew Research Center for the Press, *The Diminishing Divide: American Churches, American Politics,* study released June 25, 1996 (Washington, DC: Author), pp. 1–2.
14. Ibid., p. 7.
15. "Christian Right Defies Categories," *New York Times,* July 22, 1994, p. 1.
16. Pew Research Center, *Diminishing Divide,* p. 13.
17. For more on the definitions and history of evangelicalism, see, e.g., James Davison Hunter, *American Evangelicalism: Conservative Religion and the Quandary of Modernity* (New Brunswick, NJ: Rutgers University Press, 1983); Mark A. Noll, David W. Bebbington, and George A. Rawlyk, eds., *Evangelicalism* (New York: Oxford University Press, 1994); and Mark A. Shibley, *Resurgent Evangelicalism in the United States* (Charlotte: University of South Carolina Press, 1996).
18. See "The *Christianity Today*–Gallup Poll: An Overview," *Christianity Today,* Dec. 21, 1979.
19. Princeton Religion Research Center, *Religion in America 1992–93, 1994 Supplement* (Princeton, NJ: Author, 1996).
20. George Barna, *The Index of Leading Spiritual Indicators* (Dallas: Word, 1996), p. 3.
21. Ibid., p. 33.
22. "Church Attendance Drops Again as Boomers Cut Church from Schedule," *EP News Service,* March 22, 1996.
23. Shibley, *Resurgent Evangelicalism,* p. 27.
24. Ibid., p. 134.

Notes to Chapter 2

∽

1. For background on evangelical politics in the post–World War II period, see my *Roads to Dominion* (New York: Guilford Press, 1995), chap. 4.
2. Karen M. Hawkins, "Diamond Days: Facets from the First 75 Years," in National Religious Broadcasters, *1996 Directory of Religious Media,* p. 34.
3. National Religious Broadcasters, *1997 Directory of Religious Media,* p. 178.
4. "Christian Radio Stations, Riding a Wave of Change, Keep Their Popularity," *New York Times,* Jan. 10, 1994.
5. National Religious Broadcasters, *1997 Directory,* p. 222.
6. National Religious Broadcasters, *1996 Directory of Religious Media,* p. 285. The 1997 NRB *Directory* does not provide statistics on cable networks.
7. John W. Kennedy, "Redeeming the Wasteland?," *Christianity Today,* Oct. 2, 1995, pp. 92–102; National Religious Broadcasters, *1996 Directory.*
8. Beth Spring, "A Study Finds Little Evidence that Religious TV Hurts Local Churches," *Christianity Today,* May 18, 1984, pp. 70–71.

9. William Fore, "Religion and Television: Report on the Research," *Christian Century,* July 18–25, 1984, p. 711.

10. See my *Spiritual Warfare* (Boston: South End Press, 1989), pp. 36–38, for some of the survey reports.

11. For brief histories of the beginnings of the religious broadcasting industry, see, e.g., Hawkins, "Diamond Days"; and Mark Ward Sr., *Air of Salvation: The Story of Christian Broadcasting* (Grand Rapids, MI: Baker Books, 1994). This book, by an editor of the National Religious Broadcasters (NRB) publications, is the NRB's official history.

12. On the early history of CBN, see "Pat Robertson and CBN," *Broadcasting,* March 6, 1978; and "I Will Pour You Out a Blessing," *Religious Broadcasting,* Jan. 1994.

13. *Broadcasting,* March 6, 1978, p. 65.

14. The story is told in "Still Shouting from the Housetops," *Charisma,* April 1983.

15. Russ Williams, "Heavenly Message, Earthly Designs," *Sojourners,* Sept. 1979; "This Way to Armageddon," *Newsweek,* July 5, 1982, p. 79.

16. Pat Robertson, quoted in "Preachers in Politics," *U.S. News and World Report,* Sept. 24, 1979, p. 39.

17. "Politics, Power, and the Christian Citizen," *Sojourners,* Sept. 1979, pp. 21–22.

18. Tapes of the *700 Club,* March and May 1984; author's collection.

19. "Pat Robertson's Network Breaks Out of the Christian Ghetto," *Christianity Today,* Jan. 1, 1982, p. 37; "CBN Cable Chooses New York Ad Agency," *Religious Broadcasting,* June 1983, p. 11.; "CBN's Image Campaign Spreads the Gospel Truth," *Advertising Age,* March 30, 1987, p. 10.

20. "Pledges Rise to 'Golden Day' Levels, CBN Says," *Virginian Pilot,* Feb. 8, 1991, p. D1; Mark O'Keefe, "Pat Robertson's Growing Business Kingdom," *Virginian Pilot and Ledger Star,* June 19, 1994, p. D2.

21. "CBN Sells Cable Network," *Charisma,* March 1990, p. 18; "Family Channel Goes Big Time," *Charisma,* Dec. 1990, p. 17.

22. The specific details of the stock deal are explained in "An Empire on Exemptions?," *Washington Post,* Feb. 13, 1994.

23. O'Keefe, "Pat Robertson's Growing Business Kingdom," p. D1.

24. "A Devilishly Good Deal for the Family Channel," *Time,* May 12, 1997, pp. 65–66.

25. "Michael Little Succeeds Pat Robertson as President of CBN," *Religious Broadcasting,* Dec. 1993, p. 30.

26. *Focus on the Family: Who We Are and What We Stand For,* 1994 pamphlet; "The Empire Built on Family and Faith," *Washington Post,* Aug. 8, 1990.

27. See Dr. James Dobson, *The New Dare to Discipline,* rev. ed. (Wheaton, IL: Tyndale House, 1992).

28. "The Empire Built on Family and Faith."

29. *Focus on the Family: Who We Are and What We Stand For.*

30. "Advice for Parents, and for Politicians," *New York Times,* May 30, 1995.

31. "His Father's Son," *Christianity Today,* April 22, 1988, p. 21.

32. "Bundy Told Dobson, 'It Was Pornography,' " *Christianity Today,* Feb. 17, 1989, p. 43.

33. "Why Psychologist without a Pulpit Is Called Religious Right's New Star," *New York Times,* June 5, 1990.
34. Dr. James C. Dobson, "Focus on the Family's New Public Policy Plan: Prepare for Victory," *Citizen,* Jan. 1989, p. 13.
35. "Radio Spots Get Hot Response," *Citizen,* Feb. 1990, p. 9.
36. Kevin Tebedo, quoted in Stephen Bransford, *Gay Politics versus Colorado and America: The Inside Story of Amendment 2* (Cascade, CO: Sardis Press, 1994), p. 52.
37. Tim Kingston, "Contents of Secret Colorado Anti-Gay Election Kit Revealed," *San Francisco Bay Times,* May 19, 1994. Focus reportedly allowed CFV to use the ministry's broadcast equipment, an in-kind contribution valued at about $8,000. See "Political Fund-Raising Claim Irks Focus on Family," *Washington Times,* April 24, 1994.
38. James Dobson letter to supporters, March 1995, p. 7; author's collection.
39. "Activists Rip GOP for Ignoring Values," *Washington Times,* March 18, 1995, p. 3.
40. "Family 'Contract' Too Mild for Many," *Washington Times,* May 29, 1995.
41. I watched TBN, sometimes frequently and sometimes sporadically, from 1977 through the mid-1990s. I also went on a tour of the TBN studio in Tustin, California, in 1988.
42. "Praise the Lord," TBN newsletter, Aug., 1994.
43. "Falwell TV Shows Pulled in Florida," *Washington Times,* Aug. 17, 1994.
44. Mark Ward Sr., "The Coming Shakeout in Christian Radio," *Religious Broadcasting,* Sept. 1994, p. 24.
45. National Religious Broadcasters, *1997 Directory,* pp. 159–162.
46. Ward, "The Coming Shakeout."
47. Perucci Ferraiuolo, "Riding the Rush," *Religious Broadcasting,* Sept. 1994, p. 20.
48. Ibid., p. 21.

Notes to Chapter 3
◦⊷

1. Dale D. Buss, "Mass Marketing the Good News," *Christianity Today,* Jan. 8, 1996, p. 58.
2. David Scott, "Notes from the Alternative Nation," *National Review,* June 17, 1996, pp. 49–50.
3. "Forty-Four Years and Counting," *Religious Broadcasting,* July–Aug. 1993, pp. 12–13.
4. "CBA Welcomes Broadcasters to the 44th Annual CBA International Convention," *Religious Broadcasting,* July–Aug. 1993, p. 14.
5. Gwen Ellis, "Changes in the Women's Market," *Bookstore Journal,* Dec. 1995, p. 39.
6. Scott Pinson, "Fishers of Men," *Marketplace,* March 1997, p. 31.
7. "CBA's Largest Untapped Market?," *Marketplace,* March 1997, p. 32.

8. "Home School Market Continues to Expand," *Bookstore Journal*, February 1996, p. 33.
9. Jeff Houten, "Tapping the Homeschool Market," *Bookstore Journal*, June 1996, pp. 94–99.
10. "Word Dominates Best-Seller List," *Bookstore Journal*, April 1996, p. 49.
11. "Premier 100," *Marketplace*, March 1997, p. 44.
12. "Premier 100," *Bookstore Journal*, March 1996, p. 41.
13. "Premier 100," *Marketplace*, March 1997, p. 44.
14. Jeff Hooten, "Reclaiming Absolute Truth," *Bookstore Journal*, Nov. 1995, p. 63.
15. "Statement of Ownership," *Charisma*, Jan. 1997, p. 87. At the end of 1996, the magazine reported an average monthly circulation of 227,994 copies.
16. EP News Service, Feb. 10, 1995, p. 9.
17. Lisa Gubernick and Robert La Franco, "Rocking with God," *Forbes*, Jan. 2, 1995, p. 40.
18. Nicholas Dawidoff, "No Sex, No Drugs. But Rock 'n' Roll" *New York Times Magazine*, Feb. 5, 1995, p. 42.
19. "Christafari," *Bookstore Journal*, March 1995, p. 100.
20. April Hefner, "Don't Know Much about History," *Contemporary Christian Music*, April 1996.
21. Paul A. Creasman, "Sanctified Entertainment: Contemporary Christian Music Radio," *Religious Broadcasting*, April 1996, p. 26.
22. Ibid.
23. "Duo Offers Solid Hope to Generation X," *Charisma*, Sept. 1996, p. 80.
24. Mark A. Smeby, "Longing for Reality," *Contemporary Christian Music*, April 1996, p. 37.
25. Dawidoff, "No Sex, No Drugs," p. 66.
26. EP News Service, Sept. 1, 1995; Sept. 8, 1995.
27. Marcia Ford, "Patty's Critics Are Few, Despite Affair," *Charisma*, Nov. 1995, pp. 16–17.
28. Advertisement, *Charisma*, March 1996, p. 71.
29. Bob Briner, "Housewives Take the Offensive," *Contemporary Christian Music*, March 1996, p. 58.
30. Todd Hafer, "Erasing Racism," *Contemporary Christian Music*, March 1996, pp. 51–55.
31. "DC Talk Smashes Record; Sales Boom," *Bookstore Journal*, Jan. 1996, p. 113.
32. Bill Anderson, "Music Plays a Vital Role in CBA Industry," *Bookstore Journal*, May 1995, p. 7.
33. Deborah Evans Price, "Perspectives on Christian Music Industry Changes," *Bookstore Journal*, May 1995, pp. 30–34; Jim Long, "Can't Buy Me Ministry," *Christianity Today*, May 20, 1996, pp. 20–28.
34. John M. De Marco, "Sunday School Will Never Be the Same," *Charisma*, Sept. 1996, p. 40.
35. Jimmy Stewart, "The Rock of Our Salvation," *Charisma*, Sept. 1996, p. 38.
36. Ibid.

37. Singer Mike Roe, quoted in "Too Holy for the World, Too Worldly for the Church?," *Christianity Today,* Oct. 7, 1996, p. 84.
38. Ibid., p. 85.
39. "Pro-Lifers on the Edge," *Citizen,* Oct. 16, 1995, p. 5.
40. Ibid.
41. "Frank Peretti," *Bookstore Journal,* September 1995, p. 97.

Notes to Chapter 4

⮜

1. On the historical antecedents of the Christian Right, see my *Roads to Dominion* (New York: Guilford Press, 1995), chap. 4.
2. On the New Right, see my *Roads to Dominion,* chap. 5.
3. Joel Carpenter, "Geared to the Times, but Anchored to the Rock," Christianity Today, Nov. 8, 1985, p. 44. See also my *Spiritual Warfare* (Boston: South End Press, 1989), pp. 10–11, regarding some of the Youth for Christ leaders who remained prominent within religious broadcasting and missionary circles.
4. C. Peter Wagner, " 'Church Growth': More than a Man, a Magazine, a School, a Book," *Christianity Today,* Dec. 7, 1973, pp. 11–14.
5. "The New Rebel Cry: Jesus Is Coming!," *Time,* June 21, 1971, pp. 56–63; "Whatever Happened to the Jesus Movement?," *Christianity Today,* Oct. 24, 1975.
6. "Whatever Happened to the Jesus Movement?," p. 46.
7. Ibid., pp. 46–47.
8. "Campus Crusade: Into All the World," *Christianity Today,* June 9, 1972, p. 38.
9. On the Here's Life campaign, see *Christianity Today,* Feb. 4, 1977, and July 18, 1980.
10. On Third Century, see "Politics from the Pulpit," *Newsweek,* Sept. 6, 1976, pp. 49–50; and Jim Wallis and Wes Michaelson, "The Plan to Save America," *Sojourners,* April 1976.
11. "Born Again!," *Newsweek,* Oct. 25, 1976, p. 68.
12. Wade Clark Roof, *A Generation of Seekers: The Spiritual Journeys of the Baby Boom Generation* (San Francisco: Harper, 1993), pp. 99–100, 111–112.
13. E. J. Dionne, *Why Americans Hate Politics* (New York: Simon & Schuster, 1991), p. 227.
14. Ibid., p. 234.
15. See esp. Catherine A. Lugg, *For God and Country: Conservatism and American School Policy* (New York: Peter Lang, 1996), pp. 84–89.
16. Ibid., p. 341.
17. On the ERA, see, e.g., Flora Davis, *Moving the Mountain: The Women's Movement in America since 1960* (New York: Simon & Schuster, 1991), pp. 121–136; and Donald G. Mathews and Jane Sherron De Hart, *Sex, Gender, and the Politics of ERA* (New York: Oxford University Press, 1990).
18. Mathews and De Hart, *Sex, Gender, and the Politics of ERA,* pp. 50–51.

19. O. Kendall White Jr., "Mormonism and the Equal Rights Amendment," *Journal of Church and State*, 1989, p. 251. For more details on the role of the Mormons against the ERA, see my *Roads to Dominion*, pp. 167–168.
20. Miscellaneous issues of the *Phyllis Schlafly Report*, 1972–1974; author's collection.
21. *Phyllis Schlafly Report*, Sept. and Dec. 1974; author's collection.
22. "The New Activists," *Newsweek*, Nov. 7, 1977, p. 41.
23. See Joseph R. Gusfield, "Political Ceremony in California," *Nation*, Dec. 9, 1978, pp. 633–635.
24. "Christian Voice Gains Visibility Following Realignment of New Right," *Christianity Today*, Nov. 7, 1986, p. 47.
25. Mark Tapscott, "The Battle of Kanawha County Is Not Over," *Conservative Digest*, April 1976, p. 24; Alan Crawford, *Thunder on the Right* (New York: Pantheon Books, 1980), pp. 156–157.
26. Thomas Byrne Edsall and Mary D. Edsall, *Chain Reaction: The Impact of Race, Rights, and Taxes on American Politics* (New York: W. W. Norton, 1991), pp. 131–132.
27. "The IRS Pins 'Badge of Doubt' on Tax-Exempt Private Schools," *Christianity Today*, Jan. 5, 1979, p. 42.
28. Edsall and Edsall, *Chain Reaction*, p. 132.
29. Ibid., p. 132.
30. Ibid., pp. 133–134.
31. See Lugg, 1996, *For God and Country*.
32. Jerry Falwell, *Strength for the Journey: An Autobiography* (New York: Simon & Schuster, 1987), p. 359; Dinesh D'Souza, *Falwell: Before the Millenium* (Chicago: Regnery Gateway, 1984), pp. 109–112.
33. Robert C. Liebman, "Mobilizing the Moral Majority," in Robert C. Liebman and Robert Wuthnow, eds., *The New Christian Right* (New York: Aldine, 1983), pp. 54–55.
34. Liebman, "Mobilizing the Moral Majority," pp. 67–68.
35. Ibid., p. 61.
36. James K. Guth, "New Christian Right," in Liebman and Wuthnow, eds., *New Christian Right*, p. 37.
37. Liebman, "Mobilizing the Moral Majority," p. 71.
38. "Evangelicals in Washington: A Call to Action," *Christianity Today*, March 26, 1976, p. 36.
39. "Washington for Jesus: Revival, Fervor and Political Disclaimers," *Christianity Today*, May 23, 1980, p. 46.
40. "Linking Religion and Politics," *Washington Post*, Aug. 24, 1980.
41. "A Tide of Born-Again Politics," *Newsweek*, Sept. 15, 1980.
42. Ronald Reagan, quoted in "Reagan Strongly Backs Traditional Values," *Conservative Digest*, Sept. 1980, p. 21.
43. "Is Morality All Right?," *Christianity Today*, Nov. 2, 1979, p. 77.
44. "Christian Voice Political Action Group Plans Massive Drive on Reagan's Behalf," *Los Angeles Times*, March 6, 1980.
45. "The New Lobbies Solicit Endorsements from Pulpit," *Christianity Today*,

March 21, 1980; "Evangelical Group Plans Nov. 2 Political Appeal at Churches," *Washington Post,* Oct. 5, 1980.

46. Guth, "New Christian Right," p. 37; Kevin Phillips, *Post-Conservative America* (New York: Vintage, 1983), p. 191; "The Religious Right: How Much Credit Can It Take for Electoral Landslide?," *Christianity Today,* Dec. 12, 1980, p. 53.
47. On the 1980 election generally, see my *Roads to Dominion,* pp. 209–210, 376, note 17.
48. "Evangelical Leaders Hail Election and Ask Continuation of Efforts," *New York Times,* Jan. 28, 1981; "Evangelicals Debate Their Role in Battling Secularism," *New York Times,* Jan. 27, 1981.
49. Tim LaHaye, *The Battle for the Mind* (Old Tappan, NJ: Fleming H. Revell, 1980), p. 26.
50. Ibid., p. 181.
51. Ibid., p. 194.
52. "Is Morality All Right?," *Christianity Today,* Nov. 2, 1979, p. 76.
53. Matthew C. Moen, *The Christian Right and Congress* (Tuscaloosa: University of Alabama Press, 1989), p. 108.
54. On this point, see, generally, my *Roads to Dominion.* On the question of why the Christian Right fared poorly in Congress, see Moen, *The Christian Right and Congress.*
55. I discussed this project in-depth in my earlier books, *Spiritual Warfare* and *Roads to Dominion.* Here I have omitted the details of the freedom fighter project.
56. *Washington Post,* Feb. 4, 1984.
57. "Christian Fundamentalists Press Own Campaign within the G.O.P. Drive," *New York Times,* Aug. 17, 1984.
58. "Religious Right Makes Political Arena Its Major Battleground," *Los Angeles Times,* March 29, 1986.
59. See my *Spiritual Warfare,* pp. 69–70, and the sources cited therein.
60. For details on the surveys, see Moen, *The Transformation of the Christian Right,* pp. 22–24.
61. For more details on the Freedom Council's financial and political dealings, see Jeff Gerth, "Tax Data of Pat Robertson Groups Are Questioned," New York Times, Dec. 10, 1986; and Charles R. Babcock, "Robertson: Blending Charity and Politics," *Washington Post,* Nov. 2, 1987.
62. See my *Spiritual Warfare,* pp. 73–74.
63. Charles R. Babcock, "FEC Fines Robertson Campaign $25,000," *Washington Post,* Dec. 31, 1988.
64. "Robertson Urges Policy to Increase Birth Rate," *New York Times,* Oct. 24, 1988; "Robertson Would Ban Atheists," *San Francisco Chronicle,* Sept. 21, 1987; "Military Blockade of Libya Urged by Pat Robertson," *Los Angeles Times,* Jan. 27, 1987; "Robertson Comes under Fire for Asserting that Cuba Holds Soviet Missiles," *New York Times,* Feb. 16, 1988.
65. "Robertson Blames Bush for Scandal," *Washington Post,* Feb. 24, 1988.
66. Here I have summarized the Oral Roberts, Jim Bakker, and Jimmy Swaggart scandals. The details were reported in the press throughout 1987–1988.

67. "Rift Widens in GOP between Traditionalist and Evangelical Wings," *Wall Street Journal,* Aug. 16, 1988.
68. "Robertson Forces Seeking to Control State Parties," *Washington Post,* Feb. 14, 1988.
69. "Robertson Exhorts Followers to Run for Local Offices," *Los Angeles Times,* March 7, 1988.
70. The story is told in Ralph Reed, *Politically Incorrect: The Emerging Faith Factor in American Politics* (Dallas: Word, 1994), pp. 1–4.
71. Ibid., p. 25.
72. *Christian American,* Spring 1990, vol. 1, no. 1.
73. "Robertson Regroups 'Invisible Army' into New Coalition," *Christianity Today,* April 23, 1990, p. 35.
74. *Christian American,* Spring 1990, vol. 1., no. 1.
75. *Christian American,* Fall 1990, p. 5.
76. For details on some of the local groups scattered around the country, see "Religious Right Drops High-Profile Tactics, Works on Local Level," *Wall Street Journal,* Sept. 26, 1989.
77. Advertisement in *Christian American,* Fall 1990, p. 7.
78. *Christian American,* Winter 1990, p. 1.
79. *Christian American,* Nov.–Dec. 1991, p. 3.
80. The memo was obtained and circulated by People for the American Way, 1986.
81. On the 1990 San Diego elections, see Frederick Clarkson, *Eternal Hostility: The Struggle between Theocracy and Democracy* (Monroe, ME: Common Courage Press, 1997), pp. 22–23.
82. Ralph Reed, quoted in Frederick Clarkson, "The Christian Coalition: On the Road to Victory?," *Church and State,* Jan. 1992.
83. Ibid.
84. Pennsylvania Christian Coalition manual, 1992, pp. 9.1, author's collection.
85. "Christian Coalition Expands Agenda," *Charisma,* Oct. 1993, p. 64.
86. This was my observation at the 1994, 1995, and 1996 Christian Coalition conferences.
87. Rob Boston, "Stealth Strategy," *Church and State,* Oct. 1995, pp. 8–10.
88. "Statement of Ownership," *Christian American,* Nov.–Dec. 1995, p. 3.
89. Roberta Combs, "Organizing Your Neighborhood," speech delivered at the Christian Coalition conference, Sept. 16, 1994.
90. Alice Patterson, tape-recorded "Chapter Leader Briefing," Christian Coalition conference, Sept. 17, 1994.
91. I attended the 1995 legislative lobbying briefing and reported on it in the *Nation,* Oct. 9, 1995.
92. CWA's *Family Voice,* May 1996, p. 16.
93. "CWA Wins Equal Access Case for Maine Church," *Family Voice,* Oct. 1991, p. 17.
94. "Michigan Passes Informed Consent Law," *Family Voice,* Oct. 1993, p. 18.
95. "Field Report," *Family Voice,* May 1996, p. 16.
96. "Politicians Find a Window into the Heart of the Christian Right," *New York Times,* Nov. 1, 1995.

97. Ibid.
98. Gary Bauer, monthly letter to supporters, March 7, 1995, p. 2, author's collection.
99. "Foster Controversy Grows with Revelation of Syphilis Experimentation on Black Men," EP News Service, March 3, 1995.
100. Family Research Council, *Washington Watch*, Feb. 21, 1995.
101. "Religious Landlady Loses Cases," *San Francisco Chronicle*, April 10, 1996.
102. Alliance Defense Fund, letter to supporters, June 1996, author's collection.
103. Alliance Defense Fund, introductory brochure, pp. 3, 5, author's collection.
104. *ADF Briefing*, newsletter, Aug. 1995, p. 1, author's collection.
105. "Conservatives' New Frontier: Religious Liberty Law Firms," *New York Times*, July 8, 1995.
106. Mark I. Pinsky, "Attorney Convert Wins Again," *Los Angeles Times*, June 8, 1993; Paul Thigpen, "Christians in Court," *Charisma*, Dec. 1990, pp. 66–76.
107. Sekulow, quoted in an ACLJ press release, Feb. 1994; author's collection.
108. Mark I. Pinsky, "Legal Weapon," *Los Angeles Times*, Sept. 2, 1993.
109. *Law and Justice*, ACLJ newsletter, Feb. 1993.
110. ACLJ "1996 Year End Report"; *Law and Justice*, Jan. 1997, p. 6.
111. For the details on Hirsh's article and his departure from the ACLJ, see Clarkson, *Eternal Hostility*, pp. 144–148.
112. Keith Fournier, "Religious Cleansing in the American Republic," ACLJ, 1993, p. 7.

Notes to Chapter 5
ᵇ

1. Ralph Reed Jr., "Casting a Wider Net," *Policy Review*, Summer 1993, p. 31.
2. Ibid., p. 35.
3. On the Buchanan–Rosenthal feud, see Eric Alterman, "The Pat and Abe Show," *Nation*, Nov. 5, 1990, pp. 517–520.
4. I discuss this post–Cold War conflict on the Right in some detail in *Roads to Dominion* (New York: Guilford Press, 1995), chap. 12.
5. William F. Buckley Jr., "In Search of Anti-Semitism," *National Review*, Dec. 30, 1991.
6. From "Why I'm Running for President," Patrick Buchanan's Dec. 10, 1991 announcement speech; printed in *Human Events*, Dec. 28, 1991.
7. "Buchanan Wants to Jail Some of the Homeless," *San Francisco Chronicle*, Dec. 25, 1991.
8. "Buchanan Calls AIDS 'Retribution,' " *San Francisco Chronicle*, Feb. 28, 1992.
9. *National and International Religion Report*, Feb. 24, 1992.
10. "Bush Less Than Loved among Religious Right," *New York Times*, March 1, 1992.
11. "Buchanan Looks Back—And Ahead," *Human Events*, June 13, 1992, p. 6.
12. "What Buchanan Has Achieved for Conservatives," *Human Events*, March 28, 1992.

13. Patrick Buchanan, "The War for the Soul of America," speech delivered May 9, 1992, at Liberty University; printed in *Human Events,* May 23, 1992.
14. "Conservatives Address the Convention," *Human Events,* Sept. 5, 1992, p. 10.
15. *USA Today,* Aug. 14, 1992.
16. "Platform Leans to Right of Bush," *San Francisco Chronicle,* Aug. 18, 1992, p. 6.
17. Ralph Reed, "The Good News," *Christian American,* Nov.–Dec. 1992, p. 29. See also "Seeking Common Ground," *Christianity Today,* Dec. 14, 1992, pp. 40–62.
18. "A Republican God?," *Christianity Today,* Oct. 5, 1992, p. 51.
19. "Religious Right Intensifies Campaign for Bush," *New York Times,* Oct. 31, 1992.
20. Christian Coalition, *Voter Guide '92.*
21. "Christian Conservatives Counting Hundreds of Gains in Local Votes," *New York Times,* Nov. 21, 1992.
22. People for the American Way, 1992 election report.
23. "Points of Light on a Dark Night," *Citizen,* Dec. 21, 1992.
24. On the Iowa anti-ERA campaign, see "Learning from Our Victories," *Citizen,* March 15, 1993.
25. "Pat Robertson Was on Target Regarding Feminism," *Human Events,* Sept. 26, 1992, p. 10.
26. "Christian Coalition, Shifting Tactics, to Lobby against Clinton Budget," *Washington Post,* July 18, 1993; "Christian Right Puts New Focus on Economy," *Washington Times,* July 15, 1993.
27. Ralph Reed, quoted in "Christian Coalition to court Minorities," *Washington Times,* Sept. 10, 1993, p. 5; and "Minority Myths Exploded," *Christian American,* Oct. 1993, p. 1.
28. Ibid.
29. "Conservative Coalition Targets Nominee for Surgeon General," *Washington Times,* June 27, 1993.
30. Heidi Scanlon, "Medicine, Politics Don't Mix," *Christian American,* Sept. 1993, p. 8.
31. See *Christian American,* Feb., March, and April 1994.
32. Jeremiah Films, letter to author, Oct. 28, 1994.
33. Author's collection of mailings from Jeremiah Films.
34. Sidney Blumenthal, "The Friends of Paula Jones," *New Yorker,* June 20, 1994, pp. 38–43. See also "Clinton's Visceral Opposition," *Los Angeles Times,* July 5, 1994; and "The Clinton Hater's Video Library," *Time,* Aug. 1, 1994.
35. "Station Replaces Falwell's 'Politics,' " *Christianity Today,* Oct. 3, 1994, p. 68.
36. Author's monitoring of *Randall Terry Live,* summer 1996.
37. "Key House Democrat Lashes Out at Christian Conservatives," *Washington Times,* June 22, 1994; "GOP Senators Urge Clinton to Disown Attack," *Washington Times,* June 24, 1994; "87 Lawmakers Seek Ouster of Joycelyn Elders," *San Francisco Chronicle,* June 25, 1994; "Clinton Calls Show to Assail Press, Falwell, and Limbaugh," *New York Times,* June 25, 1994.

38. For more discussion on this point, see my *Roads to Dominion,* pp. 305–306 and passim.
39. The Wirthlin study was cited in "Joining the Cause," *Citizen,* Oct. 17, 1994, p. 4.
40. John C. Green, James L. Guth, Lyman A. Kellstedt, and Corwin E. Smidt, "Evangelical Realignment: The Political Power of the Christian Right," *Christian Century,* July 5–12, 1995, pp. 676–679.
41. Ibid.
42. Ibid.
43. Larry J. Sabato and Glenn R. Simpson, *Dirty Little Secrets: The Persistence of Corruption in American Politics* (New York: Times Books, 1996,) pp. 129–138.
44. Ibid., pp. 137–138.
45. Ibid., pp. 138–139.
46. Ralph Reed, *Active Faith* (New York: Free Press, 1996), p. 184.
47. Ibid., pp. 184–185.
48. Ibid., p. 197.
49. Ibid., p. 198.
50. "Gingrich Vows to Pursue Christian Coalition Agenda," *Washington Post,* May 18, 1995.
51. "Family 'Contract' Too Mild for Many," *Washington Times,* May 20, 1995.
52. "FEC Files Suit over Christian Coalition Role," *Washington Post,* July 31, 1996; "Federal Election Commission Sues Christian Group on Political Aid," *New York Times,* July 31, 1996.
53. Norman Mailer, "Searching for Deliverance," *Esquire,* Aug. 1996, p. 118.
54. Ibid., p. 123.
55. Ibid., p. 120.
56. "Buchanan, in Unfamiliar Role, Is under Fire as a Left-Winger," *New York Times,* Dec. 31, 1995, p. 1.
57. David Frum, "Patrick J. Buchanan, Left-Winger," *Weekly Standard,* Nov. 27, 1995, pp. 33–35.
58. "Buchanan, Beset by Many Critics, Still Unbowed," *New York Times,* Feb. 17, 1996.
59. "Buchanan Remains a Force in GOP," *Human Events,* March 22, 1996, p. 7.
60. "Social Issues Give Buchanan Boost, A New Poll Finds," *New York Times,* Feb. 27, 1996, p. 1; "Buchanan Win Shows Social Issues Critical," *Human Events,* Feb. 16, 1996, p. 3.
61. "Robertson's Team Puts Dole Over," *Human Events,* Feb. 23, 1996, p. 3.
62. For background on the formation of the U.S. Taxpayers Party in 1991, see my *Facing the Wrath* (Monroe, ME: Common Courage Press, 1996), pp. 188–191. Later, I attended a spring 1996 meeting of reconstructionists in San Jose, California, at which Phillips spoke about having converted to reconstructionism in the mid-1970s after he read works by R. J. Rushdoony.
63. Frederick Clarkson, "Out on the Fringes," *In These Times,* Sept. 16, 1996, pp. 24–26.
64. See newspaper dispatches for the first week of August 1996, e.g., "G.O.P.

Denial Is Accepted by Buchanan," *New York Times*, Aug. 1, 1996; "Unhappy Buchanan Says He Might Walk," *San Francisco Chronicle*, Aug. 1, 1996.

65. "Dole Calls for 'Tolerance' in GOP Abortion Plank," EP News Service, June 14, 1996.
66. Tom Hess, "The Team that Beat 'Tolerance,'" Focus on the Family *Citizen*, Sept. 23, 1996, pp. 1–3.
67. Ibid., p. 3.
68. "With Abortion Scarcely Uttered, Its Opponents Are Feeling Angry," *New York Times*, Aug. 15, 1996.
69. James M. Penning and Corwin Smidt, "What Coalition?," *Christian Century*, Jan. 15, 1997, p. 37.
70. Ibid.
71. "Religious Right's '96 Defeats Called 'A Portent,'" *National Catholic Reporter*, Nov. 15, 1996.
72. "What Difference Will We Make? An Open Letter to Conservatives from Gary Bauer," published by the Family Research Council in *Human Events*, Nov. 15, 1996; *Christian American*, Jan.–Feb. 1997.
73. Ibid.
74. "105th Congress: Unfinished Business," *Christian American*, Jan.–Feb. 1997, pp. 21–22.
75. "Christian Coalition Revamps Agenda to Reach Out to Inner Cities," *Washington Post*, Jan. 31, 1997.
76. "Church Burnings Continue," EP News Service, July 5, 1996, p. 2.
77. "Firebombed Churches Thank Re-Building Donors," *Christian American*, Jan.–Feb. 1997, p. 12.
78. "Christian Coalition Is Reorganizing, Trimming Staff," *Washington Post*, Dec. 20, 1997; "Christian Coalition Drops Black Outreach," *Washington Times*, Dec. 23, 1997.
79. "Christian Coalition Revamps Agenda to Reach Out to Inner Cities," *Washington Post*, Jan. 31, 1997.
80. "Christian Coalition Launches 'Samaritan Project,'" *Christian American*, March–April, 1997, p. 12.

Notes to Chapter 6

～

1. "CDF March Aims to Stem Cutbacks on Youth," *Washington Times*, May 30, 1996; "Conservatives Hit Rally for Children," *Washington Times*, June 1, 1996; "Rally in D.C. on Problems of Children," *San Francisco Chronicle*, June 1, 1996; "Children's Rally Draws 200,000 to U.S. Capital," *San Francisco Examiner*, June 2, 1996.
2. P. J. O'Rourke, "Mrs. Clinton's Very, Very Bad Book," *Weekly Standard*, Feb. 19, 1996, p. 20.
3. Kay Coles James, "Transforming America," *Family Voice*, July 1996, pp. 4–6, author's collection.

4. Judith Stacey, *In the Name of the Family: Rethinking Family Values in the Postmodern Age* (Boston: Beacon Press, 1996), p. 6.

5. "Two-Parent Families at Record Low—25% of Homes," *San Francisco Chronicle,* Nov. 27, 1996, p. 1.

6. Stacey, *In the Name of the Family,* p. 7.

7. Ibid., p. 9.

8. "Parents Know Best," *Citizen,* Sept. 18, 1995, p. 6.

9. " 'The Right to Parent': Should It Be Fundamental?," *Christianity Today,* April 29, 1996, p. 57.

10. "Colorado Has Rights of Parents on Ballot," *Washington Times,* Sept. 10, 1996; "Colorado Voters Ask: Whose Kids Are They?" *World,* Oct. 26, 1996, p. 16; "Colorado PRA Defeated," *Home School Court Report,* Nov.–Dec. 1996, p. 3.

11. Legislative packet received from Rep. Steve Largent (R-OK), fall 1996, author's collection.

12. Legislative packet received from Rep. Steve Largent (R-OK), fall 1996, author's collection.

13. *Barna Report,* vol. 1, no. 1, 1996, author's collection.

14. "Can Government Save the Family?," *Policy Review,* Sept.–Oct. 1996, pp. 43–47.

15. " 'No Fault' Divorce under Assault," *Christianity Today,* April 8, 1996, pp. 84–87.

16. Ibid. Also, "Florida Looks at Repealing No-Fault Divorce," *San Francisco Examiner,* Dec. 29, 1996.

17. Sandra Felton, "Living with a Messie," *Focus on the Family,* Feb. 1996, pp. 2–4.

18. Trudy Hutchens, "Marriage: The State of the Union," *Family Voice,* Oct. 1996, pp. 5–6, author's collection.

19. Bob Yandian, "The Question of Submission," *Charisma,* Oct. 1994, p. 63.

20. Rosaline Bush, "The End of Innocence," *Family Voice,* Feb. 1996, pp. 4–5, author's collection.

21. Ibid., p. 5.

22. Ibid., p. 10.

23. Trudy Hutchens, "The Failure of Feminism," three-part series in *Family Voice,* March, April, and May 1995, author's collection.

24. Dr. James Dobson, Focus on the Family, letter to supporters, Aug. 1995, author's collection.

25. Dr. James Dobson, Focus on the Family, letter to supporters, Oct. 1995, p. 2, author's collection.

26. "Non-Sexual Revolution," *World,* Dec. 11, 1993; "Staking Their Lives on It," *World,* Aug. 13, 1994.

27. "Ring Symbolizes Teen's Commitment," *Good News Journal* (Columbia, MO), May 1994, p. 1.

28. "Matters of the Heart," advertisement, *New Man,* Sept. 1996, p. 69.

Notes to Chapter 7

ᠬᠥ

1. "Reagan Strongly Backs Traditional Values Based on Religious View of Morality," *Conservative Digest,* Sept. 1980, pp. 20–21; "Pro-Lifers on the March, Gaining Converts," *Conservative Digest,* Aug. 1980, p. 16.
2. Michele McKeegan, *Abortion Politics: Mutiny in the Ranks of the Right* (New York: Free Press, 1992), p. 43.
3. Mark Tapscott, "Reagan Fights the Good Fight for the Unborn," *Conservative Digest,* Sept. 1982, p. 8.
4. "The Abortion Front: End of the 'Phony War,' " *National Review,* March 2, 1973, pp. 249–250.
5. Andrew H. Merton, *Enemies of Choice: The Right-to-Life Movement and its Threat to Abortion* (Boston: Beacon Press, 1981), pp. 91–131.
6. Connie Paige, *The Right to Lifers* (New York: Summit Books, 1983), pp. 149–150.
7. Dallas A. Blanchard and Terry J. Prewitt, *Religious Violence and Abortion* (Gainesville: University of Florida Press, 1993), p. 36.
8. "Reagan Condemns Arson at Clinics," *New York Times,* Jan. 4, 1984; "U.S. Clinic Bombing Inquiry Now Pleasing More Groups," *New York Times,* Jan. 20, 1985; "Violence against Abortion Clinics Escalates Despite the Opposition of Prolife Leaders," *Christianity Today,* Feb. 1, 1985, pp. 44–45.
9. James Ridgeway, "Unholy Terrorists," *Village Voice,* Jan. 15, 1985, p. 18.
10. "No Conspiracy Seen in Clinic Attacks," *New York Times,* Jan. 3, 1985; "Men with Ties to Church Arrested for Abortion Clinic Bombings," *Christianity Today,* March 1, 1985, pp. 34–35.
11. "How Anti-Abortion Groups Harassed Mondale, Ferraro," *Oakland Tribune,* Oct. 4, 1984.
12. Joseph M. Scheidler, *Closed: 99 Ways to Stop Abortion* (Westchester, IL: Crossway Books, 1985).
13. Joseph M. Scheidler, quoted in Randy Frame, "Prolife Activists Escalate the War against Abortion," *Christianity Today,* Nov. 9, 1984, pp. 41–42.
14. Randall Terry, quoted in "Pro-Lifers Disrupt New York Clinic: Police Arrest 500," *Washington Times,* May 3, 1988, p. 12.
15. Susan Faludi, "Where Did Randy Go Wrong?," *Mother Jones,* Nov. 1989, pp. 61–62.
16. For background on Randall Terry, see Robert Nolte, "Siege on Abortion," *Charisma,* Jan. 1989, pp. 42–47.
17. *Operation Rescue NewsBrief,* Dec. 1988, p. 1, author's collection.
18. Ibid., p. 2.
19. "Falwell Joins Atlanta Abortion Protest," *San Jose Mercury News,* Aug. 11, 1988.
20. Operation Rescue newsletter, Sept. 1988, author's collection.
21. Ibid.
22. This conclusion is based on data gathered by the National Abortion Federation, cited in a self-published monograph by Tom Burghardt, *Low-Intensity Warfare:*

An Anti-Abortion Strategy of Terror (San Francisco: Bay Area Coalition for Our Reproductive Rights, Jan. 1994), p. 20.

23. "Abortion Opponents Seized as They Protest with Fetus," *Washington Times,* July 7, 1988.
24. Randall A. Terry, *Higher Laws,* a pamphlet distributed by Operation Rescue in 1988, author's collection.
25. Paulk, quoted in Nolte, "Siege," p. 46.
26. Rev. Charles Stanley, quoted in "The New Pro-Life Offensive," *Newsweek,* Sept. 12, 1988, p. 25.
27. Tom Hess, "Three Tough Questions for Randall Terry," Focus on the Family *Citizen,* June 1989, pp. 4–5.
28. Ibid., pp. 5–6.
29. "Supreme Court, 5–4, Narrowing Roe v. Wade, Upholds Sharp State Limits on Abortions," *New York Times,* July 4, 1989, p. 1. For details on the *Webster* case, see Karen O'Connor, *No Neutral Ground? Abortion Politics in an Age of Absolutes* (Boulder, CO: Westview Press, 1996).
30. Brian Johnston, "California in the Wake of Webster," *California Capitol Report,* inserted into the Focus on the Family *Citizen,* Aug. 1989.
31. The National Abortion and Reproductive Rights Action League, *Who Decides? A State-by-State Review of Abortion and Reproductive Rights,* 6th ed. (Washington, DC: Author, 1997), p. 62.
32. McKeegan, *Abortion Politics,* pp. 147–149; David Wagner and Frank York, "The Aftermath of *Webster,*" Focus on the Family *Citizen,* Sept. 1989, pp. 6–7.
33. National Abortion . . . League, *Who Decides?,* pp. i–ii.
34. "Holy Week Rescues Show Movement Still Active," *Christianity Today,* Aug. 29, 1991.
35. See, e.g., "Leader of Abortion Protest Jailed after Refusing to Pay $1,000 Fine," *New York Times,* Oct. 6, 1989; "Pro-Life Leader Labors in Prison, Will Miss March," *Washington Times,* Jan. 22, 1990; "Freed Pro-Life Leader Closes Office, Charges 'Persecution,' " *Washington Times,* Feb. 1, 1990.
36. "Nomadic Group of Anti-Abortionists Uses New Tactics to Make Its Mark," *New York Times,* March 24, 1992.
37. Sara Diamond, "Trench Tactics on the Anti-Abortion Front," *Z Magazine,* Dec. 1992, p. 40.
38. See John Goetz, "Missionaries' Leader Calls for Armed Militias," *Front Lines Research* (Planned Parenthood newsletter), Aug. 1994, pp. 1–5.
39. Frederick Clarkson, "Operation Poseur: Wolves in Sheep's Clothing?," *Front Lines Research,* May 1995, p. 2.
40. Frederick Clarkson, *Eternal Hostility* (Monroe, ME: Common Courage Press, 1997), pp. 144–146.
41. Goetz, "Missionaries' Leader Calls."
42. NAF data, reported in Burghardt, *Low-Intensity Warfare,* pp. 19–20.
43. Memorandum, *Incidents of Violence and Disruption against Abortion Providers in 1996: A Report of the National Abortion Federation,* Jan. 16, 1997.
44. *To Vote for Bill Clinton Is to Sin against God,* pamphlet circulated by Randall Terry to supporters, Oct. 1992; author's collection.

45. Dallas A. Blanchard, *The Anti-Abortion Movement and the Rise of the Religious Right* (New York: Twayne, 1994), p. 118.

46. Details of the No Place to Hide campaign come from the December 1992 newsletter of Operation Rescue of California.

47. Randall Terry and Joseph M. Scheidler, quoted in "Abortion Foes Strike at Doctors' Home Lives," *Washington Post,* April 8, 1993.

48. See Karen Houppert, "John Burt's Holy War," *Village Voice,* April 6, 1993; and Paul Gray, "Thou Shalt Not Kill," *Time,* March 22, 1993.

49. *Time,* March 22, 1993, p. 45.

50. Quotes from all those quoted in this paragraph come from the *National and International Religion Report,* March 22, 1993, pp. 6–7.

51. Judie Brown, "Cast Not the First Stone," *Life Advocate,* May 1993, p. 44.

52. Joseph Foreman, quoted in "Common Ground: Both Sides Blame Clinton," *Life Advocate,* May 1993, p. 14.

53. Steven J. Pruner, "In Defense of Others," *Life Advocate,* May 1993, p. 46.

54. See "Arrests Few in Pro-Life Acts across U.S.," *Washington Times,* July 11, 1993, p. 3; and "Anti-Abortion Turnout Much Smaller than Expected," *San Francisco Chronicle,* July 12, 1993, p. 3.

55. Golden Ohlhausen and Cathy Ramey, "Rescue and 'Use of Force' Debate Part of Conference," *Life Advocate,* Aug. 1993, p. 24.

56. Ibid.

57. "Christian Ousted from Church for Griffin Support," *Life Advocate,* July 1993, p. 40.

58. Ibid.

59. Paul J. Hill, "Who Killed the Innocent—Michael Griffin or David Gunn?," *Life Advocate,* Aug. 1993, p. 41.

60. Ibid., pp. 41–42.

61. Arthur H. Matthews, "Who Is Paul Hill?," *World,* Aug. 13, 1994, p. 17.

62. Gary North, *Lone Gunners for Jesus: Letters to Paul J. Hill* (Tyler, TX: Institute for Christian Economics, 1994).

63. Ibid., p. 6.

64. Ibid., p. 41.

65. Rev. Michael Bray, *A Time to Kill: A Study Concerning the Use of Force and Abortion* (Portland, OR: Advocates for Life, 1994), p. 147.

66. Ibid., p. 148.

67. *Prayer and Action News,* January 1996, author's collection.

68. For background on conflicting claims, by prochoice and antichoice spokespersons, on whether hundreds or thousands of partial birth abortions are performed each year, see, e.g., Roy Rivenburg, "Partial Truths," *Los Angeles Times,* April 2, 1997, p. E1.

69. "As Promised, President Clinton Vetoes Bill to Ban 'Partial Birth' Abortions," *EP News Service,* April 19, 1996; "U.S. House Overrides President Clinton's Veto, but Senate Lets Partial-Birth Abortion Continue," *EP News Service,* Oct. 4, 1996.

70. " 'Partial-Birth' Abortion Ban Again Passes House," *Los Angeles Times,* March

21, 1997; "Senate Passes Partial-Birth Abortion, but Margin Insufficient to Overturn Veto," EP News Service, May 23, 1997.
71. "Clinton Vetoes Ban of Partial-Birth Abortions," EP News Service, Oct. 17, 1997.
72. "Senate Passes Partial-Birth Abortion, but Margin Insufficient to Overturn Veto," EP News Service, May 23, 1997.
73. Rivenburg, "Partial Truths."
74. "Anti-Abortion Centers' Ads Are Attacked as Misleading," *New York Times,* July 16, 1986; "Pregnancy Centers: Anti-Abortion Role Sets Off Controversy and Challenge," *New York Times,* Jan. 23, 1987; "Attracting Clients and Controversy," *Christianity Today,* Sept. 18, 1987.
75. Crisis pregnancy centers listed under "Abortion Alternatives," Alameda County, California, Yellow Pages, 1997.
76. "Inside Crisis Pregnancy Centers," *Christianity Today,* Aug. 17, 1992, p. 22.
77. "Focus' CPC Ministry Helps the Unborn," *Focus on the Family* magazine, Jan. 1997, p. 13.
78. Tim Stafford, "Inside Crisis Pregnancy Centers," *Christianity Today,* Aug. 17, 1992.
79. Information packet from Care Net, 1996; author's collection.
80. Thomas Glessner, quoted in Steve Schwalm, "Conservative Spotlight: National Institute of Family and Life Advocates," *Human Events,* Sept. 6, 1996.
81. "Saving Babies—and Their Moms—in the 90s," Focus on the Family *Citizen,* March 25, 1996, pp. 6–7.
82. Frederica Mathewes-Green, "Saving the Baby from Abortion Is Good—But Then What?," *Human Events,* Aug. 2, 1996, pp. 12–13.
83. Ibid.
84. Marcia Ford, "When Abortion Comes to Church," *Charisma,* July 1996, pp. 58–62.
85. Ibid.

Notes to Chapter 8
⌒

1. Beverly LaHaye, fundraising letter, Feb. 1991; author's collection.
2. Chris Bull and John Gallagher, *Perfect Enemies: The Religious Right, the Gay Movement, and the Politics of the 1990s* (New York: Crown, 1996), p. 18.
3. Ibid., p. 21.
4. Ibid., p. 257.
5. On this point, see esp. Jean Hardisty, "Constructing Homophobia," in Chip Berlet, ed., *Eyes Right: Challenging the Right Wing Backlash* (Boston: South End Press, 1995), pp. 86–104. Hardisty enumerates the many national organizations whose leaders played a role in Colorado's 1992 antigay ballot initiative.
6. David Colker, "Anti-Gay Video Highlights Church's Agenda," *Los Angeles Times,* Feb. 22, 1993, pp. 1, 16.
7. "Challenging the Homosexual Agenda," Focus on the Family *Citizen,* April 19, 1993, p. 5.

8. Michael Weisskopf, "Energized by Pulpit or Passion, the Public Is Calling," *Washington Post*, Feb. 1, 1993.

9. June, 1993, fundraising letter from Dr. D. James Kennedy, Coral Ridge Ministries; author's collection.

10. "How the Right Stirs Black Homophobia," *Newsweek*, Oct. 18, 1993, p. 73; Peri Wetherington, "Minorities Speak Out against Gay Rights," Focus on the Family *Citizen*, Nov. 15, 1993, p. 13.

11. For a thorough deconstruction of the "no special rights" rhetoric, see Didi Herman, *The Antigay Agenda: Orthodox Vision and the Christian Right* (Chicago: University of Chicago Press, 1997), Chap. 5.

12. Will Perkins, quoted in "Recognizing a Ruling, and Battles to Come," *New York Times*, May 21, 1996.

13. Bull and Gallagher, *Perfect Enemies*, pp. 40–43.

14. Ibid., pp. 44–58.

15. Ibid., p. 60.

16. Ibid., pp. 103–104.

17. Ibid., p. 110.

18. Hardisty, "Constructing Homophobia," pp. 92–96.

19. Ibid., pp. 97, 102.

20. Ibid., pp. 167–174; 193–194, and passim.

21. "Anti-Gay Rights Leaders Talk of Repeating 1993 Success," *Washington Times*, May 19, 1994, p. 3; "In Petition Drives, Anti-Gay Rights Groups Fall Short," *Washington Times*, July 12, 1994, p. 8.

22. People for the Anerican Way, *Hostile Climate, 1995: A State by State Report on Anti-Gay Activity* (Washington, DC: People for the American Way, 1995).

23. Larry Witham, "Movement Puts Major Focus on Changing Homosexuals," *Washington Times*, Feb. 3, 1995, p. 2.

24. See Richard Shumate, "Divine Intervention?," *Out*, Nov. 1995; Justin Chin, "Saved," *Progressive*, Dec. 1995.

25. "Once Gay, Always Gay," *Focus on the Family*, March 1994, pp. 2–3.

26. On LaBarbera's background, see Robin Stevens, "Fighting Words," *Out*, April 1994.

27. *Lambda Report*, miscellaneous issues, 1993 and 1994.

28. "And Now . . . The 'Leather Agenda,' " *Lambda Report*, Aug. 1994, p. 3.

29. Paul Cameron, *Medical Aspects of Homosexuality*, 1984 pamphlet; author's collection.

30. "Anti-Gay Adviser Stirs Controversy," *San Francisco Chronicle*, Aug. 19, 1985; Mark E. Pietrzyk, "Queer Science," *New Republic*, Oct. 3, 1994.

31. "AIDS: A Clear and Present Danger for Civilization" (interview with Paul Cameron), *New American*, March 17, 1986, p. 24.

32. "Anti-Gay Adviser Stirs Controversy."

33. Paul Cameron, *The Gay 90s: What the Empirical Evidence Reveals about Homosexuality* (Franklin, TN: Adroit Press, 1993), pp. 41–49, and passim.

34. "Colorado: 1998," a one-page sheet inserted into the newsletter of Colorado for Family Values, 1993; author's collection.

35. The April 1994 TVC conference, including the scheduled appearance of Spenser

Hughes, was advertised in the March–April 1994 *Traditional Values Report*; author's collection.
36. Kevin E. Abrams, "Preface," in Scott Lively and Kevin Abrams, *The Pink Swastika: Homosexuality in the Nazi Party* (Keizer, OR: Founders, 1995), p. iv.
37. April and May 1996 mailings from the National Campaign to Protect Marriage; author's collection.
38. "Fists Are Bared in the Fight for Religious Right's Votes," *New York Times*, Feb. 10, 1996; "Unholy Matrimony," *World*, April 6, 1996, p. 17.
39. "Senate OKs Gay Marriage Restrictions," *San Francisco Chronicle*, Sept. 11, 1996.
40. "Judge OKs Same-Sex Marriages," *San Francisco Chronicle*, Dec. 4, 1996.
41. *Law and Justice*, ACLJ newsletter, Jan. 1997, p. 6, author's collection.
42. Family Research Council, *Washington Watch*, March 26, 1996, p. 1, author's collection.
43. "A Word from Will Perkins," *CFV Report*, March 1996, p. 6, author's collection.
44. Charles Colson, "Why Not Gay Marriage," *Christianity Today*, Oct. 28, 1996, p. 104.
45. Ibid.
46. Keith Fournier, "In Defense of Marriage," *Law and Justice*, Jan. 1997, pp. 4–5, author's collection.

Notes to Chapter 9

⤙

1. John W. Kennedy, "Mixing Politics and Piety," *Christianity Today*, Aug. 15, 1994, p. 42; Susan Olasky, "Homeschool Hotline," *World*, March 5, 1994, pp. 18–19.
2. Michael Farris gave me his estimate of one million homeschooled students when I spoke with him at an August 1994 homeschooling conference in Danville, California. The 1994 Department of Education figures come from an August 1994 phone interview with Patricia Lines, who is the department's in-house expert on homeschooling. Patricia Lines's data as of 1997 is contained in a March 1997 working paper she graciously sent me, titled "Homeschooling: An Overview for Education Policymakers."
3. Lines, "Homeschooling," p. 7.
4. Statistics on the average homeschool family come from Brian Ray, *Marching to the Beat of Their Own Drum: A Profile of Home Education Research* (Home School Legal Defense Association, 1992). See also John W. Kennedy, "Home Schooling Grows Up," *Christianity Today*, July 17, 1995, pp. 50–52, and Lines, "Homeschooling," pp. 6–8.
5. Ray, *Machine*, p. 7; Also, Lines, op cit., pp. 9–10; and "Advocates hail test scores of home schooled students," *Washington Times*, Jan. 17, 1995, p. 3.
6. Ray, *Marching*, p. 5.
7. Kennedy, "Home Schooling," p. 52.

8. A-Beka Book Home School Catalog, 1994, p. 3; author's collection.
9. Ibid., p. 70.
10. Ibid., p. 65.
11. Judy Hull Moore and Laurel Hicks, *The History of Our United States* (Pensacola, FL: A-Beka Book, 1990), pp. 41–43.
12. Ibid., pp. 197–198.
13. Laurel Elizabeth Hicks and Judy Hull Moore, *New World History and Geography in Christian Perspective* (Pensacola, FL: A-Beka Book, 1992), pp. 14–15.
14. Christopher J. Klicka, *The Right Choice: Home Schooling* (Gresham, OR: Noble Publishing Associates, 1993), p. 24.
15. Ibid., pp. 75–92.
16. Ibid., pp. 172–179.
17. "Abolishing the Federal Role in Education," *Teaching Home*, Jan.–Feb. 1997, p. 23.
18. Christian Coalition, *Contract with the American Family*, 1995, pp. 13–21.
19. "How to Get Students Involved in the Election Process," *Teaching Home*, Sept.–Oct. 1996, p. 17.
20. "Getting Out the Vote," *Teaching Home*, Sept.–Oct. 1996, p. 35.
21. Michael P. Farris, "Freedom Works: Ask Home Schoolers," *Teaching Home*, May–June 1994, p. 66.
22. Ibid., pp. 66–67.
23. Douglas W. Phillips, "The Father's Role in Teaching Government," *Teaching Home*, May–June 1994, pp. 41–42.
24. Andy and Betsy Barth, "Cover Family," *Teaching Home*, May–June 1996, pp. 9–10.
25. Author's notes from August 1994 homeschooling conference held in Danville, California.
26. "Schools Become Religious War Zone," *Washington Post*, May 4, 1993; and "In N.Y. School Board 'Holy War,' Vote Is Split but Civics Triumphs," *Washington Post*, May 21, 1993.
27. Sarah Henry, "How One Town Took on the Religious Right—and Won," *Ms.*, March–April 1995, pp. 86–90.
28. "Battle over Patriotism Curriculum," *New York Times*, May 15, 1994, p. 12; "Florida Votes Thrash Religious Right, 'America-First' Curriculum," *San Francisco Chronicle*, Oct. 8, 1994, p. A6.
29. Ralph Reed, quoted in "Floridians Seize Initiatives in the Culture War," *Human Events*, May 27, 1994, p. 6.
30. Hans Johnson, "School Board Crusade," *Church and State*, July–Aug. 1995, pp. 9–12.
31. "School Board Says Yes to Abstinence Videos," *Citizen*, March 21, 1994, p. 15.
32. "Parents Create Sex Respect Option," *Citizen*, July 17, 1995, p. 15.
33. "Mom's Homework Proves Persuasive," *Citizen*, Oct. 16, 1995, p. 15.
34. "School Board Ousts Planned Parenthood," *Citizen*, Sept. 19, 1994, pp. 14–15; "Courageous School Board Keeps Moving," *Citizen*, Jan. 15, 1996, p. 13.

35. Elizabeth Shogren and Douglas Frantz, "School Boards Become the Religious Right's New Pulpit," *Los Angeles Times*, Dec. 10, 1993, p. 38.
36. Citizens for Excellence in Education, brochure distributed to the public in 1997; author's collection.
37. Sonia L. Nazario, "Crusader Vows to Put God Back into Schools Using Local Elections," *Wall Street Journal*, July 15, 1992, p. 1.
38. National Association of Christian Educators/Citizens for Excellence in Education, *President's Report*, Dec. 1995, p. 5.
39. See William Lowe Boyd, Catherine Lugg, and Gerald L. Zahorchak, "Social Traditionalists, Religious Conservatives, and the Politics of Outcome-Based Education: Pennsylvania and Beyond," *Education and Urban Society*, vol. 28, no. 3, May 1996, pp. 347–365.
40. These two phrases come from subtitles of two anti-OBE reports published, respectively, by Concerned Women for America and by the Family Research Council.
41. William Spady, quoted in "Parents Edgy over Classroom Groupthink," *Christianity Today*, Sept. 13, 1993, p. 52.
42. Ibid., p. 53.
43. Author's collection of anti-OBE materials from Eagle Forum, CWA, and CEE. See also Chris Pipho, "Opposition to Reform," *Phi Delta Kappan*, March 1994, pp. 510–511.
44. "Alice Walker Story Pulled from State Test," *San Francisco Chronicle*, Feb. 19, 1994; "Author Alice Walker Blasts Educators," *San Francisco Chronicle*, Feb. 23, 1994; "Furor Grows over Decision on Alice Walker Story," *San Francisco Chronicle*, Feb. 25, 1994.
45. The Capitol Resource Institute described its use of radio stations to arouse public opposition to CLAS in "The Battle for CLAS," *California Citizen*, inserted into Focus on the Family *Citizen*, June 20, 1994; "California's Dream Team," *California Citizen*, inserted into Focus on the Family *Citizen*, Dec. 19, 1994.
46. Quote from United States Justice Foundation, press release, received April 1994; author's collection.
47. Rutherford press releases; author's collection.
48. "Tepid Response as CLAS Test Made Public," *San Francisco Chronicle*, July 19, 1994.
49. "Teachers Take on Tough Challenge," *San Francisco Chronicle*, July 8, 1994, p. 1; "Wilson Says No to Retool of CLAS Test," *Sacramento Bee*, Sept. 28, 1994, p. 1.
50. Robert O'Harrow Jr., "Christian Group's Push Felt in Move against Gay Paper," *Washington Post*, Oct. 1, 1993.
51. People for the American Way, *Hostile Climate: A State by State Report on Anti-Gay Activity in 1994*, pp. 74–75.
52. Fall 1995 mailing from FFL, author's collection.
53. Larry Witham, "Public Library Watchdogs Go National with New Family Group," *Washington Times*, Oct. 20, 1995.
54. Scott DeNicola, "What Lurks in the Library?," Focus on the Family *Citizen*, Sept. 18, 1995, p. 6.

55. Ibid.; Withham, "Public Library Watchdogs."

56. Karen Jo Gounaud, "Banned, Canned, and Planned Books: How Pro-Gay Elites Are Using the Library to Change the Culture," *Lambda Report on Homosexuality*, Oct. 1995–Jan. 1996, p. 15.

57. Phone conversation with Karen Jo Gounaud, April 18, 1997. Also, Family Friendly Libraries, Summer 1996, a newsletter that lists FFL contact people in sixteen states and reports on sporadic successes by FFL activists in getting libraries to restrict access of "adult" material to minors.

58. Catherine Elton, "Balanced Books," *New Republic*, May 5, 1997, p. 12.

59. Donald Wildmon's April 5, 1989 letter is reproduced in Richard Bolton, ed., *Culture Wars: Documents from the Recent Controversies in the Arts* (New York: New Press, 1992), p. 27.

60. Martin Booe, "What Does the NEA Mean by 'Decency'? Justice Department Challenges Agency's Standard for Arts Funding," *Washington Post*, Feb. 4, 1994.

61. See mainstream press coverage of ongoing NEA budget conflicts, including the following *Washington Post* articles by Jacqueline Trescott: "Arts Agencies Escape as Cuts May Still Come in Budget Battle," Feb. 4, 1994; "House Panel Votes to Kill Arts Agency," May 11, 1995; "The NEA's Half-Victory: Agency Still Alive, but Budget Cuts Will Hurt," Oct. 1, 1995.

62. David Richards, "Dispatch from the Culture War," *Washington Post*, Jan. 29, 1995.

63. John Frohnmayer, *Leaving Town Alive: Confessions of an Arts Warrior* (New York: Houghton Mifflin, 1993), pp. 175–176. Early issues of the Christian Coalition's newsletter, the *Christian American*, featured articles on the NEA controversy.

64. Bruce Seleraig, "Rev. Wildmon's War on the Arts," *New York Times Magazine*, Sept. 2, 1990, p. 43.

65. Ibid.

66. Steve Beard, "Tupelo Tornado," *World*, Nov. 27, 1993, p. 22.

67. On each of these specific AFA campaigns, see, respectively, Frederick Clarkson, "Don Wildmon: He's No Jim Bakker," *In These Times*, July 4–17, 1990; Seleraig, "Rev. Wildmon's War," p. 52.; "AFA Action Forces Cancellation of Homosexual Mini-Series Sequel," *AFA Journal*, June 1994, p. 3.; "AFA Boycott Helps Drop Kmart Profits, Force Closing of 110 Stores," *AFA Journal*, Nov.–Dec. 1994, p. 1.

68. Beard, "Tupelo Tornado," p. 22.

69. AFA Action Page, July 1994. *Christianity Today* reported that forty ABC affiliates had refused to carry *NYPD Blue*. See also "Violence Foes Take Aim," *Christianity Today*, Feb. 7, 1994, p. 40.

   In a May 22, 1997 phone interview, ABC Communications director Janice Gretemeyer said that the network could "neither confirm nor deny" Wildmon's claim that AFA cost ABC $20 million in lost advertising revenues for *NYPD Blue*. Gretemeyer said that advertisers were "skittish" about the program during its first season but that its long-running success shows that Wildmon has little impact on network programming and advertising.

70. *AFA Journal*, Jan. 1996, p. 6.
71. *AFA Journal*, Sept. 1996 and Sept. 1995.
72. Donald Wildmon, quoted in Seleraig, "Rev. Wildmon's War," p. 24.
73. "Violent Reaction," *Time*, June 12, 1995, p. 26; "Corp Killa," *World*, June 17–24, 1995.
74. Author's attendance at the 1995 Christian Coalition conference.
75. Robert Hughes, "Pulling the Fuse on Culture," *Time*, August 7, 1995, pp. 61–68.
76. Beard, "Tupleo Tornado," p. 24.
77. People for the American Way, *Attacks on the Freedom to Learn*, 1994–95, list on inside front cover.
78. Carol Innerst, "Group Sees School Censorship Everywhere," *Washington Times*, Sept. 1, 1994, p. 4.
79. Marc Herman, "The Book-Banning Racket," *Harper's*, Oct. 1996, pp. 21, 24.
80. Carol Innerst, "Activist Groups War over School 'Censors,' " *Washington Times*, Aug. 31, 1995.
81. Deborah Mendenhall, "Nightmarish Textbooks Await Your Kids," Focus on the Family *Citizen*, Sept. 1990, pp. 1–7.
82. Rob Boston, "Fact or Fantasy?," *Church and State*, May 1991, pp. 4–7.
83. "Chasing *Impressions* Out of the Schools," Focus on the Family *Citizen*, Jan. 21, 1991, p. 5.
84. "The Parents Fight Back—In Court," Focus on the Family *Citizen*, Feb. 1991, p. 3.

Notes to Chapter 10

ᴄ⌒⊃

1. "Are We Headed for Doomsday? An Interview with Pat Robertson," *Charisma*, Nov. 1995, p. 76.
2. On the many versions of end-times theology, see esp. Paul Boyer, *When Time Shall Be No More: Prophecy Belief in Modern American Culture* (Cambridge, MA: The Belknap Press of Harvard University Press, 1992).
3. Ibid., pp. 303–304; Sara Diamond, *Roads to Dominion* (New York: Guilford Press, 1995), pp. 246–248.
4. "Prophecy Books Become Big Sellers," *Christianity Today*, March 11, 1991, p. 60.
5. John F. Walvoord, *Armageddon, Oil, and the Middle East Crisis* (Grand Rapids, MI: Zondervan, 1990), p. 15.
6. See Paul Thigpen, "The Second Coming: How Many Views?," *Charisma*, Feb. 1989, p. 42, and, in the same issue, an interview with Edgar Whisenant, pp. 58–50. For a critique of Whisenant and other date-setters, see B. J. Oropeza, *99 Reasons Why No One Knows When Christ Will Return* (Downers Grove, IL: InterVarsity Press, 1994.)
7. "End Times Prediction Draws Strong Following," *Christianity Today*, June 20, 1994, pp. 46–47; "Camping Misses End-Times Deadline," *Christianity Today*, Oct. 24, 1994, p. 84; "The Man Who Prophesied the End of the World," *San Francisco Chronicle*, March 12, 1995.

8. I was a regular listener to Hank Hanegraaff's *The Bible Answer Man* radio program in 1994 during the controversy over Harold Camping.
9. James Horvath, *He's Coming Soon!* (Orlando, FL: Creation House, 1995), p. 121.
10. Peter Lalonde and Patti Lalonde, *Left Behind* (Eugene, OR: Harvest House, 1995).
11. The poll is found in a small box under the heading "Vox Pop," *Time*, May 17, 1993, p. 13.
12. "The Christmas Covenant," *U.S. News and World Report*, Dec. 19, 1994, p. 63.
13. "Mobilizing for the Millennium," *Christianity Today*, July 17, 1995, p. 53; "Christians from 20 Countries Gather to Reach the World by the Year 2000," *EP News Service*, May 19, 1995, p. 6.
14. A.D. 2000 and Beyond, literature packet provided in April 1996; author's collection.
15. "Millions to Pray in Worldwide Rally," *Christianity Today*, Oct. 2, 1995, pp. 106–107.
16. Sept. 14, 1994, press release from A.D. 2000 and Beyond; author's collection.
17. Ibid.
18. "Joshua Project 2000," brochure provided by A.D. 2000 and Beyond, April 1996; author's collection.
19. Ibid.
20. "Millions to Pray in Worldwide Rally," *Christianity Today*, Oct. 2, 1995, p. 106.
21. "Spiritual Mapping: A Powerful New Tool or an Overhyped Spiritual Distraction?," *EP News Service*, Nov. 3, 1995, pp. 5–8.
22. Ibid. These included Mission America 2000, DAWN Ministries, and the Sentinel Group.
23. Kim A. Lawton, "An Invasion of Mercy in the Caribbean," *Charisma*, Jan. 1995, pp. 22–26.
24. *Charisma*, Jan. 1995.
25. John A. Siewert and John A. Kenyon, eds., *Mission Handbook: A Guide to USA/Canada Christian Ministries Overseas* (Monrovia, CA: MARC, 1993), p. 60.
26. Ibid., p. 59.
27. Ibid., pp. 55–57.
28. Ibid., pp. 55–56.
29. Ibid., pp. 73–70. The countries to which more than seven hundred North American missionaries were sent were: Brazil, Colombia, Ecuador, France, French Guiana, Germany, Indonesia, Japan, Kenya, Mexico, Papua New Guinea, and the Philippines.
30. "House Subcommittee Hears Testimony about Worldwide Christian Persecution," *EP News Service*, March 1, 1996, pp. 4–5.
31. Laurie Goodstein, "Evangelical Christians Seek Action; Administration, Congress React to Call to Fight Persecution," *Washington Post*, Sept. 22, 1996.
32. Julia Duin, "Pass the New Wine," *Charisma*, Aug. 1994, pp. 20–28; Daina

Doucet, "What Is God Doing in Toronto?," *Charisma*, Feb. 1995, cover story. See also James A. Beverly, "Toronto's Mixed Blessing," *Christianity Today*, Sept. 11, 1995. *Charisma* magazine has been favorable in its news coverage and editorials about holy laughter. For an entirely critical perspective, see Hank Hanegraaff, *Counterfeit Revival* (Dallas: Word, 1997).

33. Wimber died in 1997 at age sixty-three. "Charismatic Leader John Wimber Dies, Founded Influential Vineyard Churches," *EP News Service*, Nov. 21, 1997.
34. J. Lee Grady, "Does the Church Need Heresy Hunters?," *Charisma*, May 1995, pp. 47–52.
35. "Vineyard Severs Ties with 'Toronto Blessing' Church," *Christianity Today*, Jan. 8, 1996, p. 66.
36. Barbara J. Woerner, "Holy Spirit Moves Worldwide," *Christian American*, Jan. 1995, p. 19.
37. "Pat Robertson and CBN Promoting 'Holy Laughter,' " *Christian News*, Feb. 29, 1995, pp. 1, 16.
38. Hank Hanegraaff, *Christianity and Crisis* (Eugene, OR: Harvest House, 1993.)
39. In *Spiritual Warfare* (Boston: South End Press, 1989), I wrote extensively about shepherding, because it was a major controversy in the 1980s. What follows is a brief summary and update.
40. During the 1980s, I interviewed a number of defectors who told me about the psychological pain they suffered, as well as their fear, instilled in them by "shepherds," that they would spend eternity in hell for having left the group.
41. "Mumford Repents of Discipleship Errors," *Charisma*, Feb. 1990, pp. 15–16.
42. "An Idea Whose Time Has Gone?," *Christianity Today*, March 19, 1990, pp. 38–42.
43. On reconstructionism, see my *Roads to Dominion*, pp. 246–248, and the sources cited therein.
44. I attended the April 1996 birthday celebration and Reconstructionist conference in San Jose, California.
45. Dan O'Neill, "The Supernatural World of Frank Peretti," *Charisma*, May 1989, p. 50.
46. Angela Kiesling, "The Lady Is a General," *Charisma*, March 1994, p. 26.
47. Generals of Intercession conference brochure; author's collection.
48. Cindy Jacobs, *G.I. News*, third quarter, 1994, p. 2.
49. Steven Lawson, "Defeating Territorial Spirits," *Charisma*, April, 1990, p. 49.

Notes to Chapter 11

✑

1. See "The 'Memphis Miracle,' " *Ministries Today*, Jan.–Feb. 1995, pp. 36–38; "Pentecostals Move toward Unity after Decades of Racial Division," *New York Times*, Oct. 23, 1994; and "Pentecostals Renounce Racism," *Christianity Today*, Dec. 12, 1994, p. 58. See also the Oct. 31, 1994, issue of the *National and International Religion Report*.

2. On the history of pentecostalism, see Harvey Cox, *Fire from Heaven* (Reading, MA: Addison-Wesley, 1995).
3. Joe Maxwell, "Black Southern Baptists," *Christianity Today*, May 15, 1995, pp. 27–31; "Racist No More? Black Leaders Ask," *Christianity Today*, Aug. 14, 1995, p. 53.
4. "Christian Coalition Calls Summit on Church Burnings," EP News Service, June 21, 1996, pp. 4–5.
5. "Church Burnings Continue," EP News Service, July 5, 1996, p. 2.
6. EP News Service, June 21, 1996, p. 4.
7. EP News Service, July 5, 1996.
8. "Minority Myths Exploded," *Christian American*, Oct. 1993.
9. On the charismatic renewal, see, e.g., Margaret Poloma, *The Charismatic Movement: Is There a New Pentecost?* (Boston: Twayne, 1982).
10. Joe Maxwell, "Healing the Rift between the Races," *Charisma*, April 1993, pp. 19–24.
11. C. Peter Wagner, "A Season of Reconciliation," *Charisma*, March 1996, pp. 61–63.
12. Ibid., p. 63.
13. Joe Maxwell, "When Love Crosses the Line," *Charisma*, June 1995, pp. 30–34. The photos featured a white man married to a black woman, and their three children. In the August 1995 issue, *Charisma* published four letters to the editor on the piece. Two letter writers praised the article, and two said they were "disappointed" and "highly offended" by the idea of interracial marriage.
14. Much has been written about Promise Keepers. See, among other sources, Joe Maxwell, "Looking for a Few Good Men," *Charisma*, July 1993, pp. 20–24; Andy Butcher, "Melting Men's Hearts," *Charisma*, May 1995, pp. 23–27; Don Lattin, "Christian Warriors," *San Francisco Chronicle*, May 28, 1995; "Men Crowd Stadiums to Fulfill Their Souls," *New York Times*, Aug. 6, 1995; "Full of Promise," *Time*, Nov. 6, 1995; and Joe Conason, Alfred Ross, and Lee Cokorinos, "The Promise Keepers are Coming," *Nation*, Oct. 7, 1996.
15. See, e.g., the cover story, "God of Our Fathers," *Time*, Oct. 6, 1997.
16. "Will the Walls Fall Down?," *Christianity Today*, Nov. 17, 1997, p. 62.
17. Ibid.
18. This and the following impressions are based on my attendance, as a journalist, at the Promise Keepers rally in Oakland, California, in September 1995.
19. "Racial Reconciliation Emphasis Intensified," *Christianity Today*, Jan. 6, 1997, p. 67.
20. Joe Maxwell, "'Til Race Do Us Part?," *New Man*, Jan.–Feb. 1997, pp. 27–31.
21. April 24, 1997, phone interview with Edward Gilbreath. *New Man* published three letters to the editor on the piece in its March–April 1997 issue. All three were favorable. Gilbreath said he received only one violent and hateful letter. He received several that criticized the magazine for showing a black man married to a white woman and not the reverse.
22. "Wall Busting 101," *New Man*, Sept. 1996, pp. 36–39.
23. Letters, *New Man*, Nov.–Dec. 1996, p. 12.
24. Ibid.

25. Ibid.
26. "How to Be a Real Man," *New Man,* July–Aug. 1994, p. 6.
27. Tony Evans (column), *New Man,* July/Aug. 1994, p. 20.
28. Willard F. Harley Jr., "Why Women Leave Men," *New Man,* July–Aug. 1996, pp. 68–69.
29. Gary Jackson Oliver, Ph.D., "The Power of Anger," *New Man,* Sept.–Oct. 1994, p. 64.
30. "New Women's Organizations Patterned after PK," *Southern California Christian Times,* Aug. 1996, p. 27. Also, author's collection of miscellaneous mailings from women's groups in support of Promise Keepers.
31. Peggy Leslie, "A Woman at Promise Keepers," *Southern California Christian Times,* Aug. 1996, p. 26.
32. Faith Martin, "Promise Keepers: A Volunteer's Perspective," (Pittsburgh) *Expression,* Sept. 1996, p. 9.
33. Ibid.
34. Len LeSourd, "Escape the Sexual Trap," *New Man,* July–Aug. 1994, p. 51.
35. Ibid., pp. 51–52.
36. Dr. Archibald Hart, "Sex under Control," *New Man,* Nov.–Dec. 1994, p. 38.
37. Ibid., p. 39.
38. Ibid.
39. Letters, *New Man,* March–April 1995.
40. Frederick Clarkson, "Righteous Brothers," *In These Times,* Aug. 5, 1996, p. 17.
41. Sara Diamond, "The New Man," in *Facing the Wrath* (Monroe, ME: Common Courage Press, 1996), pp. 25–30.
42. George Barna, "The Battle for the Hearts of Men," *New Man,* Jan.–Feb. 1997, p. 42.
43. Ibid., p. 43.
44. Promise Keepers 1997 men's conferences brochure, p. 25; author's collection.

Notes to Chapter 12
∾

1. "Bauer Starts New PAC," *Human Events,* April 11, 1997, p. 2.
2. "Robertson: Christian Coalition Should Emulate Tammany Hall," *Washington Post,* Sept. 18, 1997, p. A2.
3. "FEC Files Suit over Christian Coalition Role," *Washington Post,* July 31, 1996; "Federal Election Commission Sues Christian Group on Political Aid," *New York Times,* July 31, 1996.

Index

at Republication National Convention, 94–95
school board victories of, 183–184
Christian Legal Society, 85–86
Christian publishing, 44
appeals to African Americans, 45
categories of, 45–46
Christian Reconstructionism, 106
Christian Right. *See also* Right-wing movements; Social movements; specific organizations
agenda of, 7–8
antigay agenda of, 47–48
appeal to minorities, 96–97
broadening agenda of, 89–112
Buchanan's campaigns and, 14
Central America dictatorships and, 71–72
changing approaches on race and gender, 17
coalition building by, 2
congressional focus of, 71–73
in electoral politics, 1, 3–4, 8–9, 68
ERA defeat and, 64
evangelical subculture of, 1
financing of, 11–12
historical roots of, 58–59
legal strategies of, 84–88
local focus of, 95
low voter turnout and, 79
millennial thinking and, 197–199
motivations for joining, 11
outsider perception of, 5, 8
as percentage of electorate, 4
as persecuted group, 87–88
political agenda of, 11, 238–240
potential base of support for, 241
professionals *versus* amateurs in, 90
racial reconciliation within. *See* Promise Keepers; Racial reconciliation
Republican Party and, 57, 72, 79, 93–95, 99, 240
secular humanism and, 70–71
stealth tactics of, 78–79
sustaining features of, 197–215
tenacity of, 242
urban/poverty issues and, 7, 111
Christian Voice, 68–69
Christian World Liberation Front, 61
Christianity, brands of, 43
Christianity Today, 2
Christians
evangelical. *See* Evangelicals
persecution of, 207
Church attendance
religious broadcasting and, 22
statistics on, 9–10

Churches
burnings of, 218–219
growth of, 60–61
liberal. *See* Liberal churches
Citizen magazine, 1–2
Citizens for Community Values, 163, 169
Citizens for Excellence in Education, 185–186
Civil disobedience, antiabortion movement and, 136–139
Civil rights
of gays, 160
white evangelicals and, 62–63
Civil Rights Act, Bush's support of, 91
Clark, Randy, 209
Clean Air Act, Bush's support of, 91
Clinics, bombing of, 136
Clinton, Bill
Christian Right and, 95–99, 142–143
and Defense of Marriage Act, 169–170
economic focus of, 90
and military ban on gays, 159
1996 victory of, 109
reelection of, 3
and violence against clinics, 142
welfare reform and, 113
Clinton, Hillary, 113–114, 120
Clinton Chronicles, The, 98
Coalition on Revival, 212–213
Colorado, antigay ballot measures in, 35, 161, 162–163
Colorado for Family Values, 35, 161, 162–163, 167
Colson, Charles, 44, 46, 53, 55–56, 171, 172
Combs, Roberta, 80
Commission on Pornography, 85
Concerned Women for America, 2, 22, 42, 110
Christian Coalition and, 81–82
feminism and, 126–130
lobbying by, 82–83
public schools and, 186–187
Congress, Christian Right and, 71–73
Congressional elections, 99–103
Contemporary Christian Music, 48–53
Contract with the American Family, 102–103, 110, 180
Converts, religious, 20. *See also* Missionaries
Corporate donors, New Right and, 59
Corporations, censorship and, 193–194
Cripes, Dolores, 184
Cripes, Tim, 184
Crisis pregnancy centers, 152–155
Crouch, Jan, 22, 26, 37
Crouch, Paul, 22, 26, 28, 37–38